CAMBRIDGE STUDIES IN
INTERNATIONAL AND COMPARATIVE LAW: NEW SERIES

General Editor:
SIR ROBERT Y. JENNINGS,
Judge of the International Court of Justice
Formerly Whewell Professor of International Law, University of Cambridge

TORTIOUS LIABILITY FOR UNINTENTIONAL HARM IN THE COMMON LAW AND THE CIVIL LAW

VOLUME I

TORTIOUS LIABILITY
FOR UNINTENTIONAL HARM
IN THE COMMON LAW
AND
THE CIVIL LAW

Volume I: Text

BY

F.H. LAWSON

D.C.L., F.B.A.

of Gray's Inn, Barrister;
formerly Professor of Comparative Law, Oxford

B.S. MARKESINIS,

D.IUR. (ATHEN.), M.A., PH.D (CANTAB.)

of Gray's Inn, Barrister;
Fellow of Trinity College, Cambridge;
Lecturer in Law of the University of Cambridge

CAMBRIDGE UNIVERSITY PRESS

CAMBRIDGE

LONDON   NEW YORK   NEW ROCHELLE

MELBOURNE   SYDNEY

Published by the Press Syndicate of the University of Cambridge
The Pitt Building, Trumpington Street, Cambridge CB2 IRP
32 East 57th Street, New York, NY 10022, USA
296 Beaconsfield Parade, Middle Park, Melbourne 3206, Australia

First published 1982

Printed in Great Britain at the University Press, Cambridge

Library of Congress catalogue card number: 81–10230

British Library Cataloguing in Publication Data
Lawson, F.H.
Tortious liability for unintentional harm in the Common law and the Civil
law. – (Cambridge studies in international and comparative law. New series)
Vol. 1: Text
1. Torts – Law and legislation – Europe
I. Title II. Markesinis, B.S.
342.63'094

ISBN 0 521 23585 5

CONTENTS

v

Contents

GENERAL EDITOR'S FOREWORD TO THE NEW SERIES

A series of *Cambridge Studies in International and Comparative law*, under the general editorship of H.C. Gutteridge, H. Lauterpacht and Sir A.D. McNair, was launched in 1946 with the first edition of Professor Gutteridge's important monograph on *Comparative Law: An Introduction to the Comparative Method of Legal Study and Research*. In a general introduction to the series the editors explained that it was designed to fill certain gaps in that part of English legal literature which is concerned with international relations: and that it would involve public international law, private international law and comparative law. In fact all the subsequent volumes of the distinguished series save the last, contributed by Dr B.S. Markesinis and dealing with the controversial issue of Dissolution of Parliament, were to do with public and international law.

There was a gap during the 1970s, when the Press Syndicate felt that legal publishers were best able to publish books on law. Happily, counsels more apt to the Press of Maitland's university have now prevailed, and the series is being revived. The intention is to publish monographs mainly on public international law; but it is a happy coincidence that this first work of the revived series is again about the comparative method of legal study and research.

The general editors of the original series said, in April 1946, that 'at present the literature of Comparative Law is scattered, fragmentary and often difficult of access'. The aim of the present volumes is precisely to make an important part of that material readily available to scholars and students, and to provide an authoritative commentary and guide to understanding it.

We are most fortunate that the new Cambridge series thus begins with work by that most distinguished Oxford scholar and teacher, Professor F.H. Lawson, in partnership with a Cambridge scholar and teacher, Dr Basil Markesinis.

Cambridge   R.Y.J.
April 1981

FOREWORD

It is a privilege to have been invited by the great old master of comparative law and his bright younger colleague to contribute a foreword to this important book. The authors are so well known as to need no introduction to the British and, indeed, the international reader. The work itself, however, calls for some comment.

This book gives a renewed life to a monograph which was written some thirty years ago by Professor Lawson and which rightly received world-wide acclaim, not least for its penetrating insights into the Civil law and, indirectly, the Common law. One might, therefore, be content to express admiration at the way Dr Basil Markesinis has expanded and reshaped this book so as to lay the main emphasis on the modern Common law and Civil law. It is, indeed, a rare feast to be able to read such a masterly treatment of a particularly complex subject. The great legal systems are throughout this book considered in a tightly interwoven fabric, enriched by valuable glances at other systems of law. The developments are always stated in an accurate and instructive manner. As regards the legal system I know best – the French system – one is amazed at the extent to which Dr Markesinis has been able to understand and expound with great lucidity the most complex aspects of the matter. I would not say that the French law of *responsabilité civile* is, as Dean Prosser once said of proximate cause, 'a tangle and a jungle, a place of mirrors and maze', since its main lines are reasonably clear and satisfactory. Nevertheless, I do subscribe to Jean Carbonnier's severe pronouncement: 'Un immense gaspillage d'intelligence et de temps, c'est peut-être le bilan que l'on dressera un jour de notre célèbre jurisprudence.' For, though the main lines are reasonably clear, they are encumbered by numerous pointless subtleties. And though their results are reasonably satisfactory, they can lead to at least 25 per cent of the victims of road accidents being left – unjustifiably in my view – without any compensation.

The question may be raised why French law is so imperfect in this matter. Probably, the reason is that it is no longer governed by the

ix

Code (which has been and remains an excellent working tool) but is left to the courts which are less experienced than their English counterparts in handling case-law. The first part of this explanation needs justification.

It is true that the Civil Code devotes five sections to the law of torts ('Des délits et des quasi-délits'). But, with the emergence of accidents as a result of the nineteenth-century industrial revolution, the greatest part of the subject was left unregulated by the Code. It looked as if the 1898 Act on Industrial Accidents had remedied the situation. The remedy, however, was a temporary one. Traffic accidents, which in France at present account for 40 deaths and some 1,000 injuries a day, are not governed by statutory rules, except to the extent that automobile liability insurance has become compulsory since 1958. Faced with such inaction on the part of Parliament, the courts decided to step in and created a law for the protection of victims of personal injuries and, especially, for the protection of traffic victims. But they could not achieve this *kind* of major adjustment of the provisions of a code, even though the drafters had been content to leave to them the task of adapting the texts to the needs of contemporary life. The situation was so new that they had to create the law out of nothing – the reference to article 1384 CC being a mere excuse. They did quite well in 1930. The decision in the *jand'heur* case was excellent and courageous. Unfortunately, however, the courts were not able to find a satisfactory solution to the secondary problems raised by its implementation. Nor were they able to reconsider it in the light of new factors, such as the compulsory automobile liability insurance. They have experience in formulating *jurisprudence* on the basis of statutory provisions, but not in developing and shaping case-law. The Cour de cassation does not lack able and innovative judges; what it lacks is proper techniques. Suffice to confess that it hands down some 15,000 judgments every year (800 in the field of civil liability; is this not, to quote Prosser again, adding smoke to fog?) and only recently has it taken steps to introduce a screening system for cases.

The reading of this book raises another question. It shows admirably that the various systems of law considered in its pages have given comparable responses to the identical needs of society. Still, they have to effect this by means of technical constructions which differ from one system to another but are no less complex and irrational than the French law which I have just criticised. Is there any good reason for this particularism? It is difficult not to have the feeling that until quite recently – and Lawson's *Negligence in the Civil Law* was one of the pioneer works – English, French and German law developed quite apart, in basic ignorance of each other, and have suffered from this narrowness of approach. Each has been a prisoner of its own traditions. Instead of considering the problems from a wider, comparative perspective, they have made them more refined and complex. They have been more anxious to refine than to recast – hence the results I have alluded to. Of course, a unification of the laws on the basis of rational rules which will be equally acceptable in the three systems under comparison will not be achieved overnight. However, one feels that this book will help open the minds of jurists, at any rate in the three countries it embraces. And it should also convince its readers, as its authors hope it will, that 'cross-fertilisation of ideas is both possible and desirable' and this, in the long run, will produce better laws to serve the people better.

André Tunc

Université de Paris I

PREFACE

This book has its origins in F.H. Lawson's *Negligence in the Civil Law* which first appeared in 1950 and was reprinted with minor corrections several times since. Indeed, much of its Roman law material has with few, mainly bibliographical, additions or alterations, found its way into the first chapter of this book. The restricted nature of the revision, however, should in no way be seen as belittling the more recent contributions that British scholars like Honoré, Nicholas, Watson, McCormack, to mention but few, have made to the study of the *lex Aquilia*, but rather as an indication of the belief that much of this ground remains, and by the nature of things is likely to remain, open to discussion and speculation. With this in mind, and given the uncertainty that shrouds much of the Roman law, it was thought fit to retain as much of the orginal material as possible since, despite differences in details, or interpretation, it remains a model of conciseness and readability.

Like all progenies, however, this book claims a character and personality of its own, in many respects fundamentally different from that of its progenitor's. For one thing, it has grown considerably in size, largely in order to accommodate the explosion in academic writing that has taken place during the last thirty years or so in the area of delictual liability. One side effect of this is that the book is now printed in two volumes: volume I containing the exposition of general principles and our conclusions on certain aspects of delictual liability for unintentional harm, and volume II reprinting a wide selection of extracts from texts, statutes and cases relevant to our subject. But, though volume II is, in a sense, a 'companion volume', it has been designed to have an independent existence and can thus be used by students and teachers as a kind of casebook on the Civil law of torts. A second consequence of this increase in size is that the old balance between 'introductory material' and 'texts' has been radically altered. For while in the first edition of *Negligence* the main focus was on the texts and the seventy-nine pages of 'Introduction' were merely 'intended to furnish the student with an intelligible order in which to read the texts', the emphasis in this book is, if anything, reversed. Thus, though both volumes are approximately the same size, the second is meant to support and authenticate the text found in the first.

A second and no less important change can be found in the switch of emphasis from the Roman law to the modern Civil law. This reflects the changing emphasis in University teaching and the growing importance of courses in foreign and comparative law. With the U.K. now firmly (?) anchored in the Common Market, this growing interest in the modern Civil law can only be welcomed as an opportunity to influence and be influenced by others. For it seems true to assert that English law, both private and public, appears to be prepared to look abroad for guidance and inspiration in a manner which has hitherto been totally unknown. But this change of emphasis did not in our opinion warrant the complete abandonment of Roman law. For not only does Roman law remain an admirable creation of brilliant and systematic minds and as such worthy of serious academic pursuit; it also provides an excellent way of introducing the Common lawyer to the modern Civil law since it forms the first stage in a long and fairly continuous historical development. The first chapter of this book is therefore entirely devoted to the *lex Aquilia* and subsequent developments, and acts as a bridge between the old and the modern Civil law.

From what has already been said it will be obvious that the great bulk of the book is new, and its purpose is to introduce the student to a general familiarity with some of the basic conceptions of most continental systems, such as an educated English lawyer ought to possess, *and* to develop through the exposition of particular rules a number of themes which seem to us particularly relevant and noteworthy. Our conclusions are briefly stated at the end of the book and it is hoped that they will provoke our readers to use the material we have supplied in the second volume to question or elaborate them. But the one thing we certainly hope that they will do is to encourage a more 'positive' approach to the Civil law and vice versa; an approach which, while conscious of the differences which exist between the systems, will, for a change, choose to explore their equally intriguing similarities. If we achieve this, we feel we shall have achieved one of the most important aims we set out to achieve.

A number of practical considerations have influenced the size of the book and this meant that a selection had to be made of what topics would be discussed. The title gives some idea of what we have excluded. We have omitted liability for intentionally inflicted harm and further restricted our discussion to certain aspects of what we in England would call the tort of Negligence (though we have opted for the less misleading title of unintentional harm). More importantly, we have omitted any extensive discussion of non-delictual rules of compensation such as insurance and social security. No doubt this will disappoint some of our readers, but something had to go, and what stayed was to some extent determined by the scope and title of the progenitor of this book and, of course, our own, personal, interests. Besides, the Pearson Committee has now reported and has not, to the distress of some and the delight of others, sounded the death-knell of the traditional law of tort. So, while the subject remains alive, there is room for its comparative discussion.

As already stated, the main part of the book is devoted to the modern law: Common law and Civil law. This last should be understood as referring mainly to modern French and German law which (rightly in our opinion) still attract the greatest attention in this country. But this does not mean that we have attempted to discuss *every* topic from the point of view of the Common law, French law and German law, since we do not regard comparative law as a long list of similarities and differences. Thus the emphasis alternates between French law and German law, depending upon which of the two presents greater originality or interest on a particular point. And, more often than not, we have also given references to other codes, notably the Austrian, Swiss, Belgian, Italian and Dutch, whenever we thought that this might be of interest to our readers. One must remember, however, that our exposition of the 'foreign law' is really an account by a Common lawyer looking at the Civil law and, hence, the possibility of our French or German colleagues viewing their own law in a different way cannot be ruled out. Still, this may not be a bad thing, especially if it prompts Civil lawyers to rethink their own law in the light of observations made by outsiders. A few more comments about the materials included in the second volume may not be out of place.

The materials reprinted in the second volume are meant to supply help to interested students, not researchers, and are broadly divided into three sections: the first includes extracts from Roman texts; the second, extracts from mostly modern Western European Codes dealing with delictual liability; the third, reproducing a selection of German and (mainly) French cases on the subject. All students of law by the comparative method must, at a very early stage, become familiar with these sources of modern law and there is no better place to start than the law of civil responsibility. Moreover, the problems that French and German lawyers have had to solve are substantially the same as those which have appeared in England in the present century and a special effort has been made to include cases (in both volumes) which bear a marked, factual, resemblance to well-known English cases. The task of comparison is thus greatly facilitated.

The preponderance of French materials found in this part of our work has not been dictated entirely by considerations of space. One important factor for this imbalance in favour of French law was the knowledge that most English students can read French better than German and, in fact, the French texts have been left untranslated on the assumption that one cannot hope to study modern law comparatively without *some* knowledge of French. At the same time, however, we have tried to ease the path of the student by explaining in appropriate places difficult terms and phrases. Passages from all other languages are reproduced in a translated form and in these translations the emphasis has not been on elegance and easy flowing style, because in a book of this kind the translation should be nothing more nor less than a 'crib'. But there is a further, important reason why we chose to give such pre-eminence to French law and this is because of its admirable ability to blend the theoretical and the practical while striving for elegance and symmetry. It thus avoids some of the theoretical excesses which can be found in the otherwise quite admirable German legal literature without reaching the opposite extreme (often found in English law) of ignoring logic, symmetry and elegance for the sake of 'practical solutions'. This, no doubt, is an important reason why French law has received and will continue to receive such pre-eminence in the syllabi of many Common Law Faculties and it has also led us to shift the balance in its favour.

One final point should be made. Keeping up to date with developments in one system is difficult enough; trying to achieve this with two, three, or more is a real nightmare. Happily we believe that the comparative approach can be and perhaps should be attempted in broad strokes, where form and shape matter more than detail, and acquiring the general feeling of a foreign system may be more important than trying to master its minutiae. Though every effort has been made to take into account the most recent materials, the above mentioned philosophy may explain and, perhaps, justify omissions which the more learned of our readers will be quick to discover.

Cambridge, 10 July 1980   F.H. Lawson B.S. Markesinis

ACKNOWLEDGEMENTS

'*Ἀμαθία μὲν θράσος, λογισμός δὲ ὄκνον φέρει.*' This, at any rate, was the view taken by Pericles in his famous Funeral Oration. For my part I am now convinced that it is this temerity which usually flows from ignorance of the difficulties that lie ahead, plus my ambition to work with Harry Lawson, that first led me to volunteer to update his pioneering work. This proved an awesome task, given the great complexity of the subject and the fact that in all the systems under comparison, a great deal has happened since Harry Lawson's books first appeared in the early 1950s. In the event, however, I was fortunate to have the help of many colleagues who, in various ways, came to my rescue. My debt to their written work has, I hope, been adequately acknowledged in the notes to this work. But it gives me great pleasure to record a less specific, but none the less great, sense of indebtedness to my 'Tort' colleagues and friends in Trinity, Jack Hamson, Tony Jolowicz and Tony Weir, as well as to my friend Micky Dias, to all of whom I owe my interest in the subject and whose ideas I am sure I have consciously and unconsciously used and elaborated in more than one place in this book.

More specific and just as sincere is my debt to Peter Stein, who kindly read the first chapter in draft form and made many a valuable suggestion; to Kurt Lipstein, eminently suited and always willing to help with some difficult German texts; to my former pupil and now colleague and friend Professor Christian Von Bar for his meticulous checking of statements and references to German law; to Dr Kurt Clausius for his untiring and valuable assistance with the German bibliography and case-law; and to Mademoiselle Marie Josef-Experton for her help with a number of points concerning French law. Thanks are also due to the Trustees of the Leverhulme Trust Fund for providing much of the financial assistance usually necessary for research work of this kind; to Messrs Carl Heymanns Verlag KG, and C.H. Beck'sche Verlagsbuchhandlung, publishers of the Entscheidungen des Bundesgerichtshofes in Zivilsachen and the Neue

Acknowledgements

Juristiche Wochenschrift respectively; and to the editors of the *Recueil Dalloz-Sirey*, *La Semaine Juridique* and the *Gazette du Palais* for their generous permission to reproduce here some of the decisions published in their learned editions. Grateful thanks are also due to the staff of the Squire Law Library and, in particular, to Mr G.G. Hughes and Mr A.C. Rawlings for their help; and, finally, to my secretaries, Mrs Mary Pomery and Mrs Rebecca Vasko, who cheerfully typed and re-typed an impeccable typescript from an illegible manuscript.

But my greatest good fortune was in securing the help of André Tunc, who proved a patient teacher as well as a great friend. For he read my manuscript with great care and by giving me the benefit of his immense knowledge saved me from many errors and omissions. And as if all this were not enough, he has kindly contributed a foreword to the book in his usual generous manner.

Last but not least I wish to record my thanks to Harry Lawson for giving me a free hand in the preparation of this book. His generosity, patience and erudition, so well known to generations of colleagues and students alike, were, for me, a source of strength and inspiration during the dark moments when the magnitude of the task made me wish I had read Thucydides more often. If this book proves a worthy successor to his own work on comparative law it will be largely due to his influence and the assistance of all the above; if it is not, then I, alone, am to blame.

B.S. Markesinis

Although this book, for which we both take full responsibility, is the product of a joint effort, by far the greater part of the work, including the selection and modification of the materials contained in my earlier work, has been done by Basil Markesinis, to whom I am most grateful.

F.H. Lawson

ABBREVIATIONS

ABGB	Austrian General Civil Code.
A.C.	Law Reports, Appeal Cases (Decisions of the House of Lords and the Privy Council from 1891).
AcP	*Archiv für die civilistische Praxis.*
A.E.F.	Cour d'appel de l'Afrique Equatoriale française.
A.J.Comp.L.	*American Journal of Comparative Law.*
A.L.J.R.	Australian Law Journal Reports.
All E.R.	All England Law Reports.
Amos and Walton	Sir M.S. Amos and F.P. Walton, *Introduction to French Law*, 3rd edn (1967) by F.H. Lawson, A.E. Anton and L. Neville Brown.
Am. Rep.	American Reports.
App. Cass.	Law Reports, Appeal Cases (1875–1890).
ATF	*Recueil officiel d'arrêts du Tribunal fédéral suisse* (can also be referred to as *BGE – Entscheidungen des schweizerischen Bundesgerichts*).
Atiyah	P.S. Atiyah, *Accidents, Compensation and the Law*, 2nd edn (1975).
B.	*Basilica.*
BB	*Betriebsberater.*
Beseler	G. Beseler, *Beiträge zur Kritik der Römischen Rechtsquellen*, I (1910); II (1911); III (1913); IV (1920); V (1931).
Bet.	*Der Betrieb.*
BGB	Bürgerliches Gesetzbuch (German Civil Code).
BGBl.	*Bundesgesetzblatt.*
BGE	*Entscheidungen des schweizerischen Bundesgerichtes* (can also be referred to as *ATF – Recueil officiel d'arrêts du Tribunal fédéral suisse*).
BGHZ	Entscheidungen des Bundesgerichtshofes in Zivilsachen (Decisions of the West German Supreme Court in civil matters).

Buckland, *Slavery*	W.W. Buckland, *The Roman Law of Slavery* (1908, 1970).
Buckland, *Text-book*	W.W. Buckland, *A Text-book of Roman Law from Augustus to Justinian*, 3rd edn revised by P. Stein (1963).
Buckland and McNair	W.W. Buckland and A.D. McNair, *Roman Law and Common Law*, 2nd edn revised by F.H. Lawson (1952, reprinted 1965, 1974).
Bull.civ.	*Bulletin des arrêts de la Cour de cassation, chambres civiles* (official reports).
Bull.crim.	*Bulletin des arrêts de la Cour de cassation, chambre criminelle* (official reports).
C.	*Codex Iustinianus.*
C.A.	Decision of the English Courts of Appeal.
Cal.L.Rev.	*California Law Review.*
Cal. Reptr. 2d.	California Reporter, 2nd series (American law reports).
Cal. Reptr. 3d.	California Reporter, 3rd series (American law reports).
Cass.	Cour de cassation.
CC	Civil Code.
C.E.	Conseil d'Etat.
Ch.	Law Reports, Chancery Division (from 1891).
Ch. Civ.	Cour de cassation, Chambre Civile.
Ch. Civ. 2^e	Cour de cassation, second Chambre Civile.
Ch. Comm.	Cour de cassation, Chambre Commercielle.
Ch. Crim.	Cour de cassation, Chambre criminelle.
Ch.D.	Law Reports, Chancery Division (1875–1890).
Ch. Mixte	Cour de cassation, Chambre Mixte.
Ch. Req.	Cour de cassation, Chambre des Requêtes.
Ch. Réun.	Cour de cassation, Chambres Réunies.
C.L.J.	*Cambridge Law Journal.*
C.L.R.	Commonwealth Law Reports.
Coll.	*Mosaicarum et Romanarum Collatio*, ed. Hyamson, 1913.
D.	Recueil Dalloz (1945–1964).
D	*Iustiniani Digesta.*
D.C.	Dalloz, recueil critique de jurisprudence et de législation (1941–1944).
Deutsch, *Haftungsrecht*	E. Deutsch, *Haftungsrecht*, 1, 5th edn (1976).
de Visscher	F. de Visscher, *Le Régime romain de la noxalité* (1947).
D.H.	Dalloz Hebdomadaire (1924–1940).

D.L.R.	Dominion Law Reports.
D.P.	Dalloz périodique (1825–1940).
D.S.	Recueil Dalloz et Sirey (1965–).
D. StR.	Deutsches Steurrecht.
EG. BGB	Einführungsgesetz zum BGB (Introductory law to the BGB).
Encyclopedia	*International Encyclopedia of Comparative Law*, XI, chief ed. A. Tunc (1975).
Esser-Schmidt, *Schuldrecht*	J. Esser and E. Schmidt, *Schuldrecht*, 5th edn, I, *Allgemeiner Teil* (1975), II, *Besonderer Teil* (1976).
Ex. D.	Law Reports, Exchequer Division (1875–1880).
Fleming	John G. Fleming, *The Law of Torts*, 5th edn (1977).
F. Supp.	Federal Supplement (American Law reports).
F. 2d.	Federal Reporter, 2nd series (American Law Reports).
G.	*Gai Institutiones.*
GG	Grundgesetz (the Constitution of Western Germany).
Giffard	A.E. Giffard and R. Villers, *Droit romain et ancien droit français (obligations)*, 4th edn (1976).
G.P.	*Gazette du Palais.*
Grueber	E. Grueber, *The Lex Aquilia* (1886).
H. & C.	Hurlston and Coltman (private reports 1862–1866).
Hart and Honoré	H.L.A. Hart and A.M. Honoré, *Causation in the Law* (1959).
Heimbach	C.G.E. Heimbach, *Basilicorum Libri LX*, vol. v (1850).
Holdsworth	Sir W.S. Holdsworth, *History of English Law*, 12 vols.
Honoré, *Encyclopedia*	*International Encyclopedia of Comparative Law* XI (chief ed. A. Tunc), ch. 7, 'Causation and Remoteness of Damage' by A.M. Honoré.
I.C.L.Q.	*International and Comparative Law Quarterly.*
J.	*Iustiniani Institutiones.*
J.C.L.	*Journal of Comparative Legislation and International Law*, 3rd series.
J.C.P.	*Juris-Classeur Périodique* (also referred to as *S.J. (La Semaine Juridique)*).
Jolowicz, *De Furtis*	H.F. Jolowicz, *Digest XLVII. 2, De Furtis* (1940).

Jolowicz and Nicholas	H.F. Jolowicz and B. Nicholas, *Historical Introduction to the Study of Roman Law*, 3rd edn (1972).
Josserand	L. Josserand, *Cours de droit civil positif français*, 2nd edn (1933).
J.S.P.T.L.	*Journal of the Society of Public Teachers of Law*.
JuS	*Juristische Schulung*.
JW	*Juristische Wochenschrift*.
JZ	*Juristenzeitung*.
Kaser, *R. PR.*	Max Kaser, *Das römische Privatrecht*, I, 2nd edn (1971).
K.B.	Law Reports, King's Bench (1901–1952).
Larenz, *Schuldrecht*	K. Larenz, *Lehrbuch des Schuldrechts*, 11th edn, I, *Allgemeiner Teil* (1976), II, *Besonderer Teil* (1977).
Lenel, *Ed.*	O. Lenel, *Das Edictum Perpetuum*, 3rd edn (1927).
L.Q.R.	*Law Quarterly Review*.
L.R. Ch. App.	Law Reports, Chancery Appeal Cases (1865–1875).
L.R.C.P.	Law Reports, Common Pleas Cases (1865–1875).
L.R. Ex.	Law Reports, Exchequer Cases (1865–1875).
L.R.H.L.	Law Reports, English and Irish Appeals (1866–1875).
L.R.Q.B.	Law Reports, Queen's Bench (1865–1875).
L.T.	Law Times Reports (1859–1947).
Macq.	Macqueen (Sc.) H.L. (private reports 1851–1865).
M. & W.	Messon and Welsby Ex. (private reports 1836–1847).
Mazeaud and Mazeaud	Henri, Léon et Jean Mazeaud, *Traité théorique et pratique de la responsabilité civile délictuelle et contractuelle*, II, 6th edn (1970).
Mazeaud and Mazeaud, *Leçons*	Henri, Léon et Jean Mazeaud, *Leçons de droit civil*, II, part I, 6th edn (1978) by F. Chabas.
Mazeaud and Tunc	Henri et Léon Mazeaud et A. Tunc, *Traité theorique et pratique de la responsabilité civile délictuelle et contractuelle*, I, 6th edn (1965).
McKerron	R.G. McKerron, *The Law of Delict*, 7th edn (1971).
M.D.R.	*Monatschrift für Deutsches Recht*.
Medicus	Dieter Medicus, *Bürgerliches Recht*, 9th edn (1979).

M.L.R.	*Modern Law Review.*
Monier	R. Monier, *Manuel élémentaire de droit romain.*
Monro	C.H. Monro, *Digest IX. 2, Lex Aquilia* (1898).
N.E.	North Eastern Reporter (American law reports).
N.I.L.Q.	*Northern Ireland Legal Quarterly.*
NJW	Neue Juristische Wochenschrift.
N.W.	North Western Reporter (American law reports).
OGH	Oberster Gerichtshof (Austrian Supreme Court).
OLG	Oberlandesgericht (Decision of a German Court of Appeal).
OR	Swiss Code of Obligations.
P.	Law Reports, Probate Division (1891–).
Pas.	*Pasicrisie Belge* (Belgian law reports).
Pernice	A. Pernice, *Die Lehre der Sachbeschädigungen* (1867).
Planiol et Ripert	M. Planiol et G. Ripert, *Traité pratique de droit civil,* 14 vols., tome VI par P. Esmein (1952).
Prosser	W.L. Prosser, *Law of Torts,* 4th edn (1971).
P. 2d.	Pacific Reporter, 2nd series (American law reports).
Q.B.	Law Reports, Queen's Bench (1891–1900; 1952–).
Q.B.D.	Law Reports, Queen's Bench Division (1875–1890).
Rabels Z.	*Rabels Zeitschrift für ausländisches und internationales Recht.*
Rev.crit.jur. Belge	*Revue critique de jurisprudence Belge.*
Rev.crit.lég. et jur.	*Revue critique de législation et de jurisprudence.*
Rev.gén.ass.terr.	*Revue générale des assurances terrestres.*
Rev.hist.dr.fr. et é.	*Revue historique de droit français et étranger.*
Rev.int.dr.ant.	*Revue internationale des droits de l'antiquité* (3rd series, 1954–).
Rev.int.dr.comp.	*Revue internationale de droit comparé.*
Rev.trim.dr.civ.	*Revue trimestrielle de droit civil.*
RGBl.	*Reichsgesetzblatt.*
RGSt.	*Amtliche Sammlung der Entscheidungen des Reichsgerichts in Strafsachen.*
RGZ	*Entscheidungen des Reichsgerichts in Zivilsachen* (Decisions of the German Imperial Court in civil matters).

Rotondi, *Scr. Giur.*	G. Rotondi, *Scritti Giuridici* (1922).
S.	Recueil Sirey.
S.A.L.J.	*South African Law Journal.*
Savatier	R. Savatier, *Traité de la responsabilité civile en droit français*, 2nd edn (1951).
S.C.	Session Cases (Scottish law reports).
S.D.H.I.	*Studia et Documenta Historiae et Iuris.*
S.J.	*La Semaine Juridique* (also referred to as *J.C.P.* (*Juris-Classeur périodique*)).
S.L.T.	*Scots Law Times.*
So.	Southern Reporter (American law reports).
Somm.	*Sommaire* (summary of French decisions in D.).
So. 2d.	Southern Reporter, 2nd series (American law reports).
StGB.	Strafgesetzbuch (German Criminal Code).
Starck	Boris Starck, *Droit civil, obligations* (1972).
S.W.	South Western Reporter (American law reports).
Trib. Civ.	Tribunal Civil.
XII T.	The Twelve Tables.
U.B.C.L.Rev.	*University of British Columbia Law Review.*
U.Ch.L.Rev.	*University of Chicago Law Review.*
U.of P.L.Rev.	*University of Pennsylvania Law Review.*
U.T.L.J.	*University of Toronto Law Journal.*
Va.L.Rev.	*Virginia Law Review.*
Vand.L.Rev.	*Vanderbilt Law Review.*
VersR.	*Versicherungsrecht.*
Weill and Terré	*Droit civil*, 2nd edn (1975).
Weir, *Encyclopedia*	*International Encyclopedia of Comparative Law* XI (chief. ed. A. Tunc), ch. 12, 'Complex Liabilities' by Tony Weir.
Winfield and Jolowicz	Winfield and Jolowicz on Tort, 11th edn by W.V.H. Rogers (1979).
W.L.R.	Weekly Law Reports.
WM	*Wertpapier-Mitteilungen.*
Z.S.S.	*Zeitschrift der Savigny-Stiftung für Rechtsegeschichte, Romanistische Abteilung.*
Zweigert and Kötz	K. Zweigert and H. Kötz, *An Introduction to Comparative Law*, II, *The Institutions of Private Law* (translated by Tony Weir, 1977).

TABLE OF STATUTES AND ARTICLES OF CIVIL CODES

English Law

Scots Law

French Law

German Law

TABLE OF CASES

xxix

Table of Cases

Chapter I

FROM THE *LEX AQUILIA* TO THE MODERN CODES

1. The *Lex Aquilia* and its Relation to Earlier Legislation

The date of the *lex Aquilia* is not known for certain. Ulpian informs us[1] that it was a plebiscite proposed to the plebs by a tribune Aquilius, from which one may safely infer that the *lex* was enacted later than 449 B.C. – the presumed date of the *lex Valeria Horatia* which made plebiscites, endorsed by the senate, binding on all. At the other end of the chronological scale we have the early part of the second century B.C. since we know that the *lex* was commented on by Junius Brutus,[2] one of the founders of the *ius civile*, who flourished about 120 B.C. Between these two dates the year mostly favoured by scholars has, for a long time now, been 287 B.C. and their views have been greatly influenced by the fact that Theophilus in his *Paraphrase* of the *Institutes* talks of the *lex* being passed at a time of secession (*diastasis*) of the plebs from the patricians.[3] This attribution, however, has been contested, mainly on the ground that Theophilus, though an admirable expositor of the law, did not have much knowledge of historical detail (even though he had access to the works of the classical jurists) and may merely have drawn an inference from Ulpian's statement and the description of the struggle between the orders given by Pomponius.[4] Nor does the reference to unwrought bronze (*tantum aes*) rather than coinage offer conclusive support in favour of this early date (287 B.C.), for 'long after bronze had ceased to be the usual form of coinage the Romans used the term *aes* for money'.[5] Despite these doubts most writers[6] still take the year 287 B.C. as the likely date of the enactment of the *lex* though, more recently, Professor Honoré, relying on 'modern numismatic opinion', places the *lex* in the economically uncertain and inflationary period that followed the major upheaval of the *second* Punic war. He thus sees the *lex* not as 'a poor man's statute, but part of a legislative programme to ensure the preservation of property rights' – as a 'measure to protect the propertied classes against the effects of inflation'.[7] Even greater uncertainty, however, shrouds the earlier law.

In the first fragment of the *Digest* title on the *lex Aquilia* Ulpian tells us that the 'lex derogavit'[8] from all earlier statutory provisions relating to damage to property, whether or not they were contained in the Twelve Tables; and although there is controversy as to the exact meaning of his remark, there is no doubt that the overwhelming importance of the *lex Aquilia* as a source of the mature law has made it very difficult to ascertain what preceded it. Literary and juristic texts supply a few references to the Twelve Tables which can be compared to provisions in the Babylonian Laws of Hammurabi, the Hittite Laws and the Hebrew Laws contained in the Pentateuch; but we have not the actual words and there is doubt as to the contents of the Twelve Tables. We know nothing of any other statutes. However, the following conclusions seem probable.

1. The Twelve Tables gave an action *de pastu* against anyone who pastured his livestock on another's land. Indeed, according to Pliny,[9] the Twelve Tables made pasturing animals by stealth at night a capital offence for an adult though, if committed by a minor, the offence would be punished by flogging at the discretion of the praetor. The action survived until the time of Justinian.[10]

2. They also gave an action,[11] which probably survived until the late classical period but afterwards disappeared, against a person who cut down another's tree close to the ground. Since the penalty, according to Pliny,[12] was only 25 *asses* per tree, the action was normally, but not invariably, side-tracked by a later praetorian action *arborum furtim caesarum*,[13] which gave full compensation.

3. If anyone burnt a house or a heap of corn placed next to a house, the Twelve Tables ordered him to be tied up, scourged, and burnt to death, but only if he had acted knowingly; otherwise, if it happened accidentally (Gaius[14] says 'negligently', but this is probably a later gloss), he was to make good the damage, or if he was too poor, to receive a light punishment.

4. The Twelve Tables imposed certain penalties for the following offences: *iniuria* (XII T., 8.4), *membrum ruptum* (*talio*, XII T., 8.2) and *os fractum* (300 *asses* if the victim was a freeman, 150 if he was a slave) (XII T., 8.3).[15] Probably *membrum ruptum* meant a complete destruction of a limb, or at any rate an injury that made it useless, whereas the damage involved in *os fractum* was a fracture or some other injury that was curable, and for which the principle 'an eye for an eye, a tooth for

a tooth' was inappropriate. The right to exact *talio* from another's slave for the breaking of one's *own* limb was, apparently, clear. It became, in fact, the basis of noxal surrender in that by breaking the limb of another's slave one deprived, in effect, the master of the services of his slave. Hence, the master was given the option of either surrendering his slave to vengeance, or of paying damages. But whether *talio* was ever exacted for the breaking of the limb of one's slave is more doubtful. In theory, the answer should be negative, since vengeance was personal satisfaction, and no slave was allowed personal satisfaction against a free man or his property (slave or animals for example); nor could the injured slave's master be allowed satisfaction, since this would not be personal. It will be noticed that this fixed system of penalties suffered from two distinct disadvantages. As a compensatory system it was unjust, for it did not distinguish injuries of differing gravity; and as a deterrent system it must have been increasingly ineffective, especially with the gradual depreciation of the monetary unit (the *as*). The story of Lucius Veratius amusing himself by slapping complete strangers in the face and then asking one of his retinue to pay the victim the prescribed penalty of 25 *asses* vividly illustrates the point.

5. There is a suggestion, based, it would seem, on wholly insufficient evidence, that the Twelve Tables imposed a general liability to make good any damage done by breaking anything belonging to another person.[16]

The provisions contained in the first four paragraphs above were far from covering all the ground, and Professor Daube has accordingly suggested[17] that some other statute must have preceded the *lex Aquilia*, imposing fixed penalties for killing cattle and slaves. We are certainly entitled to infer from Ulpian's remark that the Twelve Tables did not stand alone. Moreover, the order of the chapters in the *lex Aquilia* gives rise to problems which are best solved by assuming the existence of this later statute. Indeed Professor Daube's thesis was subsequently taken a step further by Pringsheim who, relying on the text of the *lex Aquilia* given by Gaius (G. 3,210, 215 and 217), argued that 'A careful reading of the text... reveals the impossibility of its entirely having been formed at one and the same time.'[18] Five enactments are envisaged by this author, each succeeding the other 'in a logically and historically understandable manner'. The theory is largely based on the argument that each successive 'layer' was wider than its predecessor and thus rendered it superfluous. Pringsheim's

3

hypothesis remains to be proved or disproved. But in the meantime one can, perhaps, quote Celsus (with whom Ulpian agreed) that 'there is nothing new in a statute enumerating certain things specifically and then adding a general word which embraces the specific things'.[19]

To the question what exactly Ulpian meant when he said that the 'lex derogavit' from all earlier *leges* concerning *damnum iniuria*, we shall be safest in giving the following answer. The *lex* superseded all previous *leges*, including the Twelve Tables, in so far as they dealt with damage to movable property; for there is no evidence that any other rules survived. Damage to immovables creates greater difficulties, but perhaps Ulpian regarded the *actio de pastu* and the *actio de arboribus succisis* as being not *in pari materia*, since by his time the wrongs penalised by them were more akin to theft than to damage, the wrongdoer actually gaining by his wrong. The same cannot be said of the *actio aedium incensarum*, about which, however, very little is known. Good authorities have expressed scepticism as to its survival into the classical period.[20] If it still lay for accidental burning, actions would hardly have been brought under the *lex Aquilia*, which required *culpa* in the burner; but the application of the *actio legis Aquilia* to such burnings is attested by h.t. 27,7–8.[21] On the whole, then, we should hold that Ulpian meant that the *lex Aquilia*, while it did not expressly repeal the earlier *leges* – he did not say 'abrogavit'[22] – superseded them by giving better remedies; and some support is given to this view by *C.* 3,35,6, which shows that the *lex* covered the ground of the *actio de pastu pecoris*.

2. The Contents of the *Lex Aquilia*

(a) The first chapter

The first chapter of the *lex Aquilia* imposed a penalty for the unlawful killing of slaves and four-footed animals of the type that go in herds (*pecudes*).[23] Doubtless originally only familiar farm animals were intended, but later elephants and camels were brought in (not, however, wild animals or dogs).[24] The wrongdoer was made to pay the owner the highest value which the slave or animal had had during the year preceding the injury which caused death, and this sum was doubled if the defendant denied liability, a provision which applied to both other chapters also.[25] Thus the plaintiff might receive something over and above the actual value of the slave or animal at the time of the injury, for it might have suffered some slighter injury which had reduced its value during the preceding year;[26] and, of course, if the defendant denied liability the margin would be much greater. Thus Gaius, having in mind only this latter circumstance, says that by the action on the *lex* we recover not only compensation but a penalty.[27] But the mere fact that *lis crescit in infitiantem* did not make an action penal,[28] and it is clear that even if the defendant did not deny liability but merely contested the amount of the claim, the action on the *lex* was regarded as penal.[29] However, it may be doubted whether at the time when the *lex* was passed any distinction was drawn between penalty and compensation. A penalty imposed by a *lex* was none the less a penalty if it operated merely to compensate the victim. Thus it is unlikely that the provision giving the plaintiff the highest value in the last year was inserted in order to afford him a chance of recovering something over and above compensation and so to entitle the action to be called 'penal'.[30] The *lex* only intended to compensate the plaintiff and, as Professor Daube suggests,[31] 'the "penalty" makes up for the fact that, prices being unsteady, the owner of the slave might not have sold him just at the time when the wrong was committed'. Possibly, too, there was some danger of the defendant's alleging, contrary to the truth, that the slave or animal had at the time of the fatal injury already lost much of its value owing to a previous injury. Early legislators had recourse to rough-and-ready methods of avoiding difficulties of proof.[32] It was only later that the possible margin beyond compensation was seized on as justifying the description of the *actio legis Aquiliae* as a penal action.[33]

(b) The third chapter

In his *Negligence in the Civil Law* Professor Lawson warned his readers that the problems relating to the wording and the scope of the third chapter were difficult and were still awaiting their answer. Over thirty years later the definitive solution has yet to be produced and, perhaps, too much energy is still expended by British scholars[34] on scrutinising the relevant texts.

According to Ulpian the third chapter read as follows:[35] 'Ceterarum rerum, praeter hominem et pecudem occisos, si quis alteri damnum faxit, quod usserit fregerit ruperit iniuria, quanti ea res erit in diebus triginta proximis, tantum aes domino dare damnas esto.'

The words 'praeter hominem et pecudem occisos' have long been suspect. The words sound much more like an explanatory gloss than the enacting words of a statute. They are, moreover, hardly grammatical. The grammatical objection would be lessened if 'occisos' were omitted, but the text would then make bad law, at any rate for the classical period; for it is clear that by that time the wounding of slaves and cattle fell within the chapter, whereas the amended text would exclude it. Accordingly Pernice[36] regarded the whole phrase from 'praeter' to 'occisos' as a later insertion. Agreeing with this view the late Professor H.F. Jolowicz[37] put forward the theory that the chapter originally did not deal with slaves or animals at all, but only with total destruction of inanimate objects. To this Lenel[38] replied that the words 'Ceterarum rerum' are also a latter insertion; for not only is the genitive case odd, but 'res' must allude to the second chapter as well as the first, and the only *res* in the second chapter could be an obligation, which could hardly have been considered a *res* at the time the *lex* was passed. Thus, according to the generally accepted view, everything down to 'occisos' goes, though we cannot be certain that it does not replace something else that was in the *lex*.

However, the strength of Professor Jolowicz's case lies elsewhere, namely in the penalty prescribed. The chapter has commonly been explained to mean that for any damage not falling within the first chapter the defendant was to pay the highest value within thirty days immediately preceding the injury.[39] Now this makes sense where an animal not falling within the first chapter had been killed or an inanimate thing has been totally destroyed or made useless, for in those cases no action would lie under the first chapter and, but for the third chapter, the victim would have to go without a remedy. But this interpretation is not convincing where a slave or animal has been wounded or an inanimate thing, capable of repair, has been damaged; for the difference between wounding and killing would seem to call for a greater difference than that between taking the highest value in the past year and taking the highest value in the past thirty days, a difference which would in most cases be illusory. The absence from the chapter of the word *plurimi*[40] does not improve matters, for at a later date Sabinus thought that it should be implied.[41] Lenel,[42] indeed, thought that the third chapter could have imposed this exorbitant penalty without being false to the ideas of the time, which would be eager to punish and unconcerned about exact compensation, but, as Professor Jolowicz has said of Lenel's view, it is 'so obviously unfair that one cannot believe any legislator intended it'.[43]

6

Pernice's solution,[44] that the plaintiff received the whole value but surrendered the damaged article, is no better, for it might present the plaintiff with the choice of handing over a favourite object or forgoing compensation; and there is no evidence to support it. Monro's solution,[45] on the other hand, makes excellent sense and probably gives the law as it stood in classical times, but involves the assumption that the *lex* was badly drawn. Others have doubted whether it can really be deduced from the text we have. His view is that 'quanti ea res erit' did not mean 'whatever the value of the damaged article shall prove to be' but 'whatever the matter in issue (i.e. the damage) amounts to'. So far so good. But 'whatever the damage amounts to in the preceding thirty days' is meaningless, and it seems impossible to deduce from the Latin anything to correspond to Monro's paraphrase 'the amount which the incident would have cost you if it occurred at the moment in the month at which it would have cost you the most'.[46]

Accordingly Professor Jolowicz[47] suggested that the third chapter meant that the highest value in the past thirty days should be paid in full, but that there was nothing unreasonable in this since the chapter only dealt with the *actual or virtual destruction* of articles which did not fall within the first chapter, that is to say, mainly, or perhaps only, inanimate objects. The difference between the year's and the thirty days' valuation is not explained by him, but the suggestion has been made[48] that the latter meant the highest price ruling at the three market days immediately preceding the injury. Inanimate objects would rarely have any special value as individuals at the time the *lex* was passed, as a slave would. The chief objection to the theory is that one would have expected the Romans of that period to be particularly interested in injuries to slaves and so to have included them in the *lex*; but this brings us up against the problem of the relation of the *lex* to the Twelve Tables and other earlier statutes, which is not really soluble with our present materials. We know so little about early republican law that the argument from silence is dangerous, and although the evidence for a general liability for damage under the Twelve Tables is very weak, the liability may have existed.

Thus matters stood until Professor Daube published in 1938[49] his article 'On the Third Chapter of the *lex Aquilia*'. Agreeing with Professor Jolowicz that all previous solutions should be rejected, he sided with Monro in holding that 'quanti ea res erit' refers to the damage and not to the entire value of the thing damaged. But he

7

believed that the word *plurimi* was omitted, not because the plebs expected it to be implied from its previous use in the first chapter[50] but because the thirty days had nothing to do with a valuation of the thing. Relying on similar provisions in other laws ancient and modern, he argued that the thirty days were the thirty days *after, not before,* the injury, and the purpose of mentioning them was to give sufficient time to see how the injury developed. At the end of the month one would expect to know the worst, whereas immediately after the injury one might be completely in the dark. This theory gave for the first time full effect to the future tense of 'erit', and it was no longer necessary to torture the Latin in order to get the sense 'whatever the matter in issue shall prove to be in the next thirty days'.[51] It will be observed that this theory is directly opposed to that of Professor Jolowicz, for it makes the chapter (at the time of its enactment) deal only with partial damage to slaves and animals: there is no point in waiting thirty days to see what has happened to an inanimate object, though perhaps one would know better how much it would cost to repair it.

Both theories have to assume that considerable changes took place between the date of the *lex* and the classical period, and it is difficult to see how such developments could have been forgotten in a system as strongly traditional as the Roman. On the other hand, as this is the most obscure period in Roman legal history, the difficulty may be less great than is imagined. If this is so, it may be easier to imagine the changes that Professor Daube's theory requires. In his view, the thirty days' limit was seriously undermined soon after the third chapter was extended to inanimate objects, probably some time during the second half of the first century B.C. For when an inanimate object is damaged it is purposeless to wait and see what the consequences of the damage are; they should, normally, be obvious at once. And the 'wait and see' rule may well have become neglected in practice even in the case of the wounding of slaves.[52] So, by Sabinus' time, the text no longer corresponded with the expanded scope of the chapter, and the jurist[53] felt obliged to read the word *plurimi* into it in order to solve the disparity of wording in the two chapters.

Over forty years after its appearance Daube's theory still has its followers.[54] More interestingly, perhaps, it has given rise to a number of variations which must be briefly noted. Some of these theories depart from Daube's views on the original scope of the third chapter; others, while accepting his interpretation that the thirty day period is

8

the one that follows and not precedes the accident, have attempted to ascribe to it a reason different from the one propounded by Daube. Thus, we have noted that Kelly has argued that from the very beginning damage to inanimate objects was covered by chapter three.[55] Iliffe[56] and MacCormack,[57] on the other hand, believe that this was so only in the case of 'serious' damage – insubstantial damage to inanimate objects not being recoverable at the time of the enactment of the *lex*. As for the thirty day rule, Iliffe[58] has argued that its purpose was 'in the case of inanimate things, (a) to give time for a set of values to appear from subsequent market days, (b) in later law, to mark out a reasonable period in which additions to the plaintiff's *interesse* may be admitted'. For Kelly, on the other hand, the thirty day period is meant to give the defendant time to find the money to pay the plaintiff[59] while Pugsley[60] has taken yet another view and argued that the thirty days marked the limitation period within which the action had to be brought. This is clearly no place to discuss these theories which, in so far as they are based 'on a minute examination of the surviving text may display a scrupulous accuracy in quoting legislative texts which, perhaps, was not shared by the Romans'.[61] Moreover, a recent article by Professor Honoré may have, at the very least, injected a serious element of doubt as regards the validity of some of the above theories.[62] Honoré's views thus deserve special attention.

Honoré's thesis depends on the authenticity of the words 'ceterarum rerum', which every author since Lenel[63] seems to have considered as spurious. Honoré takes a different view and on the basis of textual and other arguments believes that, at least in Ulpian's mind, the words were clearly part of the *lex*. Thus, he argues that the word '*ait*' in the opening sentence of h.t. 27,5 – 'Tertio autem capite *ait* eadem lex Aquilia' – always introduces 'an exact quotation'[64] and it is unlikely that Ulpian, or any of his republican predecessors, would have consciously altered the text. But did Ulpian know the original text? Professor Honoré thinks that he did, and adduces two arguments, 'one of language and one of social and economic context' to support this view. The linguistic argument is meant to counter Lenel's views on the meaning of 'Ceterarum rerum'.[65] The words appeared in the edict *de feris* and should clearly be translated: 'as regards matters other than...' Lenel had no objection to their use there, so one can only conclude that 'he evidently forgot the existence of the *edictum de feris* when he came to deal with chapter three of the *lex Aquilia* and argued

9

that *res* could not there have meant "matters"'. Moreover, the structure of the edict is closely parallel to that of the *lex Aquilia* and, if Professor Honoré is right as to his re-dating of the *lex* (or, more precisely, of chapter three), they are probably both of the same period.[66] Thus, in both cases 'two specific provisions, dealing with killing and wounding a freeman are followed by a residuary clause dealing with all other cases'. If this is right all the theories which limit the original scope of the *lex* go overboard and we are also presented with 'some of the earliest evidence of the capacity of Roman jurisprudence to generalise a problem and its solution'.[67]

(c) Damage to freemen

An extraordinary juristic interest attaches to the Roman slave as an entity which was at once a person and a thing. Nowhere is this greater than in the law of damage. For this Janus-like character of the slave enabled the Roman to bridge the gap between damage to property and personal injuries.

Strange as it may seem, in the earlier law slaves and freemen were treated alike as far as compensation for personal injuries is concerned, the only difference being as to the *amount* that each received.[68] But in later times the resemblance between slaves and things prevailed completely, obscuring the fact that both slaves and freemen are human beings. Thus, injury to a slave fell under the third chapter of the *lex Aquilia* because the slave was treated as a thing that could be owned; but it was none the less personal injury and to deal with it, rules sprang up which could with little or no alteration eventually be applied to freemen. Moreover, it suggested the provision of an analogous remedy to deal with personal injuries to freemen; and here another useful bridge could be found in the *filiusfamilias*, in whom, though free, the *paterfamilias* had an interest not very different in practice from his ownership of a slave.

Nothing is known about a father's action for damage to his son except that he was entitled by way of penalty to be compensated for loss of the son's earning capacity and for the cost of medical attendance.[69] The date when it was introduced is not known, nor whether it arose directly out of the *lex* or was *utilis* or *in factum*.

The peculiar nature of the penalty, which cannot have been 'value', makes it very unlikely that the action was direct and it is generally admitted that no action ever lay, apart from quasi-delict, for the death of a freeman; otherwise one might be tempted to say that the son was treated as *servi loco*. But there seems to be no strong reason for refusing to believe that the action existed in the classical period.[70] Certainly the suspicions concerning the key text (h.t. 5,3) no longer appear to be convincing since the discovery in Egypt of a parchment containing a fragment of Ulpian on precisely the same question.[71] Hence, if not according to classical law certainly according to Ulpian, an *actio legis Aquiliae* was given to a *paterfamilias* whose son was wounded or killed.

The next development, on the other hand, is generally held to be post-classical. The *actio iniuriarum* lay for personal injuries to a freeman provided they were inflicted intentionally, but not if the defendant's conduct was merely negligent.[72] This was largely the result of the unfortunate combination of offences subsumed under the *actio iniuriarum*. For the classical lawyers came to interpret the praetorian edict mainly in connection with what we would nowadays regard as defamation cases and hence, quite logically, insist on the presence of wilful injury (*dolus*). But this did nothing to help actions for personal injuries and, in practice, it meant that there was no remedy at all for the negligent killing or wounding of a freeman. The only, limited, exception to this rule (apart from the action of the *paterfamilias* for the death of his son) was the *actio de effusis et deiectis* given for the death of a freeman caused by something thrown or poured on him from a house. The householder's liability was for fifty *solidi*[73] and, this being an *actio popularis*, it could be brought by anyone, though if several wished to sue, persons interested in the deceased or related to him by marriage or kinship were given preference.[74] The position remained unchanged even in Byzantine law[75] and it was not until the Glossators interpreted or, perhaps, wilfully misinterpreted the Corpus Iuris Civilis that the change came about. In this mediaeval expansion, which owes a great deal to the work of Roffredus (a pupil of Azo and a contemporary of Accursius), *D* 9,13 and h.t. 5,3, already alluded to above, must have proved most useful tools.[76]

(d) The second chapter

Of the three chapters contained in the *lex Aquilia*, the first and third dealt with damage to corporeal things. Gaius in his *Institutes* (3,215) informs us that the second chapter gave an action against an adstipulator who had released a debt in fraud of the stipulator.[77] Why this provision was included in the *lex* at all is a matter for surprise, but is perhaps to be explained by the conjecture that some patrician debtor had recently put pressure on an adstipulator to release a debt owed to some plebeian creditor; the chapter would then be appropriate to a statute which was intended to deal with outstanding private law grievances between the orders. But it is still difficult to see why it should have been sandwiched between the first chapter, which dealt with the killing of slaves and animals, and the third, which dealt with other forms of damage to corporeal things. Perhaps a plausible solution is that advanced by Professor Daube,[78] who has suggested that an earlier statute subsequent to the Twelve Tables had introduced rules covering the same ground, though less satisfactorily, as the first two chapters, but nothing to correspond to the third. The *lex Aquilia* then re-enacted, with improvements, the first two chapters and added the third. But the whole question is wrapped in the deepest obscurity though we do know from h.t. 27,4 that by the time of the *Digest* and, indeed, almost certainly at a much earlier date, the chapter had become obsolete.

(e)   Confession and denial of liability under the *lex*

The *lex Aquilia* subjected a defendant to a double penalty if, having denied liability, he was proved liable under the first, second,[79] and, arguably, the third[80] chapters.

From the words 'dare damnum esto' and the rule that the penalty was doubled if the defendant denied liability it has been inferred that the plaintiff originally proceeded by way of *manus iniectio*, doubtless *pura*. The balance of probability is still in favour of this hypothesis,[81] but there are difficulties. It is by no means certain that *damnas* is a contraction of *damnatus* and therefore intended to subject the person who is *damnas* to a process the same as or akin to that which lay against one who owed a judgment debt (*iudicatus*).[82] Secondly, we are told by Gaius[83] that the *lex* itself imposed the double penalty in case of denial, which would have been quite unnecessary if it had prescribed the process of *manus iniectio*; to this, however, Pernice replied[84] that the only effect of a previous *manus iniectio* still surviving in the classical period was the double penalty, and that Gaius was doubtless mentioning this effect and not purporting to give the words of the *lex*. The most serious difficulty, however, is that no other case is known in which *manus iniectio* could be used to enforce a claim to an unliquidated sum; elsewhere it lay always for a *certum*. If then we are to accept the hypothesis, we must either say that the *lex* innovated or that the plaintiff was allowed to estimate in money the value of the slave or animal killed or the amount of damage done under the third chapter. If we reject *manus iniectio*, we may perhaps say that the plaintiff proceeded by way of *iudicis arbitrive postulatio*.

One piece of evidence tending in support of this thesis is the following:

The heading to *Coll.* 12,7,1 runs as follows: 'Ulpianus libro XVIII ad edictum, sub titulo si fatebitur iniuria occisum esse in simplum et cum diceret.' Giffard,[85] drawing on h.t. 26, completes this as follows: 'et cum diceret adversarium magni litem aestimare'. He thinks that the plaintiff himself estimated the amount of damage, which was inserted in the formula in the form of a *taxatio*, the judge being allowed to give judgment for less but not for more. It was then open to the defendant to admit the delict but to say that the plaintiff had made too high an estimate of the damage. It is possible that in the *legis actio* period the judge had no discretion as to the amount in issue if the defendant denied liability. This would perhaps explain why the double liability existed only when there was denial; in which case, perhaps, the *lex* gave a *legis actio per manus iniectionem contra infitiantem*, but only *per iudicis arbitrive postulationem contra confitentem*.[86]

Giffard,[87] in pursuance of a theory, which is attractive though there is not much evidence to support it, that one of the main purposes of the *lex* was to settle outstanding grievances which the plebeians had against the wealthy patricians, thinks that the doubling of the penalty against a defendant who denied liability was enacted in order to induce patricians to confess, plebeians finding it difficult to obtain witnesses against patricians. If, as seems probable, the victim could not bind himself not to sue,[88] that, too, was intended to prevent undue influence on the part of patrician wrongdoers.[89]

The rule inflicting the double penalty was buttressed by a further well-known principle that the *condictio indebiti* never lay for the recovery of money paid to avoid condemnation in a *lis crescens*.[90] Moreover, as we have seen, it was impossible to compromise the claim by pact.[91]

The question arises, what relief did the defendant's confession of liability give the plaintiff? The answer given is that the plaintiff need no longer prove that it was the defendant who had killed the slave or animal or done the damage;[92] but that if the defendant could prove – in the proceedings on the *actio confessoria*, not later – either that the slave was alive,[93] or even that, though dead, he had not been killed, he went scot-free.[94] This rule, though in itself clear, has to be read in conjunction with other rules, of a general kind, relating to *confessio in iure.* Pernice and Grueber attempt to build a general theory,[95] that the defendant was bound if he confessed what was untrue but possible, but not if he confessed what was impossible. Monro[96] finds this distinction untenable, but declines to submit an explanation of his own. Can it be that I cannot be bound by a confession which was at variance with the physical or legal status of the slave, animal, or thing which is the subject-matter of the action or for the damage caused for which I can be held responsible,[97] but that I can be bound in any other case? Thus I cannot be bound if I confess that a freeman was my slave, but I can if he belonged to someone else. I cannot be bound if I confess that a man near my own age is my son, but I can if, being of an age that would allow of his being descended from me, he was in fact *sui iuris* or in someone else's power.[98]

3. Extension by *actiones utiles* and *in factum* to other kinds of damage.[99]

The first chapter of the *lex* covered only killing (*occidere*), and this was apparently taken at first to mean killing by the direct application of some part of the defendant's body or by some weapon held by him.[100] Hardly any extension was involved in deciding that a slave was killed if a person caused his death by dropping on him, or crushing him with, a burden which he found too heavy to carry.[101] But it seems as though even in the first century A.D. an action on the *lex* was not held to lie against one who crushed a slave if another person's body was between him and the slave,[102] and it is possible that as late as the end of the century there was doubt whether administering poison, even directly, was killing and, therefore, actionable at Civil law. In h.t. 7,6, we are told that Celsus took the view that administering poison, even directly, was not killing and, therefore, not actionable under the *lex*. But in a similar case Labeo draws a distinction (which, incidentally, clearly illustrates the difference between *occidere* and *mortis causam praestare*): if a midwife gives a woman a drug 'with her own hands, she is held to have killed: but if she gave it to the woman for her to take it herself, an action *in factum* must be given;... for she furnished a cause of death rather than killed.'[103] But in the end jurists went so far as to say that if anyone pushed a slave into a river so that he was drowned, it was a case of killing, even though he did not sink at once but was eventually too exhausted to keep afloat.[104] In other words, the first chapter had very much the same limits as the action of trespass in English law.

Beyond this point jurists speak, not of *occidere* but of *mortis causam praestare*, and just as the mediaeval judges allowed actions on the case, so the praetors gave actions *in factum*.[105] These actions were not edictal but decretal, that is to say, the praetor did not say in his edict that he would give an action wherever anyone caused the death of a slave or animal, but decided on the allegations in each particular case whether to allow the formula. But the result seems to have been the same, and the limits were apparently ascertained by applying the principles of causation. These praetorian decretal actions became more frequent in classical law and this may account for what at times appears to be a more restrictive interpretation of the wording of the *lex* during the Empire. Thus a republican jurist might give an action under the *lex* where a later jurist would give an *actio in factum*.[106]

The third chapter was extended in very much the same way. There was an additional difficulty however, to start with, in that the *lex* mentioned only three ways of doing damage, 'quod usserit fregerit ruperit'.[107] But the jurists interpreted 'ruperit' to mean 'corruperit', which seems to have meant nothing more than 'spoil'.[108] One might have thought that, having gone so far, they could have allowed a direct action under the *lex* wherever anyone had by a *positive act* of misfeasance caused a thing to deteriorate, even though there was no physical contact.[109] But although the jurists differed as to the limit of the action in particular cases, they all recognised that there was a limit; and although no principle is enunciated in the *Digest*, and we are told[110] that we must no longer say that the *damnum* had to be *corpore corpori* – since the *damnum* is always the pecuniary loss to the plaintiff and not the damage done to the thing – yet it seems that Gaius and Justinian are right when they say that the damage must be done *corpore* and there must be actual physical damage to the object itself (*corpori*). Some at least of the classical jurists certainly held that there had to be an actual deterioration of the thing that was touched.[111]

Yet there seems to have been a period in the second century B.C. when another line of development was attempted. There is a suggestion that not all the *veteres* agreed in making 'ruperit' mean 'corruperit', and Brutus may perhaps have been willing to allow an action on the *lex* for consequential damage where there had been something that could by a stretch of meaning be called *ruptum*, but the thing itself had not deteriorated in consequence.[112]

No distinction was made in practice between 'fregerit' and 'ruperit';

and, indeed, it is difficult for us to know what distinction was originally intended. But the jurists kept their comments on 'usserit' separate.[113]

Where the direct action on the *lex* failed, the praetor gave actions *in factum*,[114] as in cases not covered by the first chapter; and there was the same preoccupation in the minds of the classical jurists as to the boundaries between the actions as in the minds of the English Common lawyers of the eighteenth century. Comparison between various cases however shows that the question whether a particular result can be treated as the direct or indirect consequence of the defendant's conduct is a matter on which opinions may differ. Thus in h.t. 9,3 the plaintiff is given an *actio in factum* against the person who startled a horse and thereby caused the plaintiff's slave to fall from it and be killed. The result here is regarded as indirect but in *Dodwell* v. *Burford*,[115] a case with similar facts, the injury was held to be the direct result of the defendant's conduct.[116] Any Roman jurist would thus have enjoyed dealing with the problem raised in the *Squib* case.[117] Indeed, although the introduction of remedies for *mortis causam praestare* and damage done *corpori* but not *corpore* inevitably created important problems of causation, these are as lacking in prominence in the *Digest* as in the older English reports.

The limits of the action *in factum* cannot be clearly ascertained. In Justinian's *Institutes*[118] there is a threefold classification: (1) an action on the *lex* lies for damage done *corpore corpori*, i.e. by what we should call a trespass; (2) an *actio utilis* is given if the damage is done *corpori* but not *corpore*, i.e. physical damage done without direct contact,[119] and (3) an *actio in factum* if it is *nec corpore nec corpori*, i.e. merely pecuniary damage to the plaintiff unaccompanied by physical damage to anything belonging to him. But in his *Institutes*[120] Gaius only distinguishes between (1) the direct action, where there is contact (*corpore*), and (2) *utiles actiones* where there is not, and in the *Digest* these *utiles actiones* are almost invariably termed *actiones in factum*. There is, indeed, no technical difference in the formulary system between an *actio utilis* and an *actio in factum*.[121] The former term only means that the action is not the direct Civil law action, though it is commonly applied to actions where the Civil law *formula in ius concepta* is modified by means of a fiction. *Actio in factum* would normally be used to describe an action with a *formula in factum concepta* but is often found with the meaning 'action on the case'.[122]

But Justinian's *actio in factum* is something quite different.[123] It is a general action for damage done indirectly and without any physical damage to any specific object belonging to the plaintiff. The example given is facilitating the escape of a slave or animal: there is no physical damage to the slave or animal, but its owner suffers pecuniary damage by having the value of his estate reduced.[124] Such pecuniary damage, if caused *wilfully,* had for many centuries given rise to an *actio doli,* unless, indeed, the defendant exploited the thing, in which case an *actio furti* would lie for the theft. Thus the *actio in factum* was necessary only where the damage was caused negligently.[125] Rotondi thought that this action was a late Byzantine generalisation from a small number of isolated decretal actions given by various praetors where there had been no wilful wrongdoing (and so the *actio doli* would not lie), but the defendant had acted so wantonly that he ought not to go scot-free: the action, however, being granted on the analogy of the *actio doli* – not of the *actio legis Aquiliae.*[126] He regarded this *actio generalis in factum* as essentially similar to the action given by article 1382 of the French Civil Code and as being in a fair way to absorb the direct action and the *actio utilis.* His theory has not gone unquestioned, and Buckland,[127] for instance, seems to have thought that no clear distinctions can be made between the various cases in which the praetor extended liability for negligence. It is no doubt possible, and perhaps even probable, that in early days when praetors were asked to give actions *in factum* in cases to which the letter of the *lex Aquilia* did not apply, they did not always draw logical distinctions between physical and merely pecuniary damage or, indeed, between acts of commission and acts of omission – those lines are not always consciously drawn even in modern English law.[128] But this is not to say that a praetor would have given an *actio in factum* as a matter of course whenever the plaintiff alleged that he had been harmed by the careless conduct of the defendant. There does not appear to have been a regular formula for actions *in factum* on the analogy of the *lex Aquilia,* and indeed one should think, not of a single action applicable to a large number of cases, but of as many actions as there were cases in which the praetor was prepared to give a remedy.[129] It seems likely, therefore, that the praetor always reserved the right to refuse a remedy where he thought fit to do so, and we may well believe that in any unusual case he would think twice before allowing an action.

We may probably assume then that by the end of the classical period an action was given almost as a matter of course wherever physical damage was caused, even indirectly, by a positive act, provided, of course, that it was intentional or negligent. But it has always been accepted doctrine that Roman law gave an action for omissions only in exceptional cases.[130] Indeed, if we leave to one side the obvious cases where a defendant failed to take precautions which his previous positive acts had necessitated,[131] the only clear instance is the famous case where one man lit a furnace and another, having taken over the job of watching it, negligently fell asleep and let the fire spread; and in that case it seems that the omission must be coupled with an assumption of responsibility which, to use the terminology of English law, raised a duty of care.[132] The other kind of damage which was likely to appear unusual to the praetor was purely pecuniary damage to the plaintiff unaccompanied by physical damage to any object belonging to him; and we may certainly assume, from the small number of cases which appear in the *Digest* and from the fact, as Rotondi noticed, they are usually dealt with in connexion with the *actio doli*, that no generalisation of liability under this head had taken place before the end of the classical period. In other words, although all damage which did not fall under the *lex* itself was remedied by isolated decretal actions, as a matter of substantive law liability for physical damage caused by a positive act was in fact generalised, whereas each case of purely pecuniary damage had to be dealt with ad hoc and without the aid of any general principle. We must infer the existence of this line of division: for unless by that time some reason had existed for differentiating between physical and pecuniary damage, the Byzantines would scarcely have had any reason for distinguishing between the actions brought to remedy them; since by their time all the forms of action had disappeared.

Although the Byzantine *actio in factum* for merely pecuniary damage is usually regarded as having been general in character, it is something of a mystery and we have no means of knowing how it was kept within bounds. It came at the very end of the ancient development of Roman law and is left very much in the air. But it cannot have been so universal in scope as would at first sight appear, for otherwise there would have been no need to retain the *actio doli*, which was certainly still in use and played a large part in the law of delict.[133] From the very little evidence we have, it would seem that the *actio in factum* lay only for the pecuniary damage caused by negligently procuring the loss of a specific thing belonging to the plaintiff, without causing physical damage to it.[134]

Whatever may be the truth as to this latest action, the two

distinctions here brought to light, between damage caused by a positive act and damage caused by a pure omission, and between physical and merely pecuniary damage, seem highly significant. We shall find them in most of the modern laws derived from or influenced by Roman law and they tend to cause as many problems now as they did two thousand years ago.

4. Fault as the criterion of delictual liability

(a) *Iniuria*: justification and excuses[135]

One of the most impressive achievements of the Roman legal mind is the concept of *iniuria*. Eventually subdivided into two elements (the absence of legal excuse and the blameworthiness of the wrongdoer's conduct), it was destined to withstand the passage of time. Today, almost two thousand years later, it can still be found in one form or another in the various legal systems of the Western world and its importance equals only the difficulties it has created. But Roman law not only invented the concept; it also tackled many of the problems that still puzzle us today and, invariably, produced similar solutions. Its study can thus offer useful insights besides being of interest to legal historians. A brief survey of the Roman law will therefore be attempted in this chapter while some of the contemporary solutions will be examined in greater detail in the next one.

In both the first and the third chapter of the *lex Aquilia* the defendant is said to be liable if he acted *iniuria*, that is to say, *non iure*, 'without right'.[136] In the end this came to imply that he must have acted intentionally or negligently,[137] but hardly when the *lex* was passed.[138] We know that as late as the classical period and, it would seem, in the time of Justinian, an action could be brought on the *lex* itself only if the death or injury resulted from direct contact between the body of the wrongdoer and the thing (*corpore corpori*).[139] Translated into the language of the English law this means that the *lex* penalised only trespasses. Now we know that originally all trespasses were prima facie wrongful, and that it was only at a comparatively late date that the question was squarely raised whether a voluntary act giving rise to damage which was neither intended nor reasonably foreseeable could be a trespass. So rare were the cases that the point was finally settled as late as the second half of the nineteenth century in England,[140] though earlier in America, that no action for trespass to the person would lie unless the act was wilful or negligent; but the mediaeval rule was one of strict liability, and down to the end of the eighteenth century the defendant could escape only if he pleaded and proved inevitable accident. Indeed, before the advent of firearms and swiftly moving vehicles most trespasses would naturally be wilful, and the most obvious defences would be that the defendant had acted in self-defence or was otherwise justified in what he did; and we may perhaps infer that originally the qualification of liability introduced by the word *iniuria* meant strictly that the defendant must not have acted *iure*, i.e. in pursuance of some right.[141] Even in the *Digest* title a seemingly disproportionate number of the cases turn on considerations of self-defence,[142] public office,[143] or private right,[144] and it is interesting to note that in Ayliffe's *New Pandect of the Civil Law*, published in 1734, there is only a passing reference to negligence, but many references to positive defences. But at a fairly early date, if not when the *lex* was passed, it is likely that the defendant could plead that although he had killed or injured the thing in question, he had done so under circumstances which made it impossible to do otherwise and that he was therefore not to blame;[145] and from this it was a short step to interpreting *iniuria* as requiring the presence of either *dolus* or *culpa*.[146]

Who was responsible for this innovation is difficult to state with certainty as it is difficult to say at which precise moment in the history of the republic the development took place. One can conjecture, however, that since the introduction of the fault principle meant a narrowing and not a widening of liability it is not likely that it could have emanated from the praetors. Probably, therefore, the development was the result of juristic interpretation.[147]

The Roman Law of *faits justificatifs* need not detain us for long, suffice it to say that though the treatment the subject receives is seldom generalised, there is 'sufficient material for constructing such a general theory';[148] and the solutions that were proposed are not, generally speaking, dissimilar to those accepted by our modern systems. One particular *acte d'excuse*, however, has given rise to some difficulties which modern writers know only too well – difficulties which are increased by the fact that the language used in these cases 'disguises the selection of values that is really involved'.[149] This defence, therefore, merits special notice.

The necessity of the case is sometimes set up as a justification for causing damage. One finds oneself in a position where the only way of preventing damage to something belonging to oneself (or to a third party) is to interfere with something belonging to someone else. This is not a case of legitimate self-defence, though if one's property is put in danger by the thing interfered with and the owner of that thing is to blame, the analogy is compelling and creates a good defence. In other cases, supposing damage is done to the plaintiff's property, three solutions are possible.

(1) One may say that the necessity of the case never justifies the interference or damage. This is probably what was intended by Servius[150] in deciding the question whether one may destroy another man's house: one is justified *only* if the fire reached the plaintiff's house, which would in consequence have been destroyed in any event. It is also the view held by classical Mohammedan law and the modern Soviet law subject to the important qualification contained in the second part of article 449 § 1 of the Soviet Code.[151]

(2) One may say that the necessity of the case, if properly proved, completely justifies the damage and deprives the plaintiff of all remedy. This seems to be the solution intended by Ulpian in the case which is usually compared with that of Servius.[152] It is carried even one stage further in *Cope* v. *Sharpe* (no. 2),[153] where it was held that the defence succeeded even where the jury had found that the operation in question was not actually necessary in fact, since the fire had been put out before reaching the defendant's property, but was reasonably necessary according to the information available at the time to the defendant's gamekeeper. But in the Common law the problem is complicated by the existence of a law of trespass, which is not known to other systems.

(3) Whilst allowing the owner of the thing threatened to interfere and even damage another's property, one may insist on his compensating him for any damage that he has actually caused. In the German Civil Code, which has the most detailed and most carefully considered provisions,[154] it is also enacted that the threatened damage must have been disproportionately greater than the damage caused to the thing interfered with. In French law there has been some dispute as to whether this third solution is admissible, some jurists admitting it on the terms laid down in the German Civil Code,[155] others denying it altogether as contrary to justice,[156] and others again accepting the principle as just but experiencing difficulty in providing for it a satisfactory basis in existing law.[157]

Today, most authors accept that the problem is best solved by reference to the underlying principles of the notion of fault. The interest saved and the interest sacrificed must thus be weighed against each other in order to discover what the 'reasonable man' would have done in the circumstances. But even where necessity relieves the 'actor' of all tortious liability the principle of some indemnity for the 'victim' is no longer seriously in doubt though its *legal* justification has still not been conclusively settled. A not dissimilar line of thought has also been accepted in some American jurisdictions,[158] and to support it a doctrine of 'incomplete privilege'[159] has been evolved, i.e. the defendant is privileged to commit what would otherwise be a trespass, but upon the terms that he shall compensate the plaintiff for any damage caused by him. Sir Percy Winfield,[160] while admitting that in England tortious liability was excluded, thought that a quasi-contractual action might be maintained for compensation.

(b) *Culpa*[161]

The word *iniuria*, as we have seen, probably meant at first merely the absence of some lawful excuse for the act causing death or damage – but for the classical jurists it also implied the presence of either *dolus* or *culpa*,[162] which, as we have seen, may be taken to have started quite simply as an answer to the question whether the defendant was 'to blame' for the death or damage. That question is now seen to contain two separate questions: first, whether the defendant objectively 'caused' the death or damage, and secondly, whether, if he did 'cause' it, blame can be imputed to him for causing it on the ground that he acted intentionally or carelessly or not like a reasonable man. English lawyers make a distinction between *causation* and failure to conform to a *standard* of conduct; the French distinction is between *causalité* and *faute imputable*. This distinction is never made clear by the classical jurists, if it was ever even clear to their minds; nor, indeed, if we look at the typical cases considered by them is there any very clear distinction between *culpa* and the absence of positive justification or excuse. It is said[163] that the Byzantines disengaged the subjective notion of fault and made of it an element quite distinct from the objective element which consists of the accomplishment of an unlawful act, the main purpose of the change being to emphasise the guilty state of mind which alone could warrant the imposition of a penalty.[164] There is, indeed, some evidence for this in scholia to the *Basilica*,[165] but the scholia in question are from so late a period as the thirteenth century. It seems improbable that the penal element in this particular delict should have been given such prominence in the time of Justinian. Indeed, as we have seen, the actions on the *lex Aquilia* were now classified as 'mixed',[166] which seems to show that increased attention was being paid to the element of compensation.

There is a tendency to hold that references to *culpa* in this title are often interpolated, the point apparently being that emphasis on *culpa* implies a preoccupation with the moral element which was out of place in the classical law of damage. Doubtless such references are often interpolated, but not, it is conceived, for the purpose suggested. The classical jurists were, in the passages in question,[167] concerned with the form of action and did not mention *culpa* because they assumed its presence. The compilers,[168] for whom the forms of action were no longer more than academic, could see no great significance in these passages unless they were made to turn on the presence or absence of *culpa*; but they did not by interpolation alter the law.

Another point which is often made is that even the classical jurists decided cases on the facts without considering whether the conduct of either or both of the parties was blameworthy; in other words, to do a certain act at a certain time and place was *culpa*, but at another time or place was not.[169] It may well be that in the passages concerned the reasons for holding the conduct to amount or not to *culpa* were interpolated by the compilers, but that is not to say that they were not present to the minds of the classical jurists, even if unexpressed.

There are also cases where the evidence for interpolation is hardly disputable; the compilers have inserted a reference to *culpa* where it was quite unnecessary, evidently wishing to tie up the solution to a general theory of *culpa*.[170] But there seems to be little doubt that in these cases the classical jurist had the notion of *culpa* at the back of his mind, but, according to the regular habit of his class, did not see why he should bore his readers by stating the obvious, more particularly when his purpose was to give an opinion and not to write a thesis.

In this connexion it is interesting to study the earlier texts; for there is a steady stream of cases, reported in some detail, from Q. Mucius Scaevola, through Alfenus, Labeo, Mela, and Proculus, to the jurists of the mid-classical period. These texts are, to be sure, largely suspected of interpolation, but not so much as to the actual facts or decisions as the ways in which the latter are explained and rationalised. What is fairly obvious is that when, say, Alfenus is reported as making the decision turn on alternative hypotheses of fact, it is Alfenus himself who is speaking; for that is the way in which a jurist of his time must have answered a question put to him. Moreover, there is no good reason to suppose that the reports of these hypotheses have been garbled.

We start then with a case discussed by Q. Mucius,[171] where a man pruning trees throws down a branch and hits a passer-by. The answer depends on the circumstances. An act which is innocent if done in the proper place or after due warning may be injurious if done otherwise. We already have here one of the most obvious features of negligence, whether we do or do not accept as Mucius' the statement of principle which is attributed to him in the text. The fact that an act is voluntary does not inevitably take the accident it causes out of the category of *casus*. In that case why should not the *veteres* have used the well-known term *culpa* to designate conduct which, without being malicious, led to damage which could not be called merely accidental?

Alfenus has three relevant passages in this title. In one[172] he says that if a ship runs into another ship coming towards it, the pilot or captain will be liable, but if the ship could not be restrained the owners will not be liable. We are then told that if the *culpa* of the sailors was the cause of the accident, the Aquilian action will lie. This last remark is very probably interpolated, for the emphasis on *culpa* seems exaggerated and out of place. Moreover, it is fairly clear that the discussion is truncated, and that Alfenus meant to say that not only the owners, but also the pilot and captain, will be free from liability if the ship could not be controlled. Thus the mere fact of collision would not make the latter liable unless the surrounding circumstances made their negligence evident; and, indeed, from the mere fact of collision it could not be clear which ship had been navigated negligently. The same sort of problem arises in most of the cases of contributory negligence, one of which is indeed made to turn on which of the various parties was responsible.[173]

In another case[174] Alfenus seems to carry the matter a stage farther. Liability for damage to a slave is made to turn on whether muleteers let go of a wagon 'sua sponte' or 'timore permoti ne opprimerentur'. Now in the passage just discussed it might perhaps be said that the damage done by the uncontrollable ship was not done by the sailors at all; but a muleteer who lets go of a wagon under the influence of fear certainly acts, and acts voluntarily. But it may none the less be said that he is not really responsible for the damage, which is accordingly the result, not of *culpa*, but of *casus*.

The point is made even clearer by him in a third[175] case, where damage done to a slave engaged in a game is said to occur 'casu magis

24

quam culpa'. There is no reason whatever to suspect these words unless one is influenced by preconceived ideas. Thayer[176] suggests that the consent of the plaintiff prevents recovery, and this may be an admissible way of looking at the case: in English law the maxim *volenti non fit iniuria* would probably be applied. But this is not the point here; we are not indeed told that the master consented to the game. The defendant, though he has done the damage by a voluntary act, has acted, we must assume, normally.

On the other hand Labeo[177] says that one cannot complain if one is made liable for killing a sick slave merely by striking him lightly. But here, in the absence of any special information, we must assume that the blow was at least voluntary and unjustified; and the point is the one familiar in modern law, that it is of no help to a defendant to say that he could not have anticipated the actual form or extent of the damage.

All these solutions are so clearly in line with those given by the modern law of Negligence that one is bound to infer that as soon as the Roman jurists tried to find a principle underlying them they would adopt *culpa* as its basis; and since the word *culpa* is used constantly in such authors as Cicero[178] and Livy[179] to designate responsibility for, say, a war, there seems to be no good reason for refusing the credit of this development to the *veteres*, especially when one considers their evident interest in the scientific statement of the law. And why should there be anything suspicious in the notion that a person who carelessly causes damage is morally to blame?

There is another point that emerges from these cases that deserves attention. It is obvious that the two meanings of *iniuria* were not always kept clearly distinct and in this state of confusion *culpa* often swallowed up the older meaning of *iniuria*. Thus, in *D* 47,8,2,20, a tax collector seizing cattle is said not to be liable to the 'actio vi bonorum raptorum' for 'sane dolo caret'. And a shopkeeper who blinds the thief while trying to rescue his goods is similarly absolved for the fault does not lie with him[180] (though, once again, the critical phrase 'culpam enim eo residere' is suspect of interpolation). And again, in the case of the young slave who is injured in the course of a game, the tortfeasor is absolved from liability since the injury occurred 'casu magis quam culpa'.[181] Indeed, in one text, those who obey lawful commands are excused not because of their duty to obey but because lawful obedience excludes intention or negligence.[182] Why *culpa* came to oust in these and other similar cases the earlier notion of *iniuria* is not entirely clear and, in any event, need not concern us here. What should, however, be noted is the ability of these two distinct notions of 'unlawfulness' to merge or separate as the case may be. Thus, we shall see[183] that the German concept of *Widerrechtlichkeit*, traditionally understood to have the early meaning of the Roman *iniuria*, is nowadays taken by many to include an additional element not dissimilar to the English concept of duty of care. And in France, where the concept of *illicéité* has provoked heated controversies, many would agree with M. le conseiller Georges Holleaux that 'la notion centrale de "faute civile"…est une notion qui *englobe*…les deux éléments d'illiceité et de "culpabilité", *pour les confondre dans un concept unique*, d'où…l'élément subjectif est à peu près complètement exclu'.[184]

What are we to say of the standard adopted by the Roman jurists in their assessment of *culpa*?[185] We are met at the outset by a statement attributed to Ulpian,[186] but probably interpolated and certainly taken out of a context which is now quite unascertainable, that under the *lex Aquilia* there is no question of assessing *culpa*: the slightest *culpa* suffices. It is obvious that Aquilian liability is thus distinguished from liability in contract, where the standard varies with the particular contract in question. But is *culpa levissima* slighter than *culpa levis in abstracto*, which is the slightest negligence known in contract? If so, there is a temptation to equate it with strict liability. This is clearly not the view of the compilers, who could not in that case have allowed the contrary opinion of Paul[187] (and probably Q. Mucius) to stand; for he is made to say quite clearly that *culpa* amounts to failing to foresee damage which a diligent person would have foreseen. Even if the formulation of that principle is later than Q. Mucius, it fits the decision in the particular case, and so probably represents his view. An attempt has indeed been made to prove that the term *diligens paterfamilias*, found frequently in the *Corpus Iuris*, described a state of mind and so must always be interpolated;[188] but the evidence for interpolation is often very thin, and an English lawyer, with his experience of 'the reasonable man', does not need to be told that such terms may just as easily point to an objective as to a subjective standard. In fact, Pollock[189] says roundly: 'Negligence is the contrary of diligence, and no one describes diligence as a state of mind.'

In any case, the distinction between a subjective and an objective standard cannot in practice be so clear as it is often made to be in theory; for even if liability is made to depend on the defendant's state of mind, the latter can normally be ascertained only by comparing his conduct with that of a reasonable man in the circumstances. So that even Holmes, attached as he was to the principle of 'no liability without fault', had to say:

The rule that the law does, in general, determine liability by blameworthiness, is subject to the limitation that minute differences of character are not allowed for. The law considers, in other words, what would be blameworthy in the average man, the man of ordinary intelligence and prudence, and determines liability by that. If we fall below the level in those gifts, it is our misfortune; so much as that we must have at our peril, for the reasons just given. But he who is intelligent and prudent does not act at his peril, in theory of law. On the contrary, it is only when he fails to exercise the foresight of which he is capable, or exercises it with evil intent, that he is answerable for the consequences.[190]

And, of course, conversely, the mere fact that one has to apply the standard of the reasonable man is quite compatible with a genuine desire to base liability on a guilty state of mind. Thus, the formulation attributed, rightly or wrongly, to Q. Mucius:[191] 'culpam esse, cum quod a diligente provideri potuerit, non esset provisum', is not decisive of the matter.

Even the treatment of persons suffering under a disability peculiar to themselves is not entirely conclusive. Roman law exempted from liability madmen and children who were too young to be capable of *iniuria*.[192] This solution would seem to point to an acceptance of the subjective theory. But cases such as *Escoffier c. Girel*[193] show that even where liability is not based on fault but is strict, it is still possible to exempt persons of defective mental capacity on the ground that their intervention is equivalent to *force majeure* or *cas fortuit*; and this is, in fact, the implication to be drawn from h.t. 5,2, which likens the act of a madman to that of an animal or the fall of a tile. Thus it is possible for an adherent of the objective theory to treat the exemption as a well defined exception admitted, it may well be, on grounds of hardship,[194] and, as will be shown later, to reduce its scope if the greater hardship proves to be on the injured party. To quote Holmes again:

So far as civil liability, at least, is concerned, it is very clear that what I have called 'the external standard' would be applied; so that, if a man's conduct is such as would be reckless in a man of ordinary prudence, it is reckless in *him*. Unless he can bring himself within some broadly defined exception to general rules, the law deliberately leaves his personal equation or idiosyncrasies out of account, and peremptorily assumes that he has as much capacity to judge and foresee consequences as a man of ordinary prudence would have in the same situation.[195]

Perhaps more cogent evidence in favour of the subjective theory is afforded by the Roman treatment of cases where damage is caused by the defendant's lack of strength or skill;[196] for here it is said that 'infirmitas' or 'imperitia' 'culpae adnumeratur'.[197] The solutions are, it is true, perfectly consistent with an objective theory of liability, for a man who undertakes something beyond his strength or skill is normally not acting like a reasonable man; but it is easy to see that the form in which the maxims are couched suggests a moral blameworthiness which is not emphasised in the objective theory.[198] It is worthy of notice that the maxims are attributed to Celsus[199] and Gaius,[200] both fairly early jurists; and there is no apparent reason to suspect that the attributions are due to interpolation.[201] If, then, they do point to a subjective theory of liability, they show that it was in existence before A.D. 150.

On the other hand, there is clear authority to show that certain mistakes did not exclude liability. Such were, for instance, a mistaken belief that the slave killed was a freeman,[202] though if he had been free no one could have brought an action under the *lex*; or that the slave injured belonged to the person injuring him.[203] Both cases fall into the class described by Thayer:[204] 'Harm is intended with a bad motive under a belief, reasonable or not, that the requisites do not exist for an Aquilian action.'[205] Another type of case is described by him[206] in the following terms: 'Harm is intended, but without a bad motive, involving the unreasonable belief that it is justified, which includes mistakes as to the extent of the privileges.' Thus we are told[207] that a person who removes a good party wall is liable to its owner for wrongful damage, and it must be assumed that he has done so under a mistake that it was no longer good. These instances would seem to point to an objective view of negligence. However, one has only to refer to English law to realise that they are quite compatible with either an objective or a subjective view of negligence.[208]

It is therefore not easy to decide finally whether Roman law regarded *culpa* in a subjective or an objective light. As for the modern systems, we shall see that after some initial hesitation under the influence of canon law and its secular offspring, natural law, they have now opted for a more objective standard of fault with 'a dynamic regard for social amelioration'.[209] The result: not infrequently liability which, in name only, is based on fault.[210]

In Roman law, as indeed in modern law, the notion of *culpa* has proved elusive and difficult. Complete agreement on the precise meaning is, therefore, unlikely to be reached and reconciliation of the many theories on the subject may well be impossible since the texts can be taken to give at least some measure of support to all of them. Professor MacCormack has thus vigorously supported a theory that *culpa* is best rendered as 'fault' rather than 'negligence'. Any compression of his exhaustive and interesting analysis of the texts is bound to appear crass, but, in brief, the argument runs as follows: where a Roman jurist discusses the facts of a case and draws his conclusion that there has or has not been *culpa*, he is not asking whether these facts constitute negligence but whether they amount to fault.

From this one may infer that where *culpa* is used as a criterion of liability in a general context without the addition of facts which explain what is meant, it should be taken as fault... The translation of *culpa* as negligence suggests that a principle of foreseeability operated in Roman law much as in English law, and that the jurists asked in each case, ought the defendant to have foreseen that his act or omission would cause damage?[211]

According to Professor MacCormack, such a generalisation can be made only 'through a distortion of the way in which jurists actually operated'. True, the facts upon which a jurist holds that there has been *culpa* may often disclose a case of carelessness and sometimes the matter is even discussed in terms of foreseeability. The *putator*'s case is one such example. But in such cases the correct conclusion is that carelessness may count as *culpa*, not that *culpa* is negligence. The same may be true of *imperitia, infirmitas, lascivia,* or *saevitia,* which leads the learned author to warn that '*culpa* as understood in the context of one rule might differ considerably from *culpa* as understood in the context of another'.[212]

This may well be true; and indeed the vague and undifferentiated use of *culpa* has already been alluded to, as also has the casuistic treatment of conduct by the jurists. But for the purposes of *actio legis Aquiliae* and the analogous *actiones utiles* and *in factum*, *culpa* does seem to have become specialised – though sometimes including, sometimes differentiated from, *dolus* – so as to correspond to the kind of conduct (sometimes also including an intent to harm) which is the basis of the Common law action of negligence. In both the dominant notion is carelessness, and in both the evidence of it may often – perhaps usually – be so obvious that there is no need to bother about foreseeability. Finally, the word 'negligent' is so much handier than any adjective derived from 'fault' that is in use, while the adverb 'negligently' can hardly be dispensed with. The continued rendering of *culpa* as 'negligence' in the texts reproduced in volume II of this work must therefore be understood in accordance with the points made above.

5. Causation and related problems

(a) Causation

Many modern scholars have succumbed to the temptation of analysing texts of the *Digest* in terms of modern causal theories.[213] This approach may be inevitable and, to some extent, it may even be desirable. There is little concrete evidence, however, to suggest that it is the one adopted by the Romans, who do not appear to have operated any particular theory or doctrine of causation.[214] This does not imply that their solution always differed from ours;[215] nor should it be taken to suggest that the Roman jurists did not have a firm grasp of the significance of what modern lawyers would describe as an interruption in the chain of causation, though, naturally enough, they had the same difficulty as everyone else in deciding whether it had taken place in particular cases. But their *approach* was different not only because most of their problems of causation seemed to be related to the question whether a particular state of affairs amounted to *occidere* or *rumpere* and was therefore actionable under the *lex*;[216] but also because often the outcome of such problems seemed to depend more on the presence or absence of fault on the part of the defendant than on the nature or causative potency of his conduct.[217] And the strong tendency to justify solutions by means of analogies is also significant, for this highly practical and concrete approach allows little 'scope for an investigation of causal connections'.[218] Finally, their attitude to what we would call the problem of remoteness was also different from ours in so far as they were prepared to carry liability to the full extent once initial liability had been established.[219] No Roman solution, then, helps us decide how far the chain of causation can for practical purposes be taken to extend where there is no actual interruption by the conscious act of a human being;[220] though the question becomes crucial if the test of remoteness applied to determining culpability is not available, either to put a limit to the damage for which a person is liable or to create a causal nexus sufficient to make him liable without fault.

Three irreconcilable passages – h.t. 11,3; 15,1 and 51 pr. – have caused difficulties from early times, and since they have also appeared most prominently in the works of modern writers[221] they deserve a closer look. In the first, Celsus, Marcellus and Ulpian agree that if one man gives a slave a mortal wound and another afterwards kills him, only the latter is liable under the first chapter for killing, and the former only under the third for wounding. In 15,1 Ulpian reports Julian, apparently with approval, as saying that if one man gives a slave a mortal wound and his death is hastened by the fall of a house or a shipwreck or another wound, the original wounder is, as in the former case, liable only for wounding and not for killing, since the fall of the house prevented it from being clear that he had killed the slave. But in 51 pr. Julian, in a passage taken from him directly by the compilers, says that if a slave is so wounded by one man as to make it certain that he will die from the blow and afterwards dies from a blow given by another, both are liable for killing; for if one man gives a slave a mortal wound and after an interval another strikes him in such a way as to hasten his death, both are liable for killing. How are we to reconcile these divergent solutions?

The gloss, and an almost contemporary late scholion to the *Basilica*,[222] found a way out by assuming that the mortal wound mentioned in 11,3 and 15,1 differed from that in 51 pr. in that death would not certainly have resulted from it; but this is most unlikely to be correct, since in the last sentence of 51 pr. Julian himself uses the term 'mortiferum vulnus' in a general summing-up of the law. Some good authorities regard the passages as irreconcilable, though Pernice[223] thought that for Justinian's law we can reconcile them by saying that in the first two the second blow was such that it would have killed the slave even if he had not been wounded by the first, whereas in the last passage the second blow was fatal only because the first wound had reduced the slave to a dying condition. But he doubted whether this reasoning could be attributed to Julian, mainly because Julian uses the word 'maturius' in both 15,1 and 51 pr.

However, it seems probable that this is the correct solution even for Julian. In 15,1 he is obviously thinking mainly of some external catastrophe, such as the fall of a house – which is the only case he mentions as preventing it from being clear that death resulted from the first wound – and not of the second blow, which is apparently introduced as an afterthought, possibly by Ulpian, or even the compilers, to bring the passage into line with 11,3. But even if Julian introduced it, he may reasonably be thought to have had in mind a blow as catastrophic in its nature and consequences as the fall of a house. If so, we may infer that in 15,1 he was dealing with something that clearly broke the chain of causation between the first wound and the death. In 51 pr., on the other hand, he is not at all concerned with that case, but with one where two persons had contributed to the death and there was nothing in the second wound to force one to say that the first was not a cause of death. Thus for Julian 51 pr. gives the rule and 51,1 the exception. The solution is not unlike that often proposed in the former English law of contributory negligence. It receives some measure of confirmation from the juxtaposition of 51,1 where Julian deals with the case of many contributing simultaneously to a death.

This leaves an apparent contradiction between 51 pr. and 11,3, which seems to say generally that the first wounder can never be liable for killing. It is possible, but not certain, that in 11,3 Celsus used 'exanimaverit' to mean something of the same kind as Julian seems to have meant in 15,1: Grueber[224] suggests cutting the slave's head off, Monro,[225] shooting him through the head. But it may well be that Celsus and Marcellus disagreed with Julian, as they did fairly often. 15,1 gives, as it were, the middle term. They may well have agreed with the opinion Julian expresses there, but not with that given in 51 pr.

Another way of approaching the problem is as follows: Celsus[226] puts the matter merely on the basis of actual result. The slave in fact died of the second blow. It makes no difference that he would have died of the first in any case – as he did not, the first blow was an unsuccessful attempt. Julian[227] makes the criterion the originally mortal nature of the blow (and it is only on the assumption that the delict was completed at the moment of striking that the difference in damages in h.t. 51,2 and the decision in the second case h.t. 15,1 can be explained). Consequently, if both blows were originally mortal in their nature, both assailants are liable. Julian (as reported by Ulpian)[228] is illogical. He begins by saying that the first blow is mortal, and then gives a decision that there is no liability because the fatal accident occurring afterwards made it impossible to prove that the first blow was mortal. He thus agrees with Celsus in effect, but with his own other decision in principle.

The whole question is in fact rather academic, and the jurists may easily have differed without harming anyone; for it is only a question of damages and, as Buckland and McNair[229] say, not a very important one at that. If the first wounder gave a mortal wound, the deterioration he caused in the slave amounted to the whole value of the slave, and accordingly the practical difference between killing and wounding is limited to the difference between the year's and the thirty days' valuation, i.e. it related not to compensation but to pure penalty, and may not, in most cases, have amounted to anything.

(b) Contributory negligence

Culpa and causation compete for possession of the territory which Common lawyers recognise as that of contributory negligence. At least five cases in the *lex Aquilia* title[230] raise questions of this kind, but in none of them is it possible to discover a certain principle of decision. All belong to that familiar class of cases where the conduct of the plaintiff not only seems to point to contributory negligence in himself, but also to be so unexpected that the defendant could not be held liable for failing to guard against it. All seem to yield to the simple argument on the part of the defendant: 'It was your own fault',[231] but whether the main emphasis was laid on the plaintiff's *culpa* or on a break in the chain of causation, perhaps the Roman jurists themselves did not know. We are not even told for certain that the whole of the damage was borne by one or other of the parties,[232] though we may reasonably suppose that if the solution had been to share the damage we should have heard of it.

Both Pernice[233] and Grueber[234] have come in for some unmerited abuse for their suggestion that the cases were dealt with on a basis of *culpa*-compensation. Monro[235] says:

The German expression '*culpa-compensation*', is better avoided. It uses the word compensation in a sense which ought to be English, but is not, and it seems to assume that a balance is struck by measuring two quantities of the same kind of thing one against the other. This can hardly have been the principle...

and Buckland and McNair[236] go even farther:

It is true that modern writers have invented and attributed to the Romans a theory of what they call '*culpa* compensation', into which they have attempted to force the Roman texts. It is an unsuitable name in any case, since it suggests set off (Compensatio) quantitative estimate of the negligence on each side, or, at best, our Admiralty rule rather than the common law rule. And it completely falsifies the Roman view. They seem to have applied here a theory of causation, no doubt a theory of causation which is not satisfactory, but that is not exceptional in theories of causation. The Roman view was that the negligent or intending person was liable for the harm if he caused it but not if some intervening agency prevented his act from producing its effect.

However, Pernice[237] himself says:

The true legal basis of culpa-compensation I believe must still be found in the fact that the *neglegentia* of the victim makes doubtful the causal connection between the *culpa* of the person who has injured him and the *damnum*.

But he also goes on to say[238]

for the time being it is enough to regard the compensation as something natural,

i.e. as something demanded by one's sense of natural justice. Thus the difference between Pernice and Buckland, if there be one, is not so much as to the reason for the Roman rule but as to the form it took. Pernice apparently did think that one *culpa* was set off against the other, in such a way as not to reduce but to destroy liability; and the proof of this is to be found in his further statement: 'The rule of culpa-compensation suffers an exception when the wrongdoer is *in dolo*. For only like can be set off against like. *Dolus* and *culpa* are however completely unlike.'[239] Now in the only relevant Roman text[240] we are told that even if the plaintiff was negligent the defendant must not deliberately hurt him – which seems to prove Pernice's case. Buckland and McNair deal with the difficulty as follows:[241]

The result ought logically to be the same whether my original act was intentional or merely negligent. If I did not cause the result in the one case I did not in the other. In the javelin case indeed we are told that if seeing the man crossing I intentionally throw at him, I am liable. But this would be true on any theory. I was the direct cause. I was the proximate cause. I had the last chance. His presence was the *causa sine qua non*: my act was the *causa causans*.

But what if the defendant's *dolus* had preceded the plaintiff's *culpa*? Suppose the defendant had deliberately set a trap for the plaintiff and the latter had carelessly fallen into it. Surely Roman law – for that matter English law too – would refuse to relieve the defendant of liability. And yet on a basis of causation the plaintiff should be held responsible for the damage to himself. The fact is that, in this case at any rate, we instinctively hold that the plaintiff's *culpa* cannot be set off against the defendant's *dolus*, or, what is the same thing, that a defendant cannot be heard to say that he did not cause a damage which he intended and which has actually come to pass. In other words, for some purpose at least we think in terms of *culpa*-compensation, if only to rule it out. It is by no means certain that Pernice went wrong in his interpretation of the Roman texts. The Romans were never faced with the really difficult problems, such as those which gave rise to *Davies* v. *Mann*[242] and *Loach*'s case,[243] which admittedly cannot be solved satisfactorily on a basis of *culpa*-compensation.

(c)   Penalties and measure of damages

We have seen that under the first chapter of the *lex* the defendant had to pay the highest value of the slave or animal during the past year.[244] Later the penalty was extended to include the *interesse* of the plaintiff in the survival of the slave or animal.[245] How this came about is not entirely clear. If Daube's interpretation of the third chapter[246] is correct, the *interesse* was always included in the sum which had to be paid under that chapter, and this may easily have influenced the interpretation of the first chapter also. But there is another way in which the same result may have been produced. If the plaintiff's slave was instituted heir by a third party and then killed by the defendant,[247] we may say that the plaintiff's *interesse* in his slave's survival included the value of the inheritance, for he could have ordered the slave to enter on the inheritance and so vest it in himself, a proceeding which the death of the slave had put out of his power.[248] But the same result can be obtained in another way without doing any violence to the wording of the *lex*. After the testator's death the plaintiff could have sold the slave for a sum including, besides his own intrinsic value, the value of the inheritance, and so his value must be taken at this enhanced sum. However, once this result had been reached by a reasonably strict interpretation of the *lex*, it was easy to say that the meaning of the *lex* had been extended to cover the whole *interesse* of the plaintiff, and further, to admit as part of that *interesse* all cases of *lucrum cessans*,[249] that is to say, of all gain which the plaintiff had missed through the defendant's wrongful act. But they must not be too speculative.[250]

Once the *interesse* became the measure of the penalty it is easy to see that account should also be taken of *damnum emergens*,[251] that is to say, the damage, outside the highest value of the slave or animal during the past year,[252] which the death of the slave or animal had caused to the plaintiff. But here too it is sometimes possible to treat the *damnum emergens* as equivalent to an enhancement in the value of the slave or animal. Thus if the plaintiff's animal was worth £10, had caused damage to the extent of £20 and was then killed by the defendant before the plaintiff could hand it over noxally, the plaintiff, who had now to pay £20 without the option of noxal surrender, could claim from the defendant £10, being the intrinsic value of the animal, plus £10, being the extra amount the defendant's act had cost him to satisfy the person injured by the animal.[253] But it is clear that after the animal had done the damage the actual value of the animal to the plaintiff was

£20, for it could be used to relieve him of liability to pay £20 damages to the person injured by it. However, the 'survival value' did not include the sentimental value that the slave or animal possessed for the plaintiff.[254]

Very much the same extensions would be made in connexion with the third chapter, though the occasions for applying them might be rarer. The cost of curing an injured slave might well be included in his loss of value or at any rate in *damnum emergens*.[255] But where the injured person was a freeman it became an independent, perhaps the sole, item of damage, for there could be no diminution in the market value of such a person.[256] On the other hand, very much the same result could be obtained by assessing the diminution in his earning capacity. The question would not arise in the case of a freeman's death, since no action lay at all outside one head of quasi-delict.[257]

However, the most interesting cases of *damnum emergens* and *lucrum cessans* under the third chapter are in relation to receipts and documents of title. The principle that damages can be recovered is clear, but there are difficulties in detail.[258]

Lucrum cessans and *damnum emergens* have proved permanent conquests of delictual liability;[259] but modern law has discussed other difficulties which the Romans never knew. For although the problem of remoteness has been shown to have played a part in the imposition of liability, there is only one case where it relates to the extent of the penalty the defendant had to pay.[260] Even that case is equivocal, for the new damage which was held not to be imputable to the defendant was the death of a slave whom he had previously wounded; and killing, being dealt with in a separate chapter of the *lex*, was not to be treated as a mere consequence of the wounding, but as a separate delict, for which liability, according to the decision, never came into existence.

6. The Advance Beyond Roman Law

The student who has acquired reasonable knowledge of Roman law has made a necessary step towards understanding the modern Civil law; but he has still far to go for two reasons. First, the modern Roman law contained in the Civil law is not always the same as the old law in the books of Justinian. Secondly, it is important to realise that the Civil law systems are hybrids and contain many elements which, though sometimes influenced and modified by Roman law, are not essentially of Roman origin. It is, therefore, desirable to say something about the more important changes that have taken place in Roman law in the Middle Ages and in later times.

Many of the changes have a long and fairly continuous history. The starting point may even be detected in the ancient law itself and the finishing touches only in the German Civil Code, the intermediate stages being found in the works of the mediaeval jurists, the theologians of the later middle ages, the natural lawyers of the seventeenth and eighteenth centuries, and the German Pandectists of the nineteenth century. Of all those agents, probably the most important were the natural lawyers: certainly the results bear all the marks of their activity. On the whole, few actual rules were changed,[261] at any rate by factors operating within the parts derived from Roman law; but there were changes in the direction of abstraction and generalisation, and in the process many minor differences which existed in the ancient law were ironed out. These changes, therefore, deserve a closer look.

(a)   The movement from remedies to rights and its effects on the classification of the modern Civil law

It is known that the Roman law of republican and classical times crystallised around a set of actions and conveyances. By the middle of the third century, however, these old forms were disappearing fast and making way for a type of pleading not unlike ours. The shift was progressive from form of action to cause of action, and from there to the right which the plaintiff was seeking to enforce, so that by the beginning of the nineteenth century lawyers everywhere in the Civil law world, and especially in Germany, were thinking increasingly in terms of rights and abstract concepts. This strong tendency towards a 'general theory of law from which all but the essential elements have been removed'[262] will appear to Common lawyers, accustomed to the kind of particularism which was acceptable to the classical Roman jurist, as a striking feature of the modern Civil law. The move towards abstraction, however, is equally remarkable from a negative point of view in so far as it removed from the modern Civil law all traces of the old habit of inferring rights from remedies.

As actions became subservient to the rights they were designed to enforce, they inevitably started to move away from the law of actions into the law of property or obligations. The law relating to the formation and extinction of contracts and the law of delict easily slid into the law of obligations, soon to be followed by quasi-contract, where there is little but what is remedial. But the forms of action which helped assert proprietary rights were, initially, more difficult to class. Yet there is no doubt that having shed their substantive content and, as a law of mere procedure, being thrust outside the Civil law, the real actions would go with property rather than obligations. For one thing, the judgment in a personal action was always for a money debt or a penalty or damages; the judgment in a real action was in post-classical times for return of the thing or a declaration or an injunction. Thus when the civilians, and above all the natural lawyers, began to tackle the work of classifying the law, many parts of the law went into quite different pigeon-holes from those which are familiar to Common lawyers with their memory of forms of action abolished only the day before yesterday. We must thus expect to find much of our law of torts in the Civil law of property. For not only have all the actions which have for their purpose the protection of property been brought under the head of property; so also are the extensions of actions by analogy where a Common lawyer would expect to find them in tort. The tort of Nuisance, though peripherally related to our main subject, is an example which deserves a closer look.

That the *rei vindicatio* would be naturally considered as incidental to ownership and thus end up as being classified as property is easy to comprehend. The same is equally true of the *actio confessoria* which helped protect rights less than ownership such as easements[263] and life interests, and the *actio negatoria* which was given to an owner who wished to assert the freedom of his land from an easement. But then came the extension in the mediaeval and modern law. For suppose your neighbour does not walk across your land under a claim to an easement, but merely sends fumes across your land or makes life unbearable by noise; can he not be said to be really claiming something in the nature of an easement to these things even though no such easement would be recognised by the law? On that fictitious reasoning you can claim the freedom of your land from his encroachment as if it had been an easement, and your action will be an *actio quasi negatoria*, which will sound in property and not in delict. From the substantive point of view, what will be in issue will be the ambit of ownership, not the personal duty of your neighbour not to commit a delict of encroachment. Incidentally, this attitude of mind led the German law and some of its derivatives to limit the remedy, if no fault were proved in the neighbour, to a declaration or injunction.

French and Swiss law, on the other hand, which do not take their classifications so seriously, have found it possible to award damages as well.[264] But this to us is nuisance and hence a tort, for we think instinctively, even now that we have got rid of the forms of actions, of the wrong rather than the right. To a Common lawyer, therefore, the civilian classification is not always easy to accept or understand. And it offers an excellent example of the kind of difficulty that is apt to confront him if he is at the threshold of comparative law. For he will be unable even to use the index of a foreign tort book in his attempt to find, say, the French law of nuisance unless he has a clear general knowledge of the conceptual structure of the foreign law. In our example this is, of course, all the more surprising given that 'nuisance' has its origins in old French!

(b)   The development of a general action

Another way in which the mediaeval and modern Civil law advanced beyond Roman law was by generalisation. As we have already noted, there is comparatively little generalisation in Roman law. The Roman jurists extended rules and principles from one institution to others which they felt to be essentially similar, but little more was attempted. Nowhere is this clearer than in their law of delict which, like the Common law of tort, was essentially based in separate actions designed to enforce liability for specific wrongs. But in the centuries that followed the fall of Rome all this changed, and the history of this transformation, even in its barest outline, presents an interest and fascination of its own.

There is little doubt that the older civilians regarded their law of negligent damage as a modernised version of the Roman. They were content to describe the latter with a footnote to the effect that the penal element no longer existed, though they drew attention to other points where the modern law had special rules,[265] and they were, of course, fully aware that differences between direct actions, *actiones utiles* and *actiones in factum*, had no longer any reality.

But even this partial recognition is, as Rotondi showed,[266] misleading, for this is one of the occasions on which the learned reception of Roman law by the jurists was imperfectly reflected in the practice of the courts. Long before there was any question of receiving Roman law, the courts had been administering a penal law which, like the older Civil law of Rome, made no distinction between crime and tort. As in Rome, there had been a need to buy off family vengeance by the award of compositions, of which the Anglo-Saxon wergild is a type; and about the time when Roman law began to be received, the repression of crime came to be considered the function of public authorities. In these circumstances the courts felt no need of penal actions on the Roman model, but seeing as they did that the actions for *damnum iniuria datum* had developed so as to lay greater emphasis on compensation than the penalty which occasionally accompanied it, they took over, more perhaps on the suggestion of Roman law than directly from it, a general action for reparation of damage caused *dolo aut culpa*. In so far as the rules of Roman law were appropriate to this action, they applied them. Thus the psychological element in delict, or, if we prefer, the element that relates to standards of conduct, comes from Roman law. But the external element is not really Roman. Any wrongful damage to person or property in the widest sense of the terms made the defendant liable. Thus from now on there is no need to make any distinction between personal injuries and damage to property.

Comparatively little of this development appears in the works of the jurists. From the Glossators onwards, they felt bound to adhere to the Roman law of the *Corpus Iuris*, with the limitations implicit in its scheme of actions, its penal character, and its consequent refusal to allow actions to be brought against heirs except to the extent by which the inheritance had been enriched by the delict. But there are ample indications that they felt uneasy at the archaic nature of the Roman remedies, and by a process of forced construction of the texts, they were able, by the end of the fifteenth century, to bring their law into something like conformity with court practice.

The humanistic school of the sixteenth century reacted strongly against this development, but the natural lawyers, who followed them, put the coping-stone on it. The required practical results had already been obtained, but they gave it a firm basis of theory which it had not hitherto possessed. Henceforth it was possible, even in a country which claimed to have received Roman law as a whole,[267] to justify this departure from strict Roman Doctrine. The theory of natural law is found fully stated by Grotius. In his *De Iure Belli ac Pacis*[268] he says:

> That fault creates the obligation to make good the loss.
> We have said above that there are three sources of what is owed to us, agreement, wrong and statute. Enough has been said about agreements. Let us come now to what is naturally due in consequence of a wrong.

By a wrong we here mean every fault, whether of commission or of omission, which is in conflict with what men ought to do, either generally or by reason of a special quality. From such a fault, if damage has been caused, an obligation arises naturally, namely, that it should be made good.

Some natural lawyers in Germany, such as Thomasius (1655 –1728), denied that the action for damage had anything to do with the Roman action but held that it was based on German law and on Equity.[269] This is an example of what Gierke called attention to, the revival of German legal ideas under cover of natural law.

The work of the natural lawyers culminated in a great movement for codification. In fairly quick succession were enacted the Prussian Allgemeines Landrecht (1794) the French Code Civil (1804), and the Austrian Allgemeines Bürgerliches Gesetzbuch (1811). The first and last of these were profoundly influenced by natural law ideas and ceased to exert much influence generally as the tide of natural law ebbed. Their treatment of damage is thorough, but over-complicated – the Prussian Code very much so. The provisions of the French Code, on the contrary, are over-simplified; but they show very good sense and have proved capable of development to fit the changing conditions of the nineteenth and twentieth centuries. Article 1382, which enunciates a general liability for fault, reads like a manifesto, and it is doubtless to its quality of simple inevitability that it has owed its remarkable extension throughout the world. And it has carried with it the other four articles, which are by no means so obvious. Almost every civil code that has since been enacted, except the German Civil Code of 1896, contains the gist of article 1382, with very little, if any, modification.

Selected further reading

Albanese, B., 'Actio utilis e actio in factum ex Lege Aquilia', 21 *Annali del Seminario Giuridico della Università di Palermo* (1950).

Barton, J.L., 'The *Lex Aquilia* and Decretal Actions', in *Daube Noster*, ed. A. Watson (1974), p.15.

Beinart, B., 'The Relationship of *iniuria* and *culpa* in the Lex Aquilia', in *Studi Arangio-Ruiz* (4 vols., 1953), I, 279.

'Once More on the Origin of the Lex Aquilia', *Butterworth's South African Law Review* (1956), 70.

Daube, D., 'On the Third Chapter of the Lex Aquilia', 52 *L.Q.R.* (1936), 253.

'On the use of the Term Damnum', *Studi Solazzi* (1948), 93 *et seq.*

Dias, R.W.M., 'Obscurities in the Development of *Damnum*', *Acta Juridica* (1958), 215.

'Policy Differences in Remoteness of Damage', *Acta Juridica* (1976), 193.

Feenstra, R., 'The Historical Development of Delictual Liability for Killing and for the Infliction of Bodily Harm', *Acta Juridica* (1972), 227.

'Théories sur la responsabilité en cas d'homicide et en cas de lésion corporelle avant Grotius', *Etudes d'histoire du droit privé offertes à Pierre Petot* (1959), 151.

'L'Actio legis Aquiliae utilis en cas d'homicide chez les Glossateurs', *Essays in Commemoration of the Sixth Lustrum of the Institute for Legal History of the University of Utrecht* (1979).

Honoré, A.M., 'Linguistic and Social Context of the *Lex Aquilia*', 7 *Irish Jurist* N.S. (1972), 138.

Iliffe, J.A., 'Thirty Days hath Lex Aquilia', 5 *Rev. int. dr. ant.* (1958), 493.

Kelly, J.M., 'The Meaning of the Lex Aquilia', 80 *L.Q.R.* (1964), 73.

Levy-Bruhl, H., 'Le Deuxième Chapitre de la loi Aquilia', 5 *Rev. int. dr. ant.* (1958), 507.

MacCormack, G., 'Aquilian Studies', 41 *S.D.H.I.* (1975), 1.

'Culpa', *38 S.D.H.I.* (1972) 123.

'Aquilian Culpa', in *Daube Noster*, p. 200.

'On the Third Chapter of the Lex Aquilia', 5 *Irish Jurist.* N.S. (1970). 164.

Pringsheim, F., 'The Origin of the "Lex Aquilia"', *Mélanges Lévy-Bruhl* (1959), 233.

Powell, R., ' "Novus actus interveniens" in Roman Law', 4 *Cur. Leg. Prob.* (1951), 197.

Pugsley, D., 'The Origins of the Lex Aquilia', 85 *L.Q.R.* (1969), 50.

'Damni Injuria', 36 *Tijd* (1968), 371.

'Causation and Confessions in the *Lex Aquilia*', 38 *Tijd* (1970), 163.

Robertis, F.M. de, 'Quanti ea res erit – id quod interest nel sistema della grande Compilazione', 32 *S.D.H.I.* (1966), 114.

Rotondi, G., 'Dalla Lex Aquilia all' art. 1151 Cod. Civ.: richerche storico-dogmatiche', *Scritti Giuridici*, II (1922).

Chapter 2

FIXING THE BOUNDARIES OF TORTIOUS LIABILITY

1. Policy factors and the law of torts*

American scholars have, for some time now, been arguing that 'the courts cannot and should not escape taking into consideration in the determination of tort or other cases the interests of "we the people" at large, or important groups whose interests are identified within the interests of the social order'.[1] This 'third phase' of the judicial process, which goes far beyond the interests of the immediate parties to the litigation, is dominated by wider considerations of policy which, until recently, were deliberately obscured behind such elusive concepts as duty, unlawfulness, *faute*, foreseeability, remoteness and the like.

In England, ideas not dissimilar to these have, from time to time, been echoed by a number of academics.[2] Dennis Lloyd, for example, in his monograph on public policy argued that it is 'difficult to resist the conclusion that the law of tort has been developed by the English judges very largely on the basis of their feelings as to what the public interest demands'.[3] Yet he excluded from the scope of his comparative monograph the law of torts on the ground that it was only in the law of contract that judges (both in England and France) were prepared to admit *openly* that their decisions were based on public policy.[4] His reasons for this omission, valid some twenty-five years ago, seem to have lost some of their force since, in recent years, certain members of the judiciary have become increasingly willing to refer to various reasons of 'policy', the 'public interest', the 'demands of society' etc. when formulating their judgments.

This 'judicial legislation or interpretation founded on the current needs of the community'[5] is, undoubtedly, helping develop both the

*This section is very largely based on a lecture delivered by the second of us in Cambridge in a programme of study sponsored by the Canadian Institute for Advanced Legal Studies. It was subsequently published with the other papers in *The Cambridge Lectures: Selected Papers of the Canadian Institute for Advanced Legal Studies*, Butterworths (1981), pp. 199 *et seq.*

43

Civil law and the Common law and bring it in tune with the economic and social demands of our times. However, differences in judicial styles,[6] as much as anything else, make it difficult to find in Civil law *judgments* the type of explicit and, it is submitted, helpful, pronouncements that one can find in many modern Common law decisions (though in France the annual reports of the Cour de cassation, submitted to the Garde des Sceaux since 1968, throw a great deal of light on the importance the Supreme Court attaches to these wider policy factors in its attempts to adapt the law to the demands of modern society). But, whether admitted or not, considerations of wider policy and social advantage play a decisive role in determining a quantitatively small but qualitatively crucial number of cases. Discovering and evaluating these policy factors involves an inquiry into, amongst other things, the whole method of judicial thinking and style. It is thus a topic which does not lend itself to facile generalisations; nor is it within the scope of this work. Yet it is desirable to look, however briefly, at some of these policy factors which appear to have played an unusually important role in the determination of negligence litigation. Three reasons can be advanced for this.

One reason for wishing to bring into the open some of the policy reasons which lie behind these judgments is the belief that this can lead to a more intelligent discussion of the real issues involved. A second reason is purely didactic since a policy-orientated approach can help students realise that the various concepts they encounter in their books and in judgments are often little more than verbal devices, 'means of formulating conclusions'[7] but not the reasons that dictate them. This in turn can help students appreciate the considerable equivocation that exists between many of these concepts; and it can also minimise their use – especially in circumstances where it is clear that they have become little more than judicial fictions. (The term 'foreseeability' immediately springs to mind as a most apposite illustration of such use.) For present purposes, however, the most important reason for emphasising this policy-orientated approach is the belief that it can facilitate the comparison of the various legal systems. For it can prevent the student from adopting a barren comparison of different abstract concepts and encourage him, instead, towards a functionally-orientated method of examining the different legal systems.

Two additional observations must be made at this stage. The first is that it would appear that nowadays lawyers seem to have recourse to these policy factors whenever their aim is to *limit* rather than *expand* delictual liability. Since in the law of torts in general and the law of Negligence in particular the crucial problem is that of limitation of liability, the study of policy reasons that help achieve this goal thus acquires an added dimension. The above is increasingly true of the Common law and, in many instances, of German law as well. French law, on the other hand, already broader in its conception of delictual liability than the other two systems, appears to be utilising broader policy arguments in order to extend its law of delict even further. The decisions of the Chambre Mixte of the late 1960s and early 1970s bear witness to this tendency and, as the Court itself put it in its annual report to the Garde des Sceaux of 1975, 'la Cour marque aujourd' hui moins d'hésitation et prend moins de temps que par le passé, à revenir sur telle ou telle décision de principe, dès lors qu'il lui apparaît que cette décision n'est plus adaptée à l'évolution générale des mœurs, de l'ordonnancement social ou des institutions'. Secondly, to return to the Common law, policy may intervene to prevent the imposition of *all liability* or it may affect the right of a *particular plaintiff* to recover, *or* to recover a *particular item of loss*. In both cases, policy factors play the dominant part, but for didactic if no other reasons it might be better to discuss these two situations separately. In the next paragraph of this chapter we shall therefore examine the devices used to achieve the first result; whereas the concepts used to prevent a *particular* plaintiff from recovering the damage *in suit* will be the subject of discussion of the next chapter.

It could be argued that amongst the most frequently encountered policy factors are the following: the 'administrative factor'; the 'superior value factor'; the 'environmental factor' and the 'insurance factor'. None of them are mutually exclusive and, more often than not, there is considerable overlap.

(a) The 'administrative factor'

Courts, especially though not exclusively in countries with uncodified systems, are notoriously fearful of the risk of being flooded by large numbers of claims – some of them, no doubt, fictitious – which the legal and economic system would not be able to support.[8] This is what MacCormick[9] calls a 'consequentialist' type of argument and it is not limited to negligence actions only. It could, for example, be argued that the gradual erosion of the imaginative rule in *Rylands* v. *Fletcher*[10] is, surely, as much due to the traditional dislike of the idea of liability without fault as it is to the fear that the new right of action might, if not carefully circumscribed, get out of control.[11] The courts' treatment of nervous shock and economic loss, however, offers better and more appropriate examples of how such fears can help defeat claims.

The number of persons who can suffer some form or other of mental distress through seeing or hearing an accident can clearly be greater than the number who can be injured in the accident itself, hence the anxiety of the courts both in Common law and Civil law jurisdictions to find effective means of keeping potential liability under control.

As a policy decision this may be intelligible. In a small crowded island (like England), on whose 100,000 miles of road some seven or eight thousand people are killed every year and another 100,000 are seriously injured, it is obvious that many people must witness some very distressing scenes on the road... It would probably be undesirable to attempt to compensate all those who suffer some small degree of distress, even if some slight pecuniary loss were suffered as a result – for instance if a person witnessing an accident had to go home and lie down for the afternoon instead of going to work. Certainly the claims of such a person must have a low priority when it is remembered that thousands of victims with physical injury go uncompensated every year because they are injured in accidents not caused by negligence.[12]

To this problem the 'impact theory',[13] widely accepted by Common law systems, originally provided a crude but effective solution. But as the social pressures to increase the number of persons entitled to claim damages grew, and the 'impact theory' was progressively questioned, the search for new means of control intensified. For English lawyers, the answer seemed to lie in the use of the concepts of duty and foreseeability.[14] The advantage of such an approach is that it involves the use of known concepts which are flexible enough to yield the desired results; and it also confers an *appearance* of consistency since it gives the *impression* that whenever a person can foresee damage to another (be it physical injury or mental distress) he is under a duty to take care. These advantages, however, are bought at the price of using these notions in an extremely artificial manner which prevents the intelligent discussion of the true policy issues that lie behind these cases. So, for example, our courts appear to have been more concerned to prevent such actions in general getting out of hand – and in the process imposing arbitrary limitations – than to try to distinguish between the more serious consequences of shock (such as were experienced in *Hay (Bourhill)* v. *Young*)[15] which deserve compensation, from the more trivial forms of distress which are commonly experienced by the witnessing or hearing of tragic accidents. One wonders, however, if the time has not come to say that if the plaintiff, as a result of the defendant's conduct, has suffered some kind of serious and 'recognizable psychiatric illness'[16] he should be allowed to recover damages irrespective of his relationship with the victim, his physical position at the time of the accidents, or even his personal propensities towards such type of injury.[17] Indeed, the law may be slowly moving in that direction.

The fear that a chain reaction of claims may follow an isolated negligent act has been voiced even more strongly in cases of pure economic loss. This anxiety lay behind the rule in *Winterbottom* v. *Wright*[18] and was echoed in *Donoghue* v. *Stevenson* by Lord Buckmaster when he said 'If one step, why not fifty?'[19] Perhaps too much has been made of this 'consequentialist' argument since it is, after all, the function of the courts to draw the line and distinguish the deserving from the undeserving case. But however over-emphasised this fear may be, it has, nevertheless, been voiced with some measure of frequency during the last fifteen years in important 'economic loss' cases both in England and in Germany. In *Weller and Co.* v. *Foot and Mouth Disease Research Institute*,[20] for example, Lord Widgery stressed the fact that in an agricultural community (such as the one involved in the case) the escape of foot and mouth virus could be a tragedy which could foreseeably affect almost every business in that area. Yet how decisively this fear weighed in his mind and led him to decide the case in favour of the defendants can only be a matter of conjecture, since he cautiously added that such fears 'should not be allowed to deprive the plaintiffs of their rights'.[21] In *Spartan Steel and Alloys, Ltd.* v. *Martin & Co. (Contractors), Ltd*,[22] on the other hand, Lord Denning M.R. was more forthright.

...if claims for economic loss were permitted for this particular hazard, there would be no end of claims. Some might be genuine, but many might be inflated, or even false. A machine might not have been in use anyway, but it would be easy to put it down to the cut in supply. It would be wellnigh impossible to check the claims...Rather than expose claimants to such temptation and defendants to such hard labour...it is better to disallow economic loss altogether, at any rate when it stands alone, independent of any physical damage.[23]

Whatever the value of such fears, the fact is that they are voiced not in this country alone. So, for example, in one of the leading 'cable cases' in Germany, the courts had to decide whether article 18 III of the

Baden-Württemberg Building Code (a local by-law) was a *Schutz-norm*, i.e. a rule intended to protect an individual against the infliction of pure economic loss. This was necessary since the claim was based, *inter alia*, on paragraph 823 II BGB. The Court of Appeal held that the by-law was not a *Schutzgesetz*. In the absence of a clear legislative indication to the contrary, the Federal Supreme Court refused to assume that article 18 III entitles individual electricity consumers to compensation claims for which no provision is made by the general stipulations, *'particularly in view of the fact that this would be bound to result in a considerable and unreasonable extension of liability'*.[24] A year later the BGH,[25] once again, relied on this type of 'consequentialist' argument. The facts were quite similar to those of the earlier case, though this time the argument proceeded on a different basis. The defendant/contractor had an agreement with a local body (*Zweckver-band*) to excavate in a particular area. The contractor was warned against the risk of damaging submerged electricity cables and, when one of them was, in fact, severed as a result of the negligence of one of his workers, the plaintiff (a nearby factory owner) sued him for the economic loss which he suffered as a result of the consequent power failure. We shall note further down that similar claims made by earlier plaintiffs and framed in tort (either para. 823 I or II BGB) had been rejected by the BGH; so here the plaintiff tried to put his claim on a contractual basis. His argument was that the contractor, by ignoring the warning, was in breach of his contract with the local body and that this contract, especially in view of the warning, should be taken to have protective effects vis-à-vis third parties, including the plaintiff. The BGH objected to this use of the contractual approach, inter alia[26] on the grounds 'that the extension of contractual obligations is prevented by the fact that defective workmanship or neglect of safety measures may damage any persons imaginable – householders, tenants, industrialists – so that contractual protection would be extended to an unlimited circle of persons which it would no longer be possible to encompass'.

In *Rondel* v. *Worsley*,[27] one finds yet another and, for present purposes, the last illustration of this policy factor, this time with an interesting variation. The 'opening of the floodgates' argument is to be found emphasised in varying degrees in some judgments[28] but policy appeared to militate against the plaintiff in another, and stronger, way. For the judges were not only anxious to spare the courts from other, *similar*, actions but also eager to shield them from the otiose task of having to re-try the *same* case. As Lawton J. put it at first instance: 'many who had been convicted of criminal offences and who had unsuccessfully exhausted all their rights to appeal would seek, maybe years later, to get a retrial by means of an action for negligence against the advocate who had defended them. There would be no end to litigation.'[29] This argument must have carried a great deal of weight in the Court of Appeal, for its members opted for a more radical solution to the problem before them by holding that this was a situation where policy prevented the rise of *any* duty of care. The alternative approach, proposed by the plaintiff's solicitor,[30] that a duty should in principle be recognised to exist and the control of the court limited to an investigation in each case whether it had been breached, was thus rejected, presumably on the ground that it was a less efficient measure for giving effect to the courts' decision of policy. The case is therefore interesting not only because it illustrates how policy (and the administrative factor in particular) can be openly invoked to decide a particular claim; but also because it shows how (and why) the courts decide through which abstract concept they will exercise their controlling function.

(b) The 'superior value factor'

A prime concern of any legal system is the protection of certain things (tangible or not) which are of value to human beings. Not all these things can have the same value; nor can they always be given efficient protection against all invasions. A hierarchy is thus dictated by moral, economic and other considerations with the result that the law affords better protection to the better things in life. We can, in fact, 'see how highly the legal system rates a thing by checking how much protection the law gives to it relatively to other good things. We know, for example, that liberty is more highly rated than property because habeas corpus is a better remedy than detinue. We know that the integrity of a person is more important than the integrity of property because the victim of assault can claim from the Criminal Injuries Compensation Board (and the same is also true under the equivalent German Act of 11 May 1976) whereas the victim of theft cannot, and because you must have insurance against liability for causing personal injury with your car but need not have insurance against liability for causing property damage; (and the same preference for life and health over property lies behind section 2 (1) and (2) of the Unfair Contract Terms Act 1977, which prohibits clauses which exclude or restrict liability for "death or personal injury" but is willing to accept them (under certain conditions) if they refer to "other loss or damage"). The carrier by air must pay more for killing or injuring a passenger than he need pay for losing or damaging his property; and since he need pay nothing at all for mere financial loss, as by delaying the passenger or his property, we can infer that wealth is in fact rated lower than property or person. This last point is evident also from the fact that taxation, or the imposition of financial loss, is more acceptable then expropriation, or the taking away of property. It is clear also from the relative strength of the remedies which protect tangible property, namely conversion and detinue, as compared with the remedies for unjustified enrichment.'[31] This kind of hierarchy, which is not necessarily immutable, not only determines the degree of protection afforded to the various interests; it also resolves potential clashes between them. A few examples can show how this kind of reasoning, concealed behind abstract legal terminology, has often dictated the outcome of negligence litigation.

This first example comes from France and it involves a clash between the idea of 'sanctity of marriage', which every civilised society accepts as one of its cornerstones, and the right to be indemnified for loss suffered as a result of another person's harmful conduct (art. 1382 CC). In France this clash reached quite considerable proportions and, perhaps, one could even say that no other system has felt so strongly in its law the effects of fluctuations in ideas about marriage and extra-marital relationships. The reasons for this last-mentioned phenomenon, quite widespread in practice, are far too complex to relate here but may, paradoxically, be partly due to the simultaneous idealisation and repression of women during the peak of the romantic movement in the nineteenth century. For, in practice, the flowering of the romantic ideal separated rather than brought closer together man and wife, while the Catholic Church, preaching an austere conception of marriage with the procreation of children as its main if not sole aim, unwittingly contributed to adultery becoming what a distinguished scholar has described as an 'almost inevitable' institution.[32] Such adulterous relations had some bearing on the criminal law and some parts of the Civil law (mainly family law, legitimation and, to a lesser extent, the law of succession) but, on the whole, left the law of civil responsibility untouched. The position, however, was very different in the case of more permanent relationships with 'kept women' (*concubinage*), for here serious financial loss could be proved by such women when deprived through accidents of the financial support of their paramours. Initially, such claims were tolerated (so long as the relationship was long and the damage 'certain')[33] but by the early 1930s fears were expressed that such extra-marital cohabitations were on the increase and that compensation of mistresses only helped undermine the sanctity of marriage.[34] This 'hommage posthume au concubinat', as Josserand branded it in 1932, was, to him at any rate, legally indefensible and represented 'la victoire du fait sur le droit, de l'union libre sur l'union légitime'.[35] Five years later, Josserand, who by then had joined the Cour de cassation, was able to give effect to these ideas by prompting the Supreme Court to adopt his views and to deny a mistress's claim for compensation on the grounds that she did *not* possess an 'intérêt légitime juridiquement protégé'.[36] This requirement that the plaintiff's claim be 'juridiquement protégé' was clearly a gloss on the basic text (art. 1382 CC) introduced solely in order to frustrate the mistresses' claim and it was not until 1970 that this extraneous requirement was excised, no doubt under the pressure of altered social and economic conditions.[37]

The clash between property and its free enjoyment on the one hand and the right to be indemnified for damage caused by such uninhibited use of land on the other offers a different and equally interesting setting for a potential clash of values. Nowadays such a competition has a frightening ring about it though more and more people would, almost certainly, be inclined to favour the latter value rather than the former. But in days gone by, and certainly during the eighteenth and nineteenth centuries, the balance was often tipped in favour of property and its free exploitation. For it was felt that any other solution would, above all, place a heavy burden on business by obliging landowners to incur great expense in order to take preventive action. Though not without force, especially in its day, this argument is, nevertheless, unsatisfactory in so far as it implies that the courts would expect landowners to ensure the safety of entrants rather than take reasonable precautions to protect them against injury. No doubt control through the concept of reasonable care would have meant a more flexible standard, lower perhaps in the nineteenth century, higher in the twentieth. But, as in *Rondel* v. *Worsley*[38], the courts obviously felt that the concepts of reasonableness or careless breach of duty were not as effective a way of blostering the prevailing policy as was the complete denial of any duty in the first place. It was not until the early 1970s when, as a result of a considerable change in the environment, the harsh rule towards trespassers was finally overruled. Lord Reid frankly acknowledged this when he declared that 'legal principles cannot solve the problem (of child trespassers). How far occupiers are to be required by law to take steps to safeguard such children, must be a matter of public policy.'[39] Thus Lord Pearson, for example, openly referred to the changes in the social environment which dictated the abandonment of the old, harsh, rule.[40]

A not dissimilar clash of values can be seen projected in an even more dramatic way in the development of the doctrine of Abuse of Rights in France. Apart from its inherent interest, the subject has given rise to great doctrinal controversy and so, we feel, a small excursus is called for at this point.[41]

It seems that the Roman law of the classical period took the same line as English law,[42] and in principle paid no regard to the motive with which a defendant exercised his rights, though in isolated cases a defence might be valid only if the defendant had acted in good faith.[43] However, certain tags appear in the Corpus Iuris – they were probably inserted by the compliers – out of which a general principle could be constructed. Thus Celsus, after giving his opinion that a *bonae fidei possessor* is not allowed, in the exercise of his *ius tollendi*, wantonly to strip the walls of a house, is made to justify it in the words 'neque malitiis indulgendum est';[44] and Ulpian is made to say that a landowner cannot have an *actio doli* against his neighbour for intercepting underground water 'si non animo vicino nocendi, sed suum agrum meliorem faciendi id fecit'.[45]

Canon law helped this more liberal doctrine to predominate, and the older French jurists, so far as can be judged, regarded as actionable the malicious exercise of a right.[46] It was not until the Revolution that a return was made to the purely individualistic doctrine that, so far as his rights extend, a man may do what he likes with his own. Article 544 of the Code Civil embodied such ideas when it proclaimed boldly that 'La propriété est le droit de jouir et disposer des choses de la manière la plus absolue...' It was the heart of *laissez-faire* doctrine that a man must be trusted to make the best use of his property, for was not private selfishness a public virtue? For the most part, the courts adhered to this doctrine for the first half of the nineteenth century, but the older ideas were not hard to disinter when they were needed.

The change came earlier than one would have expected, for as early as 1855 the court of Colmar[47] made a man liable for building a chimney with the sole object of spoiling his neighbour's view. The passage in which the court gave its reasons and which marked the triumph of article 1382 CC over article 544 CC as well as the death of yet another extreme doctrine of the revolutionary period, reads as follows:

Considérant que s'il est de principe que le droit de propriété est un droit en quelque sorte absolu, autorisant le propriétaire à user et abuser de la chose, cependant l'exercise de ce droit, comme celui de tout autre, doit avoir pour limite la satisfaction d'un intérêt sérieux et légitime; que les principes de la morale et de l'équité s'opposent à ce que la justice sanctionne une action inspirée par la malveillance, accomplie sous l'empire d'une mauvaise passion, ne se justifiant par aucune utilité personnelle et portant un grave préjudice à autrui; qu'ainsi c'est le cas, tout en reconnaissant l'affranchissement de la propriété de l'appelant de tout droit de servitude de vue, de maintenir la décision des premiers juges quant à la démolition de la fausse cheminée...

Since that decision there has never been any doubt that any exercise of a right that could be attributed *only* to a malicious motive is actionable. This doctrine was clearly enunciated in the famous *Schikaneverbot* of the German Civil Code.[48] However, it is seldom that a man injures another out of pure spite, in circumstances where he himself stands to obtain no tangible benefit from his act; he is much more likely to be trying, like the defendant in *Mayor of Bradford* v. *Pickles*,[49] to put pressure on the plaintiff to accept onerous terms; and the intentional harm he does, though it brings him no immediate benefit, is certainly intended to be highly advantageous. Thus little use has been made of paragraph 226 BGB (in connection with paragraph 823 II BGB). Much better results have been obtained by applying paragraph 826 BGB,[50] which requires of malicious damage to be merely *contra bonos mores*, a formulation that side-tracks the defence that the damage was done in the exercise of a right. Similar results can be obtained from article 2 of the Swiss Civil Code;[51] and indeed the French courts have shown themselves perfectly prepared to penalise conduct identical with that of Mr Pickles.[52]

Nevertheless, a doctrine founded exclusively on malice has not proved perfectly satisfactory. It is not always easy to infer malice in a given situation (though the absence of any self-interested motive helps), and it is by no means clear that proof of malice should be allowed to defeat the exercise of rights so long as they are considered to be in principle absolute. Ought moral issues to be allowed so much scope in matters of compensation?

If, however, we take up our usual standpoint in judging the civil quality of conduct, namely, the reasonable expectations of the rest of the world, we shall find that malicious acts, like negligent acts, are abnormal. Let us then concentrate on the abnormality of conduct in abuse of a right, and we shall find not only that it is more easily established, but that the extent of liability can be made much wider. We have still, of course, to find some way of determining what is a normal and what an abnormal exercise of a right.

The most elaborate theory, that of Josserand,[53] though not widely accepted in France, has found echoes elsewhere. According to it, every right has its own spirit, and every act done in exercise of it that is consistent with the spirit is normal, and all other acts are abnormal. In other words, rights are in principle not absolute but relative. The English lawyer will perhaps say rather that all rights are in the nature of powers of which the repository is a trustee. Nevertheless distinctions must be made. It may be clear enough that the right is conferred in the interest of some other person or of the general public; in which case the trust notion is appropriate enough. But the right may be, in Josserand's terminology, egoistical, established in the interest of the person on whom it is conferred. Generally speaking, property rights are of this kind, and all that is asked is that they shall be exercised, not altruistically, of course, for selfishness is here intended, but without malice. The presence of malice will be inferred if no genuine self-seeking motive can be detected. This seems reasonable enough, were it not that Mr Pickles would have said with justice that his motives were self-seeking in the highest degree. It is therefore said that a clear intention to cause damage is an abuse of the right. French jurists are also bound to find room for a third category, comparable with the absolute discretions of English public law. Here it is admitted that no question of abuse can possibly arise. The right is so absolute that it cannot be abused.[54] This will not be inferred in the absence of an express legislative text.

In France this has all been the work of the jurists and the courts, a foundation being found for it in the Code by treating every abuse as an instance of *faute* under article 1382. Later codes, as we have seen, deal with the abuse of rights expressly. The most famous statement of principle is probably that which introduces the Soviet Civil Code of 1922 namely, 'Civil rights are protected by law, except where they are exercised in a manner contrary to their economic and social purpose.'[55]

It is entirely appropriate that this provision should occur in the code of a socialist or communist state, for it could be argued that as soon as the theory of abuse of rights passes the stage where subjective malice is the sole test, it could be seen to be a socialist doctrine. For it can imply that a man's right is no longer, as it were, a sphere within which he is sovereign, over which he may dispose according to his own view of his interests and his own ideas of right and wrong; it is to be subject to the control of society in the person of the judge, who exercises a veto over his decisions in accordance with what he considers to be the purpose for which society has conferred the right. To express this in the technical language of the English law, most rights take on the character of powers coupled with a trust; or we may think of the consequences that might ensue from an intensified interference with freedom of contract by the courts on grounds of public policy. But in reality the nearest analogues in English law to rights regarded in this light are governmental discretions committed to public authorities, which may only be used to effect the purposes for which they have been conferred and in exercise of which no extraneous considerations may be taken into account. In France, too, the new doctrine is modelled on the *détournement de pouvoir*, which had long been known to administrative law and plays a great part in the *jurisprudence* of the Conseil d'Etat.

Further, it is clear that the 'socialistic' overtones of the modern doctrine has made for it enemies as well as friends. Thus some French jurists, dreading the freedom offered to the courts to apply political or social doctrine in determining whether a right has been exercised in accordance with its nature, but at the same time recognising that the law in its former state played into the hands of the unscrupulous man of property, would prefer to have the legislature create new rights in favour of the weak against the strong and let the courts work out a balance by empirical means.[56]

On the whole, the parts of the law where the doctrine has been applied with greater success are those where the relevance of malice has been admitted, or at least discussed, in English law.[57] Thus it is important (and useful) in litigation (e.g. *exercise abusif d'une voie de recours*), labour disputes, and the use of land. But French law does not face the obstacles which the English courts set up in the 1890s: there is no *Mayor of Bradford* v. *Pickles*[58] and no *Allen* v. *Flood*.[59] And the right of action for abuse of legal process extends far beyond the malicious institution of a prosecution or of bankruptcy or winding-up proceedings, so as to cover ordinary civil litigation and the levying of execution.

Another area in which the doctrine has been used (especially in days gone by) to impose liability is the so-called subject of *'troubles de voisinage'* which corresponds to our private nuisance. Such nuisances are properly held to arise from abnormal uses of land and hence abuses of the right of property. But this suggests, what appears on other grounds to be true, that an abuse of right can always be expressed as an excess of right.[60] All one has to do is to introduce restrictions or limitations into the definition of the right in question. If one wishes to keep the doctrine of abuse of rights within narrow bounds, this is the way to do it. But there is an undoubted sacrifice of emotional content: and it may be doubted whether without the animus attaching to the notion of 'abuse', inroads could have been made on so exceptionally well-established and buttressed a concept as the absolute right of property. In the England of the 1890s even the highly charged word 'malice' did not suffice. This then is an important difference[61] between the English and French law.

French law initially gives a wide right by statute and then restricts its antisocial use by the courts; in England, where it is the courts which announce the rights, they do it so very restrictively that there is little need for an equitable temperance of their exercise, and the legislature has either adopted the same technique or is made to do so.[62]

The final outcome of the cases is often similar and, indeed, as the number of instances where bad motives may affect the question of liability increase in English law, the similarity in results may become more pronounced. But in terms of technique the two systems are poles apart and will remain so for as long as English law (unlike French law) chooses to place the emphasis on the commission of a 'wrong' rather than the existence of a 'right'. That the techniques are diametrically opposed can be shown clearly by two cases which cry out for comparison. In *Christie* v. *Davey*[63] the defendant, annoyed by his neighbour's piano lessons, started to produce loud noises with the intention of making life intolerable for the neighbour (plaintiff). The defendant's malice was decisive in characterising the disturbance to the plaintiff as unreasonable. In a parallel French case[64] the defendant hired an orchestra to play loudly near his neighbour's boundary whenever the latter organised a hunting party on his own land. His bad motive was used to characterise the exercise of his right as abusive and he was then held liable. The comparison of these two cases is interesting not only because the same results were achieved in what were substantially similar factual situations but also because they demonstrate that whenever nuisance is linked to fault, fault plays a different role in each system: in France it has been used to characterise the defendant's conduct as 'abusive'; in England, in view of the fact that in nuisance one looks at the effect on the plaintiff and not the defendant's conduct, fault is an element which, taken with others, may render unreasonable what might otherwise be regarded as reasonable. But the French law of *troubles de voisinage* (like the English law of nuisance) covers the whole spectrum from fault to strict liability since often the defendant is held liable even though he was 'lawfully' exercising his profession or making 'reasonable' use of his land. In these instances the Cour de cassation has repeatedly held that the 'lawful' exercise of the right of property may still give rise to liability when the annoyance it creates 'exceeds the reasonable limits of the ordinary forbearance expected of neighbours'.[65] This approach does not merely replace the more fault-orientated formulations of liability with a more objective test but has also contributed to giving the theory of *troubles de voisinage* a status independent of that of its progenitor theory of *abus de droit*.

(c) The 'environmental factor'

Though there is clearly a considerable overlap between this and the previous policy factors, in this present type the emphasis is not so much on 'moral' or 'value' considerations as on the exigencies of the economic environment. Once again, lawyers and judges have, on the whole, avoided mentioning these factors in public and, instead, have chosen to conduct their argument on the basis of abstract concepts and legal doctrine. But unexpressed though these considerations may be, they are there nonetheless. Indeed, few are the cases which, once stripped of their legal technicalities, do not reveal the environmental forces that dictated their outcome. Leon Green, for example, has analysed *Rylands* v. *Fletcher*[66] as a case having to decide which of two industrial users of land (the milling or the mining industry) should bear the loss of the type of hazard encountered in that case.[67] Analysed in such a way the case can only produce the result actually reached by Blackburn (and the House of Lords), not only because the surface industrialist alone could provide protection for the mine beneath, but also because to decide otherwise would be tantamount to dealing a severe blow to the mining industry and, in the nineteenth century, to harm the mining industry would be to harm England. Such an analysis is attractive but, displaying as it does concern for loss-spreading ability and accident prevention procedures, it could be accused of transferring into the nineteenth century ideas and methods of reasoning more appropriate to the twentieth. On the other hand, there is no evidence to suggest that judges did not think in this way even though they did not express their thoughts in their judgments, in which they appeared rather to rely on analogies. And comparison with the eastern United States at that time would lend *some* indirect support for this for, as Green, once again, has observed, 'in a new country like the Atlantic seaboard, where industrial enterprise was just getting on its legs and where water storage was so important for its uses, it is quite understandable that American courts should reject the doctrine (of *Rylands* v. *Fletcher*) as unsuitable to our economic situation'.[68] It was thus only after the economic and industrial environment changed that the *Rylands* v. *Fletcher* doctrine came to be accepted and, in some instances, even to be extended.

It could be argued that a similar concern for the land-owning classes encouraged the Common law to adopt the varying and confusing standards of care owed by occupiers of land towards lawful entrants.[69] The emphasis on the plaintiff's status rather than on the nature of the defendant's land, the risks attendant to it, and his ability to prevent them, was clearly in tune with the economic demands of the time and the desire not to hinder or burden the free exploitation of one's property. But it also gave judges the extra bonus of being able to control the findings of juries on the issue of carelessness by enabling them, through the 'proper' characterisation of the plaintiff, to raise or lower the standard of care due to him. With the passage of time, however, the vagueness if not outright artificiality of these distinctions became an asset which judges were prepared to utilise in response to the exigencies of a changed economic and social environment. The use of the 'implied licence' concept thus became the 'most palpable fiction ever employed in order to impose legal responsibility',[70] and recently Lord Denning openly admitted the utility of such fictions as a means of avoiding the rigidity of the old law.[71]

The law related to industrial accidents and workers' compensation can provide us with our last example of environmental factors influencing the development of the law of torts. In the rise and fall of the doctrine of 'common employment' we can find a neat illustration of these forces at work.[72]

Priestly v. *Fowler*[73] is commonly regarded as the fons et origo of this doctrine,[74] though this must be qualified before being accepted. For, first, there is nothing in the plaintiff's declaration about an act of another servant; instead the attempt is to make the employer liable for breaking his own duty to provide a safe conveyance. Secondly, since at this period of time the tort of Negligence had not yet acquired a foothold in English law, the case could not really have been decided in tort. Certainly, counsel for the plaintiff argued his case on the basis of an implied term in the contract of employment; Chief Justice Shaw, in the almost contemporaneous decision in *Farwell* v. *Boston & Worcester Railroad Corp.*,[75] spoke the language of contract; and subsequent decisions rationalised the immunity on the basis of an implied term in the contract of employment.[76]

At this juncture, the comparative lawyer can pause for thought. A moment's reflection will remind him that about this time French lawyers, too, started to experience similar problems. In those days actions against employers had to be brought under article 1382 CC and this requires the plaintiff (employee) to prove his employer's (defendant's) fault which was (and is) more often than not impossible. For practical purposes, therefore, French law was very close to English law; for, though it recognised the existence of a 'duty' in tort (if we may use the English terminology) it did not accept easily its careless breach. Progressive lawyers tried to avoid this result – iniquitous as far as the workmen were concerned – by trying (unsuccessfully) to expand the contents of the contract of employment by implying in it a term of 'security' and 'safety' for the benefit of the worker.[77] The point at issue is not identical to that considered in the above-mentioned cases of the Common law; but the cases do show how, in the absence of an 'amenable' law of tort, civilian lawyers are tempted to expand their law of contract in order to afford a remedy to 'deserving' plaintiffs. We shall meet many more examples of this later on in this book.

But let us return to *Priestley* v. *Fowler*.[78] In his judgment Lord Abinger had no doubt that the plaintiff's claim should fail; the consequences of deciding the case otherwise were too horrible even to contemplate. In fact he gave a series of hypothetical instances to illustrate the multiplicity of actions that might ensue from the adoption of a different rule. These examples have been selected from an 'engagingly domestic'[79] scene and the author of the standard monograph on employer's liability wonders whether Lord Abinger's mind was not dwelling at that moment on his own immense household as master of Inverlochy Castle near Ben Nevis![80] Of course, one should not carry this kind of thinking too far. Roscoe

Pound,[81] for example, has warned against the danger of explaining such decisions *solely* by reference to the conscious or unconscious desires of the economically dominant class of the time. But there seems little doubt that the immunity, once accepted, could be transferred to the industrial context and there become a potent shield for employers against all legal consequences of industrial accidents. In *Hutchinson* v. *York & Newcastle Ry*,[82] Alderson B. did precisely this and it is hard to believe that this and the other cases that followed do not reflect a conscious decision *to allocate the risk* in such cases in the *economically* most suitable manner. The result was harsh on poor workers; and some judgments reveal this preference for strong economic logic to any feelings of compassion.[83] But the decision was harsh not because it refused to hold the employer liable but because the welfare system was pitifully inadequate. For if the social welfare system works properly, it can even today be argued that 'broader social responsibility' is preferable to one which taxes a particular industry for the claims of its workers.[84] Of course, which of these two possibilities is preferable, in economic and political terms, is not relevant for present purposes.

Industrial accidents posed similar problems for the Civil law. In France, attempts to improve the lot of workers through the law of contract met with little success with the courts and for the better part of the nineteenth century the possibilities offered by article 1384 CC remained unused. In a decision delivered in 1870,[85] for example, the Chambre Civile of the Cour de cassation refused to apply article 1384 CC to a case involving the explosion of a boiler installed in a laundry and, instead, insisted that recovery in such cases depend upon the plaintiff producing evidence of the defendant's fault. Commenting on this decision in Sircy in 1871,[86] Labbé let the cat out of the bag by admitting that the case simply could not have been decided otherwise. Industry, he argued, had its dangers, but it also benefited the community at large, which should therefore carry such risks. The implication is, once again, that one should not hamper unduly the gradual industrialisation of the country. Those who favoured greater protection for the working classes were still very much in the minority and the pressure for legislative reform remained weak throughout the first two decades of the life of the Third Republic. But by the end of the century increased mechanisation and a steady growth of industrial accidents demanded some modification in the approach and, through the medium of more efficient insurance, industry was becoming increasingly able to shoulder such risks. Equally important, perhaps, is the fact that this is the era of the growing strength of the socialist movements which began to generate strong pressures on the Parliaments of the day to intervene. In actual fact, the change came first from the courts[87] and some thirty years later M. le conseiller le Marc'hadour, in the celebrated *Jand'heur* case, admitted that this was the result of the 'nécessité chaque jour plus impérieuse de protéger l'ouvrier contre les conséquences des accidents survenus au cours du travail'.[88] And, lest France should be regarded as being backward in comparison with other European countries, he added: 'Déjà, à l'étranger, des lois spéciales avaient réglé la matière des accidents du travail; la jurisprudence française ne pouvait manquer d'être impressionnée par des tendances qui correspondaient à un souci évident de justice sociale...' Incidentally, the admiring reference to foreign legislation (the English Compensation Act of 1897 and the German laws of the 1870s and 1880s) is partly misconceived, for Professor Kahn-Freund amongst others has shown that the prime purpose of this legislation – which was based on inquiries which the German Consulate in London made into voluntary schemes established by the trade unions in this country – was not meant to assist the German workers but to 'take the wind out of the sails of the Social Democracy' by satisfying in advance some of its more pressing demands.[89]

(d) The 'internal balance of the code factor'

Lon Fuller has pointed out that judges are 'confronted by a problem of system. The rules applied to the decision of individual controversies cannot simply be isolated exercises of judicial wisdom. They must be brought into, and maintained in, some systematic interrelationship; they must display some coherent internal structure.'[90] This need to interrelate results is both strong and obvious in codified systems, where the outcome of a particular case may often be determined or justified by the structure of the code. In such cases to sanction a result other than that actually reached would disturb the internal balance of the code and run counter to the wider policy decisions embodied in it. The various rules on cumulation of contractual and delictual actions, invariably worked out by courts and jurists rather than by the legislatures, offer a very good illustration. The German rule allowing cumulation of actions is, for example, very largely the result of paragraphs 253 and 847 BGB and the German attitude towards damages for pain and suffering (*Schmerzensgeld*) which are only available in tort actions.[91] To prohibit cumulation would, for example, be tantamount to holding that a negligent taxi driver would be liable to pay such damages to an injured pedestrian (suing him in tort) but not to his injured passenger (who would normally sue him in contract). Yet the driver's conduct amounts to a breach of contract as well as tort and to allow the passenger to sue in tort means allowing him to recover for pain and suffering which he would not be allowed to claim if he were suing in contract. Such a solution is, in practice, just and perfectly acceptable in a system such as the German, where the BGB provides only for impossibility of performance and delay but not for positive breaches of contracts (*positive Vertragsverletzung*) and thus clearly envisages the possibility of contractors suing each other in tort.

The opposite solution obtains in French law, where most authors accept the principle of *non cumul des actions*. Once again, the internal structure of the Code makes this solution desirable if not, indeed, inevitable. The reason for this is that article 1382 CC is extremely wide and article 1384 CC is extremely strict. To allow cumulation in such circumstances would sap the law of contract of all its contents since every breach of contract could be treated as a tort.

The same risk does not arise in West Germany or the Common law where economic harm, the typical consequence of the typical breach of contract, gives rise to no liability in tort if it is caused by mere negligence. Thus in Germany admission of concurrence still leaves much to the exclusive regulation of the law of contract. In France on the other hand, the admission of concurrence would have a very different and much more serious effect, for it would mean the effective abolition of the special rules of contractual liability except in so far as they benefited the victim only.[92]

Secondly, the admission of concurrence would, in effect, make such persons as doctors and bailees liable to their patients and bailors respectively under article 1384 CC, and this would be clearly contrary to the kind of duty imposed on such persons by the law, which is invariably an *obligation de moyens* rather than an *obligation de résultat*. It is, therefore, necessary for French law to prevent recourse to the articles on delict by reserving those articles to the exclusive use of strangers or third parties.

The internal structure of the code argument can also be found in some of the economic loss cases in Germany. Thus in the leading 'cable case' mentioned earlier on[93] the Supreme Court did not allow compensation for pure economic loss under paragraph 823 II BGB by refusing to hold that the violation of an article of a building statute of Baden-Württemberg gave a right of action to factory owners affected by a power cut which was the result of damage to a nearby electricity cable. To do so, reasoned the Court, would be tantamount to allowing a *state legislator* to sanction the recovery of pure economic loss despite the contrary provision of the basic, Federal enactment (para 823 I BGB). This could clearly not have been in the mind (or the competence) of the state legislator and this was therefore an additional argument in favour of the view that the violated rule (art. 18 III of the Baden-Württemberg Building Code) was not a *Schutzgesetz*.

To a Common lawyer the above-mentioned policy factor may sound unduly restrictive – in so far at any rate as it ties down developments in the law to the prearranged structure of the Code. To some extent this is correct though, on the other hand, one should not take the civil codes too seriously since often those who have to live under them do not. For example, the French courts have so disturbed the balance between articles 1119 and 1120 of the Code as to make the recognition of third party rights in contract normal instead of exceptional, as was assuredly the intention of the compilers. The German Code, too, has received some mauling at the hands of the courts, and that too before the two world crises had placed an exceptional strain on it. Thus, the courts allow a debtor to charge his stock-in-trade in favour of a creditor without actual delivery, and without the registration which English law would require for a bill of sale. This is certainly *contra legem*. The old practice, permitted by Roman law, of alienating a thing by *constitutum possessorium*, i.e. by attorning to the alienee, has maintained itself in defiance of paragraph 1205 BGB, which insists that a pledge be accompanied by a transfer of physical possession to the pledgee. This may not worry Common lawyers unduly, but the Germans are certain that the Code is being at least evaded. However, the principal way of evading inconvenient provisions of the Code is to have recourse to other provisions which establish what Professor Gutteridge once called supereminent principles, such as paragraph 242 BGB, which provides that the performance of an obligation must be in accordance with the requirements of good faith, having regard to business usage. Obviously such a provision enables the courts to cut through many difficulties by operating on the conscience of contracting parties as the old Chancellors would have done in similar circumstances. And the courts have taken advantage of it, especially in relation to the repayment of mortgage debts in inflated currency and in the handling of frustration cases.

(e)   The 'insurance factor'

It is a well-known fact that insurance companies nowadays meet the vast majority of claims for damages for personal injury and death.[94] It is not surprising, therefore, that liability insurance has had a great impact on the law of tort which, at the very least, is now obliged to reconsider familiar problems in a new perspective. So much we can say without any hesitation. But it is less easy to be precise as to the exact way in which this influence is manifested, given a certain reluctance on the part of judges to make public what they may well be thinking in private. Certainly English and, for that matter, French and German, legal theory has it that the presence or absence of insurance should have no bearing on the imposition of liability in the case actually before the judge. Viscount Simonds, for example, has expressed himself clearly in this respect in two leading tort cases[95] and legal orthodoxy would, undoubtedly, be on his side. It would be idle, however, to assert that judges are not aware of the fact that defendants are insured, particularly against third party traffic risks, and just as futile to pretend that the law has not altered to take into account the spreading of insurance. But in the United States they have gone even beyond such simple 'awareness' and many courts and authors would agree that 'if loss administration rather than deterrence is the principal aim (of the law of torts)...then lack of insurability should be considered an important factor in *its own right* and also a reflection of the difficulties that face enterprises forced to become self-insurers by the unavailability of insurance on the market'.[96] Professor Tunc has spoken in the same vein: 'Les problèmes de responsabilité civile', he wrote a few years ago,[97]

ne doivent...plus être envisagés comme s'ils se posaient entre deux individus. La plupart du temps, aujourd'hui, l'assurance en transforme les données. Et si la solution d'un procès ne peut guère dépendre du fait que l'une ou l'autre des parties soit assurée...ce serait condamner le droit à un contenu singulièrement artificiel que ne pas en élaborer les règles en tenant compte, selon les circonstances, de ce qu'une catégorie de personnes a la possibilité de s'assurer, ou est couramment assurée, ou même est obligatoirement assurée.

The same is now true in some of the Scandinavian systems, where a distinguished member of the Danish Supreme Court has said extra-judicially that in his country, judges, while expressing themselves in terms of fault, are actually thinking in terms of who is in a better position to bear the risk.[98]

This *open* approach has yet to acquire respectability in this country[99] even though many of the controversial cases lend themselves very easily to such an analysis. The 'cable cases', for example, can be approached either in the conventional, abstract, way (presence or absence of duty; remoteness etc.) or they can be seen as deciding who is in the better position to bear the risk they involve. Put differently, the answer to these cases can be made to turn

on the practicability of insurance against various types of risk, whether of loss or liability, which can only be described in the policy in general terms. If, for example, it is a practical proposition for a business to insure against 'loss of production, however caused', there would be more to be said for a general rule of non-liability for such losses than if it is in practice necessary to specify the causes of any loss of production covered by the policy.[100]

In fact, consequential losses of the kind suffered by the plaintiffs in these 'cable cases' have come to be regarded as usual insurable risks, and loss insurance rather than liability insurance seems to be more practicable and economical.[101] It is, therefore, not surprising that the courts have so far resisted the temptation to extend tort liability to this type of situation. Whether insurance was the dominant consideration when they reached these conclusions is, however, difficult to say since they have given little away in their judgments.[102] But, as Professor Atiyah has pointed out, 'whatever motives have actuated the courts, there seems no doubt that their instincts have been sound'.[103]

There are other instances which show that a particular plaintiff may, for reasons of insurance, be regarded as a better loss distributor. Though not openly acknowledged, this factor may, nevertheless, have influenced the courts to decide against liability for water companies who failed to keep their water pressures up and thus contributed to the spreading of fires.[104] Similar reasons lie behind the so-called 'New York fire rule' 'which exempts tortfeasors (usually railroad companies) from liability for all but the first building set alight'[105] though, once again, open acknowledgement of this is sorely lacking.[106] Finally, to give one last example, this time from France: the more modern tendency of the Cour de cassation to make, where possible, each and every member of a group liable in solidum for the damage caused by one of them who cannot be discovered, can also be attributed to modern insurance practice. Originally, none of the members of the group was held liable and this was explained by reference to the theory of *conditio sine qua non* which was the theory of causation which prevailed at that time. Then the courts changed their policy and, as we shall note in chapter three, had recourse to a multitude of causal and non-causal concepts to justify this change. It is only rarely however that one finds an open allusion to the insurance factor which must have played a dominant role in this judicial *volte face*.[107]

By contrast we find some acknowledgement of the insurance factor in some recent road accident cases, probably because here insurance is compulsory. In *Launchbury* v. *Morgans*[108] the majority of the Court of Appeal were prepared to incorporate insurance arguments in their attempts to expand the area of responsibility in total disregard to the traditional reticence on the subject, though the House of Lords in that same case was much more cautious. In *Nettleship* v. *Weston*[109] Lord Denning was, once again, clearly of the opinion that in these cases the question to be asked was not whose fault had caused the damage but who was in a better position to carry the risk. 'Morally the learner driver is not at fault', he said, 'but legally she is liable to be because she is insured and the risk should fall on her.'[110]

Nettleship v. *Weston*[111] presents an additional interest in so far as it reveals yet another influence of insurance on traditional tort thinking: the willingness of modern courts to objectivise the standard of care to near strict liability standards. For since the damages are not going to be met by the defendant but by his insurer, one can afford to ignore the defendant's personal shortcoming and, instead, focus attention on the plaintiff and the consequences of his not being adequately compensated. The same is true of the tendency to approach contributory negligence in a more subjective way, and anyone reasonably familiar with the law reports will notice how judges often describe conduct as negligent but are most reluctant to describe the very same conduct as contributory negligence.

One could go on listing examples of tort rules which bear strongly the marks of insurance thinking but it would serve no further purpose. It should be noted, however, that insurance has affected rules of procedure as well as substance and, of course, the overall preventive function of the tort rules. And it has almost certainly affected the size of awards. To what extent this has actually occurred is difficult to say though such empirical evidence as exists in the United States would support the view that juries tend to award higher damages in cases of insured defendants.[112] The value of such surveys is, of course, small as far as our system is concerned though, on the other hand, it cannot be entirely ruled out that even judges are not uninfluenced by this factor. And yet, despite all the above, the influence of insurance on the law of tort still tends to be 'invisible'[113] in the sense that it is not, as a general rule, openly discussed or admitted by the Common law and Civil law courts. True, the insistence of judges to formulate their judgments in abstract and rather conventional terms has not prevented liability insurance from having the the kind of effect on torts rules which we have described above; but, it is submitted, it has, on occasion, hindered the intelligent discussion of the policy issues that lie behind all these cases. The prevailing view must, therefore, be regretted for, if the law of torts is, as most would nowadays accept, concerned with the allocation of risks and the best way to absorb them, one should be prepared to discuss in public the bearing of liability insurance and the ways in which it can help achieve these aims.[114] And it has been argued (it is submitted correctly) that this would, among other things, bring a greater degree of certainty in the law, 'for once the allocation of the most frequently recurring kinds of risk had been determined there would be little litigation. Disputes on fact would be very rare and the remaining litigation would be concerned with the question of law – on which of the parties did the risk in question lie.'[115]

2 Instances in which policy may operate to prevent the rise of all liability

In the previous paragraph we discussed *some* of the *policy reasons* which may militate against the recognition of any kind of liability arising from the defendant's conduct. We must now examine in greater detail some of these occasions and leave for the next paragraph the discussion of the conceptual *means* used by the courts to achieve these results. For didactic purposes it might be convenient to divide our material into five subheadings: the unrecognised plaintiff; the unrecognised defendant; the unrecognised manner of infliction of harm; the unrecognised type of harm; and, finally, the notion of carelessness as a device limiting liability.

(a) The unrecognised plaintiff

A variety of persons could be included under this heading of 'unrecognised type of plaintiff', which appears to be particularly characteristic of the Common law systems. In England, for instance, the Queen's enemies (and, in days gone by, outlaws);[116] wives suing for deprivation through negligence of their husbands' consortium (though the opposite is not true);[117] unborn children (until the coming into effect of the Congenital Disabilities (Civil Liability) Act 1976) were all treated as non-recognised types of plaintiffs. Until recently, trespassers were also included in this category and thus deprived of all legal protection unless they could prove that their injuries were due to the intentional or reckless conduct of the defendant/occupier.[118]

Differing, though not always convincing, considerations of policy lie behind all these disparate rules, but the central notion is common enough: in certain circumstances the plaintiff must not be allowed to recover even though the standard elements of liability (carelessness, causation and damage) appear to be satisfied. This category of non-recognised plaintiffs is, as already noted, particularly pronounced in the Common law though the comparative lawyer can, occasionally, find similar rules in civilian jurisdictions. Thus French law, through the medium of damage, has come close to achieving an analogous position in the so-called 'concubinage' cases.

The policy reasons which in 1937 led the Cour de cassation to refuse a mistress the right to claim damages from the person who had killed her paramour were briefly alluded to in the previous paragraph and need not be repeated here. But the leading case[119] is important and interesting not only because this surprising decision was reached under the guidance of one of the most liberal members of the Court (Josserand) but also because it demonstrates how the Court was prepared to distort the basic provison – article 1382 CC – in order to achieve the result which the above-mentioned policy seemed to dictate.[120] The action was thus rejected on the ground that the 'relations établies par le concubinage ne peuvent, à raison de leur irrégularité même, présenter la valeur d'intérêts légitimes, juridiquement protégés'. Now, that the plaintiff's interests must be legitimate before he can claim any compensation is beyond doubt, and no one could ever, for example, suggest that a criminal could sue for damages the person who revealed to the police his criminal activities.[121] But the 1937 decision of the Cour de cassation rejected the mistress's claim not only on the ground that 'le préjudice qu'elle invoque est immoral' but also on the ground that the extra-marital cohabitation did not give her any legal rights vis-à-vis her paramour. The requirement that the plaintiff's interest be 'juridiquement protégé' in addition to being 'légitime' was clearly a gloss which, according to most commentators, was arbitrary, useless, and often unjust. The next thirty-three years were spent in endless legal quibbles between the proponents of one school of thought which wished to uphold the 1937[122] decision, and an opposite school of thought, (championed by the criminal section of the Cour de cassation) which strove to mitigate its harshness.[123] Thus, mistresses were at times allowed to recover damages provided that the relationship with the deceased had been long and durable and so long as neither of the parties was guilty of the crime (now abolished) of adultery. Such grounds for mitigating the effects of the 1937 decision, though invariably dressed up as legal arguments, were clearly influenced by considerations of policy, as the classic work of the Mazeaud brothers has frankly admitted.[124] But they were also as unsatisfactory as the ones that in 1937 had prompted the Court to adopt the original, harsh, reasoning. For why does a mistress who has, for argument's sake, a five-year relationship with a man have an *intérêt légitime* while one who has a shorter (but perhaps emotionally stronger) link is deemed not to have one? And what justification can be found in such distinctions save the desire of the courts (especially the criminal section of the Cour de cassation) to be more generous to more deserving cases (especially those where the mistress had borne a child to the deceased)? Thus, policy considerations led to the rejection of the mistress's claim in 1937; policy considerations led some courts to mitigate the original result; and policy considerations finally prompted the Cour de cassation in 1970 to hold that 'le texte [i.e. art. 1382 CC] ordonnant que l'auteur de tout fait ayant causé un dommage à autrui sera tenu de le réparer n'exige pas, en cas de décès, l'existence d'un lien de droit entre le défunt et le demandeur en indemnisation'.[125]

It is submitted that though it may not be immediately obvious, these cases have, in fact, a parallel in the English law of liability to trespassers. True, the facts of the English trespasser cases are indisputably duller than the French concubinage disputes. But the underlying principles are quite similar. Similar in that considerations of policy (in the English context, the idea of sanctity of property) led to the development of the original rule which treated all trespassers whether innocent or guilty with the same degree of severity; and considerations of policy strongly influenced its abolition. Dissimilar only to the extent that originally, the harsh and, subsequently, the more charitable rules were introduced and justified by the presence or absence of a duty; whereas in the French law the concept that was relied upon to effect these changes was that of 'damage'. That damage would prove in France a more pliable concept for judicial activism is, however, understandable since the wide formulation of the rule of article 1382 CC allows less room for frequent recourse to any concept of duty as a means of not imposing liability. In the Common law, on the other hand, where the emphasis has historically been on *iniuria* and not *damnum* 'the purposes which the civilian lawyer was able to effectuate by means of the concept of damage had to be satisfied... by other concepts over which the judges did have control, such as duty and remoteness'.[126]

The 'identity' of the plaintiff may also be important when a legal system has to decide who will be allowed to claim for the wrongful death of another. This is, in fact, by far the most important category of potentially 'non-recognised' plaintiffs, though the solutions that the various legal systems have adopted in this matter vary from allowing anyone who was *actually* supported by the deceased to bring an action for his death to limiting the number of persons to those who actually had a *legal right* to claim support from him. A compromise solution can be found in the systems which choose to define the possible claimants by setting out the types of recognised relationships.[127] The first approach is adopted by the Romanistic group of systems, notably the French and Belgian;[128] the second is championed by Germany and can be found in the Germanically orientated jurisdictions[129] while the third is the one adopted by the Common law[130] though, very exceptionally, the list of relatives who can entertain an action against the tortfeasor may be narrower than the list of relatives legally entitled to support.[131]

(b)   The unrecognised defendant

Once again it must be noted that the Common law was, and to a lesser extent still is, particularly rich in examples of this kind though the trend, apart from one or two outstanding anomalies, is in favour of cutting down these immunities. Thus a particularly important category of non-recognised defendants included vendors and lessors of ruinous premises who were generally regarded as not liable in negligence for damage caused by defects existing at the time of sale or lease. This immunity was gradually eroded by the courts and finally by statute.[132] Statute[133] also abolished another anomalous immunity – that enjoyed by the Crown. But trade unions, whose immunity was firmly re-established by the Trade Union and Labour Relations Act 1974, are still protected against such varied torts as deceit, defamation, conversion, procurement of breach of contract, intimidation, conspiracy and even personal injury and damage to property when done in contemplation or furtherance of a trade dispute. The other remaining anomaly is the immunity which *Rondel* v. *Worsley*[134] acknowledged to barristers for negligence in connection with their conduct of a case in court. This immunity, which was subsequently extended by the Court of Appeal in *Saif Ali* v. *Sidney Mitchell & Co. and Others*[135] to the pre-trial phase, has now been restored by the House of Lords to more or less its original extent. But it is arguable that even this 'restricted' immunity for 'court work' will, eventually, be whittled away.

The civilian systems do not share the above views, and with the exception of the immunity from suit traditionally granted to Heads of State,[136] they appear to have no comparable categories of 'non-recognised defendants'. So, the liability of the central governments for delicts of its officials has, for a long time now, not been in doubt, though of course numerous specific rules and regulations govern such cases of liability.[137] Equally, trade unions have not received any *blanket* absolution from the law of civil responsibility comparable in any way to the one established by English law. The same is true for lawyers, and in France, to give but one example, statute now expressly subjects them to the law of civil responsibility and provides compulsory insurance.[138] Indeed, a long stream of cases show that though actions against lawyers are not as usual as they are against members of the medical profession, they are, nevertheless, common enough and, on the whole, the courts feel confident in their ability to value the *perte de chance* that the lawyer's negligence inevitably causes to his disgruntled client.[139] Indeed, now that English law is slowly moving in this direction, the French cases may prove useful to English courts which are unaccustomed to calculate damages for loss of chance in cases of this kind.[140]

(c) The unrecognised manner of infliction of the harm

Liability for harmful omissions has traditionally been more restricted than liability for injurious acts.[141] A number of arguments, not always clearly formulated, originally justified this distinction. To start with, causation can create greater difficulties in cases of harmful abstentions;[142] and, in mediaeval times, both the Common law and the Civil law were far too occupied in suppressing the more opprobrious forms of affirmative misconduct to have time to deal with mere inactions. Alternatively, a duty to act in favour of a third person could be considered only on the level of morality and, hence, failure to discharge it would not entail legal responsability. So legal liability for failing to act was for a long time left to what we now describe as the law of contract and, in all the systems under comparison, contract still remains the most important progenitor of affirmative duties. Later, additional arguments were advanced, especially in the United States, to support the different treatment of acts and omissions. Some were 'administrative' in nature. If, for example, more than one individual failed to come to the rescue of a drowning child, which of them should be held responsible for his death?[143] And what if the opposite occurred and a rush to comply with the law impeded rather than facilitated the rescue?[144] Others had moral and philosophical overtones. For example, it was argued that the law could not expect anyone to endanger his own life for the sake of another.[145] And, in this context, the related difficulty of defining the nature and degree of the danger which warranted intervention was also repeatedly stressed.

Yet on reflection, none of these arguments is really convincing. Modern systems have become quite accustomed to dealing with intricate problems of causation. The law is perfectly able to cope with, for instance, cases on which there are present two or more independent factors each sufficient to produce certain harm. The case of two or more men approaching a leaking gas pipe with a naked flame is often given as an example. Yet in such cases it is common sense to hold that each of the men has contributed to the result and that neither should be absolved on the unconvincing argument that the disaster would have occurred just the same, even if he had played no part in it. Could it not be argued that similar reasoning could solve the hypothetical problem of many inactive onlookers of a drowning scene? Nor is the argument about the hordes of competing but mischief-making rescuers any better, for not only in most cases can several rescuers be more effective than one; but also, in practice, people seem to die because no one bothers to rescue them rather than because too many try to help and, in the course of so doing, cause the very mischief they are trying to prevent. Finally, equally misconceived is the view that the law cannot ask people to expose themselves to risks for the sake of others. For this argument, which is probably a relic of the era which treated rescuers with unwarranted harshness, completely overlooks the fact that the modern legal systems which require intervention or affirmative conduct do so *only* if this can be done without a risk to the rescuer. In reality, therefore, the above arguments are really excuses rather than logical reasons against according similar treatment to acts and omissions. They are excuses which have been used conveniently though not successfully to conceal the true reason behind the distinction between acts and omissions: 'the extreme individualism' which is especially to be found in 'Anglo-Saxon legal thought'.[146] If to this attitude one adds the fears expressed by some during the second quarter of our century that any proliferation of affirmative duties would smack of 'an exalted form of socialism',[147] one can see why the different treatment accorded to acts and omissions remained virtually unchallenged for so long. To insist, therefore, that the plaintiff's hurt is the result of a positive act rather than of mere inaction on the part of the defendant was to impose in practice an important limitation on possible liability.

For better or for worse, however, individualism is on the wane and heightened feelings of social obligation are making the modern state and its judiciary develop an interest (according to some, too late and according to others, too great) in the needy and weak. In the circumstances the grosser instances of harmful omissions could not possibly be allowed to remain without a remedy though, we shall see, the Common law and the Civil law are not always *at idem* as to which *interests* should be protected against harmful abstentions. Certainly the words of the poet, 'thou shalt not kill but needst not strive officiously to keep alive', do not seem to haunt the Common lawyer as they obviously disturb his civilian counterparts though it is difficult to say whether this is due to ideological grounds, or to its conceptual method of discovering duties of affirmative action only when the parties in question are in some 'recognised' relationship, or to both. To this we shall return later; here suffice it to say that one of the ways used by modern lawyers to impose liability for harmful omissions was not unknown to their Roman predecessors. As the fire-watcher's case shows, the answer seems to lie in the 'discovery' of a pre-existing duty to act. For if such a duty is discovered, it matters not whether it has been breached by means of a misfeasance or a non-feasance. In this way, the manner of infliction of the injury becomes irrelevant and unity is restored in the sense that everything is made to turn on the presence or absence of a duty of care.

However, once we start talking of duty we really start thinking in terms of policy, and there may be cases where there is no obvious answer. The search for a duty of care will then be influenced by the kind of policy considerations that determine liability for positive acts and has been discussed in the previous paragraph. All that one can add is that in cases of purest omissions the systems under comparison are unanimous in rejecting a *general* duty of care. Instead, they have come to think in terms of specific, albeit ever-increasing, duty situations and the use of the plural in the German term *Verkehrssicherungspflichten* is indicative of this kind of thinking.[148] But, difficult though it may often be, the task of discovering a duty of care is not impossible, and it is considerably facilitated by generous legislative intervention. For example, numerous duties of affirmative conduct have, for obvious reasons, been imposed by statutes[149] upon employers and occupiers of premises, factories, mines, quarries and the like, in order to safeguard the physical well-being of persons working on the premises. Legislative intervention, however, is in no way limited to such cases. The Highways (Miscellaneous Provisions) Act 1961 imposes upon local authorities liability for damage caused through their failure to maintain their highways. In Canada and the United States, criminal legislation has imposed upon motorists new tort duties to render assistance to persons with whom they have been involved in an accident.[150] These so-called 'hit-and-run' statutes represent, according to the better view, an extension of the older Common law in so far as they impose such duties even where the driver has *innocently* created the initial peril. Further, numerous criminal enactments[151] now impose upon parents, husbands and children various duties of assistance which are owed to their children, wives and parents respectively though the motivation in this last case may be partly based on the desire to ease the growing burden placed on the state's welfare budget by encouraging familial support where none would be forthcoming. Enactments such as these, imposing *specific* duties of affirmative conduct, can be found in all the systems under comparison and their numbers tend to increase daily. In France, for example, as long ago as 1898 a special statute punished depriving children[152] of food and proper care; article 126 of the Code of Criminal Procedure punishes a magistrate who fails to order the release of a person unlawfully detained; and article 100 of the Criminal Code punishes anyone who fails to reveal the commission of any acts of treason against the state. But none of these enactments has the significance of the *ordonnance* of 25 June 1945 which amended article 63 of the French Penal Code.[153] The origins of this enactment[154] can be found in a statute promulgated by the Vichy Government in 1941 acting under pressure from the Germans. Its prime purpose was to punish those who failed to inform the authorities of would-be criminals as well as those who failed to assist others who were in a state of peril if they could have done so without risk to themselves. Despite their somewhat unhappy origins, the provisions of the 1941 law were re-enacted after the end of the War in an amended form and became the most important and far-reaching exception to the rule that there is no general duty to act in favour of another. Needless to say, the interpretation of this statute has not been without its difficulties and the courts are from time to time still called upon to define the precise conditions which will bring the duty into play. This, obviously, is no place to go into the details of this law; so it suffices to quote one of the most recent decisions on the matter[155] which insists that the obligation to act under article 63, alinéa 2 of the Criminal Code will only arise if '[le] danger [est] grave, imminent, constant,... nécessitant une intervention immédiate' – which 'intervention', however, does not involve any 'risque pour le prévenu ou pour un tiers'.

Before leaving this area of statutory duties for affirmative action one ought to mention, albeit briefly, a closely related subject. It is the question of potential liability for failure to exercise a discretionary power conferred by statute which has recently exercised the English courts starting with the by now famous (or notorious) *Dutton*[156] case and culminating with the House of Lords decision in *Anns* v. *Merton London Borough*.[157] The significance of these cases for the law of torts is enormous and their consequences have yet to be worked out in detail. For, apart from extending the *Donoghue* v. *Stevenson*[158] rule in a way that may henceforth make manufacturers liable to their ultimate consumers not only for the damage caused *by* their defective products but also for the damage caused *to* the products themselves, the decision in *Anns* now exposes public authorities to the risk of having to pay *damages*[159] for failure to exercise or even belatedly exercise a discretionary power. But whatever their consequences, these cases certainly illustrate how a value judgment – based on the superficial attraction of the view that a local authority should carry such losses rather than an unfortunate individual – may lead to a 'discovery' of a 'duty' to act which otherwise would not have been found to exist (*Dutton*), or the imposition of liability to compensate a person who has suffered damage as the result of a public organ failing to exercise its discretionary powers in an ultra vires manner (*Anns*).

Statutes are not the only source of duties for affirmative action. Not infrequently the task of discovering or even inventing *ex post facto* such a pre-existing duty to act falls upon judicial shoulders and this is true not only of the Common law systems which are accustomed to dealing with negligence liability in terms of duty of care but also of other civilian systems, such as the French, in which the existence or non-existence of a duty is included in, as well as obscured by, the most elusive concept of *faute*. In these systems, the question that has to be asked is whether the defendant acted as the *bonus paterfamilias* would have acted if in his position. If the defendant has failed to act where the *bonus paterfamilias* would have acted, the defendant is at fault and, if the other requirements of liability are satisfied, he is liable. As the Cour de cassation has summarily put it: 'l'abstention peut être fautive lorsqu'elle constitue l'inexécution d'une obligation d'agir'.[160] And a duty to act exists whenever, in the opinion of the court, the *bonus paterfamilias* would have felt obliged to act.

This approach has obvious advantages for, first of all, it gives the courts a considerable degree of freedom to decide each case on its merits as they see them. Secondly, it stresses the unity of the concept of *faute* which is applied alike to acts and omissions. However, it is not unlike the position English law has come to adopt, though the latter tends to express the formula in terms of duty rather than *faute*. Moreover, the manner in which *faute* is employed in these cases shows that, contrary to German accusations, the French are perfectly able to distinguish between the kind of act or omission which creates liability and the quality of the defendant's conduct which will make him liable for such an act or omission.

But though liability for acts and omissions ultimately depends on *faute* (or, in English and German law, breach of duty) this does not mean that acts and omissions are, in all respects, treated alike. For in the first place the inherent flexibility of the concepts of *faute* and duty allows the courts to look at the particular circumstances of each case and decide whether a duty *should* arise. And in practice such a duty tends to be more easily discovered when the defendant has, himself, initiated a particular activity (especially if it introduces a new danger)[161] than when he has remained entirely passive. And, secondly, the standard of care that has to be achieved may also vary from case to case. The notorious *Branly* case,[162] in which a writer was held to be at fault for omitting to mention Branly's contribution in his history of wireless telegraphy, can thus be reconciled with a subsequent decision of the Cour de cassation[163] which refused to hold a journalist liable for failing to name one of the leading advocates in his account of the proceedings of a famous trial. For it could be said that the standard of care and objectivity expected from a professional historian is higher than that expected from a reporter covering the daily news. The case, however, could also be seen as a retreat from the wide extension of liability which was established in the *Branly* case, to the horror of most academics.

The flexibility of the concepts of duty (and *faute*) enables the courts to differentiate between acts and omissions in yet another way. In the Common law, cases like *Goldman* v. *Hargrave*[164] show that though the courts are prepared to impose upon *an occupier* of land 'a *general duty*... in relation to hazards occurring on their land, whether natural or man made'[165] and thus render him liable for his failure to extinguish a fire which accidentally started on his land, they are also prepared to regard the duty as being more 'subjective' than it normally is, precisely because he did not create the risk in the first place. In other words, the standard that the occupier is expected to attain is no longer the objective standard of the man of the Clapham omnibus (which determines the standard of care in cases of harmful acts) but that which is reasonable in his own individual circumstances. This reasoning, which is clearly more favourable to the defendant, was recently reaffirmed in *Leakey* v. *National Trust*.[166] But in his judgment O'Connor J. rightly pointed out that it represents a departure from earlier practice. In *Margate Pier and Harbour Proprietors* v. *Margate Town Council*,[167] for example, the harbour proprietors were held liable for omitting to remove stinking seaweed which had been washed into the harbour and caused a nuisance to the visitors and the hoteliers in the town. The Divisional Court was not prepared to accept the defendants' view that they should not be held liable because they were merely guilty of an omission to remove it; nor, apparently, was it prepared to accept the idea that a defendant's impecuniosity or other personal circumstances could affect the scope and extent of his duties. It could be argued, therefore, that the tendency to impose upon occupiers of land new duties of affirmative action is (understandably) accompanied by the desire to lighten the requisite standard of care. Thus it may be easier for a defendant to avoid liability for an omission even if he is held to have been under a duty to act.

In Germany, too, liability for harmful omissions has come to depend on the existence of a duty to act. As elsewhere, such duty often arises from statute or contract; it can stem from a family relationship (*Verwandtschaft*); or it can come into existence as a result of a preceding dangerous activity (*vorausgegangenes gefährdendes Tun*). It was, in fact, this last heading which proved a fertile ground for expansion of the scope of paragraph 823 1 BGB. For from this last heading the courts have developed the famous *Verkehrssicherungspflichten*.[168] The term *Verkehrssicherungspflicht* cannot really be translated. But its meaning could be summarised by saying that whoever by his activity or his property establishes in everyday life (*im Verkehr*) a source of risk which is likely to affect the interests of others, is obliged to ensure their protection against the risks thus created by him. Examples are numerous and it is beyond doubt that this method of discovering a pre-existing duty to act in a certain manner has enabled the courts to impose liability in cases of omission where otherwise there would be none, while at the same time contributing to a substantial raising of the standards of human behaviour. Thus in many cases it has been decided that occupiers of premises are liable to persons injured in front of their houses as a result of their failure to keep the pavements clean from ice or snow; municipalities have been held liable for failing to maintain in proper condition roads damaged by bad weather;[169] a self-service store, in circumstances factually similar to those encountered in the recent English case *Ward* v. *Tesco Stores Ltd*,[170] has been held liable for failing to remove vegetable leaves lying on its floor when they caused the fourteen-year-old plaintiff to slip and suffer severe leg injuries;[171] and, in a case factually not dissimilar from *White* v. *Blackmore*,[172] the organisers of a motor car race have been held liable for the injuries of one of the spectators.[173] Generally speaking, however, though *Verkehrssicherungspflichten* can be found in a multitude of different situations, the concept has proved particularly useful in the area of 'occupiers' liability' (to use the English term). For it has enabled the courts to overcome the rather narrow provision of paragraph 836 BGB and to afford to all lawful visitors protection which, in most respects, is analogous to that afforded by the Occupiers' Liability Act 1957. Thus, when a young boy, while playing in a public cemetery, was injured by a collapsing tombstone, the German Supreme Court held that the local authority was under a duty to exercise due care and maintain the area properly.[174] If proper supervision had been carried out in accordance with the appropriate regulations (and this, incidentally, was not a case turning on the question of breach of statutory duty) the defect in the tombstone would have been discovered and could have been remedied. So the Court ordered further evidence on the point. In another case,[175] the plaintiff's lorry was damaged by a passing train on an unfenced railway crossing on the defendant's land. The court took the view that, quite apart from being in breach of certain statutory regulations which would render him liable under paragraph 823 II BGB, the defendant was also liable for breach of the general duty of care in view of the dangerous activity which was taking place on his land. Consequently, the defendant's failure to take appropriate measures to warn users of the road of the possible danger gave rise to liability under paragraph 823 I BGB. To give one last example, the Supreme Court has allowed[176] a tenant in the defendant's house to recover damages for injuries which he sustained when the defective banisters of the house suddenly collapsed. The Court reasoned that the defendant owed a duty of care to his tenants to provide safe premises, and this he had breached by his failure to maintain the banisters in good condition.

The similarity of the *Verkehrssicherungspflicht* concept with that of duty of care should not pass unnoticed even though it has been argued[177] that it is narrower, in that it can lead to liability only if one of the enumerated interests in paragraph 823 I BGB has been affected. In practical terms, however, this difference is almost without any real significance since the most important omission from the list of interests protected by paragraph 823 I BGB is the purely economic loss which would not be recoverable in English law either. Equally interesting, however, is the growing tendency in both countries to admit in public that the creation of such duties is clearly a question of legal policy.

In view of the above it can be argued that:

(a) most systems accept the principle that liability for acts tends to be wider than liability for harmful omissions, though they have all gone a long way towards bridging the gap which formerly existed between these two types of conduct. This is particularly true of the civilian systems though less true of the Common law in general and the English law in particular. For though English law may one day be forced to move towards the same direction, at present it is still not prepared to recognise a general duty to act to save another's life. As we have noted, the only concession towards a *generalised* duty of affirmative action can be found in connection with hazards arising from land, and here the occupier has finally been put under a general (though measured) duty to prevent those hazards from afflicting his neighbours. This different treatment of 'life' and 'land' can, of course, be attributed to the Common law's tendency to operate through the medium of 'recognised relationships' rather than 'protected interests' (as is the case with the BGB). But its strongly individualistic flavour must also account for its considerable reluctance to 'discover' such 'relationships' (and thus impose duties) between 'strangers'. This disinclination of the English law contrasts sharply with some recent American decisions like *Tarassoff* v. *Regents of the University of California*[178] in which the Supreme Court of California held that the dependents of a victim of a psychopath had a tort remedy against the analyst who had treated him and to whom the murderer had, apparently, confided his intentions to commit the murder. The Court was prepared to accept that the 'special relation that arises between a patient and his doctor or psychotherapist... may support affirmative duties *for the benefit of third persons*' with whom, of course, the analyst can hardly be said to be in any 'relationship'. Given its particular facts and the known American preoccupation with psychoanalysis, the decision may be not simply controversial but also surprising. However, as an indication of the way the law is moving vis-à-vis liability for omissions it can hardly be ignored.

(b) This *rapprochement* has been achieved through the medium of pre-existing duty (or *faute*).

(c) Finally, all the systems under comparison are willing to allow their judiciary a wide discretion in deciding whether a duty exists and, if it does exist, whether in fact the defendant's behaviour has fallen below the socially acceptable standard. Liability for harmful omissions is therefore increasingly seen as an extension of liability for injurious acts – a result which is arguably as logical as it has become inevitable.

(d) The unrecognised type of harm (or the problem of pure economic loss)[179]

Pure economic loss can result from an infinite variety of factual situations. For some systems (e.g. the French) *concurrence déloyale* is the most obvious example of an activity leading to pure financial loss. But there are many other instances. For example, pure financial loss can be occasioned to an employer who has been deprived through death or injury of the services of his employee; or, it can be suffered by individuals who, because of the defendant's conduct, lose financial support as a result of the death of the breadwinner of the family; or, it can occur in the case of the ultimate purchaser of a defective product who, though not actually injured by it, is obliged to spend a great deal of money to put it right; or, it can result from the failure to exercise a statutorily imposed duty, for example, a duty to inspect the foundations of buildings under construction; or, it can be the consequence of a negligent statement, for example, concerning the value of certain shares or the credit-worthiness of a certain company or individual; finally, it can be the result of an act which damages the property of a third person in such a way as to cause the plaintiff economic loss. All these instances give rise to a multitude of difficulties but, unfortunately, considerations of space make it impossible to discuss each of them in any great detail. Briefly, however, one could say that some systems, e.g. the French,[180] will, in principle, compensate the first type of economic loss whereas other systems, notably the English, will take a very narrow view on this matter and limit compensation to the few instances covered by the *actio per quod servitium amisit*.[181] The second type of economic loss is usually the subject of the various Fatal Accidents Acts. We said earlier on something about *who* can bring such actions but *what* exactly can be claimed often differs from one system to another.[182] The third kind of harm, being damage *to* the defective product rather than damage caused *by* the defective product is, invariably, actionable in contract, not tort, though English law has, since *Dutton*[183] and *Anns*,[184] taken a different direction in this respect. Our fourth example of economic loss is, in a sense, a variation of the third. English and German law traditionally refused to compensate it in a tort action but, once again, English law has now adopted a different view.[185] The fifth and sixth examples of pure economic loss deserve closer attention since they have figured prominently in negligence litigation.

Strictly speaking, economic loss caused by a negligent mis-statement is not a subject dealt with by the civilian law of delict. It is, instead, almost invariably discussed in a contractual context and, on this ground alone, it could be omitted from this account. Yet a brief sketch of the French and German law is useful, for it can give the Common lawyer some idea of the civilian approach to the problem.[186] And it will also afford the opportunity to explain one of the reasons which account for the greater breadth of the law of torts in Common law jurisdictions. For economic loss of this kind, along with *culpa in contrahendo* and products liability,[187] offers an excellent illustration of how and why the Common law was forced to develop its law of tort in order to deal with new problem situations which arose from modern economic and technological conditions.[188] For in all these instances, the protection of persons who were not parties to a contract could be achieved only through the notions of tort and duty, since the troublesome doctrine of consideration made even a fictitious expansion of the law of contract an impossible task. In *Hedley Byrne*, for example, Lord Devlin made this very clear when he said that the problem before him was really

a product of the doctrine of consideration. If the respondents had made a nominal charge for the reference, the problem would not exist. If it were possible in English law to construct a contract without consideration, the problem would move at once out of the first and general phase into the particular; and the question would be, not whether on the facts of the case there was a special relationship, but whether on the facts of the case there was a contract.[189]

The fact that the civilian systems are not burdened by a technical doctrine of consideration makes it easier for them to shift all these cases into the contractual field. However, this does not explain *why* they chose to do so. The answer to this question can often be found in the delict articles of the various civil codes. Paragraph 831 BGB, for example, is far too rigid and favourable to employers; true vicarious liability could thus only be established through the contractual provision of paragraph 278 BGB. Similarly, negligently inflicted economic loss is not, in principle, recoverable in tort (para. 823 I BGB) and can only be compensated in contract. For the modern civilians, therefore, the pressures were the reverse from the ones operating on their Common law colleagues and it was in their law of contract, traditionally the most important and flexible part of their law of obligations, that they were forced to seek their answers. Of course, the law of contract did not always provide entirely satisfactory solutions. For example, a plaintiff trying to circumvent paragraph 831 BGB by relying on paragraph 278 BGB would never, in view of the peculiarities of paragraph 253 BGB, be allowed to claim damages for pain and suffering. But this has been tolerated, no doubt on the principle that half a loaf is better than none. But let us turn to economic loss resulting from negligent mis-statements, remembering that broadly speaking the factual situations can include either two persons (A seeks B's advice or, on the instructions of a third person, receives B's advice; can A, in the absence of an express contract between himself and B, sue B?); or three persons (A advises B and C relies on A's advice; can C sue A?).

One consequence of what we have said up to now is that the student of comparative law has, once again, to be prepared to search for his answers in a different part of the law. More significant, however, is another consequence. Because of the different starting point, the civilian systems do not share, to the same extent at least, the Common law concern that economic loss of this kind may lead to 'liability in an indeterminate amount for an indeterminate time to an indeterminate class'.[190] For since liability in these systems has to be imposed through the law of contract, the problem is not so much how to *contain* liability (which is based on the vague notion of duty) within manageable proportions, but how to *expand* protection by means of an often procrustean extension of the law of contract. This, however, is no easy task, especially in the light of paragraph 676 BGB which lays down the general rule according to which 'a person who gives advice or a recommendation to another is not bound to compensate for any damage arising from following the advice or the recommendation without prejudice to his responsibility resulting from a contract or delict'. The picture that thus emerges from the rich case-law is uncharacteristically casuistic and one could even be excused for forming the impression that German lawyers are still somewhat unsure of the theoretical justification of their solutions. A few examples can illustrate the above observations.

In 1956 the Court of Appeal of Munich[191] had to consider the question of civil liability of a firm of accountants (defendants in the action) who had been employed by a company to prepare a statement of its financial position. To the knowledge of the defendants their report was to be shown to the plaintiffs, a firm of merchant bankers, with a view to obtaining a loan from them. The report was prepared and shown to the plaintiffs who in consequence agreed to a loan only to discover some time later that the financial position of the borrower had been negligently overstated in the report. The plaintiffs then sued the accountants for damages and in the opinion of the Court they were entitled to recover. For good faith and the special position occupied by accountants in modern society put them under a duty to take care when making such statements. Their liability towards the plaintiffs also was held to be contractual in nature. Similarly, in another case,[192] the plaintiff provided a guarantee in favour of a business firm after he had been shown a report prepared by accountants commissioned by that firm for that purpose. The report, which was negligently prepared, projected a favourable but erroneous financial picture of the firm. The truth eventually emerged and when the plaintiff was called upon to pay the guarantee he sued the accountants for damages. The court held that his action should succeed and the fact that the accountants had a contract with the firm that had commissioned the report did not prevent them from being in a contractual position with the plaintiff also, since they knew that their report would be shown to him and reliance placed on it.

It will have been noticed that in cases such as the above, the defendant made a statement (usually in the form of a report etc.) to a person who asked for it (and, invariably, paid for it) but also knew that his statement would be communicated to a third, *identified*, person (the eventual plaintiff) who would be relying on it. It is this special knowledge of the defendant's which puts him in a contractual relationship *with the ultimate receiver* of his statement.[193] But where it was not clear to the maker of the statement that his report would be shown to a person other than the one who had commissioned it or received it in the first place, than a contract (with the ultimate receiver) would not be implied.[194] It is at this stage that the problem of unlimited liability in the Cardozo sense rears its ugly head and German courts (as indeed American courts) are being forced to seek a balance between liability resting on pure foresight (or some equivalent concept) and liability based only on a form of direct nexus between the representor and the representee of the kind found in the afore-mentioned decision of the Court of Appeal of Munich or in the *Glanzer* decision. To this dilemma the Federal Supreme Court has recently proposed a compromise solution which bears considerable resemblance to the solution advocated by a number of American decisions: a contract may be implied and liability imposed upon the maker of the statement if, at the time when he made the statement, he knew that it would be shown to and relied on by a specified *group of persons* of which the plaintiff was a member. In such cases, the fact that the defendant did not know who, precisely, the plaintiff was would not prevent the imposition of liability. In that case a bank gave an investment broker a report about the financial position of one of its customers so that the broker could find potential investors for that customer. The report, which was negligently drafted and misrepre-sented the customer's financial position, was shown by the broker to a number of investors including the plaintiff, who relied on it and advanced money which he subsequently lost. The investor's action against the bank was successful even though the bank was not personally aware of his existence at the time of drafting the report. It was enough that the report be shown to a certain group of persons of which the plaintiff was a member and that it was reasonable to expect that reliance would be placed upon it.[195] The extension of the law of contract thus seems to be attempted whenever the maker of the statement occupies some 'responsible position' and/or stands to make a gain from his statement, provided always that he knows that some other person, usually though not necessarily clearly identified, is going to rely on it and (if it is wrong) suffer loss. In practice, more often than not, this is done in the sort of circumstances that would lead the Common law to discover a 'special relationship'. But in German law, if such a 'special relationship' is discovered, it will lead to the creation of a *contract* between the maker and the ultimate receiver of the statement, rather than give rise to a duty to take care which, if breached, will be actionable in tort.

If we move to French law we shall immediately note that tripartite situations of the type considered above do not appear to have occupied the attention of the courts though, in theory, there is little doubt that the contractual and tortious solutions would be available should the occasion arise. Thus, suppose that A asks B to give him information about C and B, not knowing himself, asks D to find out: D negligently reports to B that C is creditworthy though, in fact, the reverse is true. B then relays this information to A who suffers economic loss. A can sue B if he can prove that B was negligent,[196] which he will hardly be if the person he asked (D) was C's banker. So, can A sue D? We have seen that in Germany a contractual action could be made available against D if he *knew* that his statement was to be passed on to A. And on the *Hedley Byrne* principle a tortious action will lie against him if he *could reasonably foresee* that A would rely on his statement. In the absence of a decided case the French answer must be speculative, though it is clear that in theory it would not be difficult to discover a contractual relation between the parties either through the concept of agency (so long as A could show that B had to the knowledge of D acted as his agent) or through the already over-stretched notion of *stipulation pour autrui* (art. 1121 CC). But in a recent decision the court of Rennes[197] indicated, in what we regard as an *obiter dictum*, that the plaintiff (who was in a position analogous to

A in our example) might also succeed in tort (art. 1382 CC). There is no report, however, of this actually having taken place.

Where only two persons are involved (the maker and the receiver of the statement) the civilian systems base their solutions almost without exception on the law of contract. Their only concern is to discover a contract between the two parties since, we have noted, the mere giving of advice, even erroneous advice, does not, by itself, lead to liability (para. 676 BGB). This, however, they have little difficulty in achieving, especially where the maker of the statement is in some 'responsible' position (e.g. he is an accountant or a banker) and it is clear that the receiver will be relying on the advice he gets.[198] The resemblance, once again, with the requirement of special relationship of the Common law is noticeable as,[199] indeed, is the similarity of approach vis-à-vis exemption clauses incorporated in such statements. For all systems will refuse to protect a person making a fraudulent statement. And an exclusion clause which clearly violates the requirement of good faith will also fail to afford protection to the proferens, a result which *probably* tallies with those we will now have to reach under the provisions of the Unfair Contract Terms Act. One or two illustrations from French and German law may, once again, not be out of place.

In 1969 the German Supreme Court had to decide the following case.[200] The plaintiff and the defendant were two fuel-supply companies which had, over the previous ten years, closely co-operated on a variety of issues including the exchange of information about the creditworthiness of their mutual clients. One day the defendant was approached by X who asked to be supplied with fuel in an area in Germany in which the defendant did not trade so he passed on the request to the plaintiffs without, however, saying anything about the prospective purchaser's dilatoriness in settling his debts. Unaware of this the plaintiff sold him fuel on credit, and when the purchaser eventually went bankrupt, the plaintiff sued the defendants for damages. The case would have caused an English court considerable trouble, not only because it was technically one of non-feasance rather than misfeasance but also because it was a case of negligently inflicted pure economic loss. Yet the German Court had little doubt that the defendant should be held liable since, in its opinion, the long association between the parties had created a *Vertrauensverhältnisse* (a relationship of trust and confidence) which imposed upon the defendant a quasi-contractual duty to take reasonable care. This was a relationship equivalent to contract (*vertragsähnlich*) which gave rise to a duty to disclose to the plaintiff the bad characteristics of the prospective purchaser. The same result has been achieved in many other similar instances involving, for example, individuals or firms seeking written (or oral) advice from bankers about the creditworthiness of certain of their customers.[201] In all these cases the solutions have been achieved in the contractual field, though the law of delict can be brought into play where the statement has been fraudulent. In one case,[202] for example, a number of persons conspired to defraud a rich investor. In order to further these aims, they persuaded an art expert to value some paintings and convince the plaintiff of the desirability to invest by buying them. These paintings proved to be worthless and the court held that the art expert was contractually liable to the investor on the ground that he had breached the (implied) contract of advice (*Beratungsvertrag*) that regulated their relations. But the court added that if the facts alleged were to be proved, they would also render the defendant liable under paragraph 826 BGB since his activity was clearly *contra bonos mores*.

Because of the *non cumul* rule such possibility of concurrence of actions would never arise in French law. But in practice this makes little difference since the French courts are very generous in discovering contracts in situations such as the above.[203] Such difficulties as they have experienced, therefore, appear to have been limited to deciding whether the contracts in question are contracts *à titre gratuit* or *à titre onéreux* and in determining the related question of the appropriate standard of liability. The above-mentioned recent decision of the court of Rennes[204] favoured the idea of a contract *à titre gratuit*, with the practical consequence that in such cases the maker of the statement can be held liable only if it can be shown that he acted intentionally or with gross negligence. The view, however, that these are contracts *à titre onéreux* seems to be preferred by academic writers, at least in so far as requests by customers of the consulted bank are concerned.[205] The solution, however, is arguably different if a third person, not a customer of the bank, makes inquiries concerning the creditworthiness of one of the bank's customers. In 1930, in a long and well reasoned judgment, the Cour de cassation[206] decided that claims should sound in tort, not contract, though academics appear reluctant to exclude entirely even in this case the application of the law of contract.

If we now move from economic loss occasioned through negligent mis-statements to economic loss caused to the plaintiff because of damage to the property of another person, we shall immediately note a great difference between English and German law on the one hand and French on the other. This is because in the French system 'le fait qu'un dommage consiste ou non en une atteinte à la personne physique ou à la propriété du demandeur n'influence en rien ni le principe du droit à réparation ni le quantum de l'indemnisation'.[207] For the French

have been much more concerned to define the general and permanent characteristics of reparable harm than to compile a list of the types of 'dommage' that they deem worthy of compensation. Thus they tend to discuss the compensability of a particular injury by looking for the requisite general elements, such as certainty of damage or legitimacy of the interest affected, rather than by fixing on the form taken by the harm in the case under discussion as in damage to real or personal property, personal injuries, unfair competition or moral offence.[208]

The result is that factual situations such as those encountered in the 'cable cases' do not seem to have caused for them the kind of difficulties that they have provoked in both English and German law.[209] This, of course, does not mean that in these cases liability is *necessarily* open-ended; it merely means that such control as there is, is exercised through one of the other elements of liability such as causation or the requirement that the damage be 'certain' or 'direct'.[210] In contrast to French law, English and German law seem to have made up their minds that in principle, negligently inflicted economic loss should not be compensated and, though the principle is currently under attack as reflecting nineteenth-century values, it is still upheld by the courts. Yet two differences between these two systems must be noted. The first is that in the Common law the compensability of negligently inflicted economic loss may not be so very far away. Whether this is desirable or not is a different matter. The fact, however, is that cases such as *Caltex*[211] and *Dutton*[212] and *Anns*[213] have made progress towards compensation of pure economic loss much more rapid than many may have realised. There is no equivalent shift in German law, where repeated attempts to modify the principle have hitherto met with little success. The second dissimilarity can be found in the different conceptual approach adopted by these two systems, a dissimilarity which may, incidentally, be largely accountable for the greater flexibility currently demonstrated by the Common law. True enough, the reasons which led to the decision not to compensate in principle pure economic loss are broadly similar in both systems;[214]

but the legal devices used to achieve this aim are quite different. We shall see that in Germany this is done through the omission of pure economic loss from the list of interests which receive legal protection, whereas in England it is done by relying on such concepts as remoteness and duty. The vagueness of these concepts, however, makes them amenable to any attempt to challenge or modify the general principle, whereas the task of the German lawyers, who are obliged to confront an inflexible text (para. 823 I BGB), is much less enviable. Yet despite textual difficulties, they have shown considerable ingenuity in attempting to find ways to compensate pure economic loss and it is worth devoting the remaining part of this section to a brief account of these efforts.

The extreme generality and flexibility of article 1382 CC, which contributed to its popularity with almost all modern legislators, struck the Germans as very dangerous. For them such an amorphous conception of liability not only invited litigation; it also placed far too heavy a burden on the shoulders of the judges. And the lack of legislative precision naturally attracted the disapproval of the historical school and their successors, the Pandectists. So, after some initial hesitation, the BGB drafting committee adopted by a majority a resolution against the general clause technique and, in the event, paragraphs 823 I and II and 826 BGB were the closest the German draftsmen came towards adopting a general clause. But even that was not sufficient for the meticulous German legal mind, and the draftsmen proceeded to circumscribe liability even further by insisting that compensation should be limited only to damage occasioned to one of the carefully enumerated interests of paragraph 823 I BGB (life, body, health, freedom, property and other (similar) rights). From this list, a person's estate (*Vermögen*), his total pecuniary interest, was carefully and deliberately excluded and no *open* attempt was ever made to bring it under the ambiguous term *sonstiges Recht*. So, in effect, paragraph 823 I BGB deals with physical damage to person and property, pure economic loss being covered by paragraph 826 BGB which, however, makes liability dependent upon proof that the plaintiff acted *intentionally and* that his conduct was *contra bonos mores*.

The result of such legislative provisions is clear and inevitable; if the plaintiff suffers economic loss, which flows from material damage to his property, he can recover so long as requirements of causation and remoteness are satisfied. But if the defendant negligently inflicts upon him pure economic loss (*reiner Vermögenschaden*) the plaintiff is without a remedy. A decision of the Court of Appeal of Düsseldorf, subsequently approved by the Federal Supreme Court, illustrates this.[215] In that case, the defendant's servant, while negligently supervising the felling of some trees, allowed one of them to fall on a nearby electricity cable and damage it. The cable belonged to the local electricity authority and was there to serve exclusively the plaintiff's chicken farm. As a result of the power cut which lasted for some six hours the plaintiff's incubators came to a standstill and most of the eggs in them failed to hatch and had to be thrown away. The plaintiff claimed, inter alia, the profit he would have made from the sale of the chickens and was allowed to recover. Though his case was argued in different ways, the Court saw this as essentially a problem of causation and remoteness. It thus had no difficulty in holding that the defendant's conduct had caused the plaintiff material damage (the destruction of the eggs) and it mattered not that the same act had also caused damage to the property of the local electricity authority. The Court then, after rejecting the defendant's plea that the plaintiff had been guilty of contributory negligence by not having a stand-by generator to protect him from such risks, proceeded to decide what the English would call the issue of remoteness (compensability for the lost profits). In the Court's opinion the lost profits were immediately consequential upon the material damage and should be recovered. The Court also felt that it was not necessary to establish that the defendant should have actually foreseen the damage in suit or the precise manner in which it was inflicted; it was enough that damage to property was the 'typical consequence' of the defendant's conduct. The reasoning is thus remarkably similar to that found in *S.C.M.* v. *Whittal*[216] and *Spartan Steel*[217] and in the elaboration which followed *Wagon Mound*[218] of the foreseeability test, except that the test of 'typicality of consequence' used by the court may lead to a considerable extension of liability. If, however, no *material* damage had been suffered by the plaintiff, his position would have been much less enviable, for the case would have been treated as one of pure economic loss. For many this result was unjustified and in the late 1950s and in the 1960s a two-pronged attack was developed.

The first was through the new right of an established and operating business (*Recht am eingerichteten und ausgeübten Gewerbetrieb*) which was created by the Supreme Court soon after the new Code came into force.[219] Initially, this new right, which protects the economic interests of commercial enterprises, was given a subsidiary role since it was meant to fill the gaps left by special commercial enactments, e.g. the laws relating to unfair competition etc. But even in this limited role it represented an innovation in so far as it afforded protection against negligent activities which interfered with an established concern, thus relieving plaintiffs from the onerous task of having to prove the requirements of paragraph 826 BGB. This new right reached its peak with the decision of the Supreme Court in 1951 in the *Constanz Urteil* case,[220] which we should regard as a defamation case. But the right was there broadly conceived and broadly applied and it was not long before practitioners realised the possibilities it offered.

One of the most interesting decisions in this context was decided by the BGH in 1958.[221] Its facts were quite similar to those of *Spartan Steel* except that in the German case the severed electricity cable was installed exclusively for the purposes of the plaintiff's business. The plaintiff company was thus encouraged to argue that the cable, though not technically part of its property, was, in a financial sense, part of its business. But its claim for lost profits was refused on the ground that the new right of an established and operating business receives protection only against *direct* invasions. In the present case there had been no such direct invasion since the interference was the result of the damage to the electricity cable and not to any company asset. The decision was interesting for a number of reasons. First, because it reaffirmed the general principle that there is no liability for pure economic loss. Secondly, because the Court admitted in public that the new right, though included under the heading of *sonstiges Recht*, was nevertheless a judge-made right and was thus in need of careful supervision lest it got out of control.[222] In the opinion of the Court the cardinal controlling device was to be found in the requirement of directness, though the Court was prepared to admit that this was not capable of precise definition.[223] It would appear, for example, that the interference is direct if the invasion affects the enterprise itself, and not rights that it may have against others. Equally, the invasion which affects the property of others is indirect (as far as the company is concerned) even though that property presents great financial interest to the company itself; indirect, also, is any interference with the workforce of the enterprise (e.g. the injury of one of its employees). Since in the above-mentioned case the interference was with electricity cables belonging to different bodies, the requirement of directness was *not* satisfied and the plaintiffs' claims failed.[224]

It is indisputable that the test of directness is understood in a normative and not factual sense and that it is still shrouded in considerable mystery despite a great deal of learned writing on the subject. But this should cause no surprise. The term 'directness', as English lawyers have found out, may be incapable of precise definition. But in practice it has led to results very similar to those reached in England by different methods, with the consequence that only the interposition of material damage will enable the plaintiff to recover his economic loss. And a recent 'cable case'[225] has brought the systems yet closer in yet another way. For it was there argued that since the plaintiff cannot, because of statutory exemption, sue the electricity company for the power cut, he should equally not be allowed to sue the person who damages the cable which causes the power cut. The point was made by Lord Denning in *Spartan Steel* v. *Martin*[226] and though not accepted by everyone as convincing, it illustrates, once again, a certain similarity in approach.

Repeated but unsuccessful attempts to use the right of an established business to compensate pure economic loss led practitioners to the decision to explore a different avenue, that offered by paragraph 823 II BGB. The idea was ingenious since that second section of this paragraph does not distinguish between material damage and economic loss and, for a moment, it looked as if it had even gained the blessing of the Federal Supreme Court.[227] But the wider policy reasons, alluded to at the beginning of this chapter, finally won the day and practitioners found themselves back to square one. Yet the study of the case-law on the subject is not without interest since it offers a good insight into German judicial techniques.

Paragraph 823 II BGB is commendably brief and successfully avoids some of the problems that have bedevilled English lawyers in the field of statutory torts. For not only does it clarify that fault must be proved before any additional civil remedy may be given; it also spares the courts from the task of having to discover (or invent) the supposed intention of the legislator in these cases. The plaintiff's main obstacle thus lies in his duty to convince the court that the provision violated is a *Schutzgesetz*, i.e. a statutory provision intended for the protection of an individual or a class or type of individual to which the plaintiff belongs (see art.2 EG. BGB); that the kind of harm that he has suffered was the type of harm the statute was meant to guard against; and that it was inflicted upon the plaintiff in precisely the manner (*Art und Weise*) envisaged by the statute. All this sounds very familiar and in practice may be extremely difficult to prove. But once established, it will lead to the plaintiff's compensation without any further need to prove the unlawfulness of the conduct or an infringement of a protected interest.

Up to 1968, claims for the recovery of pure economic loss inflicted under circumstances similar to those of the 'cable cases' were not accepted by the courts under paragraph 823 II BGB on the grounds that the provisions which are intended to benefit the public at large but also, incidentally, benefit private individuals, are not actionable at the instance of those individuals. In 1968, however, the Federal Supreme Court[228] allowed such a claim after being asked to interpret a by-law of this type. The provision in question imposed a fine on anyone who intentionally or negligently damaged cables which formed part of the national network. The Court of Appeal and the Supreme Court took the view that the relevant statutory instrument was not merely meant to protect the electricity cables from material damage but also to safeguard, so far as humanly possible, a continuous power supply. In this context it was clearly passed in the public interest. But the Supreme Court went further and, disagreeing with the Court of Appeal, held that the public interest was really nothing more than the aggregate of individual interests and, therefore, the statutory order should be taken to afford protection to individuals as well. Certainly, reasoned the Court, there was nothing in the text itself to suggest that the legislator had expressly excluded individual electricity consumers from claiming damages as a result of a power cut resulting from damage to these cables.

This innovation was short-lived. The usual fears about liability getting out of hand were soon voiced and the old approach reasserted. In 1975 the Court of Appeal of Karlsruhe[229] and, a year later, the Federal Supreme Court[230] proceeded to attack and reject the reasoning of the 1968 decision. Much of the argument was of a technical nature turning on the wording of the instruments in question. More significantly, however, much attention was devoted to the question of how the legislator's wishes should be determined in such cases, the general argument being that if no such specific rights had been conferred upon individuals expressly, they should not be implied by the courts. Wider policy arguments, already discussed in the first section of this chapter, were quoted in favour of this cautious approach, with the result that the original policy decision not to compensate pure economic loss was firmly reasserted. The battle for compensation of economic loss still remains to be won.

(e) Fault

Whether fault is considered as a product of a moralistic age or as a protective device of nascent capitalism or, probably, as a by-product of both, it can also be seen as a limiting device of liability and, as such, mentioned in this paragraph. This can certainly be argued as long as fault is identified with moral blameworthiness. However, its understanding in increasingly objective terms has led to the opposite result, i.e. an expansion of civil responsibility. In chapter 4 we shall discuss how this has led to the imposition of near strict forms of liability.

3. Duty, fault and unlawfulness

In paragraph 1 we mentioned briefly the kind of policy arguments that have led judges to deny liability, and in paragraph 2 we discussed some of the instances where this has actually occurred. We must now conclude this chapter by saying something about the formal way in which these results are achieved. Two points, however, can be made at this stage. The first is that the concepts or verbal devices used by the courts are abstract in the extreme. In addition, they are elusive and have given rise to considerable difficulties in all the systems under comparison. They are discussed here for the sake of completeness but the comparative lawyer will do well to avoid them where possible, not least because nothing can be gained from their barren comparison. Secondly, all systems refuse to tie themselves to one particular concept in order to achieve a particular result. There is thus considerable equivocation between such concepts as duty, unlawfulness, carelessness, remoteness, and the like. Having said this, however, one should add that the systems under comparison tend to achieve the results described in the previous paragraph predominantly through the concepts of duty, fault, unlawfulness, or a list of enumerated interests which are deemed to deserve the protection of the law. We shall discuss these concepts in turn.

(a) Duty

Here we come to the core of the subject, and even the Common law, which has relied greatly on the concept, has had its doubts as to its usefulness.[231] For a long time the exact point at issue was whether the duty can be made to coincide so exactly with some other admittedly indispensable requirement that it can be treated as unnecessary; as 'the fifth wheel of a coach',[232] to quote the words in which Buckland damned it to eternity. If, for instance, it could be said that whenever a reasonable man in the position of the defendant could have foreseen damage to another if he did not take care, he is under duty to take care, the limits of the duty of care would be exactly the same as those fixed by reasonable foresight; and since, admittedly, the notion of reasonable foresight cannot be dispensed with and there is no need for new tests producing exactly the same results, the duty of care ought to go. The famous dictum of Brett M.R. in *Heaven* v. *Pender*,[233] as usually interpreted, implied the disappearance of the duty of care. It was at once dissented from by his brother judges, who drew attention to an important line of cases which showed that a manufacturer of goods owed no duty of care to anyone with whom he was not in privity of a contract.[234] When in *Donoghue* v. *Stevenson*[235] Lord Atkin made up his mind that this line of cases must be overruled, he decided that the field was now open for an improved generalisation on the lines laid down by Brett M.R., again making the duty of care coterminous with reasonable foresight. But this latter generalisation, too, broke down in the years that followed this seminal judgment. The reasons are basically two. The first and most obvious one is the continuing reluctance (shared also by German law) to discover a *general* duty to act positively in order to ward off foreseeable danger from another man, even if the act can be done easily and safely and without expense to the defendant. Thus, *de lege lata*, though Common law recognises that there are some, indeed increasing, occasions when a person is under such a duty, we must still say that duties to act remain specific. The other reason is that even despite recent decisions on the subject it is very difficult to generalise about cases concerning pure economic loss. In some instances, as we have seen, *negligently* inflicted economic loss is recoverable *provided* certain other conditions are satisfied (certainly foreseeability alone of the loss is not sufficient to impose liability on the defendant). In others, malice[236] or knowledge[237] will be required, while there may even be cases where there may be no liability whatsoever, as where one man causes another very substantial financial loss by maliciously bringing civil proceedings against him. Now that economic loss inflicted by means of a 'negligent statement' may be compensated,[238] we cannot even try to make everything depend on the nature of the damage alone and argue (as the Germans do) that one is always liable for causing physical damage carelessly, but never liable for negligently causing mere pecuniary loss. The difficulties encountered in the economic loss cases are thus formidable, but they are not the only ones that have prevented the formulation of a generalised duty of care. Policy considerations until fairly recently opposed liability even where the damage was physical and foreseeable, if it was incurred by a plaintiff who was not deemed to be worthy of the protection of the law.[239] We have noted, for example, how until *British Railways Board* v. *Herrington*[240] was decided in 1972 trespassers were not regarded as a 'recognised kind of plaintiff' and their claims against the occupier of the land where they were injured were rejected. Foreseeability of the harm was in those cases clearly insufficient to impose a duty and hence liability. The law has now changed but, on the whole, it remains safer to suggest that as soon as we overstep the line between physical damage to person or property by means of a positive act and pure financial loss we can no longer rely on a generalised duty of care; but neither can we rule out any possible duty of care. Nor can we rely on the foreseeability test alone to determine in all cases the existence or non-existence of a duty. Seen in this light, the concept of duty has been only tenuously linked to foreseeability and, in practice, its presence has depended on the policy of the law. Its function has thus been to demarcate the range of relationships and interests protected against careless interference and to control the growth of the tort of Negligence by providing a brake upon the natural tendency of juries (and some judges) to indulge their (often understandable) sympathy for accident victims without properly weighing the wider implications of their decisions.

Though the above may represent a reasonable assessment of the role played by the concept of duty during the forty odd years that have elapsed since *Donoghue* v. *Stevenson*[241] was decided, the entire picture may be about to be changed radically. For since *Dorset Yacht Co. Ltd* v. *Home Office*,[242] the House of Lords has maintained that if there is between the defendant and the plaintiff 'a sufficient relationship of proximity or neighbourhood such that, in the reasonable contemplation of the former, carelessness on his part may be likely to cause damage to the latter', then a duty of care will be discovered so long as there are no policy considerations which 'ought to negative, or to reduce or limit the scope of the duty or the class of the person to whom it is owed or the damages to which a breach of it may give rise'.[243] The two notable cases covered by this caveat are omissions and economic loss. However, a steady stream of cases[244] on the latter suggests that the day when pure economic loss becomes compensated may not be so far away, the courts increasingly appearing content to control it in specific instances through some normative theory of causation (foreseeability, scope of the rule, risk etc.).[245] The law on omissions may take longer to change, though even here in certain areas as, for example, between neighbouring land owners, the courts are becoming willing to discover fairly generalised duties of affirmative action.[246] Thus, as the instances of non-liability increase, the day when the notion of duty will become redundant may be approaching.[247] Like our French colleagues we may become content to ask: 'What was the standard of care that the defendant had to attain and did he actually attain it in the case in question?' If he did not, he should be liable, subject always to rules of remoteness. A traditional English lawyer may dismiss this as pure academic speculation. A comparative lawyer, however, should at least consider it before giving his final judgment.[248]

(b) *Faute*

If we now turn to French law we shall realise that it is much harder to ascertain the actual limits of liability for 'negligence', for the vagueness of the term *faute* is matched by the highly empirical and what would seem, even to an English lawyer, amorphous character of the law of *responsabilité civile* as disclosed in *doctrine* and *jurisprudence*. Indeed, German jurists, who long ago made up their minds as to the correct structure of the law of delict, have accused the French of failing to distinguish between the kind of act or omission which creates liability and the quality of the defendant's conduct which will make him liable for such an act or omission. Now at the end of this section on *faute* we shall see why it was logical if not inevitable for French law to adopt a single concept of fault rather than distinguish, as German law has done, between objective unlawfulness and culpability. But for a time, especially during the first half of this century, certain scholars – Planiol and Savatier notable amongst them – appeared to be moving away from this notion of fault. For their writings suggest – certainly to a Common lawyer – that, for the act or omission to be characterised as *faute*, it was not enough that the defendant should have failed to attain the standard of diligence normally shown by the reasonable man; the circumstances must also have been such as to make his failure wrongful. This kind of analysis could be taken to imply that the question of existence of a duty was separate and logically anterior to that of its careless breach and that it was thus incumbent on the courts to decide first whether the situation was such as could give rise to liability and then to determine whether the defendant's conduct had fallen below the acceptable standard. It could be argued, therefore, that French lawyers were moving towards the point of acknowledging something not very far removed from the English notion of duty. Indeed, the word *devoir* was widely used.

Those who made the above their basic premise were then forced to take the next step and either prepare an exhaustive list of acts which give rise to delictual liability or to regard the maxim *neminem laedere* as a legal rule and attempt to specify its exceptions. While the first approach was championed with great lucidity by Planiol[249] and his disciples,[250] the second line of thought was taken up by Savatier,[251] who then tried to define the exceptional cases in which a person could act freely without adverting to possible consequences to other persons. His efforts resulted in all these exceptions being brought under five headings: omissions (unless there was a duty to act); trade competition (*concurrence loyale*); lawful defence of one's or another's person or interest; petty annoyances or damage involved in the fact that one cannot help living near to other persons in society; and the right which a person normally has, within limits, of expressing himself freely to or about the plaintiff.

From a Common law point of view this approach is neither novel nor unacceptable; indeed, it bears great affinity with Pollock's doctrine of common right[252] and the wider controversy about a law of tort or a law of torts. But both theories had obvious weaknesses which have been clearly pointed out in the classic work by Mazeaud and Tunc.[253] It is, thus, the definition given by these authors which now enjoys the widest support in France. They define *faute* as an error of conduct and he is at fault who conducts himself in an antisocial manner. The term 'duty' (*devoir*) is conspicuously absent from this definition, which places all its emphasis on whether the defendant committed 'une erreur de conduite telle qu'elle n'aurait pas été commise par une personne avisée placée dans les mêmes circonstances externes que l'auteur du dommage'.[254] The presence or absence of *faute* thus depends on the answer given to two questions: 'What was in the circumstances the requisite standard of care?' (question of law)[255] and then, 'Did the defendant attain this standard?' (question of fact). The similarity here with Alderson B's definition of carelessness in *Blyth* v. *Birmingham Waterworks Co.* is notable, and one might even suggest that Professor Tunc's deep knowledge of the Common law may account for this parallel. It should not, however, conceal the fact that it clearly points towards a single concept of fault unlike German law, which distinguishes unlawfulness from fault, and English law, which separates (notional) duty from carelessness. This difference of approach can ultimately be traced to the distinction between systems which think in terms of 'torts' and systems which think in terms of 'tort'. Professor Limpens has summarised this most succinctly, so perhaps it is best to quote him here in full:[256]

The concept of 'unlawful act' fits the *case-by-case approach* well enough, but is barely conceivable when the *single approach* is taken. Under the first approach the rules of tortious liability only operate in cases expressly designated by the law. It is therefore quite logical to see a piece of tortious misbehaviour as an *unlawful act*. However, the second approach assumes that any kind of behaviour can give rise to liability, provided fault is present. The concept of fault being wider than that of unlawfulness, it is then hard to see how unlawfulness can be of any further use in this area... As the area of tortious liability gradually extends, so the concept of unlawfulness withers away. It is easy to understand why. Since unlawfulness presupposes a list of headings, it naturally tends to disappear when liability becomes so general as to make lists unnecessary.

(c)   Fault and unlawfulness in German and Swiss law

Duty, it has been noted, demarcates for English law the range of interests and relationships which are protected against careless interference. In Germany, paragraph 823 1 BGB gives, as we have seen, a clear list of the interest which receive full protection. But we have also noted that pure economic loss is not compensable since a person's estate (*Vermögen*), his total pecuniary interest, is excluded from the list of protected interests. Thus, so far as economic loss is concerned, the result which is achieved in the Common law through the medium of duty is reached in Germany through the wording of the Civil Code. In this context, a fairly exhaustive list of protected interest tends to make any notion of duty superfluous.

It is only when we move from interests to relationships (or situations) which call for care that the need for something similar to our notion of duty becomes more obvious. There is little doubt that, initially, there were important gaps in the Code,[257] notably in the area of liability for omissions, since the violation of one of the enumerated interests does not automatically satisfy the requirement of unlawfulness (*Rechtswidrigkeit*) unless it can also be shown that the defendant was in breach of a pre-existing duty to act. The various *Verkehrssicherungspflichten*, discussed earlier on,[258] have now filled these gaps and, as in the Common law so, too, in German law, a great deal now depends on the presence or absence of a duty to act carefully. But with affirmative conduct the matter is different since in this case the requirement of unlawfulness[259] is satisfied once it is shown that one of the enumerated interests has been violated by a defendant who does not have or has exceeded the limits of a legally recognised defence (*Rechtfertigungsgrund*). Once again, therefore, there appears to be little room for a duty of care concept, such policy considerations as affect the outcome of the case operating mainly through the medium of fault and remoteness. This, at any rate, was the traditional view, which still has many academic followers as well as the support of the lower courts. It held that unlawfulness depended on the harmful *result* of the conduct (*Erfolgsunrecht*) rather than on the conduct itself (*Handlungsunrecht*).[260] Unlike French law, it thus kept the element of fault (*Verschulden*) separate from that of objective *unlawfulness* (*Rechtswidrigkeit*) the first being understood as an attitude (the attitude of a person who intentionally or negligently committed an unlawful act) while the second simply indicated the violation of a legal norm in the absence of a legally recognised defence.

Modern writers, however, have challenged this approach and, inspired by various theories advanced by criminal lawyers (notably, Welzel's *Finale Handlungslehre*), have been prepared to regard the lack of care requisite in the circumstances as part of the concept of unlawfulness and to understand fault (*Verschulden*) more in the sense of imputability (*Verwerfbarkeit*). Nipperdey[261] in particular, with whom the honour of promoting such new theories largely lies, has for some time now been opposed to the traditional understanding of unlawfulness when it comes to negligently inflicted damage. He has argued that the mere violation of one of the enumerated interests of paragraph 823 I BGB, if done unintentionally, *does not necessarily* satisfy the element of unlawfulness.[262] Something more is required and this missing element can be supplied by proof that the defendant's conduct has either failed to measure up to the standard of conduct imposed by a particular imperative rule applicable to the occasion in question (*Verhaltensnorm*), or that it has violated the general duty imposed upon all human beings to take care not to inflict injury on others. The need for such a duty is obvious in every civilised society, and the scope and content of the *allgemeine Sorgfaltspflicht* should be deduced from paragraph 276 BGB, which imposes upon human beings the obligation to exercise in their ordinary daily affairs (*im Verkehr*) the care that the occasion demands.[263] So the objective approach will, once again, determine what the defendant's behaviour should have been. Moreover, in determining this standard, the social utility of the activity in question will have to be taken into account (*Sozialadäquanz*). Indeed, influential authors who on the whole favour this approach have roundly asserted that considerations of policy will (and should) determine the existence as well as the limits of such duties (it 'ist eine Frage rechtspolitischer Entscheidung', in the words of von Caemmerer).[264]

It was inevitable that a system like the German which flourishes on legal theories would respond to this novel approach (which now has the support of the Supreme Court) with a stream of legal literature accepting, condemning, or even varying the new theory.[265] Professor Larenz, for example, is inclined to restrict the application of the *Sorgfaltspflichtenverletzung* to cases of indirect invasions of the plaintiff's interests.[266] But it would be fruitless to go into these matters in any great detail, not least because in practice all these theories seem to lead in almost all instances[267] to exactly the same result. Indeed it is submitted that, apart from displaying a greater willingness to employ the term 'duty' in the context of paragraph 823 I BGB, these theories achieve little more than to show that in German law, too, there can be considerable equivocation between the various elements of liability – in this case, fault and unlawfulness. Indeed, the new understanding of unlawfulness may have gone some way towards undermining the traditional separation of fault from unlawfulness. For the most important reason for introducing the element of unlawfulness as a separate ingredient of liability was the desire to make it clear from the outset what was legally allowed and what was not. The limits were thus fixed in advance in a clear and objective manner and it was only when the element of unlawfulness was satisfied that the practitioner would move on to the more 'subjective' element of fault. We have seen, however, that the Nipperdey approach (if we may so call the new ideas about unlawfulness) characterises as unlawful an interference with one of the enumerated interests only if it has fallen below the accepted social standards of behaviour. So we are again thrown back on the definition of fault in order to discover how careless we are allowed to be in our relations to others without our conduct being objectively unlawful. The advantage (such as it is) of clear and pre-set rules of expected behaviour – supplied by the traditional understanding of unlawfulness – is thus lost.

This move towards regarding unlawfulness not merely as an act performed *non iure* (without a defence) but as a failure to attain the requisite standard of conduct (behaviour) is also evident in the development of Swiss law, and this despite the fact that the text of the revised (in 1911) Code created the impression that Swiss law was abandoning the French view on fault in favour of the Germanic approach, which separates fault from unlawfulness. The case-law there reveals that conduct is characterised as unlawful if the defendant has failed to act, or has acted badly, where he was under a duty to act or to act carefully. The problem of discovering such a duty to act carefully then becomes the crux of the matter and its solution is, once again, left to the discretion of the courts. Needless to add, the problem is more acute and the degree of judicial discretion is increased, whenever such duty is to be discovered (or denied) by relaying on what is known as *le droit non écrit* and the general provisions of the Code (e.g. art. 1, alinéa 2 of the CC; art. 2 etc.). To cope with such inherently vague concepts the judges have developed a series of tests which assist them in discovering (or justifying) such duties to act, or to act carefully. They will inquire, for example, into the 'adéquation des moyens employés au but poursuivi', 'la proportionnalité du préjudice causé et le but recherché', 'la subsidiarité de l'intérêt lésé', 'la conformité à la conduite sociale correcte' (the German *Sozialadäquanz*) and decide accordingly. Relying on such techniques the Swiss courts have been able to impose a duty to act carefully on manufacturers of defective goods;[268] persons engaged in potentially dangerous activities;[269] persons digging holes in the streets and leaving them uncovered (or unlit in the night);[270] the organisers of a hockey match in an area which exposed the spectators to undue risk;[271] and even on persons who carelessly give *des renseignements inexacts*.[272] As the Tribunal Fédéral said in this last case,

Il est vrai que l'obligation de dire la vérité n'est nulle part prescrite par la loi. Cependant,...on doit considérer comme une injonction de l'ordre juridique général que celui qui est interrogé sur des faits qu'il est bien placé pour connaître doit (s'il veut répondre à la question posée), donner un renseignement exact, dès qu'il est reconnaissable pour lui que le renseignement a ou peut avoir pour celui qui le demande une signification grosse de conséquences.

Reasoning, it is submitted, which not only bears great resemblance to the *Hedley Byrne* rule but which also illustrates how general legal principles can be skilfully utilised to create specific duty situations.

We could attempt to summarise this long chapter by stressing three points. First, all systems under comparison have often been brought to the point of acknowledging, more or less explicitly, the need for something not dissimilar to the English duty of care, though not infrequently they prefer to justify their results through some other concept such as remoteness or damage. There is considerable equivocation, however, between all these concepts in all the systems under comparison. Secondly, the discovery of such duties is left to the courts and is influenced by wider considerations of policy, which are rarely revealed in the judgments themselves. Thirdly, despite the terminological differences, the English and Germanic systems first proceed to determine what kind of act or omission creates liability and only after they have determined this issue in the affirmative do they investigate the quality of the defendant's conduct which will make him liable for such act or ommission. The Romanistic systems, on the other hand, have opted for a more unitary conception of fault.

Selected further reading

Alexander, A.V., 'The Law of Tort and Non-Physical Loss: Insurance Apects', 10 *J.S.P.T.L.* (1972–73), 119.

Ames, J.B., 'Law and Morals', 22 *Harv.L.Rev.* (1908), 97, 112.

Atiyah, P., 'Negligence and Economic Loss', 83 *L.Q.R.* (1967), 248.

Bar, Ch. von, *Verkehrspflichten: Richterliche Gefahrsteuerungsgebote im deutschen Deliktsrecht* (1980).

'Unentgeltliche Investitionsempfehlungen im Wandel der Wirtschaftsverfassungen Deutschlands und Englands'. 44 *Rabels Z.* (1980), 455.

'Das "Trennungprinzip" und die Geschichte des Wandels der Haftpflichtversicherung', 181 AcP (1981), 289.

Besser, A.G., 'Privity? – An Obsolete Approach to the Liability of Accountants to Third Parties', 7 *Seton Hall L. Rev.* (1976), 507.

Bohlen, F.H., 'The Moral Duty to Aid Others as a Basis of Tort Liability', 56 *U. of P.L. Rev.* (1908), 217, reprinted in *Studies in the Law of Torts* (1926), 291 *et seq.*

Bolgar, V., 'Abuse of Rights in France, Germany and Switzerland', 35 *Louisiana L.Rev.* (1975), 1015.

Bürge, A., 'Die Kabelbruchfälle', *Juristische Blätter* (1981), 57.

Caemmerer, E. von, *Wandlungen des Deliktsrechts, Festschrift zum hundertjährigen Bestehen des Deutschen Juristentages* 1860–1960, reprinted in *Gesammelte Schriften*, 1 (1968), 452.

'Die absoluten Rechte in 823 Abs. 1 BGB', in *Karlsruher Forum* (1961), reprinted in *Gesammelte Schriften*, 1, 554.

'Das Problem des Drittschadensersatzes' (1965), reprinted in *Gesammelte Schriften*, 1, 597.

Carbonnier, J., 'Le Silence et la gloire', D. Chron. 1954, 119.

Craig, P.P., 'Negligent Misstatements, Negligent Acts and Economic Loss', 92 *L.Q.R.* (1976), 213.

Dejean de la Batie, N., *Appréciation in abstracto et appréciation in concreto en droit civil français* (1965).

Deutsch, E., *Fahrlässigkeit und erforderliche Sorgfalt* (1963).

Ehrenzweig, A., 'Negligence Without Fault', 54 *Cal.L.Rev.* (1966), 1422.

Fixing the boundaries of tortious liability

'Assurance Oblige – A Comparative Study', 15 *Law & Contemp. Prob.* (1950), 455.

Epstein, R.A., 'A Theory of Strict Liability', 2 *J. Leg. Studies* (1973), 151.

Esser, J., *Grundlagen und Entwicklung der Gefährdungshaftung* (1941, reprinted 1969).

Fleming, J.G., 'Remoteness and Duty: the Control Devices in Liability for Negligence', 31 *Can. Bar Rev.* (1953), 471.

'More Thoughts on Loss Distribution', 4 *Osgoode Hall Law Journal* (1966), 161.

Franklin, M.A., 'Vermont Requires Rescue: A Comment', 25 *Stan.L.Rev.* (1972), 51.

Friedman, L.M. and Ladinsky, J., 'Social Change and the Law of Industrial Accidents', 67 *Col.L.Rev.* (1967), 50.

Green, Leon, 'Tort Law Public Law in Disguise', 38 *Tex.L.Rev.* (1959), 1.

'Duties, Risks, Causation Doctrines', 41 *Tex.L.Rev.* (1962), 42.

Hager, G., 'Haftung bei Störung der Energiezufuhr', *JZ* (1979), 53.

Harvey, Ch., 'Economic losses and Negligence', 50 *Can.Bar.Rev.* (1972), 580.

Hermann, G., *Zum Nachteil des Vermögens* (1978).

Hippel, E. von, 'Haftung für Schockschäden Dritter', NJW 1965, 1890.

Huber, U., 'Verschulden, Gefährdung und Adäquanz', *Festschrift E. Wahl* (1973), 301.

James, Fleming, Jr., 'Limitations on Liability for Economic Loss Caused by Negligence: a Pragmatic Appraisal', 10 *J.S.P.T.L.* (1971–72), 104.

'Accident Liability Reconsidered: the Impact of Liability Insurance', 57 *Yale L.J.* (1947–48), 549.

Jolowicz, J.A., 'Liability for Accidents', 27 *C.L.J.* (1968), 50.

'The Law of Tort and Non-Physical Loss', 10 *J.S.P.T.L.* (1972–73), 91.

Josserand, L., *De l'Ésprit des droits et de leur relativité (Théorie dite de l'abus des droits)*, 2nd edn (1933).

'L'Avènement du concubinat', D.H. 1932, 1.45.

Kahn-Freund, O., 'Comparative Law as an Academic Subject', 82 *L.Q.R.* (1966), 45.

Klein (ed.), *Deutsch-französisch-schweizerisches Colloquium über die Grundlagen und Funktionen des Haftpflichtrecht* (Basel, Stuttgart, 1973).

Landes, W.M. and Posner, R.A., 'Salvors, Finders, Good Samaritans, and Other Rescuers: an Economic Study of Law and Altruism', 7 *J. Leg. Studies* (1978), 83.

Larenz, K., *Rechtswidrigkeit und Handlungsbegriff im Zivilrecht, Festschrift H. Dölle*, 1 (1963), 169.

Lawson, F.H., 'The Duty of Care in Negligence – A Comparative Survey', 22 *Tul.L.Rev.* (1947), 111, *Selected Essays* (1977), p. 249.

Limpens, J., *Encyclopedia*, XI, ch. 2.

Linden, A.M., 'Down with Foreseeability! Of Thin Skulls and Rescuers', 47 *Can. Bar Rev.* (1969), 545.

'Tort Liability for Criminal Nonfeasance', 44 *Can. Bar Rev.* (1966), 25.

Lipstein, K., 'Protected Interests in the Law of Torts', 22 *C.L.J.* (1963), 85.

Lorenz, W., 'Das Problem der Haftung für primäre Vermögensschaden bei der Erteilung einer unrichtigen Auskunft', *Festschrift K. Larenz* (1973), 575 *et seq.*

Markesinis, B.S., 'The Not so Dissimilar Tort and Delict', 93 *L.Q.R.* (1977), 78.

Markesinis, B.S. and Bar, Ch.von, *Richterliche Rechtspolitik im Haftungsrecht* (1981).

Marshall, D., 'Liability for Pure Economic Loss Negligently Caused – French and English Law Compared', 24 *I.C.L.Q.* (1975), 748.

Marty, G., 'L'Expérience française en matière de responsabilité civile et les enseignements du droit comparé', *Mélanges Maury*, II (1961), 173.

Selected further reading

Mazeaud, H., 'La Lésion d'un intérêt légitime juridiquement protégé, condition de la responsabilité civile', D. Chron. 1954, 39.

McNiece, J.F. and Thornton, J.V., 'Affirmative Duties in Tort', 58 *Yale L.J.* (1949), 1272.

Mess, M.A., 'Accountants and the Common Law: Liability to Third Parties', 52 *Notre Dame Lawyer* (1977), 838.

Millner, M.A., 'Growth and Obsolescence in Negligence', 26 *Cur. Leg. Prob.* (1973), 260.

Musielak, H.I., *Haftung für Rat, Auskunft und Gutachten* (1974).

Nipperdey, Hans Carl, 'Rechtswidrigkeit, Sozialadäquanz, Fahrlässigkeit und Schuld in Zivilrecht', NJW 1957, 1777.

Note, 'Economic Loss in Products Liability Jurisprudence', 66 *Col.L.Rev.* (1966), 917.

Note, 'The Failure to Rescue: A Comparative Study', 52 *Col.L.Rev.* (1952), 631.

Note, 'Stalking the Good Samaritan: Communists, Capitalists and the Duty to Rescue', *Utah L.Rev.* (1976), 529.

Note, 'Where the public peril begins: A Survey of psychotherapists to determine the effects of Tarassoff', 31 *Stan.L.Rev.* (1970), 165.

Opoka, K., 'Delictual Liability in German Law', 21 *I.C.L.Q.* (1972), 230.

Pound, Roscoe, 'The Economic Interpretation and the Law of Torts', 53 *Harv.L.Rev.* (1940), 365.

Prosser, W.L., 'Misrepresentations and Third Persons', 19 *Vand.L.Rev.* (1966), 231.

Ripert, G., *La Règle morale dans les obligations civiles*, 4th edn (1949).

Rotondi, M., *Inchieste di Diritto Comparato: L'Abuso di Diritto* (collection of essays on various systems and in various languages) (Padova, 1979).

Savatier, R., 'Les Contrats de conseil professionnel en droit privé', D. Chron 1972, 137.

La Théorie des obligations en droit privé économique, 4th edn (1979).

Les Métamorphoses économiques et sociales du droit civil d'aujourd'hui, 3rd edn (1964).

Serick, R., 'La Responsabilité civile en droit allemand', *Rev.trim.dr.civ.* (1955), 560.

Shapo, M.S., *The Duty to Act. Tort Law, Power and Public Policy* (1977).

Smith, J.C., 'Classification of Duty', 9 *U.B.C.L.Rev.* (1974), 213.

Stevens, L., 'Negligent Acts causing pure economic loss', 23 *U.T.L.J.* (1973), 431.

Stoll, H., 'Penal Purposes in the Law of Tort', 18 *A.J.Comp.L.* (1970), 3.

Symmons, C.R., 'The Duty of Care in Negligence', 34 *M.L.R.* (1971), 394, 528.

Taupitz, J., *Haftung für Energieleiter störungen durch Dritte* (1981).

Tunc, A., *La Responsabilité civile* (1981) (an admirable survey of some of the basic problems of the modern low of tort).

'Les Problèmes contemporains de la responsabilité civile délictuelle', *Rev.int.dr.comp.* (1967), 16.

'The Twentieth Century Development and Function of the Law of Torts in France', 14 *I.C.L.Q.* (1965), 1089.

'L'Enfant et la balle', *J.C.P.* 1966,1.1983.

'Le Droit en miettes', 22 *Archives de Philosophie du Droit* (1977), 31.

'A Codified Law of Tort – The French Experience', 39 *Louisiana L.Rev.* (1979), 1051.

Weitnauer, H., 'Remarques sur l'évolution de la responsabilité civile délictuelle en droit allemand', *Rev. int.dr.comp.* (1967), 16

White, G.E., *Tort Law in America. An Intellectual History* (1980).

Zweigert, K., 'Des Solutions identiques par des voies différentes', *Rev.int.dr.comp.* (1966), 5.

Chapter 3

PROBLEMS OF CAUSATION AND REMOTENESS

'Le problème causal en matière de responsabilité civile', wrote Gabriel Marty many years ago, 'était fait pour séduire l'esprit des juristes d'Allemagne.'[1] There is more than mere Gallic irony in this statement, as the voluminous Germanic literature clearly demonstrates.[2] By contrast, in France, problems of causation have traditionally attracted less attention than those related to the notion of *faute* – surprisingly, perhaps, for a system which, from the turn of this century, has placed increasing emphasis on article 1384 CC and stricter forms of liability. True, the picture changed somewhat in the 1930s, when causation became the subject of a number of doctoral dissertations.[3] And, more recently, a series of articles by leading French scholars bears evidence of the ability of French writers to analyse lucidly even the more complex of causal situations.[4] Yet despite such contributions, the French approach remains essentially empirical and overtly distrustful of excess theorisation.[5] Nor is the case-law any better, since little or no assistance can be gained from judicial decisions which, in these matters, seem to be as terse and, perhaps, as obscure as can be. Between these two extremes stands the Common law. For despite the fact that its judges delight in stressing that all that is required in these cases is some common sense (which, presumably, is very uncommon), the Common law can boast of a number of important monographs[6] as well as a very rich periodical literature[7] which, at times, has displayed a Germanic ability in analysing some of these problems. Indeed, it is a Common law expert who has said that 'everything worth saying on the subject has been said many times, as well as a great deal more that was not worth saying. Proximate cause remains a tangle and a jungle, a place of mirrors and maze, and the very bewildering abundance of the literature defeats its own purpose and adds its smoke to the fog.'[8] There is a sound warning here which should be heeded. Certainly, this is not the right place to attempt any reappraisal of the various theories of causation or to indulge in any in-depth analysis of the problem. Instead, we have taken advantage of the toil and learning of others and tried to give a bird's eye view of the attitude adopted by the systems under comparison towards some key problems of causation and remoteness. And, once again, we have put the emphasis on the role that policy plays in these matters and have tried to stress, where possible, existing similarities.

1. Cause in fact

In most systems, writers adopt a bifurcated approach to problems of causation by insisting that the defendant's conduct (or the event for which he is to be held responsible) cannot claim to be a 'cause' in law of the plaintiff's harm, unless it is previously established that it is at least a 'condition' of that harm.[9] This leads to a two-phased inquiry, the first part of which aims at establishing whether the defendant's conduct played *some* role in bringing about the plaintiff's harm. Since at this point the inquiry is, basically, concerned with discovering what the facts are and what exactly happened, it is discussed under such headings as 'cause in fact', 'scientific cause' and the like. The second phase of the inquiry is based on the belief that not all 'conditions' can (or should) be legally treated as causes of the harm. As Lord Wright has put it in an oft-quoted judgment,[10] 'In the varied web of affairs the law must abstract some consequences as relevant, not perhaps on grounds of pure logic, but simply for practical reasons.' *How* this selection will be made is a matter of some considerable doctrinal controversy and will be dealt with briefly in the next section of this chapter. But there is no dispute that this is essentially a problem of law, in other words, of policy. It is this different nature of the second phase of the inquiry which, it is said, justifies the bifurcated approach to causal problems. Yet this bifurcation, though widely accepted, is not universally 'emphasised', French writers being, with a few exceptions only,[11] noted for a more 'unitary' approach. Nor do all academics share the view that the second phase of the inquiry necessarily faces problems fundamentally different from those encountered in the first. Policy, according to this view, which has found a strong advocate in Malone,[12] is as important in the determination of the first phase of the inquiry as it is for the second, the difference being merely one of 'degree rather than kind'.[13] Yet at best, the role played by policy during this first phase is marginal and, as we shall see further on, it is invariably limited to cases where the facts are in doubt or obscure.[14] For better or for worse, therefore, the bifurcated approach to causal problems seems to enjoy wide support, certainly among German and American writers, and there appears to be no valid reason against its being used as the basis for the comparative discussion that follows. This being the case, the problem arises: how should we ascertain whether the defendant's conduct was a condition of the plaintiff's hurt?

The answer to the above question has been traditionally supplied by the application of the *conditio sine qua non* rule, better known to the Common lawyer as the 'but for' test. Would the plaintiff's harm have occurred without the defendant's conduct? If it would, then the defendant's conduct is not a cause of the harm. The great merit of the test lies clearly in its ability to exclude the irrelevant from any causal discussion[15] and, not surprisingly, numerous decisions, which have either overtly or implicitly relied on it, can be given as illustrations. Thus, the negligent failure of a doctor of a casualty department to examine the plaintiff's husband when he turned up complaining of vomiting did not bring about the liability of the hospital once it was shown that the death would have occurred anyway, even if the diagnostic tests had been attempted.[16] An Italian girl, unlawfully employed by a French firm without an identity card and subsequently involved in an industrial accident, cannot make her employer liable on the ground that he failed to provide her with the requisite card if it can be shown that even if he had complied with the law this could not have prevented her injuries.[17] Where the owners of a vessel sent her to sea without duly certificated officers and a collision ensued due to the negligence of the watch officer, the question that had to be decided was whether there was any causal link between the owners' breach of statutory regulations and the collision. The evidence having shown that the watch officer was perfectly competent and could have obtained a certificate had he applied for one, but that even if he had had one, this would not have prevented the collision, the court felt that the owners' breach was not the cause of the collision.[18] A chemist who negligently renewed a prescription without previously consulting the patient's doctor was held not liable once it was shown that the doctor, had he been asked, would certainly have continued the treatment.[19] The plaintiff's inebriate condition has been held not to be a contributory negligence of his hurt when it was shown that he would have been run over anyway even if he had been sober.[20] Finally, failure to install a fire escape ladder in a hotel will not render the owner liable if it can be established that the plaintiff was suffocated by smoke while still in his bed.[21]

Cases such as these illustrate how the *conditio sine qua non* rule can weed out the causally irrelevant factors. However, this does not mean that the test is not without its difficulties and ambiguities. One which we must mention, albeit briefly, involves the cardinal question of how one should decide whether the defendant's conduct (or the event complained of) is or is not a *conditio sine qua non* of the harm. The Austrian criminal lawyer, Glaser, who was one of the earliest modern exponents of the theory of conditions, had this to say on this subject:

> If one attempts wholly to eliminate in thought the alleged author (of the act) from the sum of the events in question and it then appears that nevertheless the sequence of intermediate causes remains the same, it is clear that the act and its consequences cannot be referred to him... but if it appears that, once the person in question is eliminated in thought from the scene, the consequences cannot come about, or that they can come about only in a completely different way, then one is fully justified in attributing the consequence to him and explaining it as the effect of his activity.[22]

This has been termed the method of elimination (*Hinwegdenken*) since it assumes the notional elimination of the propositus from the scene, the other conditions remaining exactly the same. It should be contrasted with a different method – that of substitution – which, far from eliminating the propositus from the scene, assumes, on the contrary, that he was there and acted lawfully, the other conditions remaining the same except in so far as they would have been altered by the lawful conduct of the person in question.

The elimination theory, which for some time enjoyed the support of the Reichsgericht,[23] seems more acceptable when the alleged cause is a positive act. What we have to do is to reconstruct the sequence of events, omitting the tortfeasor's conduct. If, despite this, the sequence of events remains unaltered, then the conduct has no causal relation to subsequent events. If, on the other hand, the final result is changed as a result of the theoretical suppression of the tortfeasor's act, then that act must have played an active and necessary part in producing the plaintiff's harm. Thus, if A shoots B and A's shot is eliminated, then B's death goes also.[24] In the case of omissions, however, the situation is more complex, for if the 'procedure of elimination without substitution is adopted no omission can ever be treated as a *conditio sine qua non* of an event'.[25] What is necessary here is the substitution of the act that the defendant omitted. Would the harmful result nevertheless have occurred? If it would, then the defendant's omission is not the cause of the result. Let us look once again at two of our 'permit' cases, mentioned earlier on, since they offer good illustrations. We noted that in *The Empire Jamaica*[26] the English court held that the absence of a certificate of competence was not necessarily the cause of the collision in which the vessel was involved. Whether it was so depended upon whether the captain, if he had had the certificate, would have navigated more skilfully and thereby avoided the collision. We saw that the answer to that question was negative and hence the lack of the certificate was held not to be the cause of the accident. Compliance with the law would thus not have averted the harm. Similarly with the French industrial accident case.[27] For the defendant's omission, we substitute the lawful act and assume that the young plaintiff had obtained an identity card. Would the accident then have occurrred? The answer is yes, which means that the presence or absence of a card had nothing to do with the harmful result.

In the examples given up to this point the *conditio sine qua non* rule has been able to produce acceptable results. But there are many instances where the test breaks down completely. This, for example, is the case whenever it can be shown that the event complained of could have been brought about in more than one way. Suppose, for example, that two motor-cyclists simultaneously pass the plaintiff's horse in a way that makes it bolt and it is subsequently proved that either of them alone could have caused the flight of the horse.[28] Or, imagine that the defendant starts a fire which then merges with another and both of them then destroy the plaintiff's property though it can be shown that either of them alone could have brought about the same result.[29] Or, finally, a garage sells a car which has defective brakes to the plaintiff who, at the critical moment, makes no attempt to apply them.[30] Would the horse have bolted in our first example but for the conduct of the first motor-cyclist? The answer is yes, because of the way the other motor-cyclist rode quickly past it. The same reasoning can be applied to our other examples and it is clear that a strict application of the *conditio sine qua non* test would hold that neither of the motor-cyclists in the first example, nor the starters of the fire in the second, nor the driver of the car in the third, would be held liable since each of these acts was a sufficient cause of the plaintiff's hurt. But however impeccable the logic of this approach may be, the solution is patently unjust, and unless we hold liable each of the persons who has done *enough* to bring about the harmful result, the victim will remain uncompensated. The word 'enough' supplies the clue for *one* possible solution and that is the adoption of the 'substantial factor' formula which was first applied by the Minnesota court[31] some sixty years ago and has more recently been sanctioned by the American *Restatement*.[32] According to this formula, the defendant's conduct is a cause of the plaintiff's harm if it was a material element and a substantial factor in bringing it about. This formula provides an answer to the above cases as well as to other troublesome factual situations. For example, what happens if the defendant's act contributes insignificantly to the harmful result (e.g. he throws a lighted match into a burning forest)?[33] Again, what are we to say in cases where a similar but not identical result would have followed without the defendant's act (e.g. A and B each sell C a rope and C hangs himself with A's rope. B's act is not a substantial factor of C's death though this does not, necessarily, mean that A will be held responsible)?[34] It must be noted, however, that this formula does not always displace, but merely improves, the 'but for' test and, as Prosser has pointed out,[35] 'Except as indicated, no case has been found where the defendant's act could be called a substantial factor when the event would have occurred without it: nor will cases very often arise where it would not be such a factor when it was so indispensable that without it the result would not have followed.'

In our last three examples we have been faced with what have been termed 'multiple sufficient causes' in the sense that each is normally 'sufficient' to produce the harmful result. In our first two examples they have both operated *simultaneously* and have been positive in nature; in the third example, the second cause was negative in nature (i.e. failure to apply the brakes). But the most fiercely debated of 'multiple sufficient causes' are the so-called 'overtaking causes'.[36] Examples include the case of the medical practitioner who blinds the patient who would, in any event, have subsequently become blind; another is the case of a house which is damaged by a negligently caused explosion of gas but which would, in any event, have been destroyed by a subsequent bombing attack. In these cases the second cause, i.e. blindness, bomb attack (commonly referred to as the 'overtaking' cause but, in actual fact, the cause 'overtaken' by the 'operative' cause for which the tortfeasor is responsible) is sufficient by itself to produce the harmful result in question but, in fact, does not do so since the causal process initiated by the tortfeasor prevents, or has already prevented, this from happening. In such cases, can the propositus rely on the second sufficient cause and argue that he did not cause the whole or part of the harm, or that if he did so, he ought for some other reason (causal or equitable) to be relieved from at least part of the liability? One can envisage a host of possible answers ranging between two possible extremes, namely, that of completely disregarding the overtaking cause[37] and that according to which damages must always be assessed by taking into account events subsequent to the appearance of the cause of action but before trial.[38] These issues are hotly disputed and it might make for clarity of exposition if we were to discuss overtaking causes in two subsections, one dealing with internal overtaking causes (predispositions), the other with external overtaking causes.[39]

(a) Predispositions

It has already been noted that an overtaking cause is an additional cause which is capable of bringing about the harm in question which the operative cause (i.e. the tortfeasor's conduct) has actually produced. Thus, if the plaintiff suffers from dormant cancer which is activated by the defendant's conduct and thereby brings about his death, can the defendant rely on the plaintiff's predisposition in order to argue that he should not be held responsible for the entire harm? *Smith* v. *Leech Brain & Co. Ltd*,[40] from which the example is taken, denied this, so following accepted doctrine that the tortfeasor must take his victim as he finds him. In the words of Mackinnon L.J., 'one who is guilty of negligence to another must put up with idiosyncrasies of his victim that increase the likelihood or extent of the damage to him: it is no answer to a claim for a fractured skull that its owner had an unusually fragile one'.[41] Most systems share, *in principle*, this approach which postulates that the tortfeasor must take his victim as he finds him[42] with the result that overtaking causes of this kind are, *in general*, ignored when assessing the plaintiff's damages. This has been explained causally in different ways depending upon which theory of legal causation one adopts but, it is submitted, the true explanation can be found in considerations of policy. For so strong nowadays is the desire to afford the maximum possible protection to human health and life that as a matter of policy it is often felt preferable to make the tortfeasor foot such bills rather than to ask the victim (as one could legitimately do) to take extra precautions against the increased risks which result from his weak predisposition. Indeed such a philosophy, invariably disguised behind such principles as *causa causae est causa causati*, can explain the extension of the tortfeasor's liability to cover, in some cases, not only the above type of harm but also subsequent accidents or illness. Thus the Reichsgericht has held the defendant who injured the plaintiff responsible not only for his injuries but also for his death which was the result of flu contracted while he (the plaintiff) was being cared for in hospital for his original injuries.[43] An even more extreme case has held a tortfeasor liable not only for the amputation of the defendant's leg caused by the tortfeasor's act, but also for the injury suffered twenty years later due to the fact that the victim never became fully accustomed to the artificial leg fitted as a result of the first injury.[44] *Wieland* v. *Cyril Lord Carpets, Ltd*[45] offers a similar if not as exaggerated an example coming from the English courts.

However, the above-stated general rule concerning predispositions has been subject to a number of exceptions and in some systems, for example the French, court practice has vacillated from one extreme to another. In some instances the courts have exonerated tortfeasors, by having recourse to the notion of *force majeure*.[46] This jurisprudence, which enjoyed the approval of part at least of the *doctrine*, received some support in the aftermath of the decision of the Cour de cassation in the notorious shipwreck case of *le Lamoricière*.[47] For though that case was concerned with a different causal problem, it nevertheless gave impetus to the idea that damages should be shared or reduced whenever the victim's hurt was partly due to the defendant's fault and partly due to other causes, including a natural cause. The *Lamoricière*, however, is now discredited and the explanation of such results through causal concepts is not entirely convincing and, in addition, conceals the true policy reasons that lie behind such cases. Notable among them is the belief that in such cases the plaintiff himself should bear part at least of the cost of his harm since it is due to his own susceptibilities, and though he is not to blame for them he is the person who can and should guard against their consequences. This type of reasoning, however, appears excessively harsh, especially towards those who need greater protection. Quite characteristically therefore it was, until recently, ignored in the context of labour accidents where the traditional 'bias' in favour of the (weaker) employee meant that his susceptibilities and predispositions were not taken into account when assessing the damages due to him by the tortfeasor. A decision of the Assemblée Plénière of 27 November 1970,[48] however, appears to have abandoned this practice of the Chambre Sociale for a much more *nuancé* approach which, in the words of the Court, is based on the idea that '[la victime] ne doit être indemnisée que dans la mesure de son état imputable à l'accident'. The formulation of such a principle is certainly easy. Moreover it is compatible with the approach championed by the second Chambre Civile which takes into account the causative value of *le fait de la victime* (as well as of his *faute*) when determining the appropriate level of compensation. But the application of the principle enunciated by the Assemblée Plénière is not easy in practice. And, along with the case-law of the second Chambre Civile,[49] it is not easy to reconcile with the more traditional solution mentioned above and still adopted by the Chambre Criminelle and the first Chambre Civile. In the end, therefore, the case-law seems to be in a state of flux which, though it provides academics with food for thought, must, no doubt, be regretted by their practising brethren.

There are other ways of limiting the tortfeasor's liability for harm resulting in part at least from the predisposition of his victim. Some are justified by direct recourse to legislative texts, article 44 paragraph 1 of the Swiss Code of Obligations being a good example, and this has allowed the courts to allocate to victims part of the risk of extreme susceptibilities. Other methods are more 'causal' in character and a variety of them have been employed to limit the range of liability resulting especially from psychological weaknesses of the victim. This can be done, for example, by treating the victim's subsequent suicide as a *novus actus interveniens* interrupting the chain of causation;[50] by regarding the damage as not adequately caused; or by limiting recovery to certain plaintiffs who happen to be within the 'danger zone'. As already stated, the cases here basically deal with instances of nervous predisposition and the problems they raise are, by their nature, both elusive and complicated. Lack of space prevents one from discussing these interesting matters in any detail[51] though some of these 'nervous shock' cases will be looked at again in the third section of this chapter. But one last aspect of the susceptibility problem deserves a few more lines.

What is true of the physical condition of the victim is to a great extent also true of his economic position. If the tortfeasor injures a man who happens to look like a tramp but is actually a skilled neuro-surgeon he will have to pay more.[52] This may, at first sight, sound unfair and it is, undoubtedly, a relic of a highly individualistic age. And it is ill at ease with social security systems which limit disability benefits to 'average' earnings and, in the end, it may be abandoned. But for the time being, this is, with few exceptions, the position taken by most systems.[53] The greater the economic strength of the victim, the greater the size of the compensation. But if the victim's great economic robustness affects the quantum of his damages should not his weakness also be taken into account? The problem has arisen in cases which have to decide whether the victim should be allowed to claim a sum of money to buy a substitute for the property destroyed by the tortfeasor. Logically, the solution should be the same and German courts have in fact allowed victims the cost of acquiring substitute property.[54] But an English case[55] has held that the plaintiff's impecuniosity and resulting inability to purchase a substitute dredger in order to complete his contract did not enable him to claim a sum. The decision was reached on causal grounds but has not escaped criticism and is in fact difficult to justify.[56]

(b)   External overtaking causes

Let us take the case of *Performance Cars* v. *Abrahams*.[57] A damages B's car in a way that makes re-spraying necessary. Subsequently C damages the car so that there would have to be a re-spray even if there had been no previous collision. Originally, A was sued but proved to be insolvent, so B decided to turn against C. It was held on entirely proper causal grounds that C was not liable, for he had caused no new damage. More important for present purposes is the action against A. If A is sued he could argue on the 'but for' test that he is not the cause of B's damage for it would have occurred even if A had not been driving his car negligently. Yet A is liable since the overtaking cause of C is not taken into account. This is because B has a claim in respect of an interest (damage to his property, the car) which could have been realised once and for all *before* C's overtaking act occurred. But what if B is making a claim in respect of an interest such as a loss of a faculty or loss of earnings etc. which could have been exercised *after* the overtaking cause did operate? What, for example, if A injures B so that he has to give up his job and then, a year later, C injures B in such a way that he would, in any event, have had to give up his job? If the claim is against A for the full sum we could take into account the overtaking cause and make A pay for the one year and C for the rest – a solution which, incidentally, would not violate the *conditio sine qua non* rule.[58] In *Baker* v. *Willoughby*,[59] however, the House of Lords seemed to favour the view of disregarding the overtaking cause and making A liable for the entire loss. And the German Reichsgericht used to take the same view.

We have hitherto concentrated our attention on various types of 'multiple sufficient causes' which demonstrate the weakness of the *conditio sine qua non* test. Another example where the test breaks down can be found in mutually exclusive but equally possible causes. The kind of case envisaged here involves two or more persons participating in a course of conduct which, though not unlawful in itself, may involve risk to others. This risk actually materialises and the plaintiff is hurt, but it is impossible to ascertain which of the participants caused the harm. Chain collisions offer one example; the old hunting cases another. Thus, where two or more sportsmen discharged their guns and a single pellet hit the plaintiff but it could not be decided whose pellet hit him, the French courts, relying on the *conditio sine qua non* test, used to deny all liability.[60] From a causal point of view this solution is impeccable. But it is unfair and was particularly unacceptable whenever the members of the hunting group were all insured with the same insurer.[61] In these cases in particular the desire to compensate the victim was such that it led the French courts to have resort to all sorts of intriguing fictions in order to achieve the desired result. On occasion, they extended the notion of control so as to hold all sportsmen joint *gardiens* of their shotguns;[62] or, more successfully perhaps, they discovered a common fault in, for example, the organisation of the hunt.[63] In the context of *hunting* accidents these decisions have now lost much of their significance since a law of 11 July 1966 has brought into the picture the Fonds de garantie automobile and obliges them to compensate victims of such accidents whenever the hunters are not insured or the authors of the accident remain undetected. The courts will then no longer have to resort to the fictions described above in order to provide compensation to the victim.[64] But in a context other than that of a hunting accident, these cases may still retain their usefulness. Above all, however, they bear witness to the creative ingenuity of courts when hindered by legal concepts from reaching fair solutions; they also serve as an example of insurance considerations dictating a change in the case-law.[65]

The Common law reaches the same result but by means of a slightly different approach. Here, too, it is accepted that on the 'but for' test the answer is complete denial of liability. But since this solution is regarded as unfair to the victim, compensation is usually decreed. The commonest way of achieving this, where the *negligence* of all defendants is not in doubt and the only issue is that of causation, is by relaxing the normal rules as to burden of proof and placing the onus on each of the defendants to exonerate himself if he can.[66] This approach is also adopted in cases where one only of the defendants is guilty of fault but it is not clear which, as, for example, in the case of a patient injured in hospital but unable to pinpoint whose fault caused him harm.[67] But when there is no evidence of any negligence the above solution would work hardship upon an equally innocent defendant, and in such cases American courts have been very reluctant to shift the burden of proof. German law, too, makes all the perpetrators liable for the whole damage, though here the task of the courts is considerably facilitated by the existence of a specific provision in the Code. Paragraph 830 BGB expressly states that 'If several persons have caused damage by an unlawful act committed in common, each is responsible for the damage. The same rule applies if it cannot be discovered which of several participants has actually caused the damage.' A decision of the Supreme Court in 1960[68] illustrates this as well as the other requirements that must be satisfied in such cases. In that case two gangs of children had a stone-throwing battle in which one child was injured. He sued a member of his *own* gang even though no stones were thrown by one member of the gang against another member of the same gang. The BGH, however, held that, so long as there was fault on the part of the defendant and there was unity as to time and place, paragraph 830 BGB applied unless the person sued could show that the injury could not possibly have been occasioned by him. Similarly, where the plaintiff slipped on a public footpath, part of which was owned by the local community and part by the defendant, and it could not be shown on which part he was when he slipped, both would be liable.[69] Incidentally, this was one of the cases where the Court thought that the owners of the path were under a duty to maintain it in a safe condition and failure to do so would entail their legal liability. Unity or close succession of time and place was also stressed in another decision of the BGH[70] involving a car accident and further injury of the victim while he was being transported to hospital by ambulance. And the Court of Appeal of Celle[71] has, in fact, applied these rules even in the case where the injured party was one of the potential perpetrators of his harm. This, too, was a case involving an injury of a seven-year-old boy taking part in a gang battle in which he lost one of his eyes. The defendant, however, who was one of his companions, was held liable for three-quarters of the injury since the Court took the view that the injury might have been partly due to a ricochet of a stone thrown by the plaintiff himself.

2. Some theories of causation

Once it is shown that the defendant's conduct was in fact a condition of the plaintiff's harm the court has to decide whether it is also legally sufficient to render him responsible for what has occurred. 'Legal' or 'proximate' causation must also be established and this will depend on a number of vague and unspecified considerations of policy which, more often than not, will be obscured behind some abstract concept or theory of legal causation. It is with some of these theories that we shall be concerned in this section, leaving problems of special difficulty for the last section of this chapter.

(a)   The equivalence theory[72]

We encountered this theory before when we stated that an act or event can only be regarded as the cause of a harm if it is at least a condition of that harm. Some adherents of this theory, however, have extended its application to the domain of legal cause by arguing that every condition of the harm is of equal value and also a legal cause. This extensive theory of liability has, in recent times, lost most of its supporters in the sphere of Civil law, but is still accepted in the area of criminal law.[73] The reason is not difficult to discern. For though the theory has some undoubted advantages, amongst which one must count its relative simplicity,[74] it suffers from one main drawback, and that is the excessive liability which it usually entails. In the area of criminal law, fault (*mens rea*) provides a useful corrective device and this danger is, therefore, averted. But fault is not always available in the context of Civil law, especially whenever liability is openly based on such notions as risk or insurance. One is therefore faced with the choice of either using some other element of liability (e.g. unlawfulness etc.) as a corrective device or reducing the application of the equivalence theory to the problems of cause in fact. We have of course noted that even there the theory cannot always produce acceptable answers. Nevertheless, this remains the most objective and scientific test available, which probably explains its popularity in the area of cause in fact. But in the area of legal cause the equivalence theory plays a small part,[75] most systems opting for some type of combination of two or more theories of legal cause. In the pages that follow we shall restrict our observations to the five theories which nowadays attract the greatest attention.

(b)   The direct consequence theory

Sanctioned by the provisions of a number of codes[76] and prevalent in England between the years 1921 and 1961,[77] this theory postulates that the defendant should be liable for all the direct consequences of his act or the defined event for which he is responsible. This could be taken to mean either that indirect harm is not recoverable on policy grounds or that its connection with the tortfeasor's conduct is merely that of condition (not legal cause) and consequence. Taken literally this theory is excessively restrictive and unacceptably favourable to the tortfeasor in so far as it suggests that there will be no recovery if, in addition to his conduct, there is also another condition of the plaintiff's harm. Some change is, therefore, necessary, though the vagueness of the term makes it unclear what it should be. One way of re-defining indirect consequences is by saying that there are those consequences which are occasioned by acts or events *subsequent in point of time* to the tortfeasor's conduct. To deny recovery in *all* these cases, however, would be unfair, so a restriction usually imposed is that compensation will be denied only if the subsequent act is a 'free' act of a third party, or if the event is 'abnormal' in character.[78] This may produce acceptable results but, it will be noticed, the answer is no longer related to the notion of directness; instead, it is made to turn on the voluntary or abnormal character of that act or event. An alternative way of defining indirect damage is by saying that it is that which is not adequately caused.[79] This conscious or unconscious blend with the adequate theory, discussed below, can be clearly seen in a number of cases decided by the Cour de cassation dealing with injury caused by stolen cars. Since the early 1940s the view has been that, exceptional circumstances apart, the owner of the car will not be liable to the victim of the traffic accident even if the theft of the car was facilitated by the fault of its owner.[80] The result can clearly be explained on the adequate theory or the directness theory, and in the latter case the theft of the car is seen as a voluntary act interrupting the chain of causation between the first fault and the harm in suit. Yet another way of defining indirect damage is by linking it to damage by ricochet. Some of the economic loss cases in England can be explained on such reasoning[81] and from a policy point of view there may be something to be said for the view of 'channelling the claim to damages in such cases through a single plaintiff'. But such reasoning has little if anything to do with any theory of causation. Finally, some authors have frankly admitted that the distinction between direct and indirect damage is anything that the judge feels inclined to make of it and, as such, is only a screen of the judicial *ius moderandi*.[82] There may be a great deal of truth in this, and the fact that the tortfeasor's degree of fault has some bearing in these matters would support such a conclusion. But in France at any rate, an open admission of such factors is never made, since it would leave the decision exposed to the risk of being quashed by the Cour de cassation. And, on the whole, the question of directness is left to the discretion of the Courts of First Instance, the stolen car cases being the most notable example of intervention in these matters by the French Supreme Court.

(c)   The foreseeability theory

It would follow from what we have said about the direct consequence theory that unforeseeable harm may, in certain cases, be recoverable, so long as it is the direct consequence of the tortfeasor's conduct. The *Re Polemis* case offers an illustration of this as well as an example of the fears that this theory conjured up in the minds of its opponents. For was it not capable of being taken to extravagant lengths at the expense of certain tortfeasors? Possible as this danger was, it rarely materialised in practice,[83] for not only did the theory restrict itself to 'immediate physical consequences'[84] but it also never aspired to regulate the more frequent problem of *novus actus interveniens*. Both of these were left to the rival test of foreseeability which was also used to determine 'which' plaintiff could bring an action since a duty of care would not be owed to any unforeseeable plaintiff. Thus, as Professor Fleming has remarked,[85]

whatever its original potential, the Polemis rule had long become tamed to the point that, when the Wagon Mound I eventually displaced it in 1961, it was with the comment that this would actually have little practical effect on the operation of the law. The apotheosis of the foresight test was thus more in the nature of a sacerdotal rite than a harbinger of drastic change.

The reasonable foresight test was thus introduced into the Common law very largely because of the understandable attraction of the idea that everyone should, within limits, be able to calculate in advance the extent of his possible liabilities. However, it has not worked like that, and, as many authors have complained, the test itself has in many cases become little more than a simple fiction.[86] And the areas of open exceptions, where the directness test is, despite its difficulties still applied, were clearly defined in a series of cases that followed the *Wagon Mound* rule in a speed that deprived it of much of its newly found glory.[87]

(d) The adequate cause theory

A subtle variant of foreseeability is what is called in the technical language of German, Swiss and Scandinavian law the 'adequacy' theory. This can serve to achieve a compromise between the extension of liability which the theory of direct consequences is capable of producing, and the greater restriction of liability which could result from the foreseeability theory. For though the adequacy theory goes beyond what is foreseeable, it nevertheless sets realistic limits of liability by relying on common-sense notions of causal connection. The theory, first expounded by the German physiologist von Kries,[88] has, nowadays, come to mean slightly different things to different people, but its central idea is common to all the variants: the defendant must pay for damage of which his wrongful act is the 'adequate' cause, but for no more. Now, the defendant's conduct (or specified event for which he is responsible), which must be a condition of the plaintiff's hurt, will further qualify as an adequate cause of that harm if it is such that it changes or increases[89] the risk of the type of harm which actually occurs. The affinity at this stage with the risk theory discussed below is notable, though the causal element is as pronounced as the normative in so far as the theory treats the tortfeasor's intervention in the state of affairs as one which affects the existing levels of danger. This gives rise to a difficulty which has yet to receive a uniform solution. How is the increased probability of harm to be assessed: on the basis of the information and knowledge which the defendant had (or, according to a variant, ought to have had) at the time of his act (as von Kries argued); or on the basis of knowledge available to a most prudent or exceptionally perceptive man (Traeger)?[90] The theory in its latter form now generally prevails in Germany;[91] in other systems, however, such as the Dutch, Austrian, Swiss and Greek, the theory is accepted in its less rigorous form. The Germans, particularly since the Second World War, have also come to accept that the theory is not merely a technical theory of causation but also an appropriate vehicle for legal policy. As the BGH put it in a leading case: 'only if the courts remain conscious of the fact that the question is not really one of causation but of fixing of the limits within which the author of a condition can fairly be made liable for its consequences...can they avoid schematizing the adequate cause formula and guarantee correct results'.[92]

Before concluding this brief description of the adequate cause theory one must point out one or two differences from the foreseeability test discussed earlier on. For one thing, the adequate cause theory can be and is applied to all forms of tort liability and is not limited to cases of liability based on fault. The foreseeability test, on the other hand, is primarily used in negligence cases though according to *Wagon Mound* II[93] it is also the right test for remoteness in cases of nuisance. Secondly, the foreseeability theory, as applied by the Common law today in an objective sense (what the *reasonable* man would have foreseen in the circumstances), will often produce results similar to those achieved by the von Kries version of the adequate cause theory. Thus in France, where the 'milder' variation of the adequate cause theory is accepted, Professor Carbonnier[94] has remarked that the theory has introduced 'dans la recherche de la cause un critère de "raisonnabilité" et l'on peut regarder comme une de ses variantes la formule de la "prévision raisonnable", qui a été pratiquée en Angleterre'. Seen in this way, one wonders whether the difference between the French understanding of 'adequate cause' and the English 'foreseeability' theory is not almost entirely one of approach. For we start with damage and ask whether it was foreseeable, whereas the French start with cause and ask whether it was adequate. This difference of approach is, of course, nothing more than a reflection of the constant preoccupation of all English lawyers with what will happen in court, whereas the civilians (especially, of course, the Germans) think of the law as existing as an independent system and of litigation as something merely incidental. The German variant, on the other hand, can go beyond such objective tests since we have noted that it will take into account all the circumstances and all the generalisations available to mankind (including those discovered after the wrongful act) as they would have been known to a most prudent and careful man.[95] This could produce not only a different approach but, occasionally, a different result since, for example, it could be argued that on the German test, *Roe* v. *Minister of Health*[96] and *The Wagon Mound* I[97] could have been decided differently. This possibility of extended liability, however, demonstrates the weakness of the German variation of the theory. For as a controlling device of liability the theory is hardly efficient and, indeed, von Caemmerer has lent the weight of his authority to such criticism by pointing out that less than a handful of the cases decided by the Reichsgericht denied the existence of a causal link.[98] This could explain the more modern tendency of German scholars and courts to combine where possible the adequate theory with a more normative theory of causation – for example the 'scope of the rule' theory. Thirdly, the adequacy theory can be more precise and concrete than that of foreseeability in so far at any rate as 'significantly increased probability' is less vague than the notion of foreseeability. Finally, the Common law systems also possess an additional doctrine – that of the unforeseeable plaintiff. This, however, will be discussed separately under paragraph 3 of this chapter.

(e) The 'risk' and the 'scope of the rule' theories

The more factual a theory, the more causal it is; the more normative, the less causal. The theories discussed here belong to the second category, and though different in some respects, they have been grouped together under one heading because of their close affinity. There is a strong teleological element behind both these theories since the aim, unlike that of the previously mentioned theories, is not to explain or predict but to fix the limits of liability by discovering the social purposes behind the rule that is being applied.

Turning first to the 'scope of the rule' theory, independently elaborated in Germany by Rabel[99] and in the U.S.A. by Green,[100] we note that it postulates that there should be no recovery if the harm in suit is not within the scope of the rule violated. This may be because the harm is not within the protective purpose of the rule in question (*Schützzweck der Norm*) or, according to a variant, because it has not come about in an unlawful manner (*Rechtswidrigkeitszusammenhang*). The operation of this theory – which, as stated, can be found both in the Common law and German law and allied systems but not (with one exception discussed below) in French law[101] – can be best illustrated by two English cases – *Gorris* v. *Scott*[102] and *Close* v. *Steel Company of Wales*.[103] In the first, statute provided that sheep carried as deck-cargo should be enclosed in proper pens. They were not, and during rough weather the plaintiff's sheep were washed overboard. His claim for damages was refused on the ground that the purpose of the requirement of the fencing was to prevent the spreading of contagious disease amongst the animals and not to safeguard them against the perils of the sea. In *Close* v. *Steel*[104] on the other hand, the House of Lords was concerned with the proper construction of section

14 (1) of the Factories Act 1937, which provided that 'every dangerous part of any machinery... shall be securely fenced'. The plaintiff was injured by some metal pieces that flew out of the machinery. The House of Lords decided by a majority that the duty imposed by section 14 (1) was designed to prevent injury to workmen by their coming into contact with moving parts of the machine, and not to prevent injury through fragments flying out of the machine itself or out of the material being worked in it.

An illuminating application of the 'scope of the rule' theory in order to produce what, it is submitted, is the correct result can be found in some German cases dealing with problems factually similar to those encountered in the *Dutton*[105] and *Anns*[106] cases in this country. For in both instances a crucial problem was the proper interpretation of a statute requiring local authorities to inspect the foundations of buildings. If this statute was violated could the ultimate owner claim for pure economic loss? The English courts said yes, but the German BGH, in a well-reasoned decision delivered on 27 May 1963 said no.[107] Because of the intrinsic interest the full judgment is reproduced in translation in volume II, but its reasoning can be mentioned briefly. Official duties may be owed to third parties. Where this is so the range of protected persons and interests must be ascertained from the provisions of the statute read against all the surrounding circumstances. In the instant case a local authority had issued a building permit without adequately checking the architect's calculations regarding the load-bearing capacity of the building which, as a result, collapsed without, however, injuring anyone. There was no doubt, reasoned the Court, that the provisions of the statute requiring the verification of such calculations were directed to the dangers which threaten the public (including all inhabitants, owners or users of the building) from the collapse of unsafe constructions[108] – so long as the harm they have suffered is a consequence of the danger from which it is the function of the official verification of the technical specifications to protect the public and hence the individual endangered. This is not the case. True it is that the plaintiff has suffered damage as a result of the collapse of the building, but he is not a victim of the danger from which as a member of the public he was entitled to be protected by the official duties... since it was only the building itself and no other property of his which was damaged. As the same Court clarified in another judgment delivered three days later,[109] the type of harm suffered by the plaintiff was pure financial loss and this, unlike personal injury or damage caused by the defective thing (rather than damage to the thing itself), was not meant to be protected by the statute in question since it lay outside its protective scope.

A careful reader will no doubt have already appreciated the main weakness of the 'scope of the rule' theory. Though it can work well whenever it is easy to assign a particular purpose to a particular rule, it breaks down completely when it is difficult or impossible to define with precision the scope of the rule in question. Thus it works rather well in cases of tortious liability resulting from breach of statutes or subsidiary regulations and this is also true with some nominate torts like defamation or torts involving animals where it may be relatively easy to discover the kind of harm the tort is trying to prevent. But it is, as already stated, difficult if not impossible to do so in cases of negligence or tortious liability for intentionally inflicting harm *contra bonos mores*. True, it has been argued[110] that this *should not be so* since 'all rules of conduct, irrespective of whether they are the product of a legislative or are a part of the fabric of the court-made law of negligence, exist for purposes. They are designed to protect *some* persons under *some* circumstances against *some* risks.' Yet, as stated, where wrongful conduct is only vaguely defined or definable it is well-nigh impossible to ascribe a specific purpose to the rule in question, and to invite a judge to do so is to invite him to fix the limits of recovery for himself. This may be desirable whenever reasons of expediency or of policy militate for or against the imposition of liability. In these cases, the 'scope of the rule' theory has the clear advantage of making the judge aware of his quasi-legislative functions in deciding the kind of damage which shall be compensated. But this solution is more doubtful when the harm in suit is one which is clearly recognised but the manner of its infliction is dubious or unusual. Here, recourse to the probability or explanatory theories may supply better guidance.

Turning now to the risk theory we note that it, too, makes more of the purpose of the rule in fixing the limits of liability. But the reliance on the purpose of the rule in question comes, as it were, in a subsidiary or additional manner, for here the starting point is the idea that the tortfeasor should be made liable for the risks he introduces in society. For them and them alone he will be held liable, which then raises the question how are they to be determined. At this stage the inquiry approximates to the adequate cause theory, for it is held that the tortfeasor is liable for the risks which his conduct made significantly more probable. But this may not be sufficient and it may be desirable if not necessary to look further than the tortfeasor's act and examine the purpose of the isolated rule. And if this fails to provide a clear guide one might even be justified in deciding the proper bounds of liability on the loss-spreading ability of the parties. This, of course, re-states the problem in normative rather than causal terms and, seen in this light, the risk theory may in fact not only help restrict liability but, on the contrary, expand the liability of the tortfeasor beyond the limits which the adequacy or the foreseeability theories may have set.[111]

3. Particular Problems[112]

(a) Plurality of causes

The plaintiff's hurt is rarely due to one cause only; in life few damages ever are. Along with the tortfeasor's conduct there may be other causes of the harm in suit but this does not prevent legal systems from holding the tortfeasor liable in full so long as the harm is indivisible. This rule, that a tortfeasor whose conduct is one only of many causes of the plaintiff's harm is, nevertheless, responsible for the full extent of the harm thus caused may, at first sight, seem illogical and not easily compatible with some of the causal theories examined above. Such difficulties as there are, however, real or imaginary, can in practice be ignored since the real explanation behind this widely accepted rule is the desire to afford the victim of the harm the maximum possible chance of having his harm properly and fully compensated. Once this is done, the tort law has exhausted its function though, of course, there exist a variety of additional rules, some statutory and others not, some reasonable and others more questionable, which allow the tortfeasor who paid the victim to seek contribution or even an indemnity from other tortfeasors. With this aspect of the problem, interesting and complicated though it may be, we are not here concerned.[113] Our prime concern is to discuss the possible effects that various, additional, causes may have on the tortfeasor's liability. For the additional causes may affect the tortfeasor's liability either by extinguishing it altogether or merely by reducing it in size. French jurists conveniently divide these causes into three categories – natural events, act of a third party and act (usually, fault) of the victim himself – and we shall adopt this distinction in the discussion that follows.

(i) Natural events

If the plaintiff's hurt is not due to a human activity it must, to the extent that it may be traceable to any cause, be attributed to a natural event. If this event satisfies some fairly rigid criteria it will be classed as a *force majeure* (*höhere Gewalt*) and if the defendant can show that it was the cause of the plaintiff's harm, he will be free from all liability. In France, it was held for many years that a *force majeure* was either the cause of the harm or it was not. Co-existence, in a legal sense, of a *force majeure* and an act of the vicitim or a third party was thus not possible. According to this school of thought 'la force majeure absorbait, à elle seule, toute la causalité du dommage. Elle ne laissait plus de place à une autre causalité, donc à aucune responsabilité. La force majeure excluait tout lien causal entre le fait du défendeur et le dommage.'[114] The reverse of this was also true. If the defendant had committed a fault without which the plaintiff would have suffered no damage, responsibility would be entirely placed on him and there would be no reason for *force majeure*.

Because the *force majeure* doctrine had contractual origins (where stricter liability can be more common) courts were very strict when characterising an event as a *force majeure*, and in particular they would insist that the event was both unforeseeable and unavoidable. And in the context of article 1384 CC there was an additional requirement: the cause of the harm should be external to the thing which caused the harm.[115] These terms, which figure prominently in judgments of many courts, should not be taken literally and, in practice, they are often qualified by such adverbs as 'normally' or 'reasonably unavoidable'. Still, the law is fairly strict on defendants and only rarely will the judges take advantage of the inherent vagueness of the terms and characterise an event as 'unforeseeable and unavoidable', thus releasing the defendant of all liability. An alternative approach to the problem was however initiated in 1951 by the two judgments of the Cour de cassation in the *Lamoricière* case.[116] The idea was then floated that *une causalité partielle* should attract *une responsabilité partielle*. This could decrease the extent of the defendant's responsibility, or conversely, as in *Lamoricière* itself, ensure that the doctrine of *force majeure* was tempered and some compensation given to the victim of the unfortunate accident. The litigation was in that case the result of a shipwreck caused partly by an unusually violent storm and partly by the bad quality of the vessel's fuel which prevented her from overcoming (as it apparently would have done had she been supplied with superior fuel) the forces of nature. Because of the War, however, good fuel was not available and so the poor quality of the coal used by the vessel could not be treated as a fault on the part of the shipowner, since he had purchased the best he could in the circumstances. Nor could the bad quality of the fuel be treated as a *force majeure* and thus absolve the shipowner since he was being sued under article 1384 CC. The bad quality of the fuel was thus a *fait d'origine interne* and could not therefore be treated as a *force majeure*. The Cour de cassation took the view that the accident was due four-fifths to the cyclone and one-fifth to the *fait de la chose* (the vessel) and was thus able to condemn the owning company to pay one-fifth of the damages due to the victims. The principle of the *Lamoricière* case was, a few years later, taken a step further by the decision in *Les Houillères du Bassin du Nord et du Pas-de-Calais*[117] where the damage was due partly to unusually severe rainfall and partly to the defendant's fault. Liability was thus, once again, apportioned on the basis of rules of causation. With few exceptions, however, these decisions met with a very hostile reception by academics, who argued that such apportioning of causality was entirely arbitrary.[118] These decisions have thus remained *arrêts d'espèce* rather than *arrêts de principe* or, perhaps better, they can be seen as examples of a case-law which the Cour de cassation tried to introduce but eventually, and under strong academic pressure, had to abandon. Yet they did manage to initiate a prolonged controversy, and the underlying idea that a *causalité partielle* should attract a *responsabilité partielle* was taken up with moderate success in two other fields, namely, where the tortfeasor's conduct combined with the act of a third party or the fault of the victim himself. To the extent that these developments can be explained on causal grounds they have been taken to mark the triumph of the theory of equivalence of conditions, since it follows from this theory that, if each antecedent circumstance plays an equivalent role in the realisation of the damage, each of the conditions should be related to the whole of the damage actually realised.

(ii) *Act of a third party ('fait d'un tiers')*
There are other ways apart from *force majeure* by which the tortfeasor may be insulated from the harm to which he has contributed. Though technically a condition of the plaintiff's hurt, the tortfeasor's conduct may not be treated as its legal cause if the intervening conduct of another party (the third party) is regarded in law as the sole cause of

the harm. Hence when the tortfeasor's fault is comparatively slight but the third party's conduct is intentional, reckless or grossly negligent, the tendency is to hold the party whose conduct is intentional, reckless, or grossly negligent solely responsible for the harm. More important in practice is the doctrine of *novus actus interveniens*. According to this, if a third party's conduct is unreasonable or unforeseeable given the conduct of the other party, then there is a likelihood that he will be held solely responsible for the harm. Most systems accept that, on occasion, this may happen but proceed to justify it differently depending upon which theory of legal causation they adopt.[119] If the direct consequence theory prevails, the third party's conduct may either be treated as the sole cause of harm or as breaking the chain of causation; if the adequacy theory is adopted, the third party's conduct will be said to render inadequate the connection between the tortfeasor's conduct and the plaintiff's harm; if the foreseeability theory is accepted, the third party's conduct will render the harm in suit unforeseeable; if the risk theory is used, the third party's conduct will be said to fall outside the risk created by the tortfeasor, and if the 'scope of the rule' theory obtains, the third party's intervention will be treated as falling outside the scope of the rule violated by the tortfeasor. Which explanation one chooses to adopt is largely a matter of personal preference and does not matter very much since the final result remains, in its broad outlines, similar in all instances.

More often than not, however, the intervention of a third party will *not* be treated as if it exonerates the tortfeasor, and liability in such instances is invariably in solidum: each tortfeasor being responsible for the *entire* harm that his conduct has helped to produce.[120] This solution is perfectly compatible with the theory of equivalence of conditions, but is less easy to reconcile with some of the other theories of legal causation we have examined above. Thus, in the explanatory theories (e.g. the direct consequence theory) or the probability theories (e.g. the adequacy or foreseeability theories), a liability proportionate to the explanatory force or increased risk attributable to the tortfeasor and the third party would be appropriate. On the fault theory the tortfeasor's liability should logically be attenuated when the third party and the tortfeasor are both at fault, and eliminated altogether when the third person is at fault and the tortfeasor strictly liable. On the risk theory the tortfeasor's liability should be reduced proportionately to the relative social risk created by the third person and so on.

Irrespective of the causal theory they may adopt, then, the majority of the systems unhesitatingly opt for liability in solidum, and, to a very great extent, this must be attributed to the desire to afford the victim the maximum possible protection. At best, in a book such as this, one can only hope to convey a very general picture of the problems and the solutions encountered in this part of the law. So it is, perhaps, advisable to restrict the remaining observations to one system only. The French is, in this respect, as good an example as any.

The traditional view was, as already stated, that if the conduct of one of the parties was one of the causes without which the plaintiff's hurt would not have occurred, then each tortfeasor was liable for the full extent of the damage. This approach came under attack, especially after the *Lamoricière*[121] decisions. The argument that causality cannot be apportioned was countered by the argument that if it can be apportioned after payment (in the action brought by one tortfeasor against the other) why cannot it be apportioned before such payment takes place? The theory of apportionment of responsibility, however, did not receive its greatest boost from causal arguments such as the above, but from entirely different 'policy' arguments. The decision in the *Pilastre*[122] case can help to reveal them very clearly. The litigation was the result of an accident involving two motor cars. The victim/plaintiff was a non-paying passenger in one of these cars and it must be remembered that at that time the rights of the *transporté à titre bénévole* against the carrier could not be based on article 1384 CC but had, instead, to be pleaded under article 1382 CC. The other driver, however, could be sued under article 1384 CC and the issue that had to be determined was for what sum he should be made liable. After many hesitations the Cour de cassation said in the *Pilastre* case that 'le principe suivant lequel chacun des responsables d'un même dommage doit être condamné in solidum à le réparer en entier, postule que le parti lésé dispose indifféremment, contre l'un ou l'autre de ses codébiteurs, d'une action', which allows the tortfeasor who has paid to seek contribution from the other tortfeasor of an appropriate sum. In this case, however, the car driver had no action against the other driver (carrier) if the other had committed no fault and thus not engaged his responsibility vis-à-vis his non-paying passenger. To put it another way, the Court felt that if the action for contribution was not available to the one tortfeasor then his liability in solidum became untenable: the more just answer *appeared* to be to make the other driver/defendant liable only for his contribution to the plaintiff's harm. The

Pilastre case did not specify what this should be, but the cases that followed favoured equal shares. This reasoning, however, involved a *petitio principii* and in any case became unnecessary after the Cour de cassation reversed its stand on the *transport bénévole* in 1968[123] and allowed non-paying passengers to sue their carriers under article 1384 CC. And in 1969 it was openly attacked in the *Gueffier* decision[124] when the second Chambre Civile of the Cour de cassation unequivocally stated that 'dans le cas de concours de responsabilité, chacun des responsables d'un dommage, ayant concouru à le causer en entier, doit être condamné envers la victime à en assurer l'entière réparation, *sans qu'il y ait lieu d'envisager l'éventualité d'un recours à l'égard de l'autre coauteur*'.

(iii) Fault of the injured party

One point must be made clear from the outset. We are here concerned with cases where the fault of the victim is one but not the sole cause of his damage but the French term (*faute de la victime*) has been chosen, instead of the English 'contributory negligence', because it is wider in so far as it includes harm caused intentionally as well as negligently.[125] Fault of the injured party is wider than contributory negligence in yet another sense since it can be taken to include 'subsequent fault'. This type of fault, which is related to the conduct of the injured party *after* the occurrence of the initial harm, is not included in the discussion that follows, partly because of considerations of space and partly because the problems of 'mitigation of damage' tend to receive separate treatment by some systems, notably those of the Common law.

What consequences should the contributory fault of the injured party have on the conduct of the tortfeasor? Theoretically, three possibilities have been canvassed over the ages. The first found clear expression in the rule of Pomponius[126] according to which the injured party cannot recover if his injury is due to his own fault unless the tortfeasor's conduct was intentional.[127] The Common law rule, we know, was the same.[128] The second possible solution is to allow the tortfeasor a limited amount of recovery according to a number of different criteria (e.g. fault, causal contribution, equity or a mixture of all). A number of codes, including the Austrian Code[129] and the Swiss Code of Obligations,[130] have opted for this solution though, perhaps, the best illustration can be found in paragraph 254 1 BGB which decrees that 'If any fault of the injured party has contributed to the occurrence of the damage, the duty to compensate and the extent of the compensation to be made depend upon the circumstances, especially upon how far the injury has been caused predominently by the one or the other party.' Finally, according to a more modern trend, the victim's fault can, in certain circumstances, be completely ignored and, consequently, full compensation should be decreed. An early example of this rule can be found in the French Accident Compensation Law of 1898 which allowed employers to diminish their awards to their injured employees for injuries suffered in their employment only if the workman himself was at fault and his *faute* was 'inexcusable'.[131] The same idea can be found expressed in a much wider form in article 958 of the Soviet Code of 1964. This provides that only the gross negligence of the injured party shall lead to the reduction (or possible extinction) of his damages; otherwise the victim is entitled to full compensation. These three possible solutions have been adopted at different times by different systems and Professor Honoré has cautiously suggested that the comparative examination of the various systems reveals a trend towards fuller compensation as the economy of a particular state expands. Thus, 'the fault of the injured party, at first a complete bar to recovery, later leads only to a reduction of damages and, finally, is completely disregarded unless it is especially serious or flagrant'.[132] The importance of economic and social factors in shaping or changing some of the rules on this subject should not be underestimated. Yet they have received less than adequate attention, the explanation of the above rules invariably being left to theories of legal causation, most of which point towards some form or another of apportionment. For example, given that according to the equivalence theory each condition of the harm is taken to be of equal value, the natural inference is that each should be responsible for the harm to the same extent. Similarly, on the adequacy theory, if the conduct of the tortfeasor and the victim are both adequately related to the victim's harm, compensation must be apportioned between them according to how much each fault increased the risk of the harmful occurrence. It is only the old Common law rule that cannot be adequately explained by any theory of causation, and non-legal arguments (for example of an economic, moral or individualistic nature) occasionally advanced in its support have proved hardly more convincing.

In this brief sketch of the problem of contributory fault the solutions offered by the French law deserve, perhaps, to be singled out. This is because, firstly, the rule of apportionment of liability on the basis of the gravity of the respective faults has prevailed since the very early days of the Code Napoléon even though the Code itself was silent on the question of fault of the victim. Secondly, this absence of any statutory provision regulating the matter meant that, unlike Germany where the Code employs causal language to justify the rule of apportionment,[133] the French judge-made rule had to find its true justification elsewhere and many have hence chosen to fall back on wider considerations of equity rather than on any particular operation of the doctrine of causation.[134] Others have chosen to explain the diminution as a sanction, corollary to the notion of fault. Professor Starck, for example, has argued that the reduction of the victim's damages 'est conforme à l'esprit répressif auquel le droit civil, et particulièrement celui de la responsabilité, n'est pas étranger'.[135] However, the penal overtones of this explanation, though consistent with Professor Starck's general approach to the problems of civil responsibility, are not easy to reconcile with the more widely held idea that punishment is for the criminal law and not for the law of tort. The idea of deterrence may also be in the minds of some judges when ordering reduction of damages, since it can be argued that such a threat might encourage potential victims to be more careful themselves. Be that as it may, the fact is that the courts have never wavered from the view that damages should be apportioned between the tortfeasor and the victim whenever both of them are at fault. And since the middle of the 1930s the same solution has been accepted in the context of article 1384 CC in cases where the victim's damage was partly due to his own fault and partly due to the non-negligent conduct of the tortfeasor/ defendant. This represented an interesting departure from prevailing practice since earlier cases, involving the application of article 1384 CC, had held that the defendant/*gardien* of the thing that caused damage to the plaintiff should be *totally* exonerated if he succeeded in proving the victim's own fault.[136] But in 1934 the Chambre des Requêtes decided that the custodian's exoneration should only be partial given that the fault of the victim was *not* the sole cause of his damage.[137] The solution was confirmed two years later by the Chambre Civile of the Cour de cassation[138] in an *arrêt de principe* and the case-law has not altered since. Given that in this case the conduct of one of the parties only (that of the victim) is related to fault, it becomes less easy to ascribe the reduction of damages to any idea of fault or deterrence and, instead, a 'causal' explanation becomes more appropriate. Indeed, the more modern tendency of the second

Chambre Civile to take into account even *le fait de la victime*[139] (and not only his *faute*) and thereby reduce his damages, suggests that liabilities are increasingly assessed on the basis of comparative causations. This also is true of those decisions which, contrary to the more traditional approach, have relied on the predisposition of the victim (which, by definition, does not amount to *faute*) in order to reduce his damages.[140] Arguably, one could go even further and say that even in cases decided under article 1382 CC the apportionment of damages is attempted more on the basis of causal potency than the relative gravity of the respective faults. This would certainly be in accord with the prevailing tendency to base liability on causal grounds; and, incidentally, it would also bring French law closer to the German approach which, according to paragraph 254 I BGB, makes any reduction of damages depend on the injured party's contribution to his harm. For since apportionment depends on the degree of *causal contribution* of the tortfeasor's *conduct* and the victim's *fault*, it cannot make a difference whether the plaintiff's claim is based on fault, presumed fault or risk. The extent of the compensation will thus depend upon the relative causal contribution of one or the other party. Given that the adequacy theory prevails in German law, this approach creates few causal difficulties since the whole inquiry is really reduced to the question of the extent to which each party increased the risk of the harm.

(b) The unforeseeable plaintiff

The equivocation between the various elements of liability in general and of duty and legal cause in particular has already been noted. There is, undoubtedly, a certain, but not necessarily complete, overlap between these concepts which, in the tort of Negligence, can make it difficult to separate two apparently different questions: first, whether the defendant has breached a duty owed to the plaintiff and, secondly, if he has, whether a particular item of damage is recoverable. It can be strongly argued that both issues are really 'causal';[141] and the test used by English law to decide them is the same (foreseeability). To discuss, therefore, the question of the 'foreseeable plaintiff' separately from that of the 'foreseeable damage' may be unnecessary if not confusing. Yet the Common law, by adopting the doctrine of 'foreseeable plaintiff', may be doing just that while making it difficult for the non-Common lawyer to follow both his terminology and reasoning. Closer attention to the doctrine of 'foreseeable plaintiff' will only partially dispel some of these doubts though, incidentally, it may supply one possible argument in its favour.

There is no difficulty in re-phrasing problems of legal or 'proximate' cause in terms of legal duty.[142] Nervous shock and 'rescue' cases offer excellent illustrations since they are, invariably, treated by Civil law systems as cases giving rise to causal problems whereas in the Common law they are nowadays dealt with under the rubric of duty. The results, it must be noted from the outset, are in many respects the same. Nervous shock, to take one of these cases as an example, is increasingly compensated both by Civil law and the Common law systems, despite their differing theoretical approaches. This, of course, is not to deny differences. English law, for example, refuses to compensate nervous shock suffered by the plaintiff as a result of being *told* of a particular incident rather than seeing it or hearing it with his own unaided senses.[143] German law, on the other hand, more logically, one is inclined to suggest, imposes no similar limitation.[144] But these are matters of comparative detail and what is more important to underline is the growing realisation in both families of systems that the problem which really faces them is one of policy and limitation of liability rather than anything else.[145] This awareness has, in turn, led to growing dissatisfaction with existing tests (adequate cause theory), the experimentation with others more normative in content (e.g. the 'scope of the rule' theory), and the conviction that in the end arbitrary criteria will set the bounds of liability.[146] To opt in such circumstances for the 'duty' rather than the 'proximate cause' approach is only to restate the problem rather than to solve it. Yet, as Dean Prosser has remarked,[147] the 'duty' approach in some instances 'does serve to direct attention to the policy issues which determine the extent of the original obligation and of its continuance, rather than to the mechanical sequence of events which goes to make up causation in fact'. This may be particularly helpful in cases where the real issue that has to be determined is whether the defendant is under *any duty* to the plaintiff (which includes cases where the plaintiff is outside the so-called 'danger-zone')[148] and, perhaps more significantly, cases where the issue is whether the interest affected (e.g. nervous shock) deserves protection against the invasion which has actually taken place. To quote again from Prosser,[149] 'in all [these] cases the causal connection between the act and the harm is usually clear and direct, and the attempt to subdivide the indivisible by way of "proximate" only offers obstacles to the determination of the real issue'. The stock example of the train accident in which the victim's mother who witnesses the incident recovers for her nervous shock but the innocent by-stander (who also suffers nervous shock) does not, offers an excellent if gruesome illustration of Prosser's point.[150] The problem of the 'foreseeable plaintiff' is thus not essentially different from that of the 'foreseeable damage' so long as we realise that the solution of both depends upon the skilful use of strongly normative concepts. Seen in this light, it matters not which one ('duty' or 'legal cause') one chooses to adopt though for the Common law, with its traditional emphasis on the relationship between the plaintiff and defendant, the first of these notions seems the obvious one to accept.

The above observations could, for our present, limited, purposes suffice to dispose of the issue under consideration. Yet for the sake of completeness, one ought to add that the 'doctrine of unforeseeable plaintiff', as a technique for deciding 'actionability' (rather than liability in general), is not as unknown to the Civil law systems as the foregoing discussion might seem to suggest. One situation, which *is akin though not identical* to the 'doctrine of unforeseeable plaintiff' and which can be found both in the Germanically inspired systems and the Common law, is that of statutory negligence.[151] For here, too, the right of action of a particular plaintiff will be determined by the proper definition of the risk or type of harm envisaged by the statute or regulation in question. In French law, on the other hand, and subject to what will be said below, this limiting technique is almost universally rejected, at any rate in purely civil matters. Yet in a number of rather limited instances French courts have not restricted the occasional flirtation with notions like the *Rechtswidrigkeitszusammenhang*.[152] Difficulties have thus been experienced in cases dealing with erection or alteration of buildings contrary to various planning regulations in which the action was brought by disgruntled neighbours affected by these activities. In one case decided in 1956, for example, the second section of the Cour de cassation decided against one such plaintiff on the ground that 'le permis de construire [which had not been obtained by the builder] acte essentiellement administratif... n'a pas pour objet de protéger les intérêts particuliers et ne saurait être considéré comme formant le titre constitutif d'une servitude'.[153] The introduction at the end of the decision of the notion of servitude was unfortunate and led astray a number of courts which were subsequently seized of similar disputes. But the notion of 'Aquilian relativity' – as the limiting technique came to be called – was not yet abandoned. Two years later, the first section of the Cour de cassation adopted it in an even more illuminating case.[154] In accordance with special legislation (of 1913 and 1930) the château of Filières and its surrounding area were classified as a 'natural beauty spot' to be preserved unchanged for future generations. The defendant, who had acquired a small farm nearby, proceeded to fell a small wood which was part of his holding but which was within view of the château. He was sued by the owners of the château, who claimed damages and the re-planting of the area, but their action was dismissed by the Cour de cassation on the following grounds:

Attendu, qu' après avoir rappelé les termes de l'article 13 bis, l' arrêt énonce exactement que la loi du 13 décembre 1913 n'a pas pour objet de protéger les intérêts particuliers du propriétaire de l'immeuble classé ou inscrit dans les intérêts généraux de la nation et qu'il appartient à l'autorité administrative seule d'apprécier si la construction ou la modification qu'un propriétaire voisin projette d'effectuer dans le champ de visibilité d'un tel immeuble est de nature à porter atteinte aux dits intérêts généraux, d'autoriser ou d'interdire les travaux et, dans le cas où ceux-ci auraient été exécutés sans autorisation, d'exercer une action en dommages-intérêts et en remise en état des lieux.

This clear reasoning was probably the high water mark of the acceptance of the theory of Aquilian relativity in civil matters, for since the 1960s the Cour de cassation has marked a steady retreat, refusing to limit on such grounds the right of action of certain plaintiffs.[155] Thus, on 2 November, the court of Poitiers[156] in a more traditional judgment allowed the plaintiff in the action before it to claim damages from one of his neighbours who had, contrary to planning regulations, illegally erected a building too near to his own. Writing approvingly of this and other similar judgments a French scholar has summarised what is probably now the accepted view of the matter:

la relativité aquilienne ne peut être utilisée *au civil* pour déterminer la sphère d'activité du juge à l'occasion d'actions en responsabilité. La protection légale n'est réservée a priori ni à certaines victimes, ni à certains dommages. L'auteur d'une infraction à une disposition d'intérêt général ne saurait opposer à la victime de cette infraction une fin de non-recevoir tirée de la finalité de la règle reconnue.[157]

It would be a mistake, however, to take the above as signifying a complete and utter rejection by French law of the 'scope of the rule' approach since a large number of decisions dealing with a plaintiff's claim for damages as a *partie civile* in a *criminal* action can be best explained by the theory of Aquilian relativity. Given that in French law every crime can also give rise to civil liability, the question is one of great significance and the acceptance of the theory of Aquilian relativity can prove a useful device for limiting actionability in many cases. Put differently, in the restrictive approach adopted by the Chambre Criminelle in this kind of situation we can find an excellent example of the operation of the 'administrative factor' in France, the underlying idea, no doubt, being the belief that the criminal court should, so far as possible, be relieved of the 'civil aspects' of the case. The different approach in criminal matters is, in fact, facilitated by the fact that here the civil claim is not for damage, however caused, but for damages resulting from a violation of a specific criminal statute with its own scope and ambit. This is underlined by articles 2.2 and 3.2 of the Code of Criminal Procedure, which state respectively that 'l'action en réparation... appartient à tous ceux qui ont *personnellement* souffert du dommage directement causé par l'infraction' and the action 'sera recevable pour tous chefs de dommages, aussi bien matériels que corporels ou moraux, *qui découleront des faits objets de la poursuite'*. As a result of the above, one is often faced with inquiries which are analogous in nature to those encountered in our system when discussing tortious liability arising from breach of statute. Thus, if the penal statute in question has been enacted in the interests of the *ordre public classique* or the *ordre public économique*, its violation will not be actionable at the instance of a private individual.[158] If, on the other hand, the violated norm affords protection to private interests then an aggrieved party will be able to constitute himself a *partie civile* in a criminal action *provided* he belongs to the class or kind of plaintiffs the statute intended to protect, and he has suffered the kind of harm the statute was designed to prevent. An example of the first type (recognised plaintiff) can be found in cases involving the application of article 320 of the Penal Code (negligently inflicted bodily harm). The Cour de cassation has in such instances consistently held that a *victim* of a car accident can claim damages by constituting himself a *partie civile* in the criminal action against the negligent driver. But a claim by a spouse (or some other close relative) for monetary compensation for their own *préjudice moral* cannot be maintained before the criminal judge. As the Cour de cassation put it in an important judgment delivered on 29 November 1966,[159]

l'exercice de l'action civile devant la juridiction répressive est un droit qui, à raison de son caractère exceptionnel, doit être limité à la réparation du dommage directement éprouvé par la victime de l'infraction; qu'il ne saurait être étendu à d'autres personnes, dès lors qu'elles se fondent sur les conséquences dommageables du délit pour la victime, conséquences dont celle-ci poursuit elle-même la réparation.

The position appears clear with regard to the second requirement, that the damage complained of is of the type envisaged by the statute that has been violated. If it is not, it should not, in theory, be compensated. This, however, does not appear to be supported by article 3.2 of the Code of Criminal Procedure quoted above which, unlike the earlier Code d'instruction criminelle, authorises the courts to award all kinds of damage apparently without regard to the purposes or the types of damage envisaged by the violated statute. The exact meaning of this provision has not been generally agreed and one can thus find cases which rely on the purposes and scope of particular statutes in order to prevent recovery of certain items of damage. For example, on 6 March 1969,[160] the Chambre Criminelle of the Cour de cassation had to decide a case in which a husband and his wife were seriously injured in an accident. They both claimed damages for their physical injuries and the husband also claimed for *préjudice moral*, suffered by him as a result of the chronic psychiatric troubles occasioned to his wife by the accident and necessitating her admission to a psychiatric institution. The Cour de cassation refused this latter claim for reasons very similar to those given by the decision of 1966, namely that: 'le droit d'exercer l'action civile devant les juridictions répressives est un droit exceptionel qui ne peut être accordé qu'à celui-là seul qui a subi personnellement un dommage résultant directment de l'infraction'. The decision cannot be easily justified on 'causal' grounds, but is explicable as an application of the theory of Aquilian relativity: 'la loi pénale ne protège les particuliers contre les dommages d'ordre moral que dans des cas exceptionels. En dehors de ces hypothèses, nul ne saurait se constituer partie civile pour obtenir la réparation d'un préjudice moral.'[161]

Both these cases, though in fact dealing the one with the question of 'recognised plaintiff', and the other with that of 'recognised type of harm' are, in fact, manifestations of the same attitude consistently adopted by the Chambre Criminelle of the Cour de cassation since the mid 1950s and dealing with claims for *dommage moral* presented by close relatives of the injured person. As indicated, the Chambre Criminelle has consistently refused to consider them and thus found itself in conflict with the jurisprudence of the second Chambre Civile, which (with some hesitation)[162] was prepared to accept such claims as well founded. This conflict finally reached the Assemblée Plénière in 1979.[163] The Court implicitly accepted the view put forward by its Rapporteur, M. le conseiller Ponsard, that there was here no conflict of substance nor was there any question of refusing to recognise the compensability of *dommage moral*; rather it was faced with a type of 'procedural dispute', namely, whether the criminal courts were obliged to entertain such claims made by persons other than the immediate victim. The Assemblée Plénière, siding with the Chambre Criminelle, was explicit: 'le droit d'exercer l'action civile devant les juridictions répressives, dont l'un des effets éventuels est la mise en mouvement de l'action publique, n'appartient qu'à ceux qui ont personnellement souffert du dommage causé directement par l'infraction'. Notable amongst the non-technical reasons given for this result is M. Ponsard's allusion to what we have termed the 'administrative factor', for he said: 'La mission (des juridictions répressives) est d'assurer le respect de l'ordre public et de sanctionner la violation des atteintes qui y sont portées; *elle ne devrait pas être détournée de cette mission par une profusion d'actions en responsabilité civile*; si la victime directe de l'infraction peut agir, en vertu des textes du Code de procédure pénale, la portée de ceux-ci ne doit pas être élargie.' And, further down, he stressed: 'le danger que présenterait une ouverture trop large de l'action civile qui pourrait... provoquer *l'encombrement des tribunaux répressifs*.'[164]

Selected further reading

Becht, Arno C. and Miller, Frank W., *The Test of Factual Causation in Negligence and Strict liability Cases* (1961).

Boré, J., 'La Causalité partielle en noir et blanc ou les deux visages de l'obligation "in solidum", *J.C.P.* 1971, 1.2369.

Buri, von, *Die Kausalität und ihre strafrechtlichen Beziehungen* (1885).

Caemmerer, E. von, *Das Problem der überholenden Kausalität im Schadensersatzrecht* (1962), reprinted in *Gesammelte Schriften*, 1 (1968), 411.

Das Problem des Kausalzusammenhangs im Privatrecht (1956), reprinted in *Gesammelte Schriften*, 1, 395.

Calabresi, G., 'Concerning cause and the law of torts', 43 *U.Ch.L.Rev.* (1975), 69.

Chabas, F., 'Bilan de quelques années de jurisprudence en matière de rôle causal', D. Chron. 1970, 113.

L'Influence de la pluralité de causes sur le droit à réparation (1967).

Deutsch, E. and Bar, Ch. von. 'Schutzbereich und wesentliche Bedingung im Versicherungs- und Haftungsrecht', *M.D.R.* (1979), 536 *et seq.*

Dias, R.W.M., 'Trouble on Oiled Waters: Problems of the Wagon Mound (No. 2)', 26 *C.L.J.* (1967), 62.

Dupichot, J., *Des Préjudices réflechis nés de l'atteinte à la vie ou à l'integrité corporelle* (1969).

Ehrenzweig, A., 'Negligence Without Fault', 54 *Cal.L.Rev.* (1966), 1422.

Esmein, P., 'Trois Problèmes de responsabilité civile', *Rev.trim.dr.civ.* (1934), 317.

'Le Nez de Cléopatre ou les affres de la causalité', D. 1964, 205.

Fleming, J.G., 'Distant Shock in Germany and Elsewhere', 20 *A.J.Comp.L.* (1972), 485.

Selected further reading

Giovannoni, P., 'Le dommage indirect en droit suisse de le responsabilité civile, comparé aux droits allemand et français', *Z.S.R.* 96 I (1977), 31.

Goodhart, A., 'The Unforeseeable Consequences of a Negligent Act', 39 *Yale L.J.* (1930), 449.

'The Imaginary Necktie and the Rule in Re Polemis', 68 *L.Q.R.* (1952), 514.

'Liability and Compensation', 76 *L.Q.R.* (1960), 567.

Green, Leon, *The Rationale of Proximate Cause* (1927).

Hart, H.L.A. and Honoré, A.M., *Causation in the Law* (1959).

Harvard, J., 'Reasonable Foresight of Nervous Shock', 19 *M.L.R.* (1956), 478.

Hippel, E. von, 'Haftung für Schockschäden Dritter', NJW 1965, 1890.

Honoré, A.M., 'Causation and Remoteness of Damage', in *Encyclopedia*, XI, ch. 7.

Hubér, U., 'Verschulden Gefährdung und Adäquanz', in *Festschrift E. Wahl* (1973), 301.

'Normzwecktheorie und Adäquanztheorie', 1969 *JZ*, 677.

Joly, André, 'Vers un Critère juridique du rapport de causalité', *Rev.trim.dr.civ.* (1942), 257.

Kries, J. von, *Die Prizipien der Wahrscheinlichkeitsrechnung* (1886).

Ueber den Begriff der objektiven Möglichkeit und einige Anwendungen desselben (1888).

Limpens, J. 'La Théorie de la "relativité aquilienne" en droit comparé', *Mélanges Savatier* (1965), 559.

Malone, W.S., 'Ruminations on Cause-in-Fact', 9 *Stan.L.Rev.* (1956–57), 60.

Marteau, P., *La Notion de causalité dans la responsabilité civile* (1914).

Marty, G., 'La Relation de cause à effet comme condition de la responsabilité civile', *Rev.trim.dr.civ.* (1939), 685.

'Illicéité et responsabilité', in *Etudes juridiques offertes à L. Julliot de la Morandière* (1964), 339.

Morris, Clarence, 'Duty, Negligence and Causation', 101 *U. of P.L.Rev.* (1953), 189.

Nguyen Thanh Nha, Jacqueline, 'L'Influence des prédispositions de la victime sur l'obligation à réparation du défendeur à l'action en responsabilité', *Rev.trim.dr.civ.* (1976), 1.

Prosser, W.L., 'Palsgraf Revisited', 52 *Mich.L.Rev.* (1953), 1.

Puech, M., *L'Illicéité dans la responsabilité civile extracontractuelle* (1973).

Puill, B., 'Les Caractères du fait non fautif de la victime', D. Chron. 1980, 157 *et seq.*

Roy-Loustaunau, C., *Du Dommage éprouvé en prêtant assistance bénévole à autrui* (1980).

Starck, B., 'La Pluralité des causes de dommage et la responsabilité civile', *J.C.P.* 1970,1.2339.

Stoll, H., *Kausalzusammenhang und Normzweck im Deliktsrecht* (1968).

'"The Wagon Mound" – Eine neue Grundsatzentscheidung zum Kausalproblem im englischen Recht', in *Vom deutschen zum europäischen Recht, Festschrift H. Dölle*, I (1963), 371.

Stone, F.F., 'Louisiana Tort Doctrine: Emotional Distress Occasioned by Another's Peril', 48 *Tul.L.Rev.* (1974), 782.

Tercier, P., 'La réparation du préjudice réfléchi en droit suisse de la responsabilité civile', in Gedächtnisschrift – P. Jäggi (1977), 239.

Traeger, Ludwig, *Der Kausalbegriff im Straf- und Zivilrecht* (1929).

Tunc, A., 'Les Récents Developpements des droits anglais et américains sur la relation de causalité entre la faute et le dommage dont on doit réparation', *Rev.int.dr.comp.* (1953), 5.

Williams, G., 'The Risk Principle', 77 *L.Q.R.* (1961), 179.

Chapter 4

LIABILITY WITHOUT FAULT

1. The growing dissatisfaction with fault

Whatever the original foundations of delictual liability, the fact is that by the nineteenth century it had firmly come to rest upon the notion of fault. The moral and logical attractions of the proposition that a human being should make good the harm caused by his fault were (and still are) very great.[1] But the converse of this principle,[2] namely that there can be no liability where there is no fault, offered an additional attraction to an era which was more concerned in *not* making *certain* people liable than in compensating every loss (even of the most eccentric nature[3]) at the drop of a hat. So in this sense fault, like *culpa* in earlier times, could be seen as a corrective device which could help retain the boundaries of liability within manageable proportions. It is, no doubt, due to this rather unusual coincidence of morality and economic expediency that the notion of fault owes so much of its aura of soundness and inevitability. Consequently, when the first serious challenge against the notion started to materialise towards the end of the last century, it invariably had to be concealed behind presumptions or permitted inferences which the Germans usually call the *prima facie Beweis* or *Anscheinsbeweis* and the English dignify with the Latin (but not Roman[4]) term, *res ipsa loquitur.*[5]

Fault as understood in the nineteenth century clearly 'presupposed free will... and beyond that also the notion that the actor had a choice in the conduct in question between doing it in a perceptibly dangerous way and doing it in some feasible, safer way. Holmes emphasises this element of choice and reminds us that "a choice which entails a concealed consequence is, as to that consequence, no choice". Thus, legal negligence involved something of personal moral shortcoming; the man who was held liable had been guilty of ethical as well as legal wrong. And since fault involved a more or less informed choice, it was possible to see how the prospect of liability could influence the choice for the better.'[6] This last sentence underlines the social utility of the concept. For in addition to keeping liability under control, it also helped edify potential defendants by encouraging them to behave more carefully.

With the growing mechanisation of the second half of the last century and the resulting multiplication of accidents, this kind of approach came more and more under scrutiny. The moral and educative basis of the fault system was also increasingly questioned.[7] With some 35,000 deaths and 2,000,000 injuries in industrial accident in the U.S.A. alone from about 1900 onwards,[8] the idea of leaving all these victims uncompensated became morally intolerable and politically unwise and the same was true in the more advanced countries of Western Europe. But these doubts, on their own, could not have altered the system if changes in the economic environment did not also favour some reappraisal of the problem. For by that time industry was standing on its own feet and the protectionist spirit which had brought it to maturity was becoming less relevant. And, with the help of rapidly increasing insurance protection, business concerns were more and more capable of carrying such losses. The procedural devices mentioned earlier on made this shift towards the plaintiff's point of view more easy; but they were not enough. The greater use of vicarious liability and the vagueness of the notion of fault could be and were used to tilt the balance even further towards the deserving victim.

The way the law treats persons who claim to possess special skills or qualifications provided a useful inspiration. If I am held to exceptionally high standards of care and skill when undertaking a dangerous task such as a surgical operation, then, in the use or custody of peculiarly dangerous things, I can be held to even higher standards, so that I shall in fact find it difficult to explain away any damage due to their escape. Thus a legal system such as the Roman-Dutch law of South Africa, which in principle rejects[9] the rule in *Rylands* v. *Fletcher*,[10] can obtain the same results by applying the notion of *culpa*.[11] And Scots law has reached, through the same notion, results similar to those achieved by the English *scienter* rule action which is now embodied in section 2 (2) of the Animals Act 1971. In other words, given a wide extension both of the notion of *culpa* and of the use of presumptions, together with, one may conjecture, a certain hostility towards new and dangerous methods of transport and manufacture or an interference with the ordinary course of nature, and the field is open to a form of liability which in theory only is faithful to the notion of fault. This appears to have been the line of development in Scotland, where the critical decision[12] was given ten years before *Rylands* v. *Fletcher*[13] and without the benefit of any analogies from trespass or nuisance. And it is also borne out by the careful comparison of American and German cases dealing with harm caused by electric power cables. For the practical solutions reached by these two systems on this matter are quite comparable even though in Germany the result is nowadays achieved by applying a special statute imposing strict liability,[14] while in the United States it is reached through the procrustean extension of the notion of fault.[15]

As the standard of the hypothetical reasonable man became the yardstick of comparison, the study of the law of Negligence was transformed into the study of the type of mistakes the reasonable man would not be allowed to make. This was a significant change of emphasis. For not only were the standards becoming more and more difficult to attain; fault was also increasingly confused with error. Such confusion, however, is conceptually unfortunate, for fault presupposes (or, in its original sense, presupposed) a choice, whereas many of the errors which our courts treat as 'faults' are inevitable and unavoidable. The Americans, who have carried out many surveys on these matters, have shown this very clearly. For example, a study conducted by the Department of Transportation of the U.S.A. has shown that in Washington D.C. a 'good driver [i.e. one who has not committed an accident in the preceding four years] commits on average more than nine errors of four different natures in five minutes of driving'.[16] In these instances, this type of inevitable error makes the moral and educational value of a fault-based system meaningless in so far as it makes people responsible for 'faults' for which they cannot be reproached. But the confusion of the two concepts is not only intellectually untidy; it has other disadvantages as well. For one thing, it weakens the 'limiting' ability of the notion and so puts extra and often unwarranted pressure on the other elements of liability (much, for example, of the fault reasoning often reappears in discussions of causal issues). For another, it also lays upon the courts the often difficult and always expensive task of having to decide issues which do not call for legal but wider policy reasoning. Professor Tunc has, on several occasions, discussed a case which, despite its straightforward facts, brings out this point very clearly.[17]

Two boys, nine and eleven years old respectively, were playing football on their village common. One of them aimed at the ball but missed and instead, kicked mud into the other's face and injured his eye. A prolonged litigation followed, involving some forty lawyers, judges and other auxiliaries; it cost the boys' parents a small fortune and ended with a judgment of the Cour de cassation which, affirming the Court of Appeal, held that the boy had been at fault; and so had his father by letting him play without supervision on the common. The result is stunning and one may ask, along with Professor Tunc, 'where children may play together if they cannot play on the common' and 'how even a father watching his son could have prevented him missing the ball'? Yet liability in this case rested on the assumption that the *bon père de famille* would have acted otherwise.

In reality, of course, there is more behind these judgments than a simple reliance on abstract legal concepts; there is the desire to compensate an unfortunate victim.[18] This kind of reasoning can also be found behind many medical malpractice[19] suits, but its obvious desire to do justice to the plaintiff should not conceal the injustice it can cause to the defendant. Nor should we lose sight of the wider implications that such decisions can have on the legal system. Recently, the English Court of Appeal[20] in a medical malpractice suit paid great attention to these wider repercussions and to the tendency to equate negligence with error. This confusion can help deserving plaintiffs; but it also encourages inaction on the part of doctors fearful that the slightest error might attract the full rigour of the law; it also increases insurance premiums which, in turn, affect the quantum of some of the awards. In the event, the decision of the Court of Appeal was fair to the doctor who had, apparently, under great stress committed only one of those regrettable but inevitable errors. And it was welcome news to the ratepayers of the local authority who would ultimately have borne the consequences of a decision for the plaintiff.[21] But here, unlike the French case, the result was unfair to the victim/plaintiff. The fault system, apart from being an expensive system for allocating this type of loss, is thus bound to be unfair to one or other of the parties (unless, through the medium of contributory negligence, it actually manages to be unfair to both!). In cases such as the above, compensation through collective sources has obvious advantages; but it fits awkwardly into the traditional system. So, sooner or later, we realise that a fault-based system can be unfair, cumbersome and costly. These are great disadvantages since, from the social point of view, it is highly desirable that the law be so designed as to keep the cost of compensating victims as low as possible.[22] If then fault is not always the most suitable criterion of the right of compensation, what should take its place? The concept of risk, coupled with a greater willingness to take into account insurance realities, could, in part at least, provide the answer. This, according to one learned writer, would call for 'a reappraisal of the scope and function of strict liability in the law today and the imposition of strict liability upon a defendant whenever the risk of injury or damage *ought rightly to be his*.[23] A more drastic alternative may lie in the radical reappraisal of our compensation methods and their replacement by some form of an extended social security system. The likely cost of this, however, makes this alternative an unlikely possibility, at any rate for the immediate future. The Report of the Pearson Committee in England certainly points towards some kind of compromise between the tort system (based on fault *or* risk) and a social security system. This may not have satisfied the modern reformers just as it may not have entirely appeased the more traditional tort lawyers who were fearful of the initial omens. But like all compromises it may point towards a 'blend' of the various systems of compensation which may be with us for some years to come.[24]

In this work, for reasons of space as much as anything else, we have limited our scope to the *tort* ways of compensating unintentionally caused harm. Financially, this may represent a small percentage of the total sums annually handed out as compensation for all sorts of injuries. But it is still thought to have an important role to play and from an intellectual point of view it has an attraction quite of its own. In the following paragraphs, therefore, we shall concentrate on some of the ways in which the fault system has been displaced by stricter forms of liability. But the insurance and social security factor cannot be entirely overlooked even by a book which does not purport to examine them in any great detail. We have, therefore, at the end of this chapter included a *bird's eye view* of the treatment of industrial and traffic accidents – the two areas where some sort of *modus vivendi* has been worked out between these systems over the years.

2. The Romanistic and Germanic approach to strict liability

It is against this background that we must see the changing interpretation of article 1384 CC, which must surely be one of the most intriguing developments in French private law.

The compilers of the Code Civil inserted in article 1384 CC, which for the most part deals with questions of liability for the acts of other persons for whom the defendant must take responsibility, a liability for damage caused 'par le fait... des choses que l'on a sous sa garde'. A literal interpretation of the article undoubtedly gives a result comparable to – or rather more far-reaching than – that in *Rylands* v. *Fletcher*,[25] for there is nothing in the words of the article to restrict liability to cases where the defendant can be proved to have been negligent in the custody of the things, or even to things which are inherently dangerous: nor is the rule limited to things 'accumulated' on, and 'escaping' from, land. Yet for nearly a century these words were not, in fact, applied in their literal sense; and, indeed, the possibility of using them to establish a doctrine of strict liability seems never to have suggested itself for almost seventy years. They were, instead, treated as a mere '*élégance de style*, a transition between rules on liability for one's own acts and rules on vicarious liabilities and liabilities for one's animal or falling buildings',[26] which, no doubt, was how the drafters must have conceived them in the first place. More surprising, however, is the fact that this assumption remained unchallenged by the *courts* for so long, and one may safely attribute this to the fact that the then prevailing interpretation suited the liberal individualism of the period. Be that as it may, the risk of accidental harm from the operation of machines was treated as something that should be borne not by their exploiters but by any person who happened to be injured,[27] those subjected to the greatest danger being normally, of course, the workmen and other subordinates brought into the closest contact with the machines; though only in the Common law countries, which were the first to be industrialised, were servants made to take the risk not only of accidental damage but of damage done to them by the negligence of their fellow-servants. How inveterate this tendency to measure liability by fault had become may be seen from the traditional interpretation of article 1054 of the Quebec Civil Code. Admittedly, the article did not enunciate a doctrine of strict liability but merely created a presumption of fault, but its very moderation should have secured it from neglect: one can imagine a lawyer saying that strict liability stood so far outside the range of traditional thought as to make it inconceivable that the draftsman could have intended it, but it is hard to see anything inconceivable in the interpretation which merely shifts the burden of proof from the plaintiff to the defendant. And yet the passage in question escaped attention as long as, if not longer than, the corresponding passage in the French Code. It was not until 1920 that the Privy Council gave it the interpretation that one would have supposed was predestined for it.[28] Throughout the intervening period it had been assumed as an article of faith that fault had to be proved, even where the instrument of the damage subjected the public to unusual dangers. Neither the French nor the Quebec Civil Code, which contained this reference to the custody of things, was thus seen to differ from the Prussian and Austrian Codes, which contained nothing of the kind.

Then the change came, though, interestingly enough, the first attempts to give an independent status to the opening words of article 1384 CC were made in Belgium, not France. In 1870 the powerful explosion of a boiler caused the death of twelve innocent workmen and provoked in the Brussels region an emotional reaction which had been rarely experienced in the past. In the Court of First Instance M. le substitut Faider argued[29] that the defendant company should be held liable unless it could prove that it was not guilty of fault. Invoking article 1384 CC the court of Brussels had this to say on the matter:

si l'on se pénètre de l'esprit de cette disposition, l'on acquiert la conviction que cette responsabilité prend naissance du moment où, du seul fait de la chose, il résulte un préjudice; qu'il est, en effet, natural et logique que le propriétaire d'une chose sur laquelle il a droit et devoir de surveillance et de direction, soit légalement présumé en état de faute dès l'instant où cette chose cause un préjudice...

The Court of Appeal, however, would have none of this. In three brief *attendus* it flatly rejected the innovation though, by discovering fault in the defendants' conduct, it stopped short of reversing the actual result. But the seed was sown and five years later the Belgian jurist Laurent argued in the first edition of the twentieth volume of his *Principes de droit civil* that article 1384 established a presumption of fault in favour of the plaintiff. Three years later Laurent, who in the meantime had been charged with the task of revising the Belgian Civil Code, even produced a draft provision which put the whole matter beyond any doubt by proclaiming that: 'On est responsable du dommage causé par le fait des choses que l'on a sous sa garde. Il en est ainsi d'une machine à vapeur qui fait explosion. Le propriétaire est présumé en faute, sauf preuve contraire.' The timing, however, was wrong. Laurent's commission to revise the Code was withdrawn in 1884 and in 1889 the Belgian Cour de cassation unequivocally rejected the new approach.[30] It was not until 1904 that a change was once again to be attempted – this time by the Cour de cassation itself.[31] The key words of article 1384 CC were then resurrected, though limited to cases where the accident was due to an inherent vice of the thing in question. Thus, paradoxically, the Belgians, who had initiated the development of article 1384 CC, were destined to settle for a watered-down version of their original ideas.[32]

While the above developments were taking place in Belgium, the French were trying to solve the problem of industrial accidents through their law of contract or even by means of legislation. Neither of these attempts, however, were successful and little of significance happened until the close of the nineteenth century. Then came a decision of the Conseil d'Etat in 1895[33] and, a year later, a seminal judgment of the Cour de cassation.[34] In the latter case the Court, in tune with academic criticism[35] directed against the above-mentioned narrow application of article 1384 CC, awarded damages to the widow of a stoker who was killed by the explosion of a boiler in the custody of his employer. The plaintiff's case was, clearly, unenviable if she were to rely on article 1382 CC, for the Court of First Instance had held as a matter of fact that, though the welding of the boiler had been defective, its owner (the defendant) neither knew this nor could he have been expected to be aware of such inherent vice. Nevertheless, the Court of First Instance found for the widow, by-passing the obvious difficulty concerning the proof of fault by analogically extending article 1386 CC. This reasoning was accepted by the Court of Appeal which, in addition, was prepared to discover in the contract of employment an implied obligation to compensate the victim of such an explosion. The Cour de cassation, though upholding the result, chose to justify it in a different way, namely, by giving the first paragraph of article 1384 CC a force of its own. Though the wording of the decision was not entirely unequivocal, the impression it made was that the Court was veering towards adopting a strict theory of risk. But this was not to be. A year later, the Chambre des Requêtes[36] allowed the defendant – once again the owner of a boiler which exploded and killed the plaintiff's husband – to escape liability by proving that the boiler had in this case been properly constructed and maintained and that, therefore, the defendant was guilty of no fault. Article 1384 CC was thus taken to establish a presumption of fault. The fault principle was not abandoned; the burden of proof had merely been reversed. In 1898, the legislature finally intervened to remedy the situation which had given rise to these decisions by passing the Workmen's Compensation Act, very much on the lines of the English Act of the previous year. It was then thought by the more conservative jurists, who had not been entirely unsympathetic towards the public policy involved in the Cour de cassation decision, that, the most pressing cause having been dealt with, a return should be made to the traditional interpretation of the article. This might conceivably have happened for, it will be remembered, the Court, in its 1897 decision, had not accepted the extreme theory of risk. Motor accidents, however, were destined to revive the problem (and with it article 1384 CC) in another and, perhaps, more extreme form.

In the earlier stages of this development, before 1914, there was a general tendency to apply the doctrine of fault, and even to insist that fault should be proved by the victim.[37] The reason was simple: the courts were reluctant to extend the application of article 1384 CC to cover damage caused by things moved or operated by human beings. So the best that the advocates of article 1384 CC could do was to convince the courts to apply it to accidents caused by the defective state of the car but not when the accident was caused while the driver was operating or controlling it, in which case article 1382 CC applied.[38] This approach, however, could lead to ludicrous results, for it meant that if the brakes of a stationary car suddenly failed and, as a result, it rolled down a slope and injured the plaintiff, he could rely on the presumption of article 1384 CC and, almost certainly, make the owner liable; but if it actually ran him down while driven by its owner the success of the action would depend upon the plaintiff's proving the driver's fault. The Cour de cassation put an end to this practice in 1927 when it quashed a decision of the court of Besançon which had relied on this distinction. But, in so doing, the court introduced a new distinction: that of dangerous and non-dangerous things. The case, however, once again reached the Cour de cassation and this time the plenary session[39] put an end to the prolonged controversy by condemning all previous distinctions and by holding that article 1384 CC 'connects responsibility with the guard of the thing and not the thing itself'. It was thus held to establish not a mere 'presumption of fault' but a 'presumption of responsibility' which could not be rebutted by evidence of no fault or lack of explanation of the cause of the damage, but only by clear, positive evidence that the damage was due to an event (which could be a natural event or a *fait* or *faute* of the victim or a third party) unforeseeable and external both to the *gardien* and to the thing which made the accident unavoidable. Only then will the *gardien* be *exonerated*. However, his liability will be *reduced* to take into account the *faute or fait* of the victim himself, the reduction being calculated on the basis of the causative potency of the victim's conduct. So, in Professor Tunc's words,

the law developed on the basis of article 1384 rests on two foundations: (a) a rule of evidence: a presumption of fault or, more precisely, a presumption of causation, which can be rebutted by evidence that the damage was caused by a '(normally) unforeseeable and irresistible' external event; and (b) a rule of substance: an absolute liability for the damage resulting from a defect of the thing or a failure (even health failure) of one of the parties (the failure of the injured party discharging, of course, the keeper).[40]

Since article 1384 CC is capable of being applied, and has in fact been applied, to a vast variety of 'inanimate objects', (moving or inert, inherently dangerous or not)[41] the decision of the plenary session represented a huge leap forward towards strict liability. Understandably, therefore, some academics – notably Josserand – saw the judgment as the vindication of their life-long beliefs. Indeed, this eminent French jurist even went so far as to affirm that since accidents seldom happen without the intervention of some 'thing' the theory of *risque créé* (based on article 1384 CC), which he had advocated for a long time, had entirely displaced the liability for fault based on article 1382 CC.[42] An assertion which even his arch opponent – Ripert – seemed to accept when, with a mixture of irony and incredulity, he wrote[43] that

Il faudrait supposer une collision entre deux individus pratiquant le nudisme intégral pour qu'il y eût lieu à l'application de l'article 1382! Encore se trouvera-t-il bien un jurist pour dire que le corps n'est qu'une chose sous la garde de la volonté, et qu'il faut par conséquent appliquer l'article 1384 au dommage dû au fait corporel de l'homme!

Yet neither of these predictions finally materialised and in the years that have followed *Jand'heur* the French courts, free from any strict theory of precedent, have vacillated quite remarkably on a number of important issues. Though this is no place to discuss this fascinating subject in any great detail, one or two points of particular interest deserve closer attention.

The first is related to the applicability of article 1384 CC to persons incapable of discernment. French law, like all other Civil law systems,[44] never experienced any difficulty in making a lunatic's keeper responsible for damage done by him, at any rate if his escape was due to his keeper's fault. But what if no liability can be imposed on a third party? Until the passing of the 1968 Act, the French answer was that lunatics could not be held personally liable under article 1382 CC because their lack of discernment made them incapable of committing a fault. But could they be made liable under article 1384 CC, which does not require fault as one of its elements? In 1947 the Cour de cassation gave a negative reply to this question by allowing a lunatic to treat his mental state as *force majeure* and thus shield himself behind one of the recognised defences of article 1384 CC. The solution could cause hardship, especially when the person who had caused the damage was well-to-do and the victim poor. There is no obvious justice in such cases of letting the loss lie where it falls. And so the German Civil Code[45] empowers the judge to take into consideration the relative financial positions of the parties and then award the plaintiff such compensation as equity requires, but so as not to render the defendant incapable of supporting himself or other people for whose support he is responsible. This principle, which can be found in many codes,[46] including the Belgian Civil Code,[47] which is still for the most part identical to the French, has failed to gain open support in France. In 1947 the Cour de cassation, in a case involving the application of article 1384 CC, expressed its sympathy for it but felt that the technique implied in it could be introduced only by express legislation.[48] So, if a madman were to be found liable under either article 1382 or 1384 CC, there would be no way out of mulcting him of the full damages.[49]

In 1964 the Cour de cassation changed its mind and held that the defendant was liable under article 1384 CC for the damage he had caused with his car while suffering an attack of epilepsy.[50] The lack of discernment, produced by the epileptic seizure, was not, in the opinion of the Court, a *cause étrangère exonératoire*. The Court also implied that the defendant's state did not deprive him of the quality of *gardien* of the 'thing'. As the Cour de cassation subsequently put it: 'celui qui exerce sur une chose les pouvoirs d'usage, de direction et de contrôle, conserve la qualité de gardien, même s'il n'est pas en mesure d'exercer correctement lesdits pouvoirs'.[51] So, between 1964 and 1968, the only way of holding a lunatic civilly responsible was by means of article 1384 CC. But, even after the coming into force of the 1968 Act,[52] the above-mentioned case-law of the Cour de cassation may still be useful. For the elements of liability are different in articles 1382 CC and 1384 CC and, on occasion, it may be in the interest of the victim to frame his action on article 1384 CC and thus avoid having to prove the other elements of fault (apart, of course, from the capacity of discernment which is no longer required).

The ebbing and flowing of article 1384 CC can also be witnessed in the treatment accorded by the French courts to the problem of *transport bénévole*. The initial attitude of the courts was that the gratuitous passenger could not sue his carrier by relying on article 1384 CC but had to prove his fault before succeeding in his action.[53] The reasons given for this were basically two: first, that article 1384 CC was only meant to assist the victim of harm caused *by* a particular 'thing' and not anyone injured while making *use of* the thing itself; secondly because the victim, by agreeing to make gratuitous use of the thing in question, was aware of the risks involved and had consented to take them. Yet neither of these arguments could really stand up to serious scrutiny and it was not long before academics started to admit in public that the solution was one dictated by considerations of policy rather than supported by any convincing legal arguments. As Capitant put it:[54]

En réalité la jurisprudence a été guidée par un argument d'équité: les tribunaux ont estimé qu'il était choquant de permettre à celui auquel un service gratuit a été rendu d'assigner celui qui lui a rendu ce service sur le terrain de l'article 1382, al. 1er, alors qu'il ne peut prouver ni une négligence ni une imprudence commise par celui qui a rendu le service.

Statements such as the above, which abound in the various textbooks,[55] demonstrate yet again how policy considerations operate behind the terse legal façade of a French judgment. They also explain the willingness of the courts to discover fault in the defendant (the theory of *faute virtuelle*)[56] in order to enable the plaintiff to recover. And it will be noticed that by so acting the French courts were in fact indulging in precisely the kind of judicial manoeuvring that the English courts had to adopt before 1972 in order to discover implied licences and mitigate the rigour of the old law towards trespassers.

The pressure to change the law thus gained momentum and in 1968 the treatment of *transport bénévole* was brought into line with article 1384 CC. The judgment of the Cour de cassation,[57] along with the quite remarkable conclusions of the avocat général, are reproduced in volume II. Here, suffice it to note the brevity of the leading decision which overnight overruled forty years of almost uniform case-law. For once, however, the lack of a long and reasoned judgment cannot be entirely attributed to the French judicial style; equally important was the obvious lack of *legal* reasons to support the view that was being overturned. The change of heart, however, in this matter (as well as in the treatment accorded to lunatics) should not lead the Common lawyer to think that the theory of risk is now prevalent or that the courts have lost all means of control over article 1384 CC. The concept of *garde* and the element of causation have both ensured that neither of these things has actually happened.

It will be remembered that in the *Jand'heur* case the Cour de cassation left no doubt that liability attached not to the thing itself but to its (defective) guard. The definition of this relationship between *gardien* and thing is crucial but far from easy to define since one can derive but little guidance from apparently related notions such as *propriété, possession, détention*, and *occupation*. One suggestion made was that the *gardien* is the person 'qui a matériellement la direction de la chose', even if he is not the owner. An unacceptable side-effect of this was to render chauffeurs liable for the car accidents that they caused while driving their masters' cars; and the solution was also incompatible with the definition of *garde* given in article 1385 CC which stated that the *gardien* remains liable for damage caused even by animals which had escaped his control.[58] The criterion of *droit de direction* was thus advanced in an attempt to avoid the defects of the criterion of *direction matérielle*. The emphasis here was placed on the *right* to direct the thing and, since in our previously mentioned example of the accident caused by the chauffeur-driven car the *right* of direction rested with the master, it was he rather than his servant who would be called upon to make compensation. But what if the car was stolen? If the criterion of *droit de direction* applied, then the owner, who alone has the right to direct it, would remain liable for damage caused while his car was in the possession of the thief. The same iniquitous result was reached by the criterion of 'profit' which was strongly advanced by the partisans of the theory of risk. The idea behind this test was simple enough – *ubi emolumentum ibi ius*. Unfortunately for its proponents, however, this test, though easy to expound, was difficult to apply whenever two or more persons (e.g. hirer and letter) derived, in different ways, a benefit from the use of the same thing, and the determination of the *gardien* was disputed. And it required a short step from there to assert, as Josserand did,[59] that though bailment divested the bailor of *la garde de la chose*, theft did not; the victim of the theft still retained the *garde juridique*, and so remained liable for any damage caused by it whilst in the hands of the thief. This startling extension, though initially upheld by the civil section of the Cour de cassation,[60] met with great opposition in the various Courts of Appeal and, finally, it was rejected by the plenary session of the Cour de cassation in the long-drawn-out litigation in *Connot c. Franck*.[61]

In some respects *Connot c. Franck* marked the high-water mark of the *Jand' heur* case. For during the next twenty years or so the courts were anxious to uphold or carve out of article 1384 CC areas of exception. The treatment initially accorded to lunatics and to gratuitous passengers were the most notable examples, though these restrictions, as we have seen, were eventually removed. But in *Connot c. Franck* the Cour de cassation did more than merely decide the liability (or, as it turned out, the non-liability) of the owner of a stolen car, for it also provided the standard definition of *garde* which is connected with 'l'usage, la direction et le contrôle de la chose'. This formula, however, though repeated many times since, has given rise to much discussion.[62] For did the Chambres Réunies attribute the *garde* to anyone who has the 'usage, direction et contrôle' of the thing in question? Or did it attribute it to the *owner so long as he had not been deprived* of its 'usage, direction et contrôle'? The second version is, probably, to be preferred, not only because it fits in better with the language of the actual decision in *Connot c. Franck*, but also because it is more consistent with the (previous and subsequent) practice of the Court to look at the *owner* of the thing *first* and then consider whether he has lost the *garde*.[63] But this trilogy of concepts raises further difficulties. For example, should one consider one of them (say that of *contrôle*) to be of greater significance (as some decisions suggest) in that the loss of it by the owner implies that he has also ceased to be the *gardien de la chose*? Or must the owner lose all three (i.e. the *usage*, the *direction* and the *contrôle*) for the *garde* to be transferred away from him?[64] Clearly, here we can only raise these problems and refer the reader to the specialist literature rather than attempt (even assuming that this were possible) to provide the definitive answer. And, as if all these complications were not enough, subsequent elaboration of the notion of *garde* showed that it was also capable of subdivision. A distinction thus came to be drawn between the *garde du comportement* and the *garde de la structure* so as to hold that the thing in question could, for some purposes, be deemed to be *sous la garde* of one person and, for other purposes, *sous la garde* of another. This distinction, which has received varied support from the Cour de cassation, appears to have been finally sanctioned in the prolonged litigation that became known as the 'liquid oxygen' case.[65] Its application, however, has given rise to serious difficulties partly because it is often difficult for the victim to choose which of the *gardiens* to sue – difficulties which diminish the advantages that are meant to flow from the 'presumption of responsibility established in his favour' – and, more importantly, because in many cases (especially involving automobiles) the accident is due both to the *comportement and the structure*. In practice, however, it could be said that the courts take advantage of these ambiguities to attribute the *garde* to whomever *they* think is in a better position to discover the defect or control the thing that caused the harm. This empirical approach, inevitably, takes into account the litigant's particular circumstances and his ability to carry the risk, and, in general, leaves great room for judicial manoeuvre. But all this also adds to the immense refinement and detail of the case-law built round article 1384 CC in a way that adds credence to Professor Carbonnier's condemnation of this *jurisprudence* as 'un immense gaspillage d'intelligence et de temps'.[66]

The final controlling device is the concept of causation and, as is usual in cases of strict liability, this tends to play an exaggerated role in the determination of liability. What is interesting, however, is that in the requirement that the damage be the result of *le fait de la chose* the courts have, in the view of some authors at any rate, come close to reintroducing the concept of fault. This 'borderline area' appears in cases dealing with inert objects.

That 'la chose incriminée doit être la cause du dommage' has, of course, always been an obvious proposition. But in the middle of the 1930s the Cour de cassation was prepared to accept this as proved once the plaintiff had demonstrated that the thing in question had materially participated in the creation of the harm.[67] This interpretation, particularly when related to inert objects, came very close to substantiating Ripert's fears.[68] But it led to undesirable extensions of liability and in the forties it was abandoned in favour of another test, namely, that the 'thing' had proved to be the active cause of the damage.[69] If the 'thing' had merely played a 'passive' role it would not be considered as the cause of the damage. 'Passive' here does not mean 'inert', since the courts have held that moving objects may play a passive role (e.g. a moving vehicle on which a pedestrian falls in an attempt to commit suicide) and, conversely, inert objects may play an active role in the realisation of the harm (e.g. a stationary and unlit vehicle on which a cyclist falls). This does not mean that the distinction between moving and inert objects loses all its significance, for, it seems, in the case of a moving object the plaintiff merely has to prove the intervention of the thing in question and it is then for the defendant (*gardien*) to demonstrate that the thing merely played a passive role in the realisation of the damage. But in the case of an inert object the plaintiff must further establish the active role of the thing in order to invoke article 1384 CC. So, if the 'thing' played a purely passive role in the realisation of the harm – and this is whenever it is shown that 'la chose était placée et utilisée dans des conditions normales' – the presumption of article 1384 CC is destroyed. As already indicated, it is tempting to see in this development a disguised reappearance of the notion of fault, since the courts, by allowing the *gardien* to rebut the presumption of causation through evidence that the thing was being used in a normal way, are, in a sense, allowing him to rebut the 'presumption of responsibility' of article 1384 CC by proving that he (the *gardien*) did not commit any fault. And this is reinforced by the observation that often, the abnormal behaviour of the thing is evidence of a careless attitude on behalf of the *gardien*. Yet this view should not be pressed too much, not only because the burden of proof, as we have seen, is not the same in article 1382 and 1384 CC, but also because *position anormale* does not necessarily coincide with fault.[70] True, one can say that whenever the thing was well placed or used (and, therefore, played a passive role in the realisation of the damage) no fault can be attributed to its *gardien*. Conversely, a *gardien* who though his carelessness leaves a thing in a state which is likely to cause damage, is guilty of *faute*. However, a thing may be in a position which is likely to cause an accident *without* its *gardien* being guilty of any fault. For example, a folding chair belonging to a café may be knocked down during the night by a passer-by or mischievous children. A passer-by subsequently trips over it and is injured. The facts do not, necessarily, suggest fault on the part of the *gardien* (owner of the café) since it may well be that in the circumstances he has taken all the precautions expected from a *bon père de famille*. Nevertheless the chair is in a *position anormale*, has played a *rôle actif* in the realisation of the damage, and article 1384 CC may be applied. The same is true of an exploding bottle where no fault of its *gardien* can be established and of an accident resulting from the plaintiff's tripping over the loose end of a carpet in a carefully maintained block of flats.[71] Indeed, the cases which show that a thing may be the cause of an accident even though its *gardien* has committed no fault are so clear that the point need not be laboured further. What can be repeated, however, is that the cases once again confirm that within the framework of article 1384 CC liability is based on causality.

If we now turn to German law we shall see that, apart from

paragraph 833 BGB, which introduces strict liability for certain types of animals, and paragraph 836 BGB,[72] which deals with collapsing buildings or other structures and adopts a mild form of liability for presumed fault, strict liability has been introduced by a long series of specific statutes dealing with a wide variety of problems.[73] The start was made in 1838 when the *Prussian Railway Law* came into being, imposing in article 25 strict liability on railroad companies 'for all damage that takes place during transportation on a train, both to persons and things being transported and to other persons and things'. Passed before the Industrial Revolution had really started in Prussia and the power was still in the hands of the land-owning classes, this pioneering enactment was to provide the model for the subsequent and, in most respects, more far-reaching Imperial Law of Liability (*Reichshaftpflichtgesetz*) of 7 June 1871 which applied to the whole Reich. This statute, which has been amended and extended several times since its enactment,[74] did not merely deal with railways and tramways but also with other forms of industry (such as mines, quarries and factories of any kind) which involve risks. Close on its heels followed Bismarck's social insurance legislation – notably the *Krankenversicherungsgesetz* (Sickness Insurance Act) 1883 and the *Unfallversicherungsgesetz* (Accident Insurance Act) 1884 – introducing accident, health and old age insurance, thereby making the concerns in each industry (*Berufsgenossenschaften*) combine to insure their employees against various forms of industrial hazards. This legislation is remarkable not only because it provided Germany (at that time one of the fastest rising capitalist economies) with the first 'socialist' legislation of its kind, but also because it was based on the practices of the British trade union movement of the middle nineteenth century, which the German Consulate in London had been asked to discover and report on.[75] These enactments proved a great success, so the road to further statutory intervention was now open. Notable amongst the Acts that followed are: the Road Traffic Act (*Strassenverkehrsgesetz*) of 3 May 1909, amended several times since;[76] the Air Traffic Act (*Luftverkehrsgesetz*) of 1 August 1952, as amended;[77] the Act on the Peaceful Use of Atomic Energy and Protection against its Dangers (*Gesetz über die friedliche Verwendung der Kernenergie und den Schutz gegen ihre Gefahren*) of 23 December 1959 [78] and the Act dealing with matters of Water Supply (*Wasserhaushaltsgesetz*) of 1957.[79] These Acts, which in most cases have equivalents in Switzerland[80] and Austria, impose various forms of strict liability and obviously cannot be discussed here in detail. Suffice it to make the following brief points about them.

First, it must be noted that statutes that deal with the same subject-matter in different countries may delineate the ambit of liability in a different manner. The German Imperial Law of Liability, for example, imposes strict liability for harm caused 'through the operation of the railway' which includes harm caused through sudden braking, derailing, sparks etc. but excludes harm caused by *force majeure*, which, as always, refers to external and elemental forces as well as unavoidable acts of third parties. In Switzerland, on the other hand, the equivalent Act – the Loi Fédérale sur la responsabilité civile des entreprises de chemin de fer et de bateaux à vapeur et des postes – makes 'l'exploitant' of such enterprises strictly liable for 'l'exploitation, la construction et les travaux accessoires impliquant les dangers inhérents à l'entreprise'.[81] Despite various limitations that the courts have built into this provision over the years,[82] it scope remains very wide and, on occasion, it has led to some strange results.

Secondly, and related to the previous point, is the fact that, generally speaking, the German statutes do not exclude the application of the common rules of civil liability, and hence the claims for compensation are invariably based on both the special provisions of the particular statute in question and paragraph 823 I BGB. This is, for example, true for claims arising from traffic accidents. The reasons for this concurrence of actions are not difficult to find, for, to begin with, a claim under the Road Traffic Act cannot include an item for pain and suffering, and also, the Road Traffic Act, along with most of these German enactments, fixes maxima for the defendant's liability. These maxima, which are periodically re-adjusted to take inflation into account, do not, however, provide for cases where there is more than one victim in a particular accident with the result that, where this is the case, the sums awarded have to be scaled down accordingly. In Switzerland, on the other hand, the Road Traffic Act[83] fixes no maximum for awards made under it; nor does it exclude claims for pain and suffering and, in view of both these results, its exclusion of the ordinary rules of civil responsibility does not appear to be harsh but, on the contrary, logical and welcome.

Finally, in view of the exceptional nature of strict liability, German courts have repeatedly refused to extend analogically the provisions of the various statutes and, instead, have been content to leave reform, such as and when it is needed, to the legislature. Thus, in 1912, the

Reichsgericht, in a famous case of an accident involving one of Count Zeppelin's airships, refused to extend the provisions of the Imperial Law of Liability and the Road Traffic Act to the case before it, even though the circumstances were exceptional and the operation involved an unusually high degree of risk.[84] Such flexibility as the courts felt able to demonstrate was thus channelled through the concept of *culpa* and, on occasion, by raising the expected standard of care the courts have been able to do justice to particular plaintiffs.[85] The Austrian Oberste Gerichtshof, on the other hand, has felt no such qualms and has on many different occasions extended, through analogy, the provisions of strict liability of particular statutes.[86]

3 Noxal and vicarious liability

It could be, and in fact, has been argued[87] that vicarious liability is not inconsistent with the principle of no liability without fault since the fault of the employee is a necessary pre-condition of the liability of the employer. A more traditional way of looking at the problem, however, puts the emphasis on the employer, and many systems are, for obvious reasons of policy, prepared to make him liable for the torts of his employees even if *he* himself is completely blameless. The Common law and Romanistic legal families take this view, but the Germanic group of systems does not. There, the 'master's tort' theory prevails and stricter forms of liability for the acts of third persons is only introduced through reliance on contractual provisions. This 'peculiarity' may be largely due to the prolonged and often misleading influence that Roman law had on early German law, and so, perhaps, we could start this section with a brief excursus into Roman law.

(a)   Roman law

Questions arose at Rome as elsewhere whether and in what circumstances one person could be held liable for harm caused by another. Let us confine ourselves for the moment to the *lex Aquilia*. Liability would normally be restricted to cases where the wrongdoer was the slave or son *in potestate* of the defendant and would allow the alternative of noxal surrender.[88] The noxal action seems to have been given by the *lex* itself in cases of delicts covered by it[89] and was subject to the restriction[90] that the master was liable to pay the *litis aestimatio* only once if several of his slaves combined to cause the damage, though if he chose not to pay it he had to surrender all the malefactors. The only other rule worth mentioning in this connection is the odd one[91] that the owner of a runaway slave remained liable to the noxal action, which is not given against anyone who may happen to have come into bona fide possession of him. This solution is in direct contradiction to the usual rule, according to which it was the person in actual control of the slave at the time of the action who was noxally liable,[92] and it has been explained as being probably due to the wording of the *lex*, which may have used the word 'erus' to designate not only the plaintiff in the actions under the first and second chapters, but also the defendant in the noxal actions.[93] It is tempting to see in the master's or father's liability the beginning of vicarious liability, but to do so would be tantamount to ignoring the fact that the liability was that of the wrongdoer and not (subject to what is said in the next paragraph) of the master or father, with the result that the injured person could seek vengeance on the wrongdoer. 'This', however, 'produced a clash between the right of vengeance of the injured person and the *potestas* of the master or father' and it was only 'resolved by allowing the latter as it were to "buy off" the injured person by paying the penalty'.[94]

The problem of noxal liability was further complicated by the likely existence of a direct action[95] against a master who had ordered or authorised the wrongful conduct. For this purpose the *lex* itself seems to have drawn the line between damage done with and without the master's knowledge,[96] but we are told elsewhere that knowledge entails the personal liability of the master only if coupled with power to stop the slave's acts.[97] We are further told that if the slave acted with the master's knowledge, the victim had the option of bringing the direct or noxal action, the jurists being averse to relieving the slave of liability that would, if he was still a slave at the time action was brought, make him run the risk of being subjected to the power of his victim and, if he had already been manumitted, would make him personally liable for the damage.[98] Thus Labeo held that if a slave committed *iniuria* even by his master's order, he could be sued personally after manumission, though he could not be prosecuted under the *lex Cornelia* if he had killed.[99] In all these cases, however, the master's liability was primary, not vicarious. And a man would also be primarily liable for wrongful damage done by a *free* person provided that the latter was acting under his orders.[100] Normally the 'agent' would be liable too,[101] though not if the principal had a *ius imperandi* and the act was not of an atrocious kind.[102] There are a number of other situations in which one person could be held liable for the harm caused by another. For instance, a number of passages deal with the liability of a person who employs a messenger to return an object lent or supplied for some other reason by another person.[103] If the object is lost before it reaches the 'supplier', liability will rest with him if he prescribed the manner by which the object would have to be returned. But liability will rest with the 'sender' (i.e. the person returning the object) if, to use the terminology of the modern literature, he has been guilty of *culpa in eligendo* in selecting the messenger.

Another group of cases arises from the contract of *locatio conductio* and here the relevant texts examine the liability of the *conductor* for damage caused by his employees or slaves to the property of the *locator*. Even Justinian's law on the subject is not entirely clear, but it seems that for him the general principle was that a master was always liable if he had been negligent in his choice of servants, whether slaves or freemen (*culpa in eligendo*)[104] but that he was not otherwise liable for damage caused by a free servant. If, however, a slave had caused damage, then, if there had been no *culpa in eligendo*, the master could, even if sued in contract, surrender the slave noxally.[105] However, there are texts which make an employer absolutely liable on his contract for the *culpa* even of free servants or of persons whom he has admitted to his premises.[106]

The classical law on this subject probably cannot be reconstructed with certainty. Doubtless the classical jurists would have agreed in making any employer liable in an *actio locati* for *culpa in eligendo*, but it seems very unlikely that they applied the same rules to all kinds of contracts that could be enforced by that action. It must always be remembered that while the *actio locati* was, for pleading purposes, one action, it sheltered a large number of contracts of completely different economic content, such as tenancy of land or houses, work done on a thing, services and even carriage of persons and of goods of widely differing kinds. Now although in all contracts that could be brought under the umbrella of *locatio conductio* the parties were required to show *bona fides*, their reciprocal rights and duties were regulated by what we should call the express and implied terms of the contract; and the implied terms must have been fixed, partly by trade custom, but partly by a sense of what the contract really meant. We must therefore suppose that in some cases a party was taken to have promised to do his best to see that objects entrusted to him were not damaged by his own act or omission, sometimes to see that his servants were careful too, to guarantee their diligence, but sometimes to have the thing delivered or redelivered safe and sound in any event. It looks as though contracts of the last-mentioned class were commoner in the classical period than under Justinian,[107] and indeed that where they appear in the *Digest* it is because the compilers have forgotten to alter the passages in which they occur.[108] Moreover, passages can be found where alterations of that kind can be detected without much doubt.[109]

It will have been noticed that in all these cases the master was made liable because of his *culpa in eligendo*. These are not, therefore, true cases of vicarious liability, at any rate in the sense that modern English and French law understand the concept. It is otherwise, however, with the cases of the master of a ship or the keeper of an inn or a livery stable, all of whom were held by the *edict* to be strictly liable for damage caused to property entrusted to their care.[110] True, the jurists invariably justified this liability by arguing that the *nauta, caupo* and *stabularius* were guilty of *culpa* for employing the services of *mali homines*. Yet there is no mention of *culpa* in the edict itself, which, in fact, made it clear that no inquiry could be made as to the care with which the employees had been selected.[111] These, therefore, *appear* to be true cases of vicarious liability since the employer is made liable not for his own fault but for that of his employees, and, though the reasons for such liability are nowhere expressly mentioned, it is not unreasonable to suggest that they must have been broadly similar to those nowadays advanced to explain the institution of vicarious liability.

(b) Modern law

Noxal liability seems to have had no influence on the development of the modern law;[112] but otherwise the Roman rules survived in the Common law (*gemeines Recht*) of Germany. The Pandectists in fact convinced themselves that from the fragmented rules discussed above the Romans had erected a *doctrine* of *culpa in eligendo* which made masters liable *only* if they themselves had been guilty of some fault. This, however, was wrong not only because it ascribed a degree of abstraction and generalisation to Roman law which was totally unknown to the casuistic and practical Roman legal mind; but also because it paid insufficient attention to the edictal liability of the *nauta, caupo, stabularius, habitator* and *publicani* for the delicts committed by certain persons under their control which, we have noted, was strict liability. Alongside these doctrinal ideas there was also the fear shared by many that a change of approach would put too great a burden on industry, and on smaller firms in particular. So, in the end, apart from special rules applicable to special trades and apart from the obvious liability of a person for a wrong which he had ordered to be committed, paragraph 831 BGB based liability on a presumption of *culpa in eligendo vel custodiendo*.[113]

Whatever the origins of this provision and whatever the motives behind its adoption, in practice it has proved most unfortunate in so far as it makes it easier for the 'real' employer to avoid liability. True, with the passage of time, the courts have been more prepared to put greater pressure on employers by requiring them to prove (more or less as in *Wilsons & Clyde* v. *English*[114]) that their overall organisation, their system of work and supervision, as well as their internal allocation of authority, are adequate (which can be made to mean whatever the courts wish to make it mean).[115] But in practice, nevertheless, and despite the original concern about small firms, it is they who are placed in the worst position since their larger brethren are usually in a better position to satisfy the courts as to the 'adequacy' of their organisation. And where they fail to do so, and fault is discovered, it is usually attributable to someone who stands in a hierarchically intermediate position (for example, the foreman who engaged or was supervising the negligent 'servant'). This system of 'decentralised exoneration' (*dezentralisierter Entlastungsbeweis*), which substitutes the intermediary employee for the 'real' master and makes him liable in his stead is clearly economically and socially undesirable and Swiss law, which has also had to wrestle with a similar provision on vicarious liability, has avoided this doctrine of 'decentralised exoneration'[116] by making the 'real' master liable for the torts of the intermediary employee if it is due to his fault that a servant of the company has caused some damage. Problems such as these have thus led to an almost universal condemnation of paragraph 831 BGB, which has been coupled with considerable ingenuity to eschew its application. In this battle, paragraph 278 BGB has proved an invaluable ally.

To understand how this works in practice one must first compare the two provisions of the Code and discover the limitations of each. Under paragraph 831 BGB, once it is held that the master was negligent in his choice of servant, he is liable for any damage caused, even if the servant happens to be protected by some sort of delictual incapacity. Conversely, the employer will not be liable if he can prove that he 'has exercised ordinary care in the selection of the employee and, when he has to supply appliances or implements or to superintend the work, has also exercised ordinary care as regards such supply or superintendence; nor will he be liable if the damage would have arisen notwithstanding the exercise of such care'. Paragraph 278 BGB, on the other hand, provides that 'a debtor is responsible for the fault of his statutory agent, and of persons whom he employs in fulfilling his obligation, to the same extent as for his own fault'. It thus imposes *strict* liability for harm caused by the persons who are used by the debtor in the course of fulfilling his *contractual* obligations. It is clear that the two provisions do not entirely overlap. For on the one hand, paragraph 278 BGB is wider than paragraph 831 BGB in so far as it can render the debtor (employer) liable not only for the acts of his 'servants' but also for the acts of persons who, in England, would be classed as independent contractors.[117] On the other hand, however – and this is a crucial point – an action based on paragraph 278 BGB cannot (in view of paragraph 253 BGB) include a claim for 'pain and suffering'. Moreover, paragraph 278 BGB applies to persons who are used by the debtor to fulfil his (contractual) 'obligations' whereas paragraph 831 BGB is applicable whenever the employee is used 'to do *any* work on behalf of his employer'. In the absence of such a contract, therefore, paragraph 278 BGB is useless. So the courts embarked upon expanding the notion of contract in two different directions, namely, expanding the contract itself to the pre-contractual phase and expanding the contract or, at any rate, its effects, to persons who were not parties to the original transaction.

Extending contractual remedies to the pre-contractual phase of negotiations was achieved through the concept of *culpa in contrahendo*. The doctrine, initiated by the famous German jurist Rudolf Jhering,[118] was, after some hesitation, taken over by the Supreme Court and firmly applied to what were in essence delictual situations. In the leading case,[119] for example, a prospective purchaser entered a store, asked to inspect some carpets and, while doing so, was injured by two rolls which fell from the shelf. The Court took the view that the demand to see the carpets and the fulfilment of this demand resulted in a relationship preliminary to the sale and similar to a contract and imposed reciprocal duties of care with respect to the person and property of the parties. Similar protection has been given not only to the prospective contracting party but to other persons accompanying him at the time of the accident. In a very recent case,[120] for example, a woman entered a supermarket to purchase some goods. While she was waiting in the queue to pay for the goods she had selected (i.e. no contract had yet been concluded with the store) her young child slipped on a vegetable leaf which was lying on the floor and injured herself. The Court was prepared to hold the store liable not only for breach of the *Verkehrssicherungspflicht* but also on the grounds of *culpa in contrahendo*. The protection which was due to the mother/ prospective purchaser was thus extended to her child.

Extending the protective umbrella of contract to persons who were not parties to the original transaction was, at first, achieved through the notion of contracts in *favorem tertii* and paragraph 328 BGB. This enabled the German courts to provide a satisfactory solution to the problem presented to the House of Lords in *Cavalier* v. *Pope*[121] and which remained in this country unsolved until fairly recently. In one case[122] the defendant rented a room to a club to hold a special celebration. One of the members of the club slipped and hurt herself on the floor. In the action that followed she was held entitled to recover *contractual* damages. In another case,[123] X, the plaintiff's employer, contracted with a firm to service a gas water-heater. The firm did the repairs badly and, as a result, the plaintiff, a charwoman employed by X, was injured. She, too, was held to have a *contractual* action against the repair firm for their negligence. As of late, however, the courts have adopted a more subtle approach and instead of discovering a contract between the plaintiff and the defendant they choose to extend the ambit of the contract to cover other persons besides the contracting parties (*Drittschadensersatz* or *Drittschadens-liquidation*). In all these cases, however, it will be obvious that the defendant is made liable not because he is in breach of a specific contractual duty but because he has broken the general duty of care imposed by the law of delict. As Professor Kötz has rightly observed:[124]

The position of German law may be excused by the necessity caused by the unfortunate policy of para. 831 BGB, but the comparative lawyer has to classify problems according to the true significance of their actual facts. These cases must therefore be put in the law of tort, as is done everywhere else in the world. In doing so, the comparatist must realise that it may be necessary to study a person's contractual relations with third parties in order to discover to whom he owes his delictual duties of care not to cause harm.

But despite all these objections, the shift towards the law of contract did succeed in taking the pressure off paragraph 831 BGB, which, perhaps, explains why despite all the adverse criticism it has been left unaltered for so long. But it is tempting to suggest that the same move towards contract might have occurred even in the Common law (despite the doctrine of consideration) had the strong delictual rule *respondeat superior* not been accepted from early times. Sir Frederick Pollock was certainly prepared to speculate on this when reviewing in 1916[125] Thomas Baty's book on vicarious liability (which could find no rational justification for the English rule). Pollock prophetically said:

It would be an amusing speculative question, if one had time to pursue it, what would have been the result of the law taking the course Dr Baty would have liked. Denial of the superior's responsibility in tort would surely have let to a luxuriant and perplexed growth of contracts implied in law, for which the substance of justice would have been no better from any point of view, and the science of law much the worse.

Pollock would, no doubt, have been satisfied to see that his speculations have been vindicated by the development of the German law on this matter.

The French Code,[126] by contrast, enacted a rule which almost exactly corresponds to that of English law, a master being strictly liable for all damage done wrongfully by his servant in the performance of the functions for which he is employed. The history of this provision is still obscure at many points and its juristic basis has been as hard to explain as that of the English rule.[127] There is no clear statement in Domat,[128] and the rule first appears clearly in Pothier,[129] who makes a distinction between a person's liability for his children and apprentices, which is excluded if he can show he could not have prevented the damage, and his liability for his servants, which was not subject to any such limitation. Since Pothier was not an original jurist, we must assume that the distinction had already been worked out in the practice of the courts; and in fact Bourjon[130] cites a decision to this effect of the Châtelet of Paris. One can only, therefore, infer that the rule sprang up about the same time as in England and for much the same reasons. We do know that the compilers of the Code tried to suppress the distinction and create only a presumption of fault against a master for wrongful damage done by his servants; but the Tribunat insisted on a restoration of Pothier's rule on practical grounds.[131]

Apart from this important difference between the Germanic systems on the one hand, and the English and French on the other, the systems under comparison are, in their broad outlines, quite similar. The differences that exist are differences of terminology, emphasis or degree rather than of substance or legal technique. In all systems, for example, vicarious liability presupposes a master-servant relationship and all seem to employ very similar tests in distinguishing servants (for whose act a master is, invariably, liable) from independent contractors (for whom, invariably, there is no liability). English law, however, is, apparently, more willing than other systems to experiment with a host of other criteria apart from the famous test of 'direction or control'.[132] But there is a growing tendency everywhere to use neutral terms such as 'subordination' which can be made to cover more easily the *possibility* of control as well as actual control. And for the same reason it is invariably accepted that subordination can be intermittent and need not be constant; and that actual and not legal subordination will suffice to create the necessary relationship.[133] All these notions thus facilitate the extension of vicarious liability in an era of modern technology and entrepreneurial activity; and, furthermore, help 'remove from the centre of vicarious liability the defects of the master's will and replace it with the master's risk'.[134] Put differently, vicarious liability is made to extend to cover the maximum of risks that society feels it can impose on a particular type of employer. And this kind of reasoning had led a number of Common lawyers and Civil lawyers to suggest that in cases of 'borrowed servants' the victim should be allowed to 'sue both employers and leave them to dispute among themselves who should bear the burden'.[135] In practice, this will usually be the general employer and both English and French case-law acknowledge this by accepting the above as the general proposition and then placing on the general employer the heavy task of shifting liability on to the temporary employer.[136]

The master's liability will only be invoked if there is a sufficient nexus between the occurrence of the tort and the activity for which the 'servant' was engaged. This is expressed in a variety of ways ('dans les fonctions auxquelles ils les ont employés' (1384. 5 French CC); 'á l' exécution des fonctions' (1054 Quebec CC); 'in Ausübung ihrer... Verrichtungen' (OR art. 55 para. 1); 'in Ausführung der Verrichtung' (para. 831 BGB); in the 'course' or 'scope' of employment (Common law)), and behind these bewildering and not very informative expressions lies the most often litigated aspect of the whole law of vicarious liability. Nevertheless, the courts appear to find less difficulty than writers when striving to reconcile the morass of often irreconcilable cases[137] and, perhaps, one could try to simplify the problem by saying that in practice there is one rule: either the servant is within the course of his employment (and so, the other conditions being satisfied, renders his master liable) or he is not (in which case there is no liability for the master). Whether he is in the course of his employment or not is really a question of fact and, in a sense, the situation is not dissimilar from that found in negligence where, also, there is a simple rule: if a person has behaved carelessly, he is liable (subject to certain other conditions being fulfilled); if he was not careless, he is not liable. The question whether his behaviour was careless or not is one of fact. Just as there are guidelines (not rules) to help in determining carelessness, so there are guidelines, and no more, which help in determining 'scope of employment'. The decision is, therefore, often impressionistic and the only permissible generalisation is that the area of activity falling within the 'scope of employment' seems to be widening daily, partly as a result of the increase in car traffic (and the compulsory insurance schemes that go with it) and partly because the scope of acceptable risk has widened as legal entities have taken over from human beings the position of 'master'. Having said this, however, one must qualify it by stressing that in some systems (e.g. the German) courts still tend to give the phrase a narrow interpretation, insisting either that the employee must have been employed to do the very act which directly caused the damage or that the act fell within the type of measure which is normally incidental to the performance of the work entrusted to the servant.[138] Thus, unlike French law, German law is reluctant to consider an act expressly prohibited to the employee as being still within the course of his employment;[139] nor will it be sufficient to show that his employment merely gave the opportunity to cause the harm in question. Only French cases – particularly those decided by the criminal section of the Cour de cassation – have with little hesitation held employers liable for delicts committed by their employees simply because they were committed in the place of work or during office hours.[140] But this generous interpretation of the phrase 'dans l'exercice des fonctions' to include delicts committed 'à l'occasion' of the servant's work, adopted, as we have seen, by the Chambre Criminelle of the Cour de cassation, has been in clear opposition to the more restrictive approach taken by the second Chambre Civile.[141] This conflict, apart from the uncertainty which it has injected into the practice of the lower courts, offers an excellent illustration of some of the points made in chapters 2 and 3, and so it deserves a brief excursus.

For the Chambre Criminelle the master is liable even if his servant is guilty of an *abus de fonctions* so long as the plaintiff/victim is unaware of this *and* there is a *lien de connexité* between his *fonction* and the *acte illicite*.[142] The result, prompted as we shall see by reasons of 'equity', was drily justified by reference to the 'causal' theory of equivalence of conditions. The second Chambre Civile, on the other hand, reached the more restrictive solution by means of the adequate cause theory. Whatever the respective merits of each approach, the practical consequences of this conflict between the two sections of the highest court were considered unfortunate and in 1960 the plenary session of the Supreme Court, then called the Chambres Réunies, was seized of this dispute and pronounced itself in favour of the view traditionally taken by the second Chambre Civile.[143] The formulation of the decision was not, however, in terms appropriate to an *arrêt de principe* (faint echoes here of the distinction between *ratio* and *obiter*) and less than a year later the Chambre Criminelle was able to defy the superior 'moral' authority of the plenary session of the Court and to revert to its old practice.[144]

Seventeen years after its 1960 decision, the Assemblée Plénière (successor to the Chambres Réunies) reverted to this point and repeated its earlier opinion though in more general and clearer terms. It thus held that 'le commettant n'est pas responsable du dommage causé par un préposé qui utilise, sans autorisation, à des fins personnelles, *le véhicule à lui confié pour l'exercice de ses fonctions*'.[145] To this new prompting to toe the line the Chambre Criminelle responded only partially. For in a manner which a Common lawyer would both appreciate and understand, the Chambre Criminelle abandoned its old case-law only *where the 'abus de fonctions' was related to the use of cars;*[146] *in all other cases of 'abus de fonctions',* it refused to conform to the more restrictive view advocated by the Chambre Civile and the Assemblée Plénière.[147] This fine casuistry is from a legal point of view unsatisfactory; and it only partially improves the position as far as the lower courts are concerned since they are still faced (in matters *not* involving car accidents) with the same conflicting case-law from the highest court. Nevertheless, there is some 'fairness' (if not legal logic) in this distinction in so far as it is supported by wider considerations of equity and insurance practice. For the victim of the traffic accident will receive compensation from the Fonds de garantie and therefore will not suffer so much by not being able to sue the master of the negligent servant. In all other cases, however, of *abus de fonctions*, and in the absence of Fonds de garantie (or any other automatic compensation system), the restrictive approach on vicarious liability could often mean that the victim would have no one to sue apart from the usually impecunious servant.[148]

3. A bird's eye view of the French and German law relating to injuries at work and on the road

(a) Work injuries

Since 1884 Germany has had a no-fault compulsory insurance scheme covering accidents at work. This has been repeatedly amended and expanded in various ways by subsequent enactments and now forms part of a wider and more comprehensive system of social security that covers such things as permanent incapacity for work as well as sickness. Here we shall limit our comments to the treatment given to accidents at work, a phrase which should be taken to include not only injuries sustained while actually at work but also accidents occurring while travelling to and from work.

Compensation in the above cases is made through various schemes which are administered by trade co-operatives or institutes, (*Berufsgenossenschaften*) which are separate legal entities, usually in close contact with each other, and under the general supervision and responsibility of the Minister of Labour and Social Security. The institutes function on a territorial basis and are organised to cover different commercial or other activities. There are in all some thirty-four industrial accident insurance institutes; nineteen agricultural institutes; thirteen municipal accident insurance organisations; eleven state funds; four federal insurance institutes; and a number of other smaller autonomous funds – some ninety institutes in all (the first two of these, however, are the most important, covering between them some 90 per cent of work accident insurance). These institutes are self-governed by boards or councils, usually composed of equal numbers of employers and employees. Every employer is automatically a member of the institute appropriate to his firm's activities in the locality in which it carries on its business. Institutes may provide voluntary insurance for the self-employed in their areas and some actually make this compulsory.

The financing of the various institutes is a complicated affair. Generally speaking, revenue from taxes funds those institutes which insure public employees; and the funds of agricultural institutes are subsidised by the central (Federal) Government. The thirty-four industrial accident insurance institutes, on the other hand, derive their funds entirely from contributions from employers, though there is the possibility (realised once only) of mutual financial help. The contributions vary depending on the risk factor attendant to the branch of industry to which the member belongs as well on the risk-rating of the firm in question. These figures are reviewed periodically and contributions tend to vary from 1 to 12 per cent of earnings.

The awards are made by the officials of the appropriate institutes and there is an intricate system of appeals to local State and Federal courts. A basic assumption of the system is that, save in cases of intentionally inflicted injury, the injured victim *cannot* claim any further compensation by relying on the ordinary tort rules of the BGB. To make up for this, the system of awards tends to be closely connected with the victim's pre-accident earnings and the sums recoverable can thus often be quite generous. Moreover, pensions and other periodic payments are index-linked. Awards are made to all those in paid employment (whether German nationals or not) and, since 1971, children and students have been covered by the schemes. What is awarded depends largely upon whether the case is one of personal injury or death.

Awards for personal injuries will cover medical costs, including the costs of nursing, convalescence and rehabilitation. The vast majority of cases will be dealt with under the *general* sickness insurance schemes (which are financed by contributions from *both* employers and employees). But the accident insurance institutes will meet *all* costs after the eighteenth day and, in about 15–20 per cent of the cases, depending on the type and seriousness of the injury, they take over responsibility from the outset and handle the case through their own specialists and hospitals. The institutes will also pay varying sums for loss of wages depending on the degree of invalidity incurred and the period it lasts, but during the first six weeks of incapacity the employer remains responsible for paying the victim's wages. Total incapacity will usually produce approximately 65 per cent of the pre-accident wages for the first thirteen weeks of the incapacity and from then onwards a pension equal to two-thirds of the pre-accident wages within certain maximum limits. In the case of partial incapacity, the sums payable represent the proportion of the sum payable in the case of total incapacity that corresponds to the *actual* degree of incapacity and these sums are increased by small amounts if the injured person has dependants. In the case of fatal accidents, a sum equal to one month's earnings plus the funeral expenses become payable immediately. In addition to this sum, a widow would receive a pension which is usually 30 per cent of the deceased husband's pre-accident income; but this sum can be increased to 40 per cent where the widow is over the age of forty-five, or her own earning capacity is reduced by at least 50 per cent, or if she has children to look after. Children can also receive a pension which is higher where both parents are dead and lower if one of the parents has died. The sums are, once again, calculated on the pre-accident earnings of the parent, are index-linked, and cease to be paid when the child becomes eighteen. A widower, too, can claim a pension, but only where he can show that his wife was mainly responsible for the maintenance of the family and that he is, through incapacity, unable to support himself. Naturally, this applies if the wife died in an industrial accident as defined above.

In its broad outlines the French system is not dissimilar to the German. There, too, there is a no-fault accident insurance system which, though introduced later than the German one, has also been expanded with the passage of time and, since 1945, fully integrated in to the wider system of social security. In France, too, this system operates to the exclusion of the tort system, unless the injury is the result of an intentional act of the employer *or* a fellow employee, in which case an action in tort can be maintained. But the tort system may also be invoked if the injury is due to the conduct of a *third* party (e.g. a workman who, while on his way to work, is run down by a stranger.)

The French system, mostly found in the Social Security Code of 1945 (amended and updated several times since) covers all persons in paid employment for injuries suffered at work or while going to or coming from work. The self-employed must join a separate compulsory health insurance scheme or they may join the general scheme. Medical care for the industrially disabled is, generally speaking, free, whereas under the *general* sickness scheme the insured individual usually has to carry part of the cost. Loss of wages as a result of disablement is paid on a sliding scale depending on the type of invalidity, its degree and its duration. Thus, temporary invalidity will usually result in payments equalling half the average daily age of the injured party for a period of one month and thereafter to two-thirds of that amount. Permanent invalidity will result in benefits which will depend on the degree of disablement and the victim's gross earnings during the preceding twelve months; but there are maxima and minima in these calculations. In the case of fatal accidents, pensions are paid to the various dependants more or less in line with what has been said about the German system. For instance, a younger widow will receive less than an older one. But there is an interesting variation when it comes to remarriage. When this occurs, payments are not immediately discontinued but, instead, a widow or widower receives a sum equal to three years' benefit. And, upon further widowhood, separation or divorce, it has recently become possible to be reinstated as a claimant for a pension. French law also makes use of the concept of *faute inexcusable*, which is basically defined by the courts as a fault of exceptional gravity which is unaccompanied by any justifiable excuse. The presence of such fault can affect the payments described above in two ways: if it is the *employer* who is guilty, the permanent funds can pay additional benefits to the victims and make the guilty employer pay for the excess. But if such fault has been committed by the *claimant* then it may enable the insurance funds to reduce the payments they would otherwise have made to him. Finally, it should be noted that injury compensation schemes are financed by the employers, contributions varying on the risk factor of the particular industry. Average rates of contribution are around 4 per cent of earnings and adjustable maxima are also imposed. Awards are made by the officers of the local insurance funds and an appeal can be made before appropriate regional courts, and if an important point of law is involved, cases can even reach the Cour de cassation.

(b)   Road injuries

Traffic accident compensation is an immensely important area of tort law not only because of the problems it has given rise to and the infinite variety of solutions it has provoked, but also because some of its peculiarities (e.g. the inevitability of many accidents and the importance of the insurance factor) have prompted tort lawyers to rethink much of their traditional ideas on civil liability. A bird's eye view, even one which is limited to two systems, is bound to do the subject injustice. Our task, however, has been greatly facilitated by a number of excellent comparative accounts to which the interested reader is referred.

German law has, from the early days of this century, recognised the peculiarities of traffic accidents and has enacted specific statutes to cope with their problems. The inevitability of many of these accidents was stressed as early as 1906 when, in one of the drafts of what was to become the German Motor Car Accident Law of 1909, it was pointed out that 'although through the careful operation of vehicles many collisions may be avoided, nevertheless it is difficult to avoid them altogether, because automobiles do not run on rails and are capable of exceedingly swift movements'. A more stringent form of strict liability coupled with compulsory third party insúrance liability since November 1939 has thus led to the establishment of a *semi-independent* system of compensation. The italicised word, however, is meant to stress that these statutory solutions are not, unlike those found in other systems (e.g. the Swiss), meant to exclude the application of the ordinary rules of liability found in the BGB. This, as we shall see, has many important consequences.

The German Motor Car Law of 1909, now replaced by the Road Traffic Law of 1952 (as amended) places liability for car accidents primarily on the person in possession (*Halter*) of the car. This is the person immediately in control of the car, usually the owner, but sometimes the bailee. The liability is strict but not absolute and the holder will be discharged from his liability if he can establish that it arose from an 'unavoidable event which is due neither to a defect of the vehicle nor to any failure in its mechanism'. The same provision goes on to supply some guidance as to what is regarded as unavoidable (e.g. behaviour of the injured person, or animal, or some third person who is not himself involved in the operation). Alternatively, the driver of the vehicle may also be held liable unless he can show that he was not guilty of any negligence. This sounds mere presumption of fault and, in theory, it is; but in practice the courts have come to adopt fairly stringent standards of expected behaviour, so that, for example, the driver will avoid liability only if he can show that he displayed the diligence expected not merely from the *average* but from the highly competent driver. Liability, however, is not imposed upon the owner or possessor of a stolen car unless the use of the car was made possible through his own negligence. Damages awarded under the Act must, as we have already noted, comply with certain maxima and never include compensation for pain and suffering. This has made recourse to the ordinary provisions of the BGB inevitable though, of course, success under the general principles of delictual liability will depend upon proof of fault in the defendant.

The French approach is different from the German in a number of important respects. Cardinal amongst the differences is the absence of any specific statute on the matter, with the result that reliance is placed on the general provisions of the Code, namely, article 1382 CC and, more usually, article 1384 CC. The latter article, as we have seen, establishes a presumption of liability which can only be rebutted (and thus exonerate completely the *gardien*) if the defendant shows that the accident was due to the conduct of the victim or a third party or even a fortuitous event so long as these could not normally be foreseen and thus rendered the damage unavoidable. On the other hand, the conduct of the victim (but *not* that of a third party)[149] may reduce the liability of the *gardien* to the extent that it contributed to the plaintiff's hurt. Liability under article 1384 CC is, as we have seen, imposed on the *gardien*, but French law, like German law, is reluctant to impose liability on the 'owner' where the car has been stolen (at any rate, without his negligence). Since the early 1940s this result has not been in doubt, but in the absence of an express statutory provision it was achieved through causal principles. Its wisdom, however, in these days of compulsory insurance (compulsory insurance was introduced in France only in 1959) is rather open to doubt.

Damages in road traffic accidents can be awarded either by the civil courts or the criminal courts if the aggrieved person appears before them as a *partie civile*. If the criminal court refuses to convict the accused no civil damages will be awarded, so a fresh action, this time before a civil court, will be necessary. In the absence of any statutory provision similar to that found in German law, there are no maxima in the awards made by the courts and the normal rules about damages will determine the size of awards. The French have also created a Fonds de garantie automobile which carries out functions similar to our Motor Insurance Bureau. Generally speaking, dissatisfaction with the present system has been voiced, and the chief advocate for reform, Professor André Tunc, has strongly pressed for a no-fault system backed up by insurance and replacing the tort action. His views can be found in the famous 'projet Tunc', which attracted the great attention that its author's reputation deserves, but to date there has been no legislative response. But even in the absence of any legislative intervention the position of the traffic victim could be improved, for it would not require much courage for the Cour de cassation to curtail the defences available to drivers or, rather, their insurers, and thus create a near absolute form of liability which would fall only upon proof of an inexcusable fault on the part of the victim. This approach coupled with the reduction (or even elimination) of awards for non-economic losses – in order to ensure that insurance premiums did not get out of control – would go a long way towards compensating deserving victims of traffic accidents who at present remain without any compensation.[150]

Selected further reading

Allen, D.K., Bourn, C.L., Holyoak, J.H. (eds), *Accident Compensation after Pearson* (1979).

Ames, J.B., 'Law and Morals', 22 *Harv.L.Rev.* (1908), 97.

Ancel, M., 'La Responsabilité sans faute en droit français', *Travaux de l'Association Henri Capitant* II (1947), 249.

Atiyah, P., *Vicarious Liability in the Law of Torts* (1967).

Bach, L., 'Réflexions sur le problème du fondement de la responsabilité civile en droit français', *Rev.trim.dr.civ.* (1977), 17 *et seq.*

Britton, P., 'The Guest. Plaintiff, the Code Civil and the Cour de cassation', 25 *I.C.L.Q.* (1976), 826.

Calabresi, G., *The Costs of Accidents* (1970).

Calabresi, G. and Hirschoff, J.T., 'Toward a Test for Strict Liability in Torts', 81 *Yale L.J.* (1972), 1055.

Department of Transportation (U.S.A.), *Driver Behavior and Accident Involvement – Implications for Tort Liability* (1970).

Causation, Culpability and Deterrence in Highway Crashes (1970).

Ehrenzweig, A., 'Assurance Oblige – A Comparative Study', 15 *Law and Contemp. Prob.* (1950), 455.

'Negligence Without Fault', 54 *Cal.L.Rev.* (1966), 1422.

Epstein, R.A., 'A theory of Strict Liability', 2 *J. Leg. Studies* (1973), 151.

Esser, J., *Grundlagen und Entwicklung der Gefährdungshaftung* (1941).

'Zweispurigkeit unseres Haftpflichtrechts', 8 *JZ.* (1953), 129.

Eörsi, G., *Encyclopedia*, XI. ch. 4.

Fleming, J.G., 'The Role of Negligence in Accidental Law', 53 *Va.L.Rev.* (1967), 815.

'Accident Liability reconsidered. The impact of liability insurance', 57 *Yale L.J.* (1948), 549.

Goldman, B., *De la Détermination du gardien responsable du fait des choses inanimées* (1947).

'Garde de la structure et garde du comportement', *Mélanges P. Roubier*, II (1961), 51 *et seq.*

Hamson, C.J., 'The Moral Law and Professor Tunc', 32 *C.L.J.* (1973), 52.

Hassler, Théo, 'La Responsabilité des commettants', D. Chron. 1980, 125.

Isaacs, N., 'Fault and Liability', 31 *Harv.L.Rev.* (1918), 954.

James, Fleming, Jr., 'An Evaluation of the Fault Concept', 32 *Tenn.L.Rev.* (1965), 394.

'The Future of Negligence in Accident Law', 53 *Va.L.Rev.* (1967), 911.

Jolowicz, J.A., 'Liability for Independent Contractors – a Suggestion', 9 *Stan.L.Rev.* (1957), 690.

'Liability for Accidents', 27 *C.L.J.* (1968), 50.

Jørgenson, S., 'Liability and Fault', 49 *Tul.L.Rev.* (1975), 329.

Malone, W.S., 'Ruminations on the role of fault in the history of the common law of torts', 31 *Louisiana L.Rev.* (1970), 1.

O'Connell, J. and Henderson, R.C., *Tort Law, No-Fault and Beyond* (1975).

Oftinger, K., 'L'Evolution de la responsabilité civile et son assurance dans la législation suisse la plus récente', *Mélanges Savatier* (1965), 723.

Posner, R.A., 'Strict Liability: A Comment', 2 *J.Leg.Studies* (1973), 205.

'The Economic Approach to law', 53 *Tex.L.Rev.* (1975), 757.

Ripert, G., *La Règle morale dans les obligations*, 4th edn (1949).

Starck, B., 'Les Cas de responsabilité sans faute', *Rev.trim.dr.civ.* (1958), 56.

Tendler, R., 'Le Rapproachement des droit français et suisse en matière de responsabilité du fait de leurs préposés', *Rev.int.dr.comp.* (1972), 677.

Tunc, A., 'Tort Law and the Moral Law', 31 *C.L.J.* (1972), 247.

'Accident Victim Compensation and the Moral Law', 32 *C.L.J.* (1973), 241.

'Fault: A Common Name for Different Misdeeds', 49 *Tul.L.Rev.* (1975), 279.

'L'Enfant et la balle', *J.C.P.* 1966,1.1983.

Pour une loi sur les accidents de la circulation (1981). (Collection of essays by different authors: gen. ed. A. Tunc.)

Encyclopedia, XI, ch. 14.

'A Codified Law of Tort – the French Experience', 39 *Louisiana L.Rev.* (1979), 1051.

'Les Causes d'exonération de la responsabilité de plein droit de l'article 1384, al. 1, du code civil', D. Chron. 1975, 83 *et seq.*

'Garde du comportement et garde de la structure dans la responsabilité du fait des choses inanimées', *J.C.P.* 1957,1.1384.

'La Détermination du gardien dans la responsabilité du fait des choses inanimées', *J.C.P.* 1960.1.1592.

'Les Paradoxes du régime actuel de la responsabilité de plein droit', D. Chron. 1976,13.

Ursin, E., 'Strict Liability for Defective Premises – one step beyond *Rowland* and *Greenman*', 22 *U.C.L.A. L.Rev.* (1975), 820.

Viney, G., *Le Déclin de la responsabilité individuelle* (1964).

Williams, G.L., 'Vicarious Liability: Tort of the Master or the Servant?', 72 *L.Q.R.* (1956), 522.

Chapter 5

CONCLUSIONS

Since we regard this book as a kind of textbook primarily intended for students interested in the comparative study of the law of tort, one of our prime aims has been to provide our readers with some *basic* information about the various substantive rules on this subject. If, after reading this book, their appetites have been whetted and their interest aroused, then the many bibliographical references in the notes and at the end of each chapter can guide them towards a deeper and more rewarding study of this subject. And in the second volume a wide selection of materials from codes, statutes, Roman texts and reported cases should provide them with some important primary sources which will familiarise them with some basic conceptions of the Civil law systems as well as enable them to develop (or question) some of our assumptions, ideas, or conclusions. This, then, was our first aim, not only because Common lawyers are at long last becoming seriously interested in acquiring some idea of the Civil law (and vice versa) but also because comparison (which was our main aim) presupposes some knowledge of the 'other' system, and this knowledge we could not assume to exist except in a very small number of advanced students. But textbooks – even the most elementary of the species – normally attempt to cover (however thinly) all the ground of their subjects and, beyond offering their authors' views on obscure or debated points, rarely venture into a more speculative, controversial, or thematic presentation of their topic. Yet this book, precisely because it is not an 'orthodox' textbook, has violated both of these principles, first by omitting topics which are, undoubtedly, the proper concern of tort lawyers and, secondly, by aspiring to offer to its readers a *thematic* approach coupled with some general reflections on the Common law of tort and the Civil law of delict. Without underestimating the importance of the first objective and the difficulties of presenting to the uninitiated reader the basic rules of the Common law and the Civil law *in constant juxtaposition* and in a manner which is both readable and concise, we have no doubt that it is the second of our objectives that deserves the greater attention. Thus, the entire treatment of our topic, with its serious but self-inflicted limitations, has revolved around a number of themes which we felt deserved special emphasis and which, like Wagnerian leitmotifs, appear and reappear with constant regularity as the exposition of the law unfolds before the eyes of the (unsuspecting) reader. Some of these ideas we should like to restate in summary form to bring them more into focus in the hope that some day some of our readers might consider taking them a step further than we have.

Cardinal amongst our themes has been the intriguing similarity between the Common law and the Civil law systems in the area of the law of delict. For the serious student of comparative law this has become during fairly recent times an increasingly obvious truth; but for many, if not most lawyers, this point has yet to be grasped and its implications fully understood. This, of course, is not to deny *important* differences which are more than obvious if a conceptual rather than functional approach is adopted. For it is the concepts that differ rather than the results or even, at times, the method or the handling of source material. These differences cannot be bridged by comparing abstract concepts and we therefore opted for a functional, policy-orientated approach which, we hope, has helped to explain why certain results are reached as well as to reveal many hitherto concealed similarities. This we have done because we felt that the time was ripe for teachers (on both sides of the Channel) to abandon their 'splendid isolation' and switch their attention to similarities, obvious and hidden, and the advantages that can be gained from that realisation that cross-fertilisation of ideas is both possible and desirable. Despite differing formulations, then, the study of the systems under comparison can, we feel, support the following general propositions.

First, while the Common law and the Germanic systems are not prepared to impose liability for every culpable act which causes harm, the French system and its derivatives are more generous in this direction. Their unitary conception of fault makes this possible but it also means that greater emphasis has to be placed on the notions of 'damage' and 'causation' for the purposes of controlling the limits of liability. The distinction between 'unlawfulness' and 'fault', 'duty' and 'careless breach', characteristic of the German and Common law systems respectively, is, on the other hand, perfectly in tune with these systems' thinking in terms of 'torts' rather than in terms of 'tort'.

But since 'unlawfulness' (to use the term broadly to encompass both systems) presupposes a list of headings (or, at least, important areas of non-liability), it tends to wither away as the area of tortious liability gradually expands. There are signs of this happening in the Common law and this trend is bringing the system ever closer to the French approach with all its advantages and disadvantages.

Second, many systems on occasion impose liability only upon proof of wrongful intent or even malice. German law in particular makes a clear and logical distinction between cases where a person may be liable for negligent conduct and those where wrongful intent must be proved and, except in cases specially provided for by statute, it does so in such a way as to exclude liability for negligence where only pecuniary damage has occurred. English law has until now taken a similarly restrictive view towards pure economic loss though there are signs that this may not last for much longer. In this sense the recognition of the compensability of pure economic loss will be yet another step towards making the notion of 'duty', if not actually redundant, certainly less important than it has been up to now. In Germany, on the other hand, the predominantly nineteenth-century philosophy of treating economic loss as a kind of harm 'inferior' to damage to the person or property has been 'fossilised' in the rigid structure of the Code in a way that hinders any advance towards its wider compensation.

Third, all systems accept that a person may be liable for a careless omission to act in a specified manner, though only on the basis of pre-existing duty to act; and though the number of duties for affirmative action are daily multiplied by courts and legislators alike, there is still in some systems (e.g. English, German) a certain reluctance to recognise the existence of a *general duty* to act in the interests of another. This could be seen as one of the longest surviving legacies of Roman law though, with the passage of time, other reasons more in tune with the liberal philosophy of the nineteenth century were advanced in order to justify the *retention* of this distinction between acts and omissions.

Finally, it is true to say that most writers in most countries nowadays accept that the prime purpose of the law of tort is the compensation of the injured plaintiff and that the admonitory function in the law of delict is attenuated, if not actually left to the criminal law. Yet though this is widely accepted, the pull between the plaintiff's interests and the defendant's interests is strong and a number of legal rules can be explained by the fact that the law is still more preoccupied with the defendant's conduct than the plaintiff's hurt. For some, like Ehrenzweig, this clash of interests forms the central theme in the history of tort law as it has always struggled for a compromise between an injurer's law based on the injurer's conduct and an injured's law satisfying the injured.[1] Thus, the emphasis on the injurer's conduct has justified the overt or concealed retention of the institution of punitive damages; the acceptance of 'fault' as the basic criterion of legal liability; the increased protection afforded to injurers (defendants) by various, normative, theories of causation; the struggle to retain or establish some measure of immunity for certain categories of defendants (e.g. insane persons); and the retention (especially by many American jurisdictions) of the older rule concerning contributory negligence (defendant absolved if plaintiff was also careless). By contrast, the emphasis on the injured person's state and the desire to compensate him has led to the extension of vicarious liability (and allied doctrines such as the concept of the 'family car'); to the increased use of *res ipsa loquitur* or similar legal presumptions; to the weakening of the 'controlling function' of fault, especially through the assimilation of fault and error (though this cuts both ways and, as the French case-law on article 1384 CC clearly shows, it can often affect the victim's compensation); to the introduction of extensive theories of causation in cases of enterprise liability (e.g. Ehrenzweig's idea of 'typicality' of harm); to the recognition of new duty situations; to the abandonment of the older rule of contributory negligence, occasionally to the extent of allowing the careless victim to recover *full* compensation so long as he is not guilty of a grave fault (*faute inexcusable*); and to the 'discovery' of new forms of strict liability which are in theory based on a provision of the Code, but in reality represent a completely new judicial creation (article 1384 CC offering, of course, the obvious illustration for this). This tilting of the scales in favour of the victim/plaintiff is very largely due to the modern highly mechanised enterprise and modern traffic conditions with their attendant risks and the increase in insurance cover. In fact it is, in one sense, quite surprising how far-reaching changes such as the above have, on the whole, been accommodated within the framework of the traditional law of tort. This, however, has been achieved at a price and the price has been the emergence of an immensely refined and complicated set of rules governing civil responsibility, and a blurring or even perversion of traditional notions together with concepts of liability. 'Negligence' (or fault), for example, has lost its original flavour of reprehensible conduct since it is now discovered in order to impose liability for inevitable results of lawful activities. 'Foreseeability' is another term which has been divorced from its natural and ordinary meaning and is often little more than a fiction. This mutation of the various concepts can lead to confusion, inconsistency, the concealment of the genuine premises of judicial decisions and, often, to results which, though fair to victims, are oppressive to tortfeasors who may be just as innocent as the victims of their activities. Alternatively, the desire to strike some kind of balance between plaintiff and defendant through the utilisation of traditional concepts (e.g. causation, contribution between joint tortfeasors etc.) can produce harsh results for the victim. We have seen, for example, how the importance currently attached by French law to 'le fait ou la faute de la victime' in the context of article 1384 CC can produce just such results, unfair to the victim and inconsistent with the basic aims of the law of torts. For the reduction of the traffic victim's damages, because of his own conduct (which often is little more than an inevitable error), blatantly frustrates the 'compensation' aim of the law of tort, while at the same time doing nothing towards accident prevention in so far as it does not deter potential defendants from killing or injuring but merely 'deters' potential victims from being killed or injured – something which is hardly necessary.[2]

This struggle between the plaintiff's and defendant's interests is thus still crying out for a compromise which would accommodate both points of view, a compromise, however, which the traditional law of 'negligence' liability is finding difficult to achieve. It is in the light of such realities and failures that the idea of making the notion of 'risk' the basis of liability or the extending of the scope of social security and/or private insurance as a means of compensating victims of inevitable accidents have gained support. However, the technical, economic, and 'political' obstacles against even a partial replacement of the traditional law of tort by some system of automatic no-fault insurance have hitherto proved difficult to surmount and, until the difficulties are sorted out, the philosophical and political arguments for and against reform of the tort system will continue to rage. One thing, however, is clear, and that is that we are now approaching the end of a long period of legal development which, as far as most European countries are concerned, started with the Roman law, reached the peak of its development with the enactments of the nineteenth-century civil codes (of which the German was one of the finest creations of the human mind), and began its decline in the face of the radical economic and social changes of our era and the proliferation of industrial and traffic accidents.

Another important theme which we have attempted to stress wherever appropriate is the considerable if not bewildering equivoca-tion between the various elements of liability. Cases which are factually similar to one another are resolved in an identical manner but with their respective judges relying on different legal concepts. For example, the noise of passing aeroplanes which causes damage to the health of foxes in silver fox farms below their path has been held to be not actionable in Canada because of the absence of any *duty*, and in Germany, because of lack of *adequate cause*.[3] If a woman witnesses a gruesome car accident and, as a result, suffers a miscarriage she will be allowed to recover, but it may be otherwise if she does not actually see the accident the moment it occurs. In England this result has been reached through the medium of duty. In France the courts have experimented with causal notions;[4] the same is true of the so-called 'rescue' cases which the Common law nowadays treats as cases raising the problem of duty (or no duty), whereas the Civil law has handled them as problems of causation.[5] This equivocation can even be found in one and the same case without, however, affecting the final outcome. In *King* v. *Phillips*,[6] for example, the Court of Appeal was unanimous in rejecting the mother's claim, though two of its members chose to do this by denying the existence of any duty towards the mother whereas the third, Lord Denning, took the view that though there was a duty, the damage was too remote. *Woods* v. *Duncan*[7] offers another illustration, and the 'cable cases' discussed in chapter 2 also provide illustrations of how duty, remoteness, causation and the like can be used interchangeably to produce the desired results. Occasionally, however, the choice of concept can materially affect the outcome of the case, and the selection may then be determined by whether the judge wishes or not to impose liability. The equivocation between the various concepts is, therefore, exten-sive and a number of conclusions can be drawn from this. *First*, appreciating the equivocation between the various elements of liability can help reveal concealed similarities in reasoning. A Common lawyer should not, for example, be surprised to see German lawyers tackle problems of nervous shock under the heading of legal cause since he himself could do it the same way and, more important, has actually done it in the past. *Second*, though this equivocation between the various elements of liability can be found in all the systems under comparison, a number of wider considerations may commend different concepts to different systems *as a means of expressing judicial policies of a more general nature.* French law, for example, has placed great emphasis on the notion of damage whereas English law has, especially during this century, stressed the notion of 'duty' when giving effect to wider policy decisions and the notion of 'remoteness' when denying recovery in specific cases. *Third*, the cases seem to support the view that though the choice of concept is often a matter of the personal taste of the judge, there is a move away from factually based concepts to concepts with a stronger normative element. The move from 'causation' to 'duty' and from there to the open acknowledgement of policy is an interesting trend noticeable in the English economic loss[8] cases and underlining the willingness to take into account a wide variety of factors when determining a particular dispute. *Fourth*, the equivocation between these concepts makes one realise that they are really nothing more than the accepted mechanisms for dealing with the infinite variety of fact situations. In other words 'they are means' of formulating conclusions but do not often dictate them.[9] *Finally*, if the above observations are correct it becomes both desirable and useful to try to discover and consider intelligently the real issues before the courts and the reasons which lead them to decide the cases before them in one way rather than another. For example, a strictly legal exposition of the law of traffic accidents which ignores modern insurance practices is bound to be one-sided and defective. All this opens new and exciting vistas which tort lawyers have hitherto failed to explore adequately and in its turn can raise further interesting issues for consideration. Notable amongst them is the question when, if at all, the judge is in a better position than the (slow-moving and overworked) modern legislator to adapt the law to changing social requirements; and where 'adaptation' ends and 'creation' begins. The discussion of all these problems lies clearly outside the ambit of this work, but perhaps enough has been said to justify the conclusion that the continued use of these concepts only helps judges to avoid articulating the real premises of their decisions.

The parallel study of tort and delict can support further propositions which are equally applicable to the law of obligations in general.

Thus, it can help dispel the erroneous but widely held belief that the existence of a code 'enables the legal profession to discover more easily what the law is on a given point'.[10] A simple glance at the abundant case-law and the importance attached to it by the legal profession will prove the fallacy of such a belief. Of course, one could say that this was inevitable given the extreme brevity of the French Civil Code in the area of the law of delict; yet it is just as true for the law of contract, which receives from all the civilian codes far greater attention. The abundant and often innovating case-law provides there, too, clear evidence of judicial creativity and belies the argument commonly advanced against codification, namely, that it 'restricts the natural development of the law'. The 'discovery' of article 1384 1 CC and the analogous expansion of article 1121 ('stipulation pour autrui') are obvious examples. Indeed, as has already been remarked, the French courts have disturbed to such an extent the balance between articles 1119 and 1120 of the Code that they have made the recognition of third party rights in contract the norm rather than the exception. Thus, yet another argument in favour of codification, *viz.*, that it encourages the 'planned'[11] development of the law, is put in doubt since neither articles 1121 CC nor article 1384 were conceived by the French legislator in the way that they are now applied by the legal profession. Thus the case-law built on article 1384 CC has come to resemble a painting by Seurat: the various legal rules developed by the courts are but points on a large canvas and one must stand back a few steps in order to detect, appreciate and also criticise the picture that emerges.

One final point must be made. The structure and general principles adopted by a code often have great bearing on the way a particular problem is tackled. We have noted, for example, the French tendency to focus on *damnum* rather than *iniuria*. Another factor, which, though it lies outside the province of the law of tort has, nevertheless, had a great bearing on its development, is the doctrine of consideration. We have on several occasions noted how this accounts for the English tendency to force into the law of tort factual situations which are akin to contract. Liability for negligent statements is an obvious example. The reverse tendency can be found in the Civil law. The wording of certain civilian provisions dealing with delictual liability was such that it made their use prohibitive to plaintiffs. Until the burden of proof was reversed in favour of the plaintiff, German law used to treat problems arising from defective products under the general rubric of contract; the wording of paragraph 823 1 BGB still makes contract the most appropriate basis for liability for negligent statements; and paragraph 831 BGB has obliged German courts and scholars to shift tortious situations into the law of contract. All in all, therefore, a Common lawyer must be prepared to trace some of his tort rules in different parts of the civil codes. This presupposes a general knowledge of the conceptual structure of the foreign system. But once this has been mastered and the 'equivalent law' has been discovered, then, more often than not, it will be found to display an intriguing similarity to his own law. More imporantly, however, it will be seen to be subject to similar stresses as it struggles to supply solutions to problems which were unthinkable only the day before yesterday.

NOTES

1. The *Lex Aquilia* and its relation to earlier legislation

1. *D* 9,2,1,1. (Henceforth references to *D* 9,2 will appear as h.t. followed by the appropriate numbers.)

2. H.t. 27, 22, 23.

3. *Ad. J.* 4,3,15. See also the Scholiast on *B.* 60,3,1. (Heimbach 5.263). The secession referred to is the third and last followed by the passing of the *lex Hortensia* which made plebiscites binding on patricians and plebs alike.

4. *D* 1,2,2,8.

5. Honoré, 7 *Irish Jurist* N.S. (1972), 138, 147.

6. For example: J.A.C. Thomas, *Textbook of Roman Law* (1976), 363 (with the latest bibliography); A.Watson, *The Law of Obligations in the Later Roman Republic* (1965), 234; Beinart, *Butterworth's South African Law Review* (1956), 70 *et seq*. Cf. W.M. Gordon, *Acta Juridica* (1976), 315.

7. Honoré 7 *Irish Jurist* N.S. (1972), 148–9. The *lex Silia* is another such enactment meant to protect moneylenders and creditors in an age of inflation. See C. St. Tomulescu, 'Origin of the Legis Actio Per Condictionem', 4 *Irish Jurist* N.S. (1969), 180, 186. Others, however, have seen the *lex* as a poor man's statute. Thus, Giffard, nos. 358 and 365, note 2. Cf. J.M. Kelly in 80 *L.Q.R.* (1964), 73, 82, who regards the *lex* as a 'humanising statute'. It should be noted, however, that in his article Honoré is particularly concerned to explain chapter *three* of the *lex* and it is therefore likely that chapters one and two were either enacted at an earlier date than chapter three, or had some forerunner of which the existing chapters one and two are successors. The historical record, however, does not provide any direct evidence of such previous statutes unless h.t. 1 is to be taken as referring to them.

8. For the meaning of 'derogavit' see *D* 50,16,102.

9. *Nat. hist.* 18,3,12.

10. *D* 19,5,14,3.

11. *G.* 4,11.

12. *Nat. hist.* 17,1,7.

13. *D* 47,7. See also *D* 12,2,28,6; 43,24,19.

14. *D* 47,9,9. According to Cicero, *De Legibus* II, 24,6, the Twelve Tables prohibited, presumably on grounds of safety, the building of funeral pyres nearer than sixty feet to another person's building without the landowner's consent.

15. *G.* 3,223; *Coll.* 2,5,5; *J.* 4,4,7.

16. Festus, 265, says 'Rupitias (in) XII significat damnum dederit', and 322, 'Sarcito in XII Ser. Sulpicius ait significare damnum solvito, praestato'. The words 'rupitias' and 'solvito' have been put together to form the core of a provision of the Twelve

Tables, imposing a general liability to make good damage. But it is by no means certain that 'rupitias' is not merely a ghost-word; and for the generality of the provision there is no evidence whatever. R.F. Girard, *Manuel élémentaire de droit romain*, 8th edn (1929),440–1.

17. Daube, 52 *L.Q.R.* (1936), 267. Cf. *Studi Solazzi* (1948), 156.
18. Pringsheim, *Mélanges Lévy-Bruhl* (1959), 232, 234.
19. H.t. 27,16.
20. E.g. T. Mommsen, *Römisches Strafrecht* (1899), 841, n. 6.
21. Still, D 2,14,7,13 does, apparently, refer to the *actio incensarum aedium* as still existing in the classical period.
22. Nor could he have used this term as far as the Twelve Tables are concerned for, constitutionally, they were created by supra-national machinery and could thus not be repealed by ordinary legislative process.
23. H.t. 2 pr.; G. 3,210; J. 4,3 pr. Kelly, 80 *L.Q.R.* (1964), 73, 76–7, has argued that 'the words *alienum alienamve* are not, in the original sense of the *lex*, adjectives qualifying slaves and quadrupeds; but either those very words, or words like them, stood in the first chapter to mean "persons *alieni iuris*", and thus included free sons and daughters'. Watson, however, (*The Law of Obligations*, 246, n. 7) disagrees. See also *infra* para. 2 (c). Cf. Pugsley, 85 *L.Q.R.* (1969), 50.
24. H.t. 2,2. Wild animals and dogs were dealt with under the third chapter, h.t. 29,6; G. 3,217; J. 4,3,1.
25. H.t. 2,1.
26. H.t. 23,3. 5–7; G. 3,214; J. 4,3,9; 4,6,19.
27. G. 4,9.
28. Buckland, *Text-book*, 586.
29. J. 4,3,9; 4,6,19.
30. E. Rabel, in Franz von Holtzendorff and Josef Kohler, *Enzyklopädie der Rechtswissenschaft*, I, 456, n. 2.
31. Daube, 52, *L.Q.R.* (1936), 259.
32. J.B. Thayer, *Lex Aquilia; On Gifts between Husband and Wife* (1929), p. 68.
33. J. 4,6,19.
34. The list includes: MacCormack in 5 *Irish Jurist* N.S. (1970), 164 and in 41 *S.D.H.I.* (1975), 1; Iliffe, 5 *Rev.int.dr.ant.* (1958), 503; Kelly, 80 *L.Q.R.* (1964), 73; Pugsley, 85 *L.Q.R.* (1969), 50; Honoré, 7 *Irish Jurist* N.S. (1972), 138. Continental lawyers on the other hand have, with few exceptions, taken the view that at the time of its enactment and during the classical period the third chapter of the *lex* provided a remedy where a slave or animal was wounded or an inanimate object destroyed or damaged. For extensive references see MacCormack, 5 *Irish Jurist* N.S. (1970), 1, note 2.
35. H.t. 27,5.
36. Pernice, pp. 14 and 240.
37. H.F. Jolowicz, 38 *L.Q.R.* (1922), 220. Jolowicz rejected *only* the words 'praeter...occisos'.
38. O.Lenel, *Z.S.S.* (1922), 43, 577.
39. Grueber, 265; F. Schulz, *Classical Roman Law* (1951), 588, 590; Jolowicz and Nicholas, 275–6 and n. 8. This view has always prevailed on the Continent. Thus, Kaser, *R.P.R.*, 620; D. Medicus, *Id quod interest* (1962), 238 *et seq.*
40. H.t. 27,5;29,8.

41. G. 3, 218; h.t. 29,8; J. 4, 3,14,15.
42. Lenel, *Z.S.S.* (1922), 43, 577, and his view is apparently shared by Schulz, *Classical Roman Law*, 590 and, more recently, de Robertis, 32 *S.D.H.I.* (1966), 114.
43. Jolowicz, 38 *L.Q.R.* (1922), 220 at 224. As Professor Watson has pointed out (8 *Rev.int.dr.ant.* (1961), 456): 'l'économie de n'importe quel pays ne pourrait supporter une telle règle qui voudrait dire que si quelqu'un cause un faible dommage à une pierre d'un bâtiment, il serait tenu de payer la valeur du bâtiment; ou si quelqu'un traverse un champ de blé, en renversant quelques brins, la valeur du champ'.
44. Pernice, p. 240.
45. Monro, pp. 36–7.
46. Monro, p. 37.
47. Jolowicz, 38 *L.Q.R.* (1922), 229–30.
48. By Sir John Miles.
49. Daube, 52 *L.Q.R.* (1936), 253.
50. J. 4,3,15; cf. also G. 3,218.
51. However, Gaius, 3,218, uses the word 'fuerit', which, if correct, would throw the calculation back into the past. Indeed, h.t. 29,8 actually uses the word 'fuit'. It becomes a question whether 'erit' or 'fuit' is a copyist's slip. Monier, II, p. 57, n. 2, thinks 'fuit' is the original.
52. So, according to Iliffe (5 *Rev.int.dr.ant.* (1958), 493 n. 1), it is more in accordance with Daube's theory to translate 'diebus triginta proximis' in the *Digest* text as the 'previous thirty days'. It has been observed however, that none of the actual cases dealt with in the *Digest* title on the *lex* is made to turn on the thirty days. A. Bernard in *Rev.hist.dr.fr. et é.* (1937), 450.
53. Apud G. 3,218; J. 4,3,15.
54. Watson *The Law of Obligations*, 234.
55. Kelly, 80 *L.Q.R.* (1964), 78 and n. 22.
56. Iliffe, 5 *Rev.int.dr.ant.* (1958), 493.
57. MacCormack, 5 *Irish Jurist* N.S. (1970), 164.
58. Iliffe, 5 *Rev.int.dr.ant.* (1958), 504–5. The same is true of inanimate things, though in this latter case the thirty day rule also provided the opportunity of discovering whether the damage got 'worse or better to the point of there being no damnum at all'.
59. J.M. Kelly in *Studi Volterra* (6 vols., 1971) I, 235 but cf. the views advanced in 80 *L.Q.R.* (1964), 78.
60. Pugsley, 36 *Tijd* (1968), 371, 383–4.
61. Jolowicz and Nicholas, 276, n. 8.
62. Honoré, 7 *Irish Jurist* N.S. (1972), 138.
63. Lenel, *Z.S.S.* (1922), 43, 577. It will be remembered that Jolowicz, 38 *L.Q.R.* (1922), 220 had not rejected the words as spurious, though, on the other hand, he had interpreted the chapter in a very narrow way.
64. Honoré, *Gaius*, xiv *et seq.* – unlike 'cavetur ut' which 'gives the text of the enactment in words which may or may not closely follow the text'. 7 *Irish Jurist* (1972), 139.
65. Professor Lawson's doubts (given above) as to the use of the genitive 'ceterarum

rerum' do not convince Honoré, who treats the usage as an archaism. *Ibid.*, 144-5.

66. Watson, *The Law of Obligations*, 282, dates the edict at about 200 B.C.

67. *Ibid.*, 145. In a nutshell, therefore, Honoré's thesis rejects Daube's limited view of the original scope of the *lex* but, apparently, leaves untouched his interpretation of the thirty day rule. It is unclear, however, to what extent this 'separation' is possible.

68. According to XII T., for example, the penalty for *os fractum* was 300 asses if the victim was a freeman; 150, if he was a slave.

69. H.t. 7 pr.

70. Though *Coll.* 2,4,1 refuses a claim for medical expenses incurred in having a slave cured.

71. On the whole matter see R. Feenstra, in *Etudes d'histoire du droit privé offertes à Pierre Petot* (1959), pp. 157-71, reprinted in *Fata Iuri Romani* (1974) pp. 223 *et seq.*; Feenstra, *Acta Juridica* (1972), 227 *et seq.* and, more recently, *Essays in Commemoration of the Sixth Lustrum of the Institute for Legal History of the University of Utrecht* (1979), 45 *et seq.* Kelly has argued (80 *L.Q.R.* (1964), 73, 76-7) that the *lex* applied from the beginning to the killing or injury of free children and relies mainly on h.t. 5,3; 6; 7; and D 9,7,4.

72. Ulpian (h.t. 13 pr.) suggests an *actio utilis* on the analogy of the *lex*, but the text would appear to be interpolated.

73. *J.* 4,5,1, *D* 9,3,1 pr.

74. *D* 9,3,5,5.

75. However, it is possible that the praetor would have occasionally given an action, on the analogy of the *actio de pauperie*, which lay for medical expenses and loss of earnings where a freeman was injured by an animal; see *D* 9,1,3.

76. On this consult the erudite works of Professor R. Feenstra quoted in note 71 above.

77. The words 'acceptum facere', however, are not entirely clear and Lévy-Bruhl (5 *Rev.int.dr.ant.* (1958), 507) has thus argued that the 'tort' of the adstipulator was not the mere release of the debtor, to the detriment of the principal creditor, but a release following *payment* of the debt to the adstipulator himself. *Contra*, Pugsley, 85 *L.Q.R.* (1969), 50, 71. For chapter two, see also Daube in *Studi Solazzi* (1948), 154.

78. Daube, 52 *L.Q.R.* (1938), 267-8. See also Pringsheim in *Mélanges Lévy-Bruhl* (1959), 233.

79. H.t. 2,1; 23,10. G. 3,216.

80. This follows from h.t. 24; otherwise there would be no point in confessing. Cf. generally, *C.* 3,35,4. *Contra*, Pugsley, 85 *L.Q.R.* (1969), 57-8.

81. It is accepted by Girard, Cuq, and Huvelin but cf. Iliffe, 5 *Rev.int.dr.ant.* (1958), 403, 505; Giffard, 'Aestimatio, taxatio, quod interest dans l'actio legis Aquiliae', *Rev.hist.dr.fr. et é.* (1933), 334 and *Rev.hist.dr.fr. et é.* (1936), 769.

82. Though a similar view has been restated by Max Kaser, *Das altrömische Ius* (1949), 128. For a discussion of the meaning of 'damnas', see Kelly, 80 *L.Q.R.* (1964), 73, but the validity of his views has been doubted by Watson in *The Law of Obligations*, 246, note 7.

83. H.t. 2,1.

84. Pernice, p. 108.
85. Giffard, *Rev.hist.dr.fr. et é.* (1933), 334.
86. Kaser, *Das altrömische Ius*, 132, thinks it was the other way round.
87. Giffard, no. 359, n. 2.
88. Paul, S. 1,19,2.
89. But the passage in Paul applies to all actions with a *lis crescens*. But see D 2,14,7,13.
90. J. 3,27,7.
91. Paul, S. 1,19,2.
92. D 42,2,4.
93. H.t. 23,11.
94. H.t. 25 pr.
95. On the basis of D 11,1,14,1.
96. Monro, p. 87.
97. D 11,1,14 pr.
98. D 11,1,13 pr.
99. For a more extensive discussion of some of the topics discussed in this paragraph see: J.L. Barton in *Daube Noster*, pp. 15–25; MacCormack, 41 *S.D.H.I.* (1975), 30–43; J. Macqueron, 'Le Rôle de la jurisprudence dans les actions en extension de la loi Aquilia', 43 *Annales de la Faculté de Droit d'Aix-en-Provence* (1950), 6–24.
100. H.t. 7,1.
101. H.t. 7,2. For an analogous illustration involving the application of chapter three see h.t. 27,23. See on this Watson, *The Law of Obligations*, 243.
102. H.t. 7,3.
103. H.t. 9 pr.1; 8 pr.
104. H.t. 7,7.
105. H.t. 7,6; 9 pr. 3; 11,1.5; 53; D 19,5,11.
106. H.t. 52,2 and cf. h.t. 7,3; But see h.t. 9,3.
107. G. 3. 217; J. 4,3,13; h.t. 27,5.
108. G. 3. 217; J. 4,3,13; h.t. 27,13 (where Ulpian attributes the extension to the *veteres*. Cf. MacCormack, 41 *S.D.H.I.* (1975), 3–9.
109. It looks very much as though Sabinus was prepared to go a very long way; h.t. 27,21. Perhaps it was Proculus (following Alfenus, 19,5,23) who reintroduced strict interpretation. See h.t. 7,3; D 41,1,55. Pomponius seems to follow Proculus against Sabinus at D 19,5,14,2; but Ulpian at h.t. 27,33 takes a wider view.
110. Daube, 'Nocere and Noxa', 7 *C.L.J.* (1948), 41–2; *Studi Solazzi* (1948), 8, 31.
111. H.t. 27,14–18; 25–8; 30,2.
112. H.t. 27,22. Perhaps the same notion accounts for the solution in h.t. 27,30. See also h.t. 39 pr. 1.
113. H.t. 27, 6–12; *Coll.* 12,7,1–10.
114. G. 3. 219; J. 4,3,16; h.t. 11,5; 27,35; 29,5; 49 pr.
115. (1670) 1 Mod. 24.
116. For further illustrations see R.W.M. Dias, *Acta Juridica* (1958), 209–15.
117. *Scott* v. *Shepherd* (1773), 2 W.Bl. 892.
118. J. 4,3,16.
119. Stock examples are given at h.t. 53; D 47,2,51; 47,8,2,20.
120. G. 3,219.

121. Lenel, *Ed.*, 203, and quite a few classical texts incorporated in the *Digest* do not support this distinction. See, for example, h.t. 7,3; 7,6; 92; 9,3; 11, 1; 27,35; 53. In these cases the injury is *corpori non corpore* and, according to the Justinian classification should give rise to *actiones utiles*; yet the texts talk of actions *in factum*.

122. See generally, Monro, App. IV, pp. 91–6.

123. For what follows see especially Rotondi, II, 444–64; Jolowicz and Nicholas, 512–13.

124. *J.* 4,3,16.

125. See G. 3, 202; D 4,3,7,7; 19,5, 14 pr.; 47,2,50,4.

126. But this is not true of G. 3, 202; nor, probably, of D 19,5,14, 1–2. Cf. Jolowicz and Nicholas, 513 where it is said that 'the connexion between the general *actio in factum* and the *Lex Aquilia* [is] shown by the application to it of the Aquilian rule that damages are doubled on denial of liability'.

127. Buckland, *Text-book*, 589. Rotondi thinks that h.t. 33,1 may have been torn from its context to represent the Byzantine 'general' indirect action (see J.B. Thayer, *Lex Aquilia: On Gifts between Husband and Wife*, p. 103) but in that case no distinction is made between physical and pecuniary damage.

128. There are even 'bridge' cases where it might well be argued that no physical damage has been done, but yet the direct action on the *lex* was allowed (cf. h.t. 27,14.19.20), and others where there was considerable doubt and dispute (h.t. 27, 21; D 19,5,14,2; 41,1,55).

129. D 19,5,11.

130. See D 7,1,13,2.

131. e.g. h.t. 8 pr.; 27,33; 30,3; *J.* 4,3,6.

132. *Coll.* 12,7,7; h.t. 27,9.

133. For a criticism of this view, which, however, seems to neglect the interest which the Byzantines still took, if not in the form, yet in the 'nature' of the various actions, see T.W. Price, 'The Duty of Care in the *Actio Legis Aquiliae*', 66 *S.A.L.J.* (1949), 171, 173–4.

134. B. Windscheid seems to have been of this opinion, *Lehrbuch des Pandektenrechts*, 9th edn by T. Kipp (1906).

135. Beinart in *Studi Arangio-Ruiz* (4 vols., 1953), I, 279 *et seq.* Cf. MacCormack, 41 *S.D.H.I.* (1975), 43–56.

136. H.t. 3–7 pr.

137. H.t. 5.1; G. 3,211; *J.* 4,3,3.

138. Cf. Monier, II, no. 44. Apart from the fact that liability in primitive systems is, invariably, strict it is worth noting that the penalties prescribed under both chapters one and three of the *lex* did not depend upon whether the injury was inflicted intentionally or negligently. This could suggest that originally they were awarded irrespective of any fault. The view expressed in the text, above, is shared by Watson, *The Law of Obligations*, 236; Beinart in *Studi Arangio-Ruiz*, I, 279; and MacCormack in *Daube Noster*, p. 201. More recently, however, MacCormack has argued (in 41 *S.D.H.I.* (1975), I, 56) that it is 'likely that from *the time of the enactment of the lex* iniuria was understood by the jurists as expressing a requirement of fault' (italics supplied).

139. Though we must not speak of *damnum corpori datum*: Daube in *Studi Solazzi*, 18.

140. *Stanley v. Powell* [1891] 1 Q.B. 86; see on this case Salmond (10th edn), **339**;

Pollock, The Law of Torts, 14th edn by P.A. Landon, 47, 114, 140; J.H. Wigmore, *Harvard Essays on the Law of Torts*, 68.

141. H.t. 5,1.
142. Including honour and property. H.t. 4; 5 pr.; 30 pr.; 45,4;52,1; *Coll.* 7,3,2; *D* 48,8,9; *J.* 4,3,2. See also *D* 43, 16, 1, 27 for the general rule.
143. H.t. 29,7; *D* 18,6,14(13);47,10,13,1.
144. H.t. 5,3; 6; 7 pr.; 7,4; 27,29; 29 pr. 1; 39 pr. 1; *D* 11,5,2; 19,2,13,4.
145. H.t. 29,3; 49,1; *D* 43,24,7,4; 19,5,14 pr.; 47,9,3,7.
146. G. 3,211.
147. In this sense, Beinart in *Studi Arangio-Ruiz*, 1,285; Dias, *Acta Juridica* (1958), 215.
148. Beinart in *Studi Arangio-Ruiz*, 1,284.
149. G. Williams, 'Defence of Necessity', 6 *Cur.Leg.Prob.* (1953), 216, 224.
150. *D* 43,24,7,4.
151. Art. 449 § 1:
    Harm caused in circumstances of extreme necessity must be made good by the person who occasioned it. Taking into account the conditions in which such harm was caused, the court may impose a duty to make it good on a third party in whose interests the person causing the harm was acting, or may wholly or partly discharge from liability both the third party and the person causing the harm.
152. H.t. 49,1. See also h.t. 29,3; 47,9,3,7.
153. [1912] 1 K.B. 496.
154. Paras. 228, 904 (which contain different requirements); see also OR art. 52, and Austrian CC 1306a. On all this see J. Limpens, *Encyclopedia*, ch. 2 nos. 170 *et seq.*
155. Mazeaud, *Traité théorique et pratique de la responsabilité civile délictuelle et contractuelle*, nos. 492–5 (4th edn). But cf. now the text of the 6th edn. The leading monograph on the subject is R. Pallard's *L'Exception de necessité en droit civile* (1949). See also R. Savatier, 'L'État de nécessité et la responsabilité civile extracontractuelle', in *Etudes de droit civil à la mémoire de Henri Capitant* (1939), pp. 729 *et seq.*
156. Lalou, no. 306.
157. Planiol et Ripert (-Esmein), no. 567.
158. Cf. *Vincent* v. *Lake Erie Transportation Co.*, 109 Minn. 456. Fleming, 92–6.
159. F.H. Bohlen, 'Incomplete Privilege', 39 *Harv.L.Rev.* (1926), 307.
160. Winfield and Jolowicz, 680–2.
161. The concept has been repeatedly and thoroughly analysed by MacCormack in *Daube Noster*, p. 201; in 38 *S.D.H.I.* (1972), 123 (both with extensive bibliographical references) and in 41 *S.D.H.I.* (1975), 1, 43; see also 'Culpa in eligendo', 18 *Rev.int.dr.ant.* (1971), 525 and B. Perrin, 'Le Caractère subjectif de l'iniuria aquilienne', *Studi de Francisci* (4 vols., 1956), IV, 265.
162. G. 3, 211. Indeed, Gaius (3,211) defined *iniuria* in terms of *dolo aut culpa*. In such cases where *culpa* is opposed to *dolus* it means carelessness. By itself, however, the term should be taken to mean 'blame, fault'.
163. E.g. Monier, 11, no. 44 1°.
164. E.g. h.t. 30,3.
165. Heimbach, 272.
166. *J.* 4,6, 19.
167. E.g. h.t. 29,2.

168. Certainly by Justinian's time.
169. E.g. h.t. 9,4; 28 pr. – 29 pr.; 30,3; 31; *J.* 4,3,4–5.
170. E.g. h.t. 29,3–4; 30,3.
171. H.t. 31; cf. *J.* 4,3,5.
172. H.t. 29,4.
173. H.t. 11 pr.
174. H.t. 52,2.
175. H.t. 52,4.
176. Thayer, *Lex Aquilia*, p. 117.
177. H.t. 7,5. The reference to *equitis culpa* in h.t. 57 may be interpolated, but is probably in line with Labeo's thought.
178. *Fam.* 3,8,6; *Att.* 15,28.
179. 35,33,3.
180. H.t. 52,1.
181. H.t. 52,4.
182. D 50,17,167,1: *Qui iussu iudicis aliquid facit, non videtur dolo malo facere, qui parere necesse habet.*
183. Below, pp. 99–102.
184. *Colloque franco-germano-suisse sur les fondements et les fonctions de la responsabilité civile*, published by the Law Faculty of the University of Basle (1973), p. 155 (italics supplied).
185. The term is here opposed to *dolus*.
186. H.t. 44 pr.
187. H.t. 31, Cf. *J.* 4,3,5.
188. W. Kunkel, 'Exegetische Studien zur Aquilischen Haftung', *Z.S.S.* (1929), 158–87. Buckland replied to this in *Studi Bonfante* (4 vols., 1930), II, 85.
189. Pollock, 350.
190. O.W. Holmes, *The Common Law*, (1911), 108–9.
191. H.t. 31. Or perhaps only to Paul.
192. H.t. 5.2.
193. The case is particularly interesting for it raised for the first time the question of liability of a mentally deranged person sued under article 1384 CC. It could not have been argued under article 1382 CC, for as the law then stood mentally deranged persons were not liable for their torts. See next note.
194. The immunity of madmen and infants, however, causes hardship to the equally innocent victim. In France, since 1968, the immunity of mentally deranged persons has been removed – another concession some would say to a more objective understanding of the notion of fault. But immunity of infants has been retained, regrettably according to some (e.g. Weil, no. 635) who see no reason why the loss should lie with the victim. Clearly policy considerations determine which of two innocent parties will bear the loss and each author is entitled to his views.
195. *Commonwealth* v. *Pierce* (1884), 138 Mass. 165, at p. 176.
196. H.t. 8,1.
197. D 50, 17, 132; *J.* 4,3,7,8.
198. The tone of h.t. 6 seems even more in favour of the subjective view. For a discussion of the relevant cases, see MacCormack in *Daube Noster*, p. 200 and conclusions at p. 219.

199. *D* 19,2,9,5.
200. *Above*, n. 196.
201. The contrary opinions of Kunkel, *Z.S.S.* (1929), 49, 162, Hayman, *Z.S.S.*, 42, 387, and Rotondi, II, 484, n. 3 seem based on *a priori* grounds.
202. H.t. 45,2.
203. H.t. 38 and note.
204. Thayer, *Lex Aquilia*, p. 66.
205. Perhaps h.t. 7,5 is another case of the same kind, since the wrongdoer mistakenly believed that what he was doing was not actionable under the first chapter, even if it was under the third.
206. *Ibid*. Cf. also *D* 47,8,2,20 and BGB para. 231.
207. H.t. 45,5.
208. A plea of inevitable mistake is quite different from a plea of inevitable accident.
209. Weir in P. Catala and J.A. Weir, 37 *Tul.L.Rev.* (1963), 613. For a comparative survey, see Mazeaud and Tunc, I, nos. 441–5.
210. See discussion in chapter 4.
211. MacCormack in *Daube Noster*, p. 202.
212. MacCormack, 38 *S.D.H.I.* (1972), 173.
213. Thus, R. Powell, 4 *Cur.Leg.Prob.* (1951), 197; Dias, *Acta Juridica* (1976), 193.
214. Supporting this view are MacCormack, 41 *S.D.H.I.* (1975), 1, 9 *et seq.* and Pugsley, 38 *Tijd* (1970), 163.
215. Cf. h.t. 11,2 and *Oliver* v. *Mills* 144 Missouri 852 (1925) and for a more detailed discussion of these problems see chapter 3 below.
216. See discussion in paragraph 3 above.
217. For example, h.t. 7,2. MacCormack in 41 *S.D.H.I.* (1975), 16–18 stresses this point and argues that similar reasoning may underly the decisions in *D* 9,2, 9,3 and *D* 47,2,50,4.
218. MacCormack, 41 *S.D.H.I.* (1975), 25. A text in point is h.t. 52,2.
219. For example, h.t. 7,5; 27,8.
220. Buckland and McNair, 378.
221. For example: Albanese, 21 *Annali Palermo* (1950), 147 *et seq.*; Powell, 4 *Cur.Leg.Prob.* (1951), 203 *et seq.*; Beinart, *Butterworth's South African Law Review* (1956), 75; Pugsley, 38 *Tijd* (1970), 163; Dias, *Acta Juridica* (1976), 205; MacCormack, 41 *S.D.H.I.* (1975), 25–30.
222. Heimbach, 319, sch. 7.
223. Pernice, p. 180.
224. Grueber, p. 36.
225. Monro, p. 16.
226. H.t. 11,3.
227. H.t. 51 pr.
228. H.t. 15,1.
229. Buckland and McNair, p. 371.
230. H.t. 9,4; 11 pr.; 28 pr. – 29 pr.; 30,4; 52 pr. See, also, h.t. 52,3; *J.* 4,3,4.
231. *D* 50,17,203.
232. Perhaps sufficient evidence is provided by h.t. 45,3., where it is stated categorically that no action can be brought in a collision until it is ascertained which of the slaves concerned was the active party.

233. Pernice, pp. 58–64.
234. Grueber, p. 228.
235. Monro, p. 14.
236. Buckland and McNair, p. 371.
237. Pernice, p. 60.
238. *Ibid.*
239. Pernice, p. 62.
240. H.t. 9,4.
241. Buckland and McNair, p. 372.
242. (1842) 10 M. & W. 546.
243. [1916] 1 A.C. 719.
244. H.t. 21 pr. 1; 23,3,5,7; 51,2; G. 3,210.
245. H.t. 21,2; J. 4,3,10. This covered, *inter alia*, loss of earnings and of earning capacity (D 9,1,3); medical expenses (D 9,1,3 and h.t. 27,17); but compensation for mental pain and suffering was not allowed: h.t. 33 pr.
246. P. 7 above.
247. H.t. 23 pr. 2; G. 3,212.
248. For some difficult problems arising out of the killing of slaves instituted as heirs, see h.t. 15,1 end; 16; 23,1–2; 36,1. They turn mainly on peculiarities of the law of succession. See Rodger, 'Damages for the Loss of an Inheritance' in *Daube Noster*, p. 289; MacCormack, 41 *S.D.H.I.* (1975), 67 *et seq.*
249. E.g. h.t. 23,4; 40; 41 pr.
250. H.t. 29,3, end.
251. G. 3,212; J. 4,3,10, which expressly attributes it to *interpretatio*.
252. H.t. 22 pr. 1; 55.
253. H.t. 37,1.
254. The line is difficult to explain, but see h.t. 33 pr. and note.
255. H.t. 27,17; 33 pr.; 45,1; *contra Coll.* 2,4,1.
256. H.t. 7 pr.; D 9,1,3.
257. P. 11 above.
258. See h.t. 40; 41 pr.; 42; D 4,3,35; D 47,2,27,2–3; 31 pr.; 32,1.
259. Prussian Code, 1.6, §§ 5–7; French CC art. 1149; German CC § 252; Italian CC art. 1223.
260. H.t. 30, 4. See also h.t. 52 pr.
261. A glance at Grotius' introductory textbook to the municipal Roman-Dutch law – his *Inleiding tot der Hollandsche Rechtsgeleertheyed* (English translation by R.W. Lee, 1926) – can confirm this.
262. J.H. Merryman, *The Civil Law Tradition* (1969), 68. Cf. J.A. Weir, 'Abstraction in the Law of Torts', *City of London Law Review* (1974), 15.
263. The term is used for its evocative quality. The Romans and modern civilians call them praedial servitudes, to distinguish them from personal servitudes such as usufruct or *usus*, which were in effect life interests.
264. Since the prevailing tendency in France is to explain the liability in terms of an abuse of rights, it seems almost ripe for transfer to the law of obligations; yet it is still dealt with in the law of property.
265. See e.g. Voet, *Compendium Juris*, ad D 9,2, *moribus.*
266. Rotondi, II, 465.

267. The technical term is *in complexu*.
268. Book II, Ch. XVII, sect. I. Domat, *Les Lois civiles dans leur ordre naturel*, tit. VIII, no. 4 (1689), expresses himself in equally wide terms.
269. Cf. the suggestive title of his work: *Larva legis Aquiliae detracta actioni de damno dato receptae in foro Germanorum* (1703).

2 Fixing the boundaries of tortious liability

1. Notable amongst them is Leon Green in 38 *Texas L.Rev.* (1959) 1, 2 (from which the quote in the text is taken); *idem.* 41 *Texas L.Rev.* (1962) 42, 45. For a similar approach see Fleming, 31 *Can. Bar Rev.* (1953), 471; Linden, 47 *Can. Bar Rev.* (1969), 545; cf. Millner's more cautious approach in 26 *Cur.Leg.Prob.* (1973), 260, 280.
2. Most recently by C.R. Symmons in his useful discussion of a number of leading cases decided in the 1960s and early 1970s in 34 *M.L.R.* (1971), 394, 528. See also M.D.A. Freeman, 'Standards of Adjudication, Judicial Law-Making and Prospective Overruling', 26 *Cur.Leg.Prob.* (1973), 166 and, more broadly, Neil MacCormick, *Legal Reasoning and Legal Theory* (1978) passim and B. Rudden's comments in 24 *Juridical Review* N.S. (1979), 193–201.
3. Dennis Lloyd, *Public Policy* (1953), xi–xii.
4. *Ibid.*
5. This is how Winfield, rather hesitantly, defined public policy in 'Public Policy in the English Common Law', 42 *Harv.L.Rev.* (1928), 76, 92.
6. The literature on this subject is immense. The following may be particularly useful for what follows: Lord Devlin, 'Judges and Lawmakers', 39 *M.L.R.* (1976), 1; A. Tunc. 'Methodology of the Civil Law', 50 *Tul.L.Rev.* (1976), 459; J.L. Goutal, 'Characteristics of Judicial Style in France, Britain and the U.S.A.', 24 *A.J.Comp.L.* (1976), 43; F.H. Lawson, 'Comparative Judicial Style', 25 *A.J. Comp.L.* (1977), 364; B. Rudden, 'Courts and Codes in England, France and Soviet Russia', 48 *Tul.L.Rev.* (1974), 1010; A. Touffait and A. Tunc, 'Pour une motivation plus explicite des décisions de justice notamment de celles de la Cour de cassation', *Rev.trim.dr.civ.* (1974), 487 (an article of seminal importance); P. Perrot, 'Le Rôle du juge dans la société moderne', *G.P.* 1977,1.91; J. Déprez, 'A Propos du Rapport annuel de la Cour de cassation', *Rev.trim.dr.civ.* (1978), 504.
7. J.G. Fleming, 31 *Can. Bar Rev.* (1953), 471, 497–8. This was acknowledged by M. Bellet, the first President of the Cour de cassation in a speech delivered on 19 December 1979 to the Société de Législation Comparée and published in *Rev.int.dr.comp.* (1980), 293.
8. The 'administrative factor', as explained and illustrated in the text above, appears to have played a very limited role in the French law of *responsabilité civile*, its most obvious applications to be found in the decisions of the Chambre Criminelle of the Cour de cassation when deciding on the *recevabilité de constitution de partie civile* in a criminal action. Further illustrations can be found in decisions limiting the circle of persons who can claim *dommage moral par ricochet*, especially whenever this appears a priori to be negligible. For another illustration, see the text at the end of chapter 3 and the revealing comments of M. le conseiller Ponsard in his Rapport in the decision of the Assemblée Plénière of 12 janv. 1979, *J.C.P.* 1980, 2.19335.
9. MacCormick, *Legal Reasoning* pp. 129 *et seq*. In brief, MacCormick's thesis is that

in complicated cases 'the adduction of the principle ...although necessary to is not sufficient for a complete justification of the decision. The ruling which directly governs the case must be tested by *consequentialist* argument as well as by the argument from "coherence"...' *ibid.* p. 250 (italics supplied).

10. (1865), 3. H. & C. 774 (Court of Exchequer); (1866), L.R.1. Ex. 265 (Court of Exchequer Chamber); (1868), L.R.3 H.L. 330 (House of Lords).

11. See, for example, Lindley L.J. in *Green* v. *Chelsea Waterworks Co.* (1894) 70 L.T. 547 at 549 and cf. G.H.L. Fridman, 'The Rise and Fall of *Rylands* v. *Fletcher*', 34 *Can. Bar Rev.* (1956), 810.

12. Atiyah, p. 78. Cf. J. Harvard, 'Reasonable Foresight of Nervous Shock', 19 *M.L.R.* (1956),478.

13. Exemplified in this country by *Dulieu* v. *White* [1901] 2 Q.B. 669 and other authorities given in Clerk and Lindsell on Torts, 14th edn, § 872. For American authorities see Prosser, pp. 327 *et seq.* See also F.F. Stone in 48 *Tul.L.Rev.* (1974), 782.

14. The Germans, fully conscious of the nature of the problem, have opted for an *apparently* mechanical application of the adequate cause theory. There is little doubt, however, that it is applied in a normative and not factual manner. On this, see E. von Hippel, NJW 1965, 1890, 1891–2; Huber, in *Festschrift E. Wahl*, 301, 318.

15. [1943] A.C. 92. In German law, as indeed in the English law, mere mental distress is not compensatable; the plaintiff must show physical or psychological manifestations of his injury. *BGHZ*, 56, 163.

16. *Hinz* v. *Berry* [1970] 2 Q.B. 40, 42 (per Lord Denning M.R.).

17. For a strong criticism of the English law see Atiyah, 75 *et seq.* In the recent case of *McLoughin* v. *O'Brian* [1981] 2 W.L.R. 1014 the limitation of liability was justified, inter alia, by open reference to policy.

18. (1842) 10 M. & W. 109, and in *Cattle* v. *Stockton Waterworks Co.* (1875) L.R. 10 Q.B. 453, the first modern case of pure economic loss.

19. [1932] A.C. 562, 577.

20. [1966] 1 Q.B. 569, 577.

21. *Ibid.*

22. [1973] 1 Q.B. 27. The same fears were voiced by Lord Kissen in the factually similar Scottish case of *Dynamo Ltd* v. *Holland and Hannen and Cubitts (Scotland) Ltd* 1971 S.C. 257 at 263.

23. *Ibid.* at pp. 38–9. Lawton L.J., on the other hand, while admitting that policy accounted for the different treatment of economic loss, was unwilling to elaborate further on the subject. *Ibid.* p. 49. See also Geoffrey Lane J. in *Electrochrome* v. *Welsh Plastics* [1968] 2 All E.R. 205 at 208. In *Hedley Byrne and Co. Ltd* v. *Heller and Partners, Ltd* [1964] A.C. 465 some of the law lords attributed the different treatment accorded to negligent acts and negligent words to the greater propensity of the latter to provoke unlimited litigation. Thus Lord Pearce, at p. 534 and Lord Reid at pp. 482–3. Others, however, could see no logic in the distinction. So, for example, Lord Devlin at p. 517. Liability for negligent mis-statements is discussed more fully in the next paragraph of this chapter.

24. BGH NJW 1976, 1740 and Emmerich, *JuS* 1977, 120. Similarly, NJW 1975, 221. French law, on the other hand, has never experienced any real difficulty with this

type of situation. For Canadian hesitations, see Harvey, 50 *Can. Bar Rev.* (1972), 580; Stevens, 23 *U.T.L.J.* (1973), 431; Smith, 9 U.B.C.L.Rev. (1974), 213.

25. BGH NJW 1977, 2208.

26. The BGH also took the view that the warning (about possible danger to submerged cables with all its consequences) was given *after* the contract was concluded and was, hence, ineffectual (I am grateful to my former student Mr Axel Tiemann for drawing my attention to this point and also to the fact that the case is more fully reported in BB 1977, 1419 – B.S.M.).

27. [1969] 1 A.C. 191.

28. [1965] 2 W.L.R. 300, 317 (per Lawton J.); [1967] 1 Q.B. 443, 504 (per Lord Denning M.R.); [1969] 1 A.C. 191, 251 (per Lord Morris).

29. [1965] 2 W.L.R. 300, 317; [1967] 1 Q.B. 443, 503 (per Lord Denning M.R.); 519 (per Salmon L.J.); [1969] 1 A.C. 191, 230 (per Lord Reid); 248 (per Lord Morris). In *BGHZ* 62, 54; *JZ* 1974, 548, the German Supreme Court relied on this 'consequentialist' type of argument to dismiss the plaintiff's claim against a medical expert commissioned by the court. For further details see: B.S. Markesinis and Ch. von Bar, *Richterliche Rechtspolitik im Haftungsrecht* (1981).

30. The plaintiff was unrepresented on the appeal but his solicitor (instructed before the appeal came on for hearing) tendered to the court a written brief setting out the arguments against barristers' immunity.

31. J.A. Weir, 'Abstraction in the Law of Torts', *City of London Law Review* (Oct. 1974), 15, 20.

32. Th. Zeldin, *France 1848–1945*, 1 (1973), 307. (This erudite work contains at pp. 285–314 a brief but most interesting description of the social and economic background of the time.) Adultery even became the subject of 'serious' monographs, e.g. P. Vernon, *Paris vicieux: le guide de l'adultère* (1883); E. Cademartori, *L'Adultère à Marseille* (1886)!

33. Ch. Crim. 28 fév. 1930, D.P. 1930,1.49 and Note Voirin; Paris, 5 juin 1923, G.P. 1923,2.417; Montpellier, 24 juin 1924, D.P. 1924,2.145 Note Savatier; Paris, 2 juin 1928, motifs, S. 1928,2.125 etc.

34. Thus Josserand, D.H. 1932,1.45; M. Nast. 'Vers l'union libre, ou le crépuscule du marriage légal', D.H. 1938,1.37. As these dramatic titles suggest, for many the phenomenon had reached cataclysmic proportions. The alarmists put the figure of *faux ménages* at 40 per cent of the population whereas a study conducted by the Church put the figure at 16–29 per cent (Le Bras, *Revue d'histoire de l'Eglise de France* (1945, 328 *et seq.*). The most recent sociological study by R. Théry, 'Le Concubinage en France', *Rev.trim.dr.civ.* (1960), 33 *et seq.*, puts the figure at a much more modest 3 per cent. Yet its author admits that since his figure is based on information supplied at the population census of 1954 it may err on the optimistic side.

35. Théry, *Rev.trim.dr.civ.* (1960) at p. 48.

36. Ch. Civ. 27 juil. 1937, S. 1938,1.321 and Note Marty; D. 1938,1.5 and Note Savatier. The view that the words 'juridiquement protégé' were really another way of saying that the *intérêt* must be *légitime* (Ch. Civ. 26 janv. 1954, D. 1954,217 and Note Levasseur) was never widely accepted. Cf. Ch. von Bar, 42 *Rabels Z.* (1978), 87, 99.

37. Cass. 27 fév. 1970, D. 1970,201. The English Fatal Accidents Act 1976 still refuses to recognise a mistress as a 'dependent in law'. But the woman's children

with the deceased may have a claim for the loss of dependency; and often the compensation will be generous. See: *K.* v. *J.M.P.Co.* [1976] Q.B.85

38. [1969] 1 A.C. 191.
39. *British Railways Board* v. *Herrington* [1972] A.C. 877, 897. For the U.S.A. see Ursin, 22 *U.C.L.A.L.Rev.* (1975), 820.
40. [1972] A.C. at p. 929.
41. A selection from the vast literature on the subject can be found in Mazeaud and Tunc, nos. 547 *et seq.*, especially notes 547 (1) and 593 (2). The pioneering French works are L. Josserand's *De l'Esprit des droits et de leur relativité (théorie dite de l'abus des droits)*, 2nd edn (1933) and *Cours de droit civil positif français* (1933). For an eloquent opposition see Ripert, *La Règle morale*, esp. 157 *et seq.* For a stimulating comparative study see P. Catala and J.A. Weir, 38 *Tul.L.Rev.* (1964), 221 *et seq.* See also Gutteridge, 5 *C.L.J.* (1933), 22–45; Scholtens, 'Abuse of Rights', 75 *S.A.L.J.* (1958), 39; Rotondi, *Inchieste di Diritto Comparato*, VII, Bolgar, 35 *Louisiana L.Rev.* (1975), 1015 and, generally, C.K. Allen, *Legal Duties* (1931), 95–118.
42. *Mayor of Bradford* v. *Pickles* [1895] A.C. 587; *Allen* v. *Flood* [1898] A.C. 1. For the Roman law see Buckland and McNair, p. 98 ('we get more than once the proposition that one who is exercising his right cannot be committing a wrong'). From the seventeenth century onwards Scottish law apparently accepted the doctrine of abuse of rights within its law of real property, but in *Bradford* v. *Pickles* Lord Watson put and end to this when he agreed with his English colleagues that Scots law was like English law (at p. 598). For further discussion see B.W. Napier in Rotondi, *Inchieste di Diritto Comparato*, 269–71.
43. Buckland and McNair, pp. 73–6; D 50,17,55; 151,155,1.
44. D 6,1,38.
45. D 39,3,1,12. For another, doubtful, case, see h.t. 39 pr.1.
46. Scholtens, 75 *S.A.L.J.* (1958). In 1577 the Parlement of Aix condemned a wool-carder for singing continuously in order to annoy his neighbour (Mazeaud and Tunc, no. 556).
47. D.P. 1856,2.9.
48. Para. 226 BGB: followed by Mexican CC art. 1912.
49. [1895] A.C. 587 at 601. See, also, Fridman, 'Motive in the English Law of Nuisance', 40 *Virginia L.Rev.* (1954), 503.
50. See also OR para. 41 ii.
51. 'Chacun est tenu d'exercer ses droits et d'exécuter ses obligations selon les règles de la bonne foi.' 'L'abus manifeste d'un droit n'est pas protégé par la loi.'
52. *Consorts Forissier c. Chaverot*, D.P. 1902,1.454; S. 1903,1.11.
53. Josserand, II, nos. 428–37; *De l'Esprit des droits et de leur relativité*, passim.
54. Such rights, however, are, if anything, steadily diminishing. The doctrine, equally, does not apply to *actes de pure tolérance* (approximately our 'licences').
55. Article 5 of the 1961 Code states that the exercise of a civil right will not be protected where it is 'contrary to its destination in a socialist society during a period of communist edification'. The Italian Civil Code contains no reference to the abuse of rights. The omission must be deliberate.
56. Morin, 'Quelques observations critiques sur le concept d'abus de droit', in *Etudes Lambert*, 11 (1938), 467–74.
57. For a good summary see Planiol et Ripert, 1, nos. 573 *et seq.*; J. Ghestin and G.

Goubeaux, *Traité de droit civil*, I (1977), 575 *et seq*; Mazeaud and Tunc, nos.
582–91. Reading these paragraphs one is inclined to agree with Gutteridge, 5
C.L.J. (1946), 35, that 'the English lawyer will find that many matters which we
regard as separate wrongs have been swept up by the French Courts into the net
of abuse of rights'. See also R.W.M. Dias and B.S. Markesinis, *The English Law
of Torts: A Comparative Introduction* (1976), pp. 152–9.

58. [1895] A.C. 587.
59. [1898] A.C. 1.
60. Thus, h.t. 39, and 45,4 and *D* 19,5,14 pr. will certainly yield to this analysis.
61. But not the only one. French law, for example, does not make the distinction
   which English law has adopted (in theory though not always in practice) between
   material damage to the plaintiff's property and interference with his enjoyment
   or use of land. But there are also many similarities. For example the 'give and
   take' rule is expressed by A. Colin and H. Capitant, *Cours élémentaire de droit civil
   français* (1939), 770 in a manner strongly reminiscent of Thesiger L.J.'s famous
   dictum in *Sturges* v. *Bridgman* (1879) 11. Ch. D. 852 at 865. See also text below.
62. Weir in Catala and Weir, 38 *Tul.L.Rev.* (1964), 238.
63. [1893] 1 Ch. 316.
64. Amiens 7 fév. 1912, 1913 D. 2.177 at 179. For what is probably the leading case
   see Ch. Req. 3 août 1915, S. 1930, 1.300.
65. Cass. 29 mai 1937, D.H. 1937, S. 1937, 1.244; Cass. 4 fév. 1971, *J.C.P.* 1971,
   16781 and Note Lindon; Durry, *Rev.trim.dr.civ.* (1971), 857; Cass. 18 juil. 1972,
   J.C.P. 1972, 17203, Rapport Fabre; Durry, *Rev.trim.dr.civ.* (1974), 609 with
   further references.
66. (1866) L.R. 1 Ex. 265; (1868) L.R.3 H.L. 330.
67. Green, 38 *Texas L.Rev.* (1959), 1,5. F.V. Harper and Fleming James, *The Law of
   Torts*, II (1956) § 14.3, though putting forward a slightly different view, also
   explain the case by reference to its economic and political environment.
   Similarly, Bohlen in *Studies in the Law of Torts* (1926), 359. This kind of
   interpretation, however, is rejected by Roscoe Pound in 53 *Harv.L.Rev.* (1940),
   365, 383–4 and Prosser in his *Selected Topics in the Law of Tort* (1953), 138–9. Cf.
   Fridman, 34 *Can. Bar Rev.* (1956), 810, 812.
68. Green, 38 *Texas L.Rev.* (1959), 5. The early milldam cases in the U.S. could,
   arguably, be used to support this. *Shrewsbury* v. *Smith*, 12 Cush. 177 (Mass.
   1853); *Livingston* v. *Adams*, 8 Cow. 175 (N.Y. 1828). This attitude remained
   unaltered even after *Rylands* v. *Fletcher*. Thus, *Losee* v. *Buchanan*, 51 N.Y. 476, 10
   Am. Rep. 623 (1873); *Marshall* v. *Welwood*, 38 N.J.L. 339, 20 Am. Rep. 394
   (1876); *Brown* v. *Collins*, 53 N.H. 442, 16 Am. Rep. 372 (1873). With some
   exceptions (e.g. *Sanderson* v. *Pennsylvania Coal Co.*, 86 Pa. 401, 27 Am. Rep. 711
   (1878); *Ball* v. *Nye*, 1868, 99 Mass. 582) the new doctrine was thus avoided by
   many courts and liability was made to rest on nuisance or negligence. The
   principle, however, is nowadays accepted by a majority of jurisdictions. For
   details see Prosser, 508 *et seq.* and in *Selected Topics in the Law of Torts* (1953), 149 *et
   seq.*
69. Fleming, 432 *et seq.* Leon Green, 'Landowner v. Intruder; Intruder v.
   Landowner. Basis of Responsibility in Tort', 21 *Mich.L.Rev.* (1923), 495.
70. Green, *ibid.*, 508.
71. *Pannett* v. *P. McGuiness & Co. Ltd* [1972] 2 Q.B. 599, 606.

72. L.M. Friedman and J. Ladinsky, 67 *Col.L.Rev.* (1967), 50.

73. (1837) 3 M. & W. 1; 7 L.J. Ex. 42.

74. Thus, Winfield and Jolowicz; J. Munkman, *Employer's Liability at Common Law*, 7th edn (1971), 7. *Contra*, F.H. Newark, 'Bad Law', 17 *N.I.L.Q.* (1966) 469, 477.

75. 45 Mass. (4 Met.) 49 (1842). For a fuller discussion of this important case see Friedman and Ladinsky, 67 *Col.L.Rev.* (1967), 54 *et seq.*

76. *Bartonshill Coal Co.* v. *Reid* (1858) 3 Macq. 266 (H.L.).

77. For example, Marc Sauzet, 'De la responsabilité des patrons vis-à-vis des ouvriers dans les accidents industriels', *Rev.crit.lég. et jur.* (1883), 596 *et seq.* and 677 *et seq.*

78. (1837) 3 M. & W. 1; 7 L.J. Ex. 42.

79. Rudden, 24 *Juridical Review* N.S. (1979), 198.

80. Munkman, *Employer's Liability*, 6. 'These instances seem to show personal apprehension rather than any principle.' Per Lord Wright in *Radcliffe* v. *Ribble Motor Services Ltd* [1939] A.C. 215 at 239.

81. Roscoe Pound, 'The Economic interpretations and the law of torts', 53 *Harv L. rev.* (1940), 365. See, also, Molloy, in 9 *U.Ch.L.Rev.* (1942), 266.

82. (1850) 5 Ex. 343. This was a tort case under Lord Campbell's Act, 1846. It was later said that 'Lord Abinger planted the doctrine of common employment. Baron Alderson watered it and the Devil gave it increase.'

83. For example, Bramwell B. in *Dynen* v. *Leach* (1857) 26 L.J. (N.S.) Ex. 221.

84. Friedman and Ladinsky, 67 *Col.L.Rev.* (1967), 50, 56.

85. D.P. 70.1.361.

86. S. 1871,1.9. It must be said that it is not clear from the *arrêt* whether the plaintiff was an employee of the defendant's or not. The head-note to the *Sirey* report talks of injury 'à un tiers' but the facts of the case are quite similar to some of the 'boiler-explosion' cases decided a few years later and indisputably dealing with injured employees. And Labbé's case-note is couched in sufficiently wide terms to be able to cover both kinds of situation. The Germanic literature has also noted the importance attached to this type of 'consequentialist' reasoning in order to favour industry. Thus, von Zeiller, *Kommentar zum ABGB* III (1812), 707 (Austria) and, more notably, J. Esser, *Grundlagen und Entwicklung* (1941), 50, 56.

87. First from the Conseil d'Etat, 21 juin 1895, D.P. 1896,3.65 and then the Cour de cassation 16 juin 1896, D.P. 1897,1.433 and Note Saleilles; S. 1897,1.17 and Note Esmein. For the subsequent developments, see chapter 4.

88. D.P. 1930,2.57.

89. K. Renner, *The Institutions of Private Law and their Social Functions* (1949), 238 (Engl. edn with an introduction by O. Kahn-Freund).

90. Lon Fuller, *Anatomy of the Law* (1971), 134.

91. Weir, *Encyclopedia*, nos. 24, 63; *RGZ* 88, 317.

92. Weir, *ibid.* §54.

93. BGH NJW 1976, 1740.

94. According to the Pearson Report, vol. II no.509 'It is estimated that claims on insurers represent about 88 per cent of the total number and about 94 per cent of the total value of all personal injury claims in tort.'

95. In *Davie* v. *New Merton Board Mills* [1959] A.C. 604, 627; *Lister* v. *Romford Ice and Cold Storage Co. Ltd* [1957] A.C. 555, 572.

96. Fleming, 10 *J.S.P.T.L.* (1972–73), 104, 113 (italics supplied). See also *Rowland*

v. *Christian*, 69 Cal. Reptr. 2d. 89,94,443; P. 2d. 561,564, 70 Cal. Reptr. 2d. 97,100 (1968). Among the scholars who have for many years advocated the substitution of the fault principle by the risk/insurance approach is A. Ehrenzweig, 15 *Law & Contemp.Prob.* (1950), 445. See also his 'Negligence Without Fault', 54 *Cal.L.Rev.* (1966), 1422. In this country the case for the risk approach has been made by, amongst others, J.A. Jolowicz, 27 *C.L.J.* (1968), 50.

97. In D. Chron. 1975,83, 86; also, 22 *Archives de philosophie du droit*, 31. For analogous views in Germany see von Bar in 181 AcP (1981), 289.

98. Trolle, *Risiko og Skyld* (1960) (quoted by S. Jørgensen, *Scandinavian Studies in Law* (1963), ed. F. Schmidt. pp. 47–8. For the Swedish Law of 1972 see J. Hellner, 'The New Swedish Tort Liability Act', 22 *A.J.Comp.L.* (1974), 1 at 6–7. For further observations on German law see Markesinis and von Bar, *Richterliche Rechtspolitik*, pp. 43ff.

99. The same is true of French law even though, once again, much of the development of the law can only be understood against the background of insurance. See Ch. Civ. 2 mai 1968, *G.P.* 1968,2.109 and, more generally, A. Tunc, *Encyclopedia*, XI, ch. 1, note 304 and in *J.C.P.* 1966,1.1983. See also ref. in note 97 and, more generally, G. Viney, *Le Déclin de la responsablilité individuelle* (1964).

100. J.A. Jolowicz, 10 *J.S.P.T.L.* (1972–73), 91,98.

101. D. Riley, *Consequential Loss Insurance and Claims*, 4th edn. (1977), §306. A.V. Alexander, 10 *J.S.P.T.L.* (1972–73), 119.

102. But see Lord Denning M.R.'s judgment in *Spartan Steel* v. *Martin & Co. (Contractors), Ltd* [1973] 1 Q.B. 27, 38, and Lawton L.J.'s remarks at p. 48.

103. Atiyah, p. 90. Cf. Millner, 26 *Cur.Leg.Prob.* (1973), 260, 272. In Germany Atiyah's view seems to be shared by G. Hager, 'Haftung bei Störung der Energiezufuhr', *JZ* 1979, 3–58 for he, too, argues that loss insurance may be cheaper to obtain than liability insurance. Professor Kötz, on the other hand, in Zweigert and Kötz, 273, believes that it would be more effective (and cheaper?) to place the risk on the building contractor. Neither of these authors, however, gives any clue as to how the German insurers actually look at this problem. See, also, Bürge in 1981 *Juristische Blätter*, 57, 70.

104. *Atkinson* v *Newcastle Waterworks Co.* (1877) 2 Ex. D. 441; *Moch Co.* v. *Rensselaer Water Co.* (1928), 159 N.E. (N.Y. Ct of Appeals).

105. *Ryan* v. *New York Central Ry Co.* (1866), 35 N.Y. 210. Similarly, insurance arguments can explain the immunity accorded to American water companies who have failed to maintain their hydrants and thereby caused damage to neighbours. See *Doyle* v. *South Pittsburgh Water Co.*, 414 Pa. 199 and 51 *Cornell L. Rev.*, 142.

106. Fleming, 4 *Osgoode Hall Law Journal* (1966), 161, 166. See also Fleming James Jr, 57 *Yale L.J.* (1947–48), 549, reprinted in Harper and James, *The Law of Torts*, II, §§ 13.2 *et seq*. On the influence of insurance on the liability of professional accountants see Besser, 7 *Seton Hall L.Rev.* (1976), 507 and especially 534 *et seq*. and Mess, 52 *Notre Dame Lawyer* (1977), 836, and especially 855 *et seq*. The important American case of *Rusch Factors, Inc.* v. *Levin* (1968) 284 F. Supp. 85, shows that American courts have these kind of economic considerations very much in mind. Thus the court asked rhetorically (*ibid.*, at p. 91), 'Isn't the risk of

loss more easily distributed and fairly spread by imposing it on the accounting profession, which can pass the cost of insuring against the risk onto its customers, who can in turn pass the cost onto the entire consuming public?'

107. Since 1966 the Fonds de garantie will idemnify victims of hunting accidents where it is impossible to discover which of the hunters involved caused the damage or where they are not covered by private insurance. The problem discussed in the text will thus no longer arise in the context of *hunting* accidents. On this and its consequences see Durry, *Rev.trim.dr.civ.* (1971), 377. A decision of the court of Grenoble of 16 May 1962 (D. 1963, 137 and Note Azard; *Rev.trim.dr.civ.* (1963), 555, Note Tunc) offers, however, an excellent example of how the insurance factor operated before the Fonds de garantie was brought into the picture. In that case, two hunters, insured with the same insurance company, negligently discharged their guns but only one pellet hit the victim. Since it was impossible to discover from which gun it had come, the court (ignoring the tendency prevailing at the time to hold both defendants responsible) refused to hold either of them liable to the plaintiff. Nevertheless, it obliged their *common insurer* to indemnify the victim in the amount specified by the terms of the insurance contract most favourable to the insurer. The plaintiff was thus compensated even though *neither* of the defendants was held liable for his hurt. OLG Oldenburg *VersR.* 1979, 91 offers an interesting German parallel and is discussed briefly by Markesinis and Von Bar in *Richterliche Rechtspolitik.*

108. [1971] Q.B. 245; [1973] A.C. 127.

109. [1971] 2 Q.B. 691. The implications of insurance were also taken into account in *Ministry of Housing* v. *Sharp* [1970] 1 All E.R. 1009, 1019 and *White* v. *Blackmore* [1972] 2 Q.B. 651, 667.

110. *Nettleship* v. *Weston* [1971] 2 Q.B. 691 at 700.

111. [1971] 2 Q.B. 691.

112. Kalven, 'The Jury, the Law and the Personal Injury Damage Award', 19 *Ohio State Law Journal* (1958), 158. The position in France may not be different. See, for example, A. Tunc. 'Logique et politique dans l'élaboration du droit, spécialement en matière de responsabilité civile', *Mélanges Jean Dabin* (1963), 317, 324.

113. The expression comes from G. Williams and B. Hepple's *Foundations of the Law of Torts* (1976), 141 *et seq.*

114. See A. Tunc, 22 *Archives de Philosophie du Droit* (1977), 31, 34 and references given in notes 100 and 101 above.

115. J.A. Jolowicz, 27 *C.L.J.* (1968), 50,63.

116. Clerk and Lindsell, § 868.

117. *Best* v. *S. Fox & Co. Ltd* [1952] A.C. 716.

118. *Robert Addie & Sons (Collieries) Ltd* v. *Dumbreck* [1929] A.C. 358; *Commissioner for Railways* v. *Quinlan* [1964] A.C. 1054. How important the identity of the plaintiff was, is shown by the case of *Videan* v. *B.T.C.* [1963] 2 Q.B. 650, where the injury suffered by a member of a recognised class (rescuer) was recoverable whereas that suffered by a member of an unrecognised class (trespasser) was not.

119. Ch. Civ. 27 juil. 1937, S. 1938,1.321 and Note Marty; D. 1938,1.5. and Note Savatier. For a more detailed discussion of the case and its consequences, see Mazeaud and Tunc, nos. 277–7 *et seq.*

120. As Professor Mazeaud has observed ('La Lésion d'un "intérêt légitime juridiquement protégé", condition de la responsabilité civile', D. Chron. 1954,39), 'Les tribunaux adoptant avec empressement tout principe dont la souplesse les rend maîtres des procès en leur laissant le contrôle de l'application des règles juridiques. Moyen commode de prendre leur revanche sur l'interdiction qui leur permet mieux de "moraliser" le droit.'

121. Weill and Terré, no. 607.

122. Ch. Civ. 2ᵉ Ch. Civ. 10 janv. 1963, D. 1963, 404; 4 mars 1964, G.P. 1964,1.392 etc. The administrative courts followed this view. So, Conseil d'Etat of 11 mai 1928, S. 1928,3.98, D. 1929,3.6; 21 oct. 1955, D. 1956,139.

123. Thus, Ch. Crim. 26 juin 1958, G.P. 1958,2.160; 24 fév. 1959, J.C.P. 1959,2.11095; 20 janv. 1959, G.P. 1959,1.210, Rev.trim.dr.civ. (1959), 534, observations by H. and L. Mazeaud; 18 fév. 1964, D. 1964 Somm. 82; 20 janv. 1966, D. 1966,184 and report Combaldieu, J.C.P. 1966,2.14870 and Note Wiederkehr; Rev.trim.dr.civ. (1966), 536, observations by R. Rodière. These decisions were in line with the leading case of 20 fév. 1863, S. 1863,1.321 at 323; D. 1864,99 at 102, which had declared that:

    l'article 1382, en ordonnant en termes absolus la réparation de tout fait quelconque de l'homme qui cause à autrui un dommage, ne limite en rien ni la nature du fait dommageable, ni la nature du dommage éprouvé, ni la nature du lien qui doit unir, au cas de décès, la victime du fait avec celui de ses ayants droit qui en demanderait la réparation.

    But a decision of the court of Paris of 18 November 1932, awarding damages to *two* mistresses of the deceased, was quashed by the Cour de cassation, Crim. 27 avr. 1934, G.P. 1934,1.927 on the understandable ground that 'le double concubinage est immoral'!

124. Mazeaud and Tunc, no. 283. The more liberal views of Professor Tunc are summarised in no. 279 note 1. See also J. Granier, 'Epouse, concubinage ou compagne', S.J. 1956,1.1299.

125. Cass. 27 fév. 1970, D. 1970,201. But for some time after this decision the courts continued to regard the *intérêt* as 'illégitime' whenever one or other of the parties was guilty of the *crime* adultery, though see Ch. Crim. 14 juin 1973, D. 1973, 585. The law was further relaxed by the subsequent decision of 19 June 1975, D. 1975,679 and Note Tunc, and finally changed by the law of 11 July 1975 which, in article 17, abolished the crime of adultery.

126. Weir in Catala and Weir, 38 Tul.L.Rev. (1964), 665.

127. The whole topic is exhaustively discussed by H. McGregor, Encyclopedia, xi, ch. 9, nos. 218 et seq.

128. *France*: Ch. Crim. 20 fév. 1863, S. 1863,1.321 and, extensively, Mazeaud and Tunc, 277–2 et seq. *Belgium*: Cass. 16 janv. 1939, Pas. 1939,1.25; Cass. 2 mai 1955, Pas. 1955,1.950. *Switzerland*: OR art. 45.3.

129. §§ 844 II and 845 BGB, which are unique in that they distinguish between an action for 'loss of support' (§ 844 II BGB) and an action for 'loss of services'. In practical terms, however, there seems to be little difference between the two. The persons legally entitled to support are defined by various articles of the Civil Code, e.g. §§ 1360, 1601, 1615a, 1736, 1739, 1757, 1762 etc. The approach of the Greek Civil Code is similar. See art. 928 CC. For Austria, see art. 1327 CC. For Scotland, see the classic statement of Lord President Inglis in *Eisten v. North*

British Railway (1870) 8 M 980,984, now restated and modified by section 1 of the Damages (Scotland) Act 1976, c. 13.

130. E.g. Fatal Accidents Act 1976.

131. Netherlands CC arts. 463, 464, and 1406.

132. *Cavalier* v. *Pope* [1906] A.C. 428 and *Bottomley* v. *Bannister* [1932] 1 K.B. 458 were the leading cases of the old law. The immunity was progressively eroded and finally abolished by *Dutton* v. *Bognor Regis Urban District Council* [1972] 1. Q.B. 373 and the Defective Premises Act 1972 sects. 1, 3 and 4. See J. Spencer, 33 *C.L.J.* (1974), 307 and 34 *C.L.J.* (1975), 48.

133. The Crown Proceedings Act 1947. The corresponding immunity enjoyed by the Swedish State was finally abolished by the Tort Liability Act of 1972. In France, on the other hand, the immunity of the state was reduced and eventually abolished by the courts. For Germany see Vogel, *Die Verwirklichung der Rechtsstaatsidee im Staatshaftungsrecht* (1977), 9 *et seq.*; Ch. von Bar, *JZ* 1979, 332 *et seq.*

134. [1969] 1. A.C. 191. It was suggested *obiter* that solicitors should enjoy a similar immunity in respect of court work. For an comparison with S. African law see D.L.C. Miller, 1977 *S.A.L.J.*, 184.

135. [1977] 3 W.L.R. 421.

136. The various immunities invariably accorded by special statutes or international conventions to Ambassadors and diplomatic officials do not fall within the ambit of this work.

137. Noteworthy however is paragraph 839 1 BGB which states that civil liability for *negligent* breach of official duty will be recognised 'only if the injured party is unable to obtain compensation elsewhere'.

138. Law no. 71–1130 of 31 December 1971, arts. 26 and 27 and Decree no. 72–783 of 25 August 1972 in Nouveau Code de Procédure Civile 1977 pp. 603 *et seq.* and 651 *et seq.* In 1980 the Bar in Annual General meeting endorsed the principle of compulsory insurance and set up a Working Party to consider detailed proposals.

139. For interesting discussions of some cases see *Rev.trim.dr.civ.* (1960), 229, no. 9; (1963), 607, no. 10; (1964), 110, nos. 15 and 16; (1965), 715, no. 5; (1970), 572, no. 3.

140. Though inspiration can, of course, be drawn from other areas of the law of tort (e.g. the older cases of valuing the chance of re-marriage of a widow) or, even, contract (e.g. *Chaplin* v. *Hicks* [1911] 2 K.B. 786 – loss of chance of taking part in a beauty contest; *Manubens* v. *Leon* [1919] 1 K.B. 208 – loss of the chance of earning tips).

141. Generally speaking this is so in all the systems under comparison though it is particularly true of the Common law. Old French law, however, was, apparently, less inclined to draw a sharp distinction between affirmative and negative conduct and it was only at a later date, under the misleading influence of criminal law, that harmful omissions came to be treated differently so as not to lead to the imposition of liability. On the whole matter see Mazeaud and Tunc, nos. 526, 531. For American law see Shapo, *The Duty to Art* (1977).

142. For French doubts on this aspect see Mazeaud and Tunc, no. 527 (with further literature). See also Honoré, *Encyclopedia*, no. 25. For further references see Limpens, *Encyclopedia*, XI, ch. 2, nos. 78, 84.

143. H.F. McNiece and J.V. Thornton, 58 *Yale L.J.* (1949), 1272, 1288.
144. R.L. Hale, 'Prima Facie Torts, Combination, and Nonfeasance', 46 *Col.L.Rev.* (1946), 196, 214–15.
145. Linden, 44 *Can. Bar Rev.* (1966), 25, 29 *et seq*. On the whole matter of tortious omissions see also Bohlen, 56 *U. of P.L.Rev.* (1908), 217, 316, reprinted in *Studies* (1926), 291 *et seq*.; Ames in 22 *Harv.L.Rev.* (1908), 97, 113 (arguing that the no-duty rule should be changed); Epstein, in 2 *J.Leg. Studies* (1973), 151, 197 (challenging Ames' views); Franklin, 25 *Stan.L.Rev.* (1972), 51 and, more recently, Landes and Posner in 7 *J.Leg. Studies* (1978), 83.
146. Bohlen, *Studies*, 294.
147. Minor, 'Moral Obligation as a Basis of Liability', 9 *Va.L.Rev.* 421, 422; Note, 'The Failure to Rescue: A Comprehensive Study', 52 *Col.L.Rev.* (1952), 631, 641. For a more recent comparative study see Kristin A. DeKuiper, 'Stalking the Good Samaritan: Communists, Capitalists and the Duty to Rescue', *Utah L.Rev.* (1976), 529. The murder of Kitty Genovese in 1964, witnessed by thirty-eight people who nevertheless failed to intervene in any way, led to an interdisciplinary conference sponsored by the University of Chicago Law School. This published the various papers in book form under the title *The Good Samaritan and the Law* (ed. J. Ratcliffe, 1966). It is notable that most of the participants expressed dissatisfaction with the present rule.
148. For French law see Mazeaud and Tunc, nos. 537, 542. For German law, equally unprepared to recognise a general duty to act in favour of others, see Larenz, *Schuldrecht*, II, para. 72 I d. But see paragraph 330 c StGB. (as amended in 1953) and article 63 of the French Penal Code.
     The most recent work on the German understanding of 'duty of care' is by Ch. von Bar, *Verkehrspflichten, richterliche Gefahrsteuerungsgebote im Deutschen Deliktsrecht* (1980).
149. For example, The Occupiers' Liability Act 1957; The Factories Act 1961; The Mines and Quarries Act 1954, etc.
150. See Linden, 44 *Can. Bar Rev.* (1966), 25, 48 *et seq.*; DeKuiper, *Utah L.Rev.* (1976), 528, 531. In the United States forty-nine states now attempt to encourage the provision of first aid by physicians by relaxing the ordinary rules of negligence, though only ten of those are prepared to extend this protection to rescuers who are not members of the medical profession. Still further goes a 1968 Act passed in Vermont which imposes statutory *criminal* liability for failure to rescue (under certain circumstances) a person in danger. See M. Franklin, 25 *Stan.L.Rev.* (1972), 51 and D'Amato, 'The "Bad Samaritan" Paradigm', 70 *N.W. U.L.Rev.* (1975), 798. For an economic analysis of the issue see Landes and Posner, 7 *J.Leg. Studies* (1978), 13.
151. For example, sect. 186 (1) of the Criminal Code of Canada.
152. Now article 321 of the Criminal Code. This obligation comes to an end when the child reaches the age of fifteen. See the tragic *affaire Monnier*, 20 nov. 1901, D. 1902,2.84. After the law of 1945 – discussed below – the case would be decided differently.
153. See also article 2368 of the Portuguese Civil Code; article 450 of the Dutch Criminal Code; article 387 of the Norwegian Criminal Code. The Belgian solutions are, in most respects, similar to the French. In Germany, on the other hand, a position similar (though not identical) to that established in France by the

Ordonnance of 1945 was only gradually achieved, in 1935 and in 1953, and can be found now in article 330 c of the Criminal Code. For the original version of the Code (article 360 number 10) only punished those who failed to come to assistance when requested by police magistrates. By contrast, nothing as generalised as the above can be found in the Common law jurisdictions, and Ames was one of the few pioneering authors to favour a limited duty to rescue. See 22 *Harv.L.Rev.* (1908), 97, 112, 113.

154. They are discussed in greater detail by Professor A.Tunc in D. 1946, *Législation,* 33 *et seq.,* and *Nouveau Répertoire,* 1 under *Abstention Délictueuse.*

155. Cour d'appel de Poitiers, 3 fév. 1970, D. 1978,34 and note by P. Couvrat.

156. [1972] 1 Q.B. 373.

157. [1977] 2 W.L.R. 1024, critically discussed by I. Duncan-Wallace in 94 *L.Q.R.* (1978), 60 *et seq.*

158. [1932] A.C. 562.

159. The general rule is that no action for damages will lie for failure to exercise a discretionary power. See S. de Smith, *Judicial Review of Administrative Action,* 3rd edn (1973), 280; also H.W.R. Wade, *Administrative Law,* 4th edn (1977), 629.

160. Ch. Civ. 18 mai 1955, D. 1955, 520 and cf. Willmer L.J.'s views in *Zoernsch* v. *Waldock* [1964] 1 W.L.R. 675 at 685. See also the pioneering decision of the Cour de cassation of 24 déc. 1924, D.H. 1925,120, where the Court made it clear that 'l'omission ne peut entrainer une responsabilité qu'autant qu'il y avait pour celui auquel on l'impute, obligation d'accomplir le fait omis'. For an even more precise and far-reaching pronouncement, see Ch. Civ. 27 fév. 1951, D. 1951,329.

161. This is clearly brought out by the so-called 'municipality cases' decided by South African courts. See, for example, *Halliwell* v. *Johannesburg Municipal Council* 1912 A.D. 590.

162. Ch. Civ. 1 fév. 27, 1951, D. 1951,329.

163. Ch. Civ. 1 juil. 1953, D. 1954,533. Arguably, however, the real reason for this decision is the Court's sensibility to the severe criticism it was subjected to for its decision on the *Branly* case. See, in particular, Professor Carbonnier's remarks in D. Chron. 1954,119.

164. [1967] 1 A.C. 645. *British Ry Board* v. *Herrington* [1972] A.C. 877 offers another good example.

165. [1967] 1 A.C. 645 at pp. 661–2.

166. [1978] 2 W.L.R. 774. Confirmed by the Court of Appeal in [1980] 2 W.L.R. 65; B.S. Markesinis, 'The Subsidence of "Mumps" or the Duties and Responsibilities of Landowners', 39 *C.L.J.* (1980), 259 *et seq.*

167. (1896) 20 L.T. 564.

168. Discussed in greater detail in: Larenz, *Schuldrecht,* II, para. 72 id; Palandt-Thomas, *BGB,* 39th edn (1980) under para. 823; Medicus, paras. 641 *et seq.* The first decision on the subject is *RGZ* 52, 373.

169. For example, *RGZ* 155, 161; *RGZ* 54, 53. Liability has also been imposed on the appropriate authority for failing to maintain a canal in navigable condition, *BGHZ* 9, 373. The earliest decision to invoke the *Verkehrssicherungspflichten* was *RGZ* 52, 373.

170. [1976] 1 W.L.R. 810.

171. BGH NJW 1976, 712.

172. [1972] 2 Q.B. 651.

173. BGH NJW 1975, 533.
174. *BGHZ* 36, 206. Cf. *Brown* v. *Cotterill* (1934) 51 T.L.R. 21, in which, however, it was the mason who erected the tombstone who was sued. In view of *Thomson* v. *Cremin* [1956] 1 W.L.R. 103, it is not clear why the Church authorities were not sued as occupiers of the yard.
175. *BGHZ* 11, 175. Cf. *Commissioner for Railways* v. *McDermott* [1967] 1 A.C. 169.
176. *BGHZ* 5, 379. Cf. *Wheat* v. *Lacon & Co. Ltd* [1966] 1 Q.B. 355.
177. Weitnauer, 16 *Rev.int.dr.comp.* (1967), 807, 812. See also Larenz, *Schuldrecht*, II, para. 72 Id; W. Fikentscher, *Schuldrecht*, 6th edn (1976), para. 103 III 1; for a different view see K. Huber, 'Verkehrspflichten zum Schutz fremden Vermögens', in *Festschrift von Caemmerer* (1979), 359 *et seq.*; Ch. von Bar, Note, *JZ* 1979, 729.
178. 17 Cal. Reptr. 3d. 425, 551 P. 2d. 334, 131 Cal. Reptr. 14. Cf. the more narrow phrasing of paras. 315–20 (especially 319) of the *Restatement (Second) of Torts*. For a commentary on Tarassoff see, inter alia, Stone, 'The Tarassoff Decision: Suing Psychotherapists to Safeguard Society', 90 *Harv.L.Rev.* (1976), 358 and Note, 'Where the Public Peril Begins: A Survey of Psychotherapists to Determine the Effects of Tarassoff', 31 *Stan.L.Rev.* (1978), 165.
179. The discussion in the text is limited to English, French and German law, but other systems have developed different methods of limiting compensation. In Sweden, for example, the causing of financial loss is actionable only if the conduct is also punishable as a crime. See Hellner, 22 *A.J.Comp.L.* (1974), 1, 5.
180. French law can, in fact, be quite generous in such cases. See, for example, Colmar 20 avr. 1955, D. 1956,723 and Note Savatier, where a football club which lost one of its players was allowed to recover at least his transfer value. See also Comporti, *Rev.int.dr.comp.* (1967), 827, 851. But liability is kept under control through the requirement that the damage must be 'direct' or 'certain'. A company has thus not been allowed to claim for its loss resulting from the accidental killing of the chief executive on the grounds that its damage was not 'directe'. Directness here is understood in the sense of remoteness and, as with us, it is very much a policy decision. See Note D. 1967,77. And a theatre cannot claim lost profits because it has been deprived through an accident of the services of its leading tenor: Ch. Civ. 14 nov. 1958, G.P. 1959,1.31. The loss here was treated as uncertain since it could have been due to 'multiples circonstances ou incidents autre que la défaillance d'un interprète de talent'. Cf. Cour d'appel de Bruxelles, 22 janv. 1955, *Rev.crit.jur. Belge* (1955), 190. The case-law on this subject is immense.
181. Thus: (a) the *actio per quod* protects only proprietory or semi-proprietory interests (*I.R.C.* v. *Hambrook* [1956] 2 Q.B. 641); (b) it is probably restricted to domestic servants (see Gareth Jones, 'Per quod servitium amisit', 74 *L.Q.R.* (1958), 39); and (c) is limited to loss of services due to injury, not death. For a more detailed comparison of English and French law see D. Marshall, 24 *I.C.L.Q.* (1975), 748, 763 *et seq.* German law is also strict and allows no analogical extension of paragraphs 844 II and 845 BGB. Deutsch, *Haftungsrecht*, 484; von Caemmerer, 'Das Problem des Drittschadensersatzes', reprinted in *Gesammelte Schriften*, I, 597, 600.
182. H. McGregor, 'Personal Injury and Death', in *Encyclopedia*, XI, ch. 9, nos. 204 *et seq.*

183. [1972] 1 Q.B. 373.
184. [1977] 2 W.L.R. 1024. Severely criticised by Duncan Wallace, 94 *L.Q.R.* (1978), 60.
185. BGH 39, 358; contrast *Dutton* and *Anns*.
186. In Germany, though the courts have been dealing with such cases since before the War, academics did not start to examine the subject seriously until the 1970s. Of the many works of that period see: H.I.Musielak, *Haftung für Rat, Auskunft und Gutachten* (1974); W. Lorenz, 'Das Problem der Haftung für primare Vermögensschaden bei der Erteilung einer unrichtigen Auskunft', in *Festschrift Larenz* (1973), 575, 584; H.P. Sheerer, 'Probleme der Haftung der Kreditinstitute für die Erteilung von Auskünften in Deutschland und Frankreich unter besonderer Berücksichtigung der Haftungsfreizeichnungsklauseln' in *Festschrift Bärmann* (1975), 801; S. Lammel, 'Zur Auskunftshaftung', AcP 1979, 337. For French law see : M. De Juglart, 'L'Obligation de renseignements dans les contrats', *Rev.trim.dr.civ.* (1945), 1; R. Savatier, D. Chron. 1972,137; G. Flécheux and F. Fabiani, 'La Responsabilité civile de l'avocat', *J.C.P.* 1974, 1.2673; G. Viney, 'La Responsabilité des entreprises prestataires de conseils', *J.C.P.* 1975,1.2750; G. Durry, *Rev.trim.dr.civ.* (1974), 151 (Note to Colmar 5 janv. 1973, *G.P.* 1973,1.537). In all these the emphasis is put on the law of contract.
187. Both were discussed briefly in 93 *L.Q.R.* (1977), 78, 97–103.
188. For this English tendency to 'shift the facts into the law of tort', see O. Kahn-Freund, 82 *L.Q.R.* (1966), 45, 50 *et seq.*
189. [1964] A.C. 465, 525.
190. *Ultramares Corp.* v. *Touche, Niven and Co.*, 1931, 255, N.Y. 170, 174; N.E. 441, 444.
191. OLG München, BB 1956, 866. Cf. *Glanzer* v. *Shepard* (1922) 135 N.E. 275. In both of these cases the extent of liability did not present a serious problem since in both there could be only one person injured. However, the solution in the former case was founded in the law of contract while in the latter it was based on tort.
192. BGH *WM* 1965, 287. See also BGH *WM* 1963, 913.
193. In BGH *WM* 1974, 685 the Court adopted a different contractual solution. A wished to advance credit to X so A asked his Bank (B) about X. B asked X's bank (C) and C told B that X was creditworthy. He was not, and A suffered loss. A sued C and, though the court was prepared to discover a contract between B and C with protective effects vis-à-vis A, A's claim failed on causal grounds. Contrast BGH Bet. 1976, 1218.
194. BGH *WM* 1966, 149; *BGHZ* 12, 105; OLG Frankfurt D. StR. 1973, 476; BGH *WM* 1966, 1148.
195. BGH *WM* 1979, 548. Cf. *Rusch Factors, Inc.* v. *Levin* (1968) 284 F. Supp. 85, 93; *Rozny* v. *Marnul* (1969) 250 N.E. 2d. 656; *Rhode Island Hospital Trust National Bank* v. *Swartz et al.* (1974) 455 F. 2d. 847; W.L. Prosser in 19 *Vand.L.Rev.* (1966), 231 and, more generally, M.A. Franklin, *Tort Law and Alternatives* (1979), pp. 1019 *et seq.* (and with American bibliography on p. 1065). But what if there is no limit to the size of the class of the actually foreseen reliants? The *Rusch* decision (*ibid.*, at p. 93) talks of an '*actually* foreseen and *limited* class of persons' (italics supplied); the German decision, while it agrees that the *identity* of the relying person need not be known to the representor, insists that he must be 'part of a calculable group of persons'. Dean Prosser, the Reporter of the *Restatement*,

addressed himself to this problem and wrote: 'What if an art expert certifies a painting as a genuine Vermeer, knowing that the dealer to whom he gives the certificate intends to publish it in a bulletin to be sent to 1,000 prospective purchasers in the hope of making the sale. Is he liable for negligence to the man who buys? The Reporter would say yes' (*Restatement (Second) of Torts, Explanatory Notes* § 552, at 16 (Tent. Draft No. 12, 1966)). This *could* imply that the size of the class of recipients could be irrelevant (provided always that they belong to an actually foreseen class). On the other hand, it is notable that in the Reporter's example only *one* person would, in the end, suffer harm. The point must, therefore, still be regarded as being open.

196. 'Chronique de droit Bancaire', *J.C.P.* 1976,1.2801 nos. 86 in finem and 87.

197. 21 mai 1974, *Rev. Banque* (1974), 848, and commentary in *Rev.trim.dr.comp.* (1974), 566.

198. See, inter alia, BGH *WM* 1955, 230; BGH *WM* 1962, 1110; BGH *WM* 1971, 817; BGH *WM* 1972, 466; BGH *WM* 1979, 771. BGH *JZ* 1979, 725 (and note by von Bar) suggests that there may even be a duty to correct a carefully supplied but erroneous statement once the maker subsequently becomes aware of its falsity. In that case, A recommended one of his employees to another firm, B. There was no contractual relationship between A and B and, at the time the reference was written, A had no reason to suspect that the employee had in fact been cheating him. A subsequently found out and, through his lawyer, asked the employee to return the stolen money. The employee did, having this time embezzled the sum from his new employer, B. When B discovered this, he sued A, alleging that A was under a duty to inform him once he had found out the activities of the employee. The action succeeded and A had to pay damages.

199. Professor A.M. Honoré thinks that this may be more than a mere coincidence. See his comments in '*Hedley Byrne & Co. Ltd* v. *Heller & Partners, Ltd*', in 8 *J.S.P.T.L.* (1965), 284, 295.

200. BGH *WM* 1969, 247. See also *RGZ* 27, 118; *RGZ* 139, 103.

201. BGH *WM* 1971, 206; *WM* 1970, 632; BB 1956, 770.

202. BGH NJW 1969, 36; BGH *WM* 1956, 1229.

203. Though, naturally, it is not only bankers who can be held liable on these grounds. See Savatier, D. Chron. 1972, 137. Moreover, it should be noted that though in most cases the giver of the information is held to be under an *obligation de diligence*, occasionally there may be an *obligation de résultat*, e.g. Ch. Req. 15 mai 1923, D. 1925,1.15. J.A. Jolowicz has argued that, on occasion, this may be true of English law as well: 10 *J.S.P.T.L.* (1972–3), 187.

204. 21 mai 1974, *Rev. Banque* (1974), 848, and commentary in *Rev.trim.dr.comp.* (1974), 566.

205. *Rev. trim.dr.comp.* (1974), 566, Note Cabrillac, Rives-Lange. In the same vein, Chambre Commerciale of the Cour de cassation 15 July 1975 (unreported), quoted by Gavalda and Stoufflet, 'Chronique de droit bancaire', *J.C.P.* 1976,1.2801, no. 87.

206. G.P. 1931,38, and Markesinis, 93 *L.Q.R.* (1977), 78, 92 n. 60.

207. G. Viney, 'La Réparation des dommages non physiques en droit français', paper delivered at the Ford Foundation Workshop, 1971 (quoted by Marshall, 24 *I.C.L.Q.* (1975), 749).

Notes to pp. 88–91

208. Catala in Catala and Weir, 38 *Tul.L.Rev.* (1964), 664, n. 2.
209. For the French, unfair competition is the typical example of pure economic loss.
210. There is a hint of this in the conclusions of the Commissaire du gouvernement in the decision of *Cie gén. de Trav.hydr.(S.A.D.E.) et Soc. Thomson-Houston-Hotchkiss-Brandt*, C.E. 1972, 168. But the Conseil d'Etat awarded the plaintiff damages for his economic loss. The case was a typical cable-case. See also Ch. Civ. 8 mai 1970, D. 1970, *Somm.* 203 though in this case some emphasis was apparently placed on the fact that the damaged pipeline served the plaintiff's firm only. Cf. in this respect *Caltex Oil v. The Dredger 'Willemstad'* [1976] C.L.R. 529 and *BGHZ* 41, 123 and *BGHZ* 29, 65.
211. 51 A.L.J.R. 270; 37 C.L.J. (1978), 27.
212. [1972] 1 Q.B. 373.
213. [1977] 2 W.L.R. 1024.
214. They have been discussed briefly at the beginning of this chapter.
215. *BGHZ* 41, 123; NJW 1964, 720. See also *ATF* 97 II 221 (though here it seems the cable belonged to the plaintiff).
216. [1971] 1 Q.B. 337.
217. [1973] 1 Q.B. 27.
218. [1961] A.C. 388; Clerk and Lindsell, §§ 344–53.
219. The first case to consider the new right and reject it as a *sonstiges Recht* was decided in 1902 (*RGZ* 56,271). Soon after, however, the position was reversed and the new right was judicially recognised first by RG JW 1902 Teil 227 and then by *RGZ* 58,24. The number of cases and the volume of the literature has not stopped growing since. The following may be useful: Buchner, *Die Bedeutung des Rechts am eingerichteten und ausgeübten Gewerbebetrieb für den deliktsrechtlichen Unternehmensschutz* (1971); Schippel, *Das Recht am eingerichteten und ausgeübten Gewerbetrieb* (1956); Suppes, *Die Rechtsprechung der BGB zum Recht am eingerichteten und ausgeübten Gewerbetrieb* (1965); E. Wolf, 'Das Recht am eingerichteten und ausgeübten Gewerbetrieb', in *Festschrift von Hippel* (1967), 665 *et seq.*; Neumann-Duesberg, 'Zum Recht am eingerichteten und ausgeübten Gewerbetrieb', NJW 1972,133 *et seq.*; W. Fikentscher, 'Das Recht am Gewerbetrieb (Unternehmen) als "sonstiges Recht" para. 823 1 in der Rechtsprechung des RG und des BHG', *Festgabe für Kronstein* (1967), 262 *et seq.*
220. *BGHZ* 3,270.
221. *BGHZ* 29,65 (factually quite similar to the earlier decision of OLG München NJW 1956, 1719 with an important note by Professor Larenz). A detailed consideration of all these cases can now be found in J. Taupitz, *Haftung für Energieleiterstörungen durch Dritte* (1981) with extensive bibliography.
222. *BGHZ* 29,65, at pp. 70 and 73.
223. *Ibid.* at p. 71.
224. The reaction to this definition was mixed: favourable from von Caemmerer, 'Wandlungen des Deliktsrechts', reprinted in *Gesammelte Schriften*, I. 452,498, and Lehmann, in NJW 1959, 670; unfavourable by, amongst others, Fikentscher, *Schuldrecht,* 5th edn (1975), 625; Emmerich, *JuS* 1977,120. *BGHZ* 29,65 has, in this respect, been consistently followed. Thus, BGH NJW 1968, 1279, 1280; BGH NJW 1976, 1740, 1741; BGH NJW 1977, 2208, 2209; OLG Karlsruhe, NJW 1975, 221.

213

225. BGH NJW 1976, 1740.
226. [1973] 1 Q.B. 27.
227. BGH NJW 1968, 1279; BGH *VersR.* 1969,542. *Contra,* OLG Karlsruhe NJW 1975,221.
228. See previous note.
229. NJW 1975,221.
230. BGH NJW 1976, 1740 and critical comment by Emmerich, *JuS* 1977,120; subsequent attempts to gain compensation through the law of contract also failed. See BGH NJW 1977,2208. Swiss law has taken a more generous view on this matter e.g. *ATF* 102 II 85. The whole attitude of the German courts towards pure economic loss has been recently criticised by Herrman, *Zum Nachteil des Vermögens.*
231. Sir Percy Winfield made the first attack on the concept in 34 *Col.L.Rev.* (1947). See also Buckland in 51 *L.Q.R.* (1935), 637 and cf. Lawson, 22 *Tul.L.Rev.* (1947), 111, 129; R.G. McKerron, 69 *S.A.L.J.* (1952), 189 and *The Law of Delict*, 7th edn, 34–5 and R.W.M. Dias, 30 *Tul.L.Rev.* (1956), 377, 400–8, where it is suggested that the controversy is the result of verbal misunderstandings.
232. Buckland, 51 *L.Q.R.* (1935), 637.
233. (1883), 11 Q.B.D. 503, 509.
234. *Ibid.* at p. 516.
235. [1932] A.C. 562, 580.
236. For example in conspiracy or injurious falsehood.
237. For example with deceit. *Derry v. Peek* (1889) 14 App.Cas. 337.
238. *Hedley Byrne and Co. Ltd v. Heller and Partners, Ltd* [1964] A.C. 465; *Mutual Life and Citizens Assurance Co. Ltd and Another v. Evatt* [1971] A.C. 793; *Esso Petroleum Co. Ltd v. Mardon* [1975] Q.B. 819; affirmed [1976] 2 W.L.R. 583.
239. Alternatively, the defendant may not be recognised by law, e.g. the *Rondel v. Worsley* [1969] 1 A.C. 191 type of situation.
240. [1972] A.C. 877.
241. [1932] A.C. 562.
242. [1970] A.C. 1004, esp. 1026–7 (per Lord Reid).
243. *Anns v. Merton London Borough* [1978] A.C. 728 (per Lord Wilberforce).
244. Thus, *Caltex Oil v. The Dredger 'Willemstad'* [1976] 136 C.L.R. 529; *Midland Bank v. Hett* [1979] Ch. 384; *Ross v. Caunters* [1979] 3 W.L.R. 605. See also *Yumerovski v. Dani* (1978) 83 D.L.R. (3rd) 558.
245. The different judgments in the *Caltex* case, above, are particularly interesting in this respect.
246. See *Goldman v. Hargrave* [1967] 1 A.C. 645; *Leakey v. National Trust* (C.A.) [1980] 2 W.L.R. 65.
247. R.W.M. Dias, 39 *C.L.J.* (1980), 45,48 adopts a slightly different view.
248. Cf. J. Limpens, *Encyclopedia*, XI, ch. 2, nos. 26–46.
249. M. Planiol, *Traité élémentaire de droit civil*, 11th edn, no. 863.
250. E.g. Rabut, *De la Notion de faute en droit privé* (1946).
251. R. Savatier, *Traité de la responsabilité civile*, 2nd edn (1951), pp. 56–134.
252. Pollock, *The Law of Torts*, 14th edn by P.A. Landon, 115–23.
253. Mazeaud and Tunc, no. 392.
254. *Ibid.* no. 439. The same 'objective' standard has also been consistently adopted by the German courts at least since *RGZ* 119,397.

255. See Aubry and Rau, *Droit civil français*, VI, 7th edn by A. Ponsard and N. Dejean de la Batie (1975), 529 and cf. Clerk and Lindsell, §899.

256. Limpens, *Encyclopedia*, XI, ch. 2, no. 46.

257. On this and related matters see von Caemmerer's seminal work, 'Wandlungen des Deliktsrechts', reprinted in *Gesammelte Schriften*, I, 452 *et seq.*, 478 *et seq*. Idem in *Karlsruher Forum* (1961), reprinted in *Gesammelte Schriften*, I, 554 *et seq*.

258. Above, pp. 78–9.

259. Originally, this requirement was inserted merely in order to remind the judge that he should not enter judgment for the plaintiff before having examined whether the defendant's act was legally justified. Like Roman law, self-defence, necessity, and superior orders were the most usual legal defences. The traditional definition of 'unlawful' as 'what is contrary to the established legal order' is tautological, and German scholars accept this, but argue that there are advantages in maintaining such flexibility. See, for example, Deutsch, *Haftungsrecht*, I, 191–2.

260. A good summary of the various views expressed on this matter can be found in Medicus, paras. 641 *et seq*.

261. 'Rechtswidrigkeit, Sozialadäquanz, Fahrlässigkeit und Schuld im Zivilrecht', NJW 1957,1777. Nipperdey's contribution in this area is expressly recognised by Larenz in *Festschrift H. Dölle*, I, 163,170 n. 2. See also Deutsch, *Haftungsrecht*, I, 193. But the true origins of the approach can be traced in works on criminal law, where it could have *practical* significance, especially for the law of aiding and abetting.

262. See the decision of the Grosser Senat in *BGHZ* 24,21. This is now the view taken by the Supreme Court though Esser-Schmidt, *Schuldrecht* I, *Allgemeiner Teil, Teilband* 2, p. 18 note 80 suggest that the older view still prevails with the lower courts. In practical terms, however, the results are the same.

263. For example *BGHZ* 41,123.

264. Von Caemmerer, *Wandlungen des Deliktsrechts*, reprinted in *Gesammelte Schriften*, I, 452,488 n. 123.

265. *Accepting* the basic lines of Nipperdey's theory: von Caemmerer, *Wandlungen des Deliktsrechts* (previous note); R. Wiethölter, *Der Rechtfertigungsgrund des verkehrsrichtigen Verhaltens* (1960); von Caemmerer in *Karlsruher Forum*, reprinted in *Gesammelte Schriften*, I, 554,572; W. Münzberg, *Verhalten und Erfolg als Grundlagen der Rechtswidrigkeit und Haftung* (1966); Eike Schmidt, 'Zur Dogmatik des 278 BGB', AcP 1970, 502 *et seq*.; V. Emmerich, *Grundlagen des Vertrags- und Schuldrechts* (1974), 496 *et seq*.; Esser-Schmidt, *Schuldrecht* I, Allgemeiner Teil, §25 IV.1.3.2 and 25.V.

    Rejecting Nipperdey's approach: Weitnauer, in *Karlsruher Forum*, pp. 28 *et seq*.; also Grenzen, 'Des Personlichkeitsschutzes', NJW 1961,107 *et seq*. and again in NJW 1962,1190 *et seq*.; Reinhardt, in *Karlsruher Forum*, pp. 3 *et seq*.

    Suggesting an *intermediate* position: Larenz, *Schuldrecht*, II, *Besonderer Teil*, §72 I.c. (p. 540); Deutsch, *Fahrlässigkeit und erforderliche Sorgfalt* (1963) and *Haftungsrecht*, 195 *et seq*.

266. Larenz, *Schuldrecht*, II, Besonderer Teil, §72. I.c.

267. In some cases – e.g. para. 831 BGB – the new theory may lead to different results since here unlawfulness clearly performs a different function from fault. Thus, *BGHZ* 24, 21. For a different view see: H. Stoll, *JZ* 1958, 137 et seq.

268. On ne doit pas mettre en danger sans necessité la vie et les biens d'autrui; celui qui crée de tels dangers agit de façon illicite; ce principe est aussi applicable à la fabrication ou la réparation défectueuse d'objets usuels lorsque les défauts peuvent compromettre la santé ou la vie des personnes qui utilisent ces objets conformément à leur destination. (*ATF* 64 II 260).
    Cf. also *ATF* 90 II 89; 77 II 151; 71 II 114.
269. Execution of public works and, until recently, traffic accidents were included under this heading.
270. E.g. *ATF* 45 II 647; *ATF* 51 II 517; *ATF* 57 II 165; *ATF* 60 II 38.
271. *ATF* 79 II 69.
272. *ATF* 57 II 81, *ATF* 41 II 77.

3 Problems of causation and remoteness
1. Marty, *Rev.trim.dr.civ.* (1939), 685, 689 .
2. A select bibliography can be found at the end of the chapter.
3. The earliest and most significant work was by P. Marteau, *La Notion de causalité dans la responsabilité civile* (1914). For the dissertations of the 1930s see Marty, *Rev.trim.dr.civ.* (1939), 700, note 5.
4. Notably by F. Chabas in D. Chron. 1970, 113; B. Starck in *J.C.P.* 1970,1.2339 and J. Boré in *J.C.P.* 1971,1.2369. For further references see the list at the end of this chapter.
5. See, for example, Joly, *Rev.trim.dr.civ.* (1942), 257, 268 et seq.
6. Notably by Green, *The Rationale of Proximate Cause*; Becht and Miller, *The Test of Factual Causation*; Hart and Honoré, *Causation in the Law*. To these one must now add Professor Honoré's erudite contribution to the *Encyclopedia* (ch. 7).
7. For references see the bibliographical list at the end of this chapter.
8. Prosser, 38 *Cal.L.Rev.* (1950), 369.
9. Prosser, 236 *et seq.*; Winfield and Jolowicz, 110 *et seq.* Fleming, 179 *et seq.*; in Germany, too, the distinction between condition (*Bedingung*) and adequate cause is firmly drawn. See, for example, L. Enneccerus and H. Lehmann, *Recht der Schuldverhältnisse*, 15th edn (1958), § 15 III, 1,2.
10. *Liesbosch Dredger* v. *Edison Steamship* [1933] A.C. 449 at 460.
11. P. Esmein is one of the exceptions and has for a long time now advocated the distinction. See his 'Trois Problèmes de responsabilité civile', *Rev.trim.dr.civ.* (1934), 317, 320 *et seq.* and 'Le Nez de Cléopatre ou les affres de la causalité', D. 1964,205. The bifurcated approach emerges indirectly in the analysis by the Cour de cassation of liability under article 1384 CC and the onus of proof thereunder. For in the 1940s a series of decisions held that the plaintiff has to prove that the 'thing' 'a participé à la réalisation du dommage' and, if this is done, then it is presumed that this 'participation été la cause génératrice' (the legal cause, we would say) of the damage *unless* the defendant can show that the thing played a purely 'passive' role in the realisation of the damage. These early cases have been discussed by M. Nast, 'La Cause en matière de responsabilité du fait des choses', *S.J.* 1941,1.221. See also Joly, *Rev.trim.dr.civ.* (1942), 257, 268 *et seq.*; Ch. Civ. 10 oct. 1979, D. 1980,1.R. 232.
12. Malone, 9 *Stan.L.Rev.* (1956–57), 60.

13. *Ibid.* at p. 97. Contrast Prosser, 237. See also Hart and Honoré, pp. 103 *et seq.*
14. Becht and Miller, *The Test of Factual Causation*, 7.85. Honoré, *Encyclopedia*, 106.
15. In France, those who advocate a bifurcated approach to causation stress this point. Thus, Esmein, *Rev.trim.dr.civ.* (1934), 316, 322.
16. *Barnett* v. *Chelsea and Kensington Hospital Management Committee* [1969] 1 Q.B. 428. For another illustration see *British Road Services Ltd* v. *Arthur V. Crutchley & Co. Ltd* [1968] 1 All E.R. 811, and *Robinson* v. *P.O.* [1974] 1 W.L.R. 1176
17. Ch. Soc. 7 mai 1943, *S.* 1943,1.106; Ch. civ. 20 oct. 1931, D.H. 1931,538; *S.* 1932,1.83 (unlicensed driver not liable towards the person he ran over if he was driving carefully).
18. *The Empire Jamaica* [1957] A.C. 386.
19. *RGSt.* 15 (1886), 151. Similarly *RGSt.* 63 (1929), 211. See also paragraph 831 BGB and article 563 of the Portuguese CC.
20. *Woods* v. *Davidson* [1930] N.I. 61 (H.L.) (Northern Ireland).
21. *Weeks* v. *McNulty*, 1898, 101 Tenn. 495, 48 S.W. 809.
22. Glaser, *Abhandlungen aus dem österreichischen Strafrechte*, 1 (1858), 298 (translated in Hart and Honoré at pp. 391–2). Honoré, *Encyclopedia*, no. 117.
23. *RGZ* 141, 365. The Bundesgerichtshof, on the other hand, has leaned in favour of the substitution method, *BGHZ* 10,6.
24. For further refinements see Honoré, *Encyclopedia*, no. 117.
25. Hart and Honoré, p. 403.
26. [1957] A.C. 386.
27. Ch. Soc. 7 mai 1943, *S.* 1943,1.106.
28. *Corey* v. *Havener*, 1902, 182 Mass. 250, 65 N.E. 69.
29. *Anderson* v. *Minneapolis, St P. & S.S.M.R. Co.*, 1920, 146 Minn. 430, 179 N.W. 45.
30. Prosser, 239, n. 25; Fleming, 183, n. 19; Becht and Miller, *The Test of Factual Causation*, 95. In such cases it is generally accepted that there is 'a breakdown of ordinary causal notions'. Liability, however, is affirmed on the ground that each of the negligent parties has, by his own negligence, deprived the plaintiff of a cause of action against the other.
31. *Anderson* v. *Minneapolis, St. P. & S.S.M.R. Co.*, above, note 29, presumably influenced by J. Smith's 'Legal Cause of Actions in Tort', 25 *Harv.L.Rev.* (1911), 103, 223. It is particularly outrageous to deny the victim redress where all the factors that contributed to his harm are culpable.
32. *Restatement of Torts*, § 432 (2. For a different justification see note 30 above. Yet another way of solving such cases is by casting the onus of proof on the defendant. Thus, para. 830 BGB; Enneccerus and Lehmann, *Recht der Schuldverhältnisse*, § 15 III, 5.
33. *Golden* v. *Lerch Bros.*, 1938, 203 Minn. 211, 281 N.W. 249.
34. Carpenter, 'Workable Rules for Determining Proximate Cause', 20 *Cal.L.Rev.* (1932), 229, 396.
35. Prosser, at p. 240.
36. Von Caemmerer, *Das Problem der überholenden Kausalität*, reprinted in *Gesammelte Schriften*, I, 411. Most Germans would treat this as a problem of amount of damages rather than one of causation.
37. *RGZ* 169, 117, 120. Cf. D 43,24,7,4.

38. *BGHZ* 10,6; Enneccerus and Lehmann, *Recht der Schuldverhältnisse*, § 17 III,3; von Caemmerer, *Das Problem der überholenden Kausalität*, 245, reprinted in *Gesammelte Schriften*, I, 411, 425.

39. For a more detailed discussion consult Honoré, *Encyclopedia* §§ 135–9; Jacqueline Nguyen Thanh Nha, *Rev.trim.dr.civ.* (1976), 1; B. Puill, D. Chron. 1980,157 *et seq.* and, more generally, F. Chabas, 'Fait ou faute de la victime', D. Chron. 1973,207.

40. [1962] 2 Q.B. 405. The harshness of this solution, however is mitigated by the fact that allowance is made for the victim's 'reduced value' which is due to his disease. Thus, *Cutler* v. *Vauxhall Motors* [1971] 1 Q.B. 418. See also Fleming, 183, 191.

41. *Owens* v. *Liverpool Corp.* [1939] 1 K.B. 394, 400–1.

42. *England: Dulieu* v. *White* [1901] 2 K.B. 669, 679 (the locus classicus) *Smith* v. *Leech Brain & Co. Ltd* [1962] Q.B. 405. *Germany: RGZ* 155, 37; *BGHZ* 20, 137; BGH NJW 1958, 1579. *Belgium:* Cass. 5 nov. 1956, *Pas.* 1957,1.227; Cass 9 juin 1951, *Pas.* 1951,1.691. *France:* Ch. Crim. 9 nov. 1933, *G.P.* 1934,1.11; 15 déc. 1966, *J.C.P.* 1967,2.15162; 21 janv. 1970, *J.C.P.* 1970,4.65; 10 avr. 1973, *G.P.* 1973,2.710; Ch. Civ. 19 juil. 1966, D. 1966, 598; 5 avr. 1973, *G.P.* 1973,1.125. See also references in note 39 above.

43. *RGZ* 105,264.

44. *RGZ* 119,204 but contrast BGH NJW 1952, 1010. (Defendant who caused the plaintiff to lose a leg not liable for his inability several years later to rush to an air raid shelter for refuge.)

45. [1969] 3 All E.R. 1006. See also Ch. Civ. 16 juin 1969, *Bull.civ.* I, no. 230, Durry, *Rev.trim.dr.civ.* (1970), 356; Ch. Crim. 14 janv. 1970, Durry, *Rev.trim.dr.civ.* (1970), 574.

46. For cases see Mazeaud and Mazeaud, no. 1613, n. 4.

47. Ch. Comm. 19 juin 1951, D. 1951, 717 and Note Ripert; S. 1952,1.89 and Note Nerson.

48. 27 nov. 1970, D. 1971,181, concl. Lindon; Durry, *Rev.trim.dr.civ.* (1971), 657.

49. Ch. Civ. II juil. 1966, *Bull.civ.* II, no. 772; 12 juin 1969, *Bull.civ.* II, no. 204. In this sense see also Poitiers, 17 déc. 1968, *G.P.* 1969,1.171; Ch. Crim. 7 fév. 1967 referred to by Durry, *Rev.trim.dr.civ.* (1971), 657. On the whole matter see references given in note 39 above.

50. *Restatement of Torts,* § 455. Policy, however, may lead a court to the opposite result, e.g. *Pigney* v. *Pointers Transport* [1957] 1 W.L.R. 1121. Would the court have adopted the same favourable attitude if the deceased had failed in his suicide attempt and, instead, increased his incapacity? The *novus actus* approach, however is clearly inapplicable to acts of the plaintiff who has been rendered insane as a result of the tortfeasor's conduct.

51. They are examined more fully by Honoré, *Encyclopedia*, nos. 183, 184.

52. *Restatement of Torts,* § 461; *The Arpad* [1934] P. 189, 202 (the 'shabby millionaire', per Scrutton L.J.). Strictly speaking this is a rule of compensation (unlike the egg-shell-skull rule which is one of remoteness of damage) since it is concerned with *unexpected cost of expected consequences.*

53. The exceptions can be found in Norway and Denmark. See Selmer, 'Limitation of Damages according to Circumstances of the "Average Citizen"', 5 *Scand. Law Studies* (1961),131.

54. *RGZ* 7,216. Cf. RG of 6 May 1924, JW 1924, 1359.
55. *Liesbosch Dredger* v. *Edison Steamship* [1933] A.C. 449.
56. Clerk and Lindsell on Torts, 14th edn. § 346.
57. [1962] 1 Q.B. 33.
58. On the whole matter see von Caemmerer, *Das Problem der uberholende Kausalität*, 21–2, reprinted in *Gesammelte Schriften*, I, 411 *et seq.*
59. [1970] A.C. 467. Fleming, 184–5.
60. Ch. Civ. 29 sept. 1941, *G.P.* 1941,2.437; *J.C.P.* 1942,2.1779; Montpellier, 8 nov. 1949, *J.C.P.* 1950,2.5519; Orléans, 17 janv. 1949, D. 1949,502; Ch. Civ. 4 janv. 1957, D. 1957,264; S. 1957,218; Ch. Crim. 22 mars 1966, *G.P.* 1966,2.46. On this subject see Postacioglu, *Rev.trim.dr.civ.* (1954),438 and Aberkane, *Rev.trim.dr.civ.* (1958), 516.
61. Grenoble, 16 mai 1962, D. 1963,137 and Note Azard; Tunc, *Rev.trim.dr.civ.* (1963) 555.
62. Cour d'appel of A.E.F., 5 avr. 1957, *J.C.P.* 1957,2.10308. See also Ch. Civ. 5 fév. 1960, D. 1960, 365, and Note Aberkane.
63. Ch. Civ. 18 mai 1955, D. 1955,520; *J.C.P.*1955,2.8793 and Note Esmein; Ch. Civ. 5 juin 1957, D. 1957,493; *J.C.P.* 1957,2.10205; Ch. Civ. 6. mars 1968, *Bull.civ.* II, no. 76, p. 52, *Rev.trim.dr.civ.* (1968), 718, observations by Durry; Ch. Civ. 19 mai 1976, *J.C.P.* 1978,2.18773.
64. Rennes, 14 janv. 1971, *J.C.P.* 1971,16733; Durry, *Rev.trim.dr.civ.* (1971), 377.
65. F. Chabas, *Responsabilité civile et responsabilité pénale* (1975), 46; Ch. Civ. 28 fév. 1939, *G.P.* 1939,1.698 and *Rev.gén.ass.terr.* 1939,509 and Note Besson, Grenoble, 16 mai 1962, D. 1963,137 and Note Azard.
66. *Summer* v. *Tice*, 1948, 33 Cal. Reptr. 2d. 80, 199 P. 2d. 1, cf. *Cook* v. *Lewis* [1952] 1 D.L.R. 1 [1951] S.C. Rep. 830. In other cases, the courts have solved this problem by finding concert of action and thus permiting recovery against all defendants. *Oliver* v. *Miles*, 1927, 144 Miss. 852, 110 So. 66 is an example.
67. *Ybarra* v. *Spangard*, 25 Cal. Reptr. 2d. 486, 154.P. 2d. 687 (1944).
68. *BGHZ* NJW 1960, 862.
69. *BGHZ* 25, 271.
70. *BGHZ* 55, 86.
71. OLG Celle 1950, NJW 1950, 951.
72. Glasser, *Abhandlungen*; von Buri in many works culminating in *Die Kausalität und ihre strafrechtilichen Beziehungen* (1885); B. Windscheid, *Lehrbuch des Pandektenrechts*, II (1902), nos. 257–8. For accounts in English see: Hart and Honoré, pp. 391 *et seq.* and P. Catala and J.A. Weir, 39 *Tul.L.Rev.* (1965), 708 *et seq.*
73. RG St. 1 (1880), 373, 374. The Bundesgerichtshof has almost consistently adopted the same view.
74. French writers have argued that the rule that independent tortfeasors are each liable in solidum to the plaintiff points strongly towards the equivalence theory.
75. Though once popular in France it is now more or less abandoned by most writers and, it seems, the courts. Thus, for example, Mazeaud and Mazeaud, no. 1441; Savatier, II, nos. 468 and especially 471 *et seq.*; Weill and Terré, no. 743.
76. *France*: art. 1151 CC (which is generally accepted as applicable in tort, too; see Mazeaud and Mazeaud, nos. 1670 *et seq.*); *Belgium*: art. 1151 CC; *Italy*: art. 1223 CC; *The Netherlands*: art. 1284 CC etc.
77. After the decision in *Re Polemis* [1921] 3 K.B. 560 (C.A.).

78. Hart and Honoré, pp. 151–70. Support for this interpretation can be found in the 5th edn of the treatise of the Mazeaud brothers written in collaboration with A. Tunc. The 6th edn (1970) on the other hand takes a different view and interprets direct consequences as necessary consequences. The authors, however, admit that the substitute concept is vague. See no. 1671 in finem.

79. Weill and Terré, nos. 606, 743.

80. Ch. Civ. 6 janv. 1943, *S.* 1943,1.51; D. 1945,117 (*Connot c. Franck*), cf. Ch. Civ. 20 nov. 1951, D. 1952,268.

81. *Cattle* v. *Stockton Waterworks Co.* (1875) L.R. 10 Q.B. 453; *Weller and Co.* v. *Foot and Mouth Disease Institute* [1965] 3 All E.R. 560.

82. Marteau, *La Notion de causalité*, 221. Cf. similar statements in Weill and Terré, no. 416; Starck, no. 747.

83. A rare and extreme example can be found in *Pigney* v. *Pointers Transport* [1957] 1 W.L.R. 1121.

84. See *Liesbosch Dredger* v. *Edison Steamship* [1933] A.C. 449.

85. Fleming, 195.

86. Ehrenzweig, 54 *Cal.L.Rev.* (1966), 1422, 1460 *et seq.* Cf. Goodhart, 39 *Yale L.J.* (1930), 449; 68 *L.Q.R.* (1952), 514; and 76 *L.Q.R.* (1960), 567.

87. Thus: 'egg-shell-skull' rule retained (*Smith* v. *Leech Brain and Co. Ltd* [1962] 2 Q.B. 405); if the 'kind' of harm is foreseeable the way in which it occurs need not be (*Wieland* v. *Cyril Lord Carpets, Ltd* [1969] 3 All E.R. 1006); and if the 'kind' of harm is foreseeable its magnitude need not be (*Vacwell Engineering Co. Ltd* v. *B.D.H. Chemicals Ltd* [1971] 1 Q.B. 88).

88. J. von Kries, *Die Prinzipien der Wahrscheinlichkeitsrechnung; Ueber den Begriff der objektiven Möglichkeit.* See also Carl Ludwig von Bar, *Die Lehre vom Kausalzusammenhang im Recht, besonders im Strafrechte* (1871).

89. Von Kries' term 'objektive Möglichkeit' is best rendered as 'objective probability'. It is thus only those conditions which objectively increase the changes of the harm in question which can be regarded as its causes. For a different (negative) formulation of the rule see Enneccerus and Lehmann, *Recht der Schuldverhältnisse*, § 15 III, 2.

90. Traeger, *Der Kausalbegriff im Straf- und Zivilrecht* (1929), 159 *et seq.*

91. Thus, Deutsch, *Haftungsrecht* 146 *et seq.*; Hermann Lange, *Schadensersatz* (1979), 57 *et seq.* with further references on this point.

92. BGH 23 Oct. 1951 *BGHZ* 3, 261, 267 (Honoré's translation).

93. [1967] 1 A.C. 617. The decision, however, is far from clear. On this see, generally, Dias, 'Trouble on Oiled Waters: Problems of the Wagon Mound (No. 2)', 26 *C.L.J.* (1967), 62.

94. J. Carbonnier, *Droit civil*, IV, p. 323.

95. For illustrations, see Honoré, *Encyclopedia*, 51;

96. [1954] 2 Q.B. 66.

97. [1961] A.C. 388.

98. 'Das Problem des Kausalzusammenhangs', reprinted in *Gesammelte Schriften*, I, 395, 402, 408 *et seq.*

99. E. Rabel in *Das Recht des Warenkaufs*, (1936), 495 *et seq.*

100. Green in *The Rationale of Proximate Cause.*

101. Note, however, the decision of the Chambre Criminelle of 14 janv. 1969, *J.C.P.* 1969,16.101; Durry, *Rev.trim.dr.civ.* (1970), 181. In that case a manufacturer of an

'elixir' represented as having dietetic qualities was prosecuted for illegally exercising the profession of pharmacist. Having proved that his substance contained no chemical or biological elements, he was acquitted on that charge. However, he was found guilty of violating article 5 of the law of 2 July 1963 prohibiting 'la publicité mensongère' and ordered to pay damages to the Ordre national des pharmaciens, which had constituted itself as *partie civile*. On appeal the decision was quashed 'au motif que la loi de 1963 a pour objet la défense des consommateurs et non la protection directe ou indirecte de l'intérêt collectif de la profession pharmaceutique' (Durry). Though the 'scope of the rule' theory is put here to successful use, the decision must be seen in the context of the restrictive approach adopted by the Chambre Criminelle in matters of 'recevabilité de l'action civile'. For further details on this topic see the discussion at the end of this chapter.

102. (1874) L.R. 9 Ex. 125.
103. [1962] A.C. 367.
104. *Ibid.*
105. [1972] 1 Q.B. 373.
106. [1978] A.C. 728.
107. BGH 39, 358.
108. In *Anns* v. *Merton London Borough* [1978] A.C. 728, 752, Lord Wilberforce said as much but did not pursue the point further. Had he done so, a result similar to that reached by the German court could have been achieved, thus avoiding the almost inevitable and, to some, undesirable, extension of the *Donoghue* v. *Stevenson* rule.
109. BGH 39, 366. Lord Denning has, extrajudicially (*The Discipline of the Law* (1979), 264), come very close to accepting that Mrs Dutton's harm was pure economic loss. In his judgment, however, he argued differently.
110. Malone, 9 *Stan.L.Rev.* (1956–57), 60, 73.
111. This has been strongly advocated by Ehrenzweig in his 'Negligence Without Fault', 54 *Cal.L.Rev.* (1966) and other writings (e.g. in 69 *Yale L.J.* (1960), 978, 989). Ehrenzweig's view is thus that the defendant should bear this consequences of the incidents which are typical to his business or enterprise and this irrespective of fault or causal principles.
112. See the references given in note 4, and Chabas, *L'Influence de la pluralité de causes*.
113. For a full comparative discussion see Weir, *Encylopedia*, pp. 40 *et seq.*
114. Starck, no. 760. More extensively: Mazeaud and Mazeaud, nos. 1540 *et seq.* (with further references in note 4).
115. Mazeaud and Mazeaud, nos. 1574–6, 1590 *et seq.*
116. Ch. Com. 19 juin 1951, D. 1951, 717 and Note Ripert; S. 1952, 1.89 and Note Nerson.
117. Ch. Civ. 13 mars 1957, *J.C.P.* 1957,2.10084 and Note Esmein; D. 1958,73 and Note Radouant.
118. For fuller references see Chabas, *L'Influence de la pluralité de causes*, pp. 2 *et seq.* But the two decisions have not been without supporters. Thus, Nerson and Radouant in their above-mentioned case-note and, more recently, Boré, 'Les Arrêts de la Chambre mixte du 20 déc. 1968' in *J.C.P.* 1969,1.2221 nos. 20—7
119. Honoré, *Encyclopedia*, nos. 189 *et seq.*
120. Starck, nos. 77 *et seq.* Mazeaud and Mazeaud, no. 1639, *Germany*: §§ 830 1 and

840 1 BGB; *Italy*: art. 2055.1. CC; *Switzerland*: art. 50.1 OR.

121. D. 1951,717.

122. Ch. Civ. 9 mars 1962, *J.C.P.*, 1962,2.12728 and Note Esmein; D. 1962,625 and Note Savatier.

123. Ch. Mixte, 20 déc. 1968 (three decisions), D. 1969,37.

124. Ch. Civ. 2 juil. 1969, *G.P.* 1969,2.311; Durry, *Rev.trim.dr.civ.* (1970), 177. The victim in this case was injured in a car accident involving a car driven by a fellow employee and a car driven by a third party. Because of art. 470 of the Code de la securité sociale he could not have sued his fellow employee driver so, instead, he sued the third party, *gardien* of the other car. The latter was held responsible for the full amount even though he would have had no right of contribution against the other driver (the fellow employee of the plaintiff). The result may appear harsh, but not once one realises that it was the insurance company of the defendant which would meet the cost. In the result therefore, if not in its reasons, the Cour de cassation thus finally appeared to be acknowledging the fact that automobile insurance had become compulsory since 1958 (unless one argues that their earlier stance was ultimately influenced by fears that insurance premiums would get out of control if they decided the cases otherwise).

125. It must be remembered, however, that 'fault' is not a term of art in the Common law. On this see F.H. Lawson, 'Fault and Contract – A Few Comparisons', 49 *Tul.L.Rev.* (1975), 295.

126. D 50,17,203. Cf. D 21,1,23,8; h.t. 9,4, 52 pr.

127. The theory of culpa-compensation, which mitigates the harshness of this rule, has been briefly discussed in chapter 1, pp. 33–4 above.

128. Though not as a result of conscious imitation.

129. Art. 1304 CC.

130. OR arts. 44, 55 and 101.

131. Tunc, *Encyclopedia*, XI, ch. 1, p. 17.

132. Honoré, *Encyclopedia*, p. 97.

133. Para. 254 1 BGB.

134. In Mazeaud and Mazeaud, nos. 1447 *et seq.* one can, once again, find an exhaustive treatment of the entire subject.

135. Starck, no. 830.

136. For example, Ch. Req. 12 janv. 1927, D. 1927,1.145 and Note Savatier; Ch. Civ. 7 déc. 1931, *G.P.*, 1932,1.363.

137. S. 1934,1.313 and Note H. Mazeaud; D. 1934,1.41 and Note R. Savatier.

138. G.P. 1937,1.157.

139. The first case which *clearly* enunciated this approach was the decision of the second Chambre Civile of 17 déc. 1963, D. 1964, 569 and Note Tunc; and others followed in close succession. Professor Starck, however, who strongly disapproves of this line of approach, has argued (Starck, nos. 837 *et seq.*) that some of these cases, though talking of 'fait de la victime', really refer to conduct which reveals some fault, albeit slight. Not all the decisions of the second Chambre Civile can be seen in this way, the decision of 1963 being one such case.

140. See above, pp. 113–14 and, in more detail, Jacqueline Nguyen Thanh Nha, in *Rev.trim.dr.civ.* (1976), 1; Puill, in D.Chron. 1980,157 *et seq.*

141. In this sense A. Tunc in *Rev.int.dr.comp.* (1953), 25 *et seq.*

142. Green, *The Rationale of Proximate Cause*, 11–43; though this hardly solves the

problem. See Prosser's masterly account of the *Palsgraf* case in 52 *Mich.L.Rev.* (1953),1.

143. *Hambrook* v. *Stokes Bros.* [1925] 1 K.B. 141, *Guay* v. *Sun Publishing Co.* [1953] 4 D.L.R. 577 (in some respects an unconvincing case); *Dillon* v. *Legg*, 68 Cal. Reptr. 2d. 728, 441 P. 2d. 912 (1968). Cf. *Archibald* v. *Braverman*, 79 Cal. Reptr. 723 (Cal. App. 1969) (mother who did not witness the accident, but came on the scene five minutes after the tragedy, allowed to recover). *Schneider* v. *Eisovitch* [1960] 2 Q.B. 430, 441, the only English case suggesting the contrary, has been criticised (Jolowicz [1960] *C.L.J.* 156). Section 4 of the Law Reform (Miscellaneous Provisions) Act of 1944 New South Wales allows the parent or spouse of the primary victim to recover for nervous shock even where the accident is not witnessed by them.

144. *RGZ* 133, 270; *RGZ* 157, 111; BGH NJW 1971, 1883. For further details see von Hippel, NJW 1965, 1890, especially note 5. See also Berg, note to LG Frankfurt, NJW 1969, 2286 in NJW 1970, 515 *et seq.*

145. Von Hippel, NJW 1965, 1890 at 1891 openly admits that the problem is not one of causation but of policy. Huber, in *Festschrift E. Wahl*, 301 *et seq.*, agrees. Thus increasing reliance can be found on more normative theories of causation (e.g. the Normzweck approach) and even the contractual concept of *Vertrag mit Schutzwirkung für Dritter* has been mentioned as a possible source of inspiration. See Berg in NJW 1970, 515.

146. One is the well-known technique of restricting claim to near relatives of the accident victim. This is now discarded by the Common law but was left open by the BGH, NJW 1971, 1883. More important and probably reasonable is the requirement that the plaintiff's distress must be accompanied by physical or psychological manifestations (*BGHZ* 56, 163). And the above-mentioned decision of the BGH (NJW 1971, 1883) appears to go even further by suggesting that 'shocks which do not exceed in intensity accustomed reactions to the news of a husband's or child's sudden death fall outside the protective ambit of the violated tort rule' (J.G. Fleming, 30 *A.J.Comp.L.* (1972), 485, 491 (an article severely critical of the BGH decision)). In contrast to the above, French law appears most generous to claims for grief and distress. Thus, for example, Rouen 27 juin 1967, *G.P.* 1967, 2 *Somm.* 20; Ch. Civ. 21 oct. 1960, *Bull.civ.* 1960, no. 594; Ch. Civ. 17 mai 1973 *G.P.* 1974, criticised by Durry in *Rev.trim.dr.civ.* (1974), 409 (interruption of pregnancy as a result of plaintiff's shock when she became aware that her husband had been involved in an accident), Caen, 2 nov. 1976, *G.P.* of 3 March 1977, criticised by Durry in *Rev.trim.dr.civ.* (1977), 327 (mother of five killed in an accident; three weeks later husband, suffering from shock, commits suicide; defendant held liable to the children for the economic consequences of the suicide). Cf. Ch. Crim. 25 avr. 1967, *Rev.trim.dr.civ.* (1967), 822.

147. Prosser, 244.

148. As in *Palsgraf* v. *Long Island Ry. Co.* 1928, 248 N.Y. 339, 162 N.E. 99; *Hay (Bourhill)* v. *Young* [1943] A.C. 92.

149. Prosser, 245. Cf. Professor P.S. Atiyah's differing views on the usefulness of the notion of duty in such cases: *Accidents, Compensation and the Law* (1975), pp. 75 *et seq.*

150. See Huber in *Festschrift E. Wahl* (1973) 301, 318.

151. Prosser, 255, suggests that 'the written law and the policy of strict construction which refuses to extend its effect beyond the legislative purpose seem definitely to set this apart from any court-made rule' (like that found in *Palsgraf* and *Hay (Bourhill)* v. *Young*). Limpens, on the other hand, does not appear to emphasise this difference: *Mélanges Savatier* (1965), 559, especially 569 *et seq.*

152. G. Marty is one of the authors who has argued this in *Etudes juridiques offertes à L. Julliot de la Morandière* (1964), 339 *et seq.* Planiol had earlier argued that 'la faute étant l'inexécution d'un devoir, ceux-là seuls peuvent se plaindre de la faute qui auraient pu exiger l'accomplissement du devoir et même, ils ne peuvent se prétendre lésés que d'une manière relative, c'est-à-dire dans ceux de leurs intérêts que la loi a voulu protéger' (Note to Ch. Civ. 7 août 1895, D. 1896,1.81).

153. *Bull.civ.* II, no. 243.

154. Ch. Civ. 17 mars 1958, *J.C.P.* 1959,2.10950.

155. Ch. Civ. 1 mars 1965, *J.C.P.* 1965,2.14134; D. 1965,560; 13 janv. 1965, D. 1965, *Somm.* 86.

156. *J.C.P.* 1968,2.15597; *Rev.trim.dr.civ.* (1969), 123.

157. M. Puech, *L'Illicéité*, 283.

158. Puech, *L'Illicéité*, 291 *et seq.*

159. *J.C.P.* 1967,2.14979.

160. Ch. Crim. 6 mars 1969, *Bull.crim.* no. 110, 271; Robert, *Revue Science Criminelle* (1969), 888; Durry, *Rev.trim.dr.civ.* (1969), 780. In the same sense Ch. Crim. 5 juil. 1967, *Bull.crim.* no. 203.

161. Puech, *L'Illicéité*, 290.

162. Some decisions of the second Chambre Civile appeared to introduce a limitation device by refusing to compensate damage which was *not* 'suffisamment grave'. Thus, Ch. Civ. 14 déc. 1972, *G.P.* 1973,2.587; Durry, *Rev.trim.dr.civ.* (1974), 600; Ch. Civ. 5 janv. 1973, Durry, *Rev.trim.dr.civ.* (1973), 775. This insistence on a 'préjudice présentant une gravité exceptionnelle' was abandoned by the Chambre Civile in its decision of 23 May 1977, *Bull.civ.* no. 139; Durry, *Rev.trim.dr.civ.* (1977), 768–70. On the whole matter, see Dupichot, *Des Préjudices*, nos. 204–13.

163. *J.C.P.* 1980,2.19335 and Rapport Ponsard.

164. *Ibid.* (italics supplied). Durry, *Rev.trim.dr.civ.* (1972), 595–6, openly states that it is these kinds of policy considerations that influenced the second Chambre Civile to adopt the restrictive approach found in the cases quoted in note 162 above.

4 Liability without fault

1. Ames, 22 *Harv.L.Rev.* (1908), 97 *et seq.*; Isaacs, 31 *Harv.L.Rev.* (1918), 954 *et seq.*; Ripert, *La Règle morale dans les obligations civiles*, 4th edn, nos. 112–32.

2. Strongly and cogently criticised amongst others by J.A. Jolowicz, 27 *C.L.J.* (1968), 50 *et seq.*

3. A. Heldrich, 'Compensating Non-Economic Losses in the Affluent Society', 18 *A.J.Comp.L.* (1970), 22.

4. It is a characteristic consequence of the Roman juristic method, which drew a sharp line between law and fact, and paid only the slightest regard to questions of evidence, that we are nowhere told where the burden of proof lay in cases of negligence. In accordance with the general rule that one who alleges a fact must prove it (Paul, *D* 22,3,2) the plaintiff must, we must assume, have had to prove

not only the damage but also the *culpa* of the defendant. Although no use is professedly made of either presumption or inference in the *Digest* title of the *lex Aquilia*, most, if not all, of the actual cases discussed would seem to yield to their application.

5. *Scott* v. *London & St Katherine Docks Co.* (1865) 3 H. & C. 596. Cf. *BGHZ* 8, 239.

6. Fleming James Jr, 32 *Tenn.L.Rev.* (1965), 394, 395.

7. For an excellent discussion with further references see: A. Tunc, *Encyclopedia*, XI, ch.I, nos. 133–53. See also references at the end of this chapter.

8. L.M. Friedman and J. Ladinsky, 67 *Col.L.Rev.* (1967), 50, 60.

9. *Union Government* v. *Sykes*, 1913 A.D. 161; *Botes* v. *Potchefstroom Municipality*, 1941 T.P.D. 149. Cf. *Eastern & South African Telegraph Co.* v. *Cape Town Tramways* [1902] A.C. 381, 393–4, where the Privy Council expressed (obiter) the opinion that the rule in *Rylands* v. *Fletcher* is not inconsistent with Roman-Dutch law.

10. (1868) L.R. 3 H.L. 330.

11. Cf. McKerron, p. 246.

12. *Kerr* v. *Earl of Orkney* (1857) 20 D. 298.

13. (1868) L.R. 3 H.L. 330.

14. The *Reichshaftpflichtgesetz* of 1871 as extended in 1943.

15. Thus, *Jones* v. *Southern Utah Power Co.*, 106 Utah 482, 150 P. 2d.376 (1944); *Ottertail Power Co.* v. *Duncan*, 137 F. 2d. 187 (8th Cir. 1943); *Chase* v. *Washington Power Co.*, 62 Idaho 298, 111 P. 2d. 872 (1941). Before the introduction of the special statutory liability the Germans adopted a similar approach. See, for example, *RGZ* 14, 353 and Esser, *JZ* 1953, 129. Ehrenzweig's works, quoted at the end of this chapter, provide further material on this point.

16. Department of Transportation, *Driver Behavior and Accident Involvement*, 177–8. In fact these accidents are so unavoidable that another report by the Department of Transportation (*Causation, Culpability and Deterrence*, 209), has suggested that attention should be shifted 'from the prevention or reduction of the number of crashes to the prevention or reduction of the human and economic losses that result from crashes'.

17. Ch. Civ. 1 déc. 1965, *J.C.P.* 1966,2.14567; *J.C.P.* 1966,1.1983; 31 *C.L.J.* (1972), 247, 253 *et seq.* See also 32 *C.L.J.* (1973), 52, 241. For an even stranger set of facts which were held to amount to *faute* see Grenoble 4 déc. 1978, *J.C.P.* 1980,2.19340.

18. Though the confusion between fault and error can also work against those victims (especially of traffic accidents) whose slight fault or error is taken into account in order to reduce their compensation. On this see Tunc, D. Chron. 1975,83.

19. Though in all the systems under comparison the courts vacillate, sometimes taking the side of the patient and thus equating error with fault, and sometimes not. Tunc, *Encyclopedia*, XI, ch. 1, no. 145.

20. *Whitehouse* v. *Jordan and Another* [1980] 1 All E.R. 650; affirm. by the H. of L. in [1981] 1 W.L.R. 246. For the U.S. see Capron, 79 *Col.L.Rev.* (1979), 618.

21. Counsel in that case estimated that the total cost would exceed £150,000 and, if the case had been allowed to proceed to the House of Lords, this sum would have been much higher.

22. The defects of the fault system from this point of view have been eloquently explored by Professor Guido Calabresi in a series of articles culminating in his

book *The Costs of Accidents* (1970). Any compression of this new approach is bound to do it injustice so perhaps it is best to leave Calabresi himself to summarise his views on the fault system:

the fault system can only be justified if what we wish to minimize is neither the sum of the costs of accidents, and their avoidance... nor 'faulty behavior',... nor both of them,... but rather only those accidents in which 'faulty' behavior is a 'but for' cause. The more one examines this proposition, the more absurd the fault system becomes (*ibid.* at p. 276).

23. Jolowicz, 27 *C.L.J.* (1968), 50, 61. For further references to literature critical of the notion, see the select bibliography at the end of this chapter.
24. But see P.S. Atiyah in Allen, Bourn and Holyoak, *Accident Compensation*, 257 *et seq.*
25. (1868) L.R. 3 H.L. 330.
26. See Tunc, 39 *Louisiana L.Rev.* (1979), 1051, 1053. See also the conclusions of M. l'avocat général Sarrut in D.P. 1897,1.433, 439 *et seq.* (16 June 1896).
27. See Labbé's note in S. 1871,1.9 but cf. his note to *De Sitter* c. *l'Etat Belge*, S. 1890,4.18.
28. *Quebec Railway, Light, Heat and Power Co. Ltd* v. *Vandry* [1920] A.C. 662.
29. *La Belgique judiciaire* 1871, 758. For a fuller account see Mazeaud and Mazeaud, *Leçons*, pp. 538 *et seq.*
30. *Pas.* 1889,1.161.
31. *Pas.* 1904,1.246.
32. See R. Dalcq, *Traité de la responsabilité civile*, 2nd edn (1967), §§2012, 2137–61. Cf. *Loescher* v. *Parr*, 324 So. 2d. 441 (La. 1975) (Louisiana Supreme Court). For further details on Louisiana law, see: F. F. Stone, 'Tort Doctrine', in 12 *Louisiana Civil Law Treatise* (1977), §§61, 310 and A. Tunc, 'Louisiana Tort Law at the Crossroads', 48 *Tul.L.Rev.* (1974), 1111.
33. 21 juin 1895, D.P. 1896,3.65.
34. 16 juin 1896, D.P. 1897,1.433, Note Saleilles; S. 1897,1.17 and Note Esmein.
35. Mainly from R. Saleilles, *Les Accidents du travail et la responsabilité délictuelle* (1897) and L. Josserand, *De la Responsabilité du fait des choses inanimées* (1897). For an earlier attempt see Sainctelette, *De la Responsabilité et de la garantie. Accidents de transports et accidents de travail* (1884).
36. 30 mars 1897, S. 1898,1.71; D.P. 1897,1.441. At the time when this case was decided (1897) the Bill, which was to become the 1898 Law, was already before the Assemblée Nationale and this *may* have been one reason why the court felt it could take a more cautious approach to the problem. Events proved it right for it was not until 1919 that the new theory was to receive new impetus (Cass. 21 janv. 1919, D. 1922,1.25 and Note Ripert).
37. Ch. Req. 22 mars 1911, D.P. 1911,1.354.
38. Besançon, 29 déc. 1925 and Lyon of 7 juil. 1927 (S. 1927,2.106) which, in fact, led to the decision of the plenary session of the Cour de cassation of 13 fév. 1930, D.P. 1930,1.57.
39. *Jand'heur* c. *Les Galeries Belfortaises*, D.P. 1930,1.57.
40. Tunc, 39 *Louisiana L.Rev.* (1979), 1051, 1070.
41. Thus: Ch. Réun. 13 fév. 1930 (cars) (see note 38); Ch. Civ. 30 janv. 1950, D. 1950,380 (locomotives); Ch. Req. 19 déc. 1927, S. 1928,1.177 (trams); Montpellier, 28 fév. 1929, D.P. 1929, 2.41 (bicycles); Paris 18 fév. 1946, D.

1947,285 (fire-arms); Ch. Civ. 26 juin 1953, D. 1954,181 (corrosive liquids); Trib. Civ. Marseille, 8 juin 1950, G.P. 1950,2.137 (radio-active materials); Chambéry, 15 fév. 1944. G.P. 1944,1.134 (ski coming off skier's boot); Ch. Civ. 24 fév. 1941, S. 1941,1.201 (chair on which passer-by stumbles); Ch. Civ. 17 janv. 1962, D. 1962, 533 (wooden board with protruding nail); Rennes, 20 juin 1975, D. 1976,351 (raincoat caught in a motor-cycle) etc. etc.

42. And Capitant regretfully agreed with him. D.H. Chron. 1930, 28, 30-2. For more recent views see the works of Savatier and Starck quoted at the end of this chapter.

43. Ripert, Note to l'affaire Jand'heur, D. 1930,1.59.III. The strange decision of the Court of Appeal of Grenoble of 4 déc. 1978, J.C.P. 1980,2.19340, though not on article 1384 CC, very nearly vindicates Ripert's fears while showing how objectively faute is understood.

44. §832 BGB; § 1309 Austrian CC; art. 2047 Italian CC.

45. §829 BGB. The Prussian Code, 1.6, §§15, 41 and the Austrian CC § 1310 had already foreshadowed this solution. It seems to go back to mediaeval German law (Sachsenspiegel, II, art. 65), was thrust into the background by the reception of Roman law and then revived by the natural lawyers from Thomasius onwards: Gierke, Deutsches Privatrecht, III, 909-10.

46. OR § 54; Soviet CC art. 406; Italian CC art. 2047.

47. Art. 1386 CC as amended by Loi 16 avr. 1935, art. 1.

48. Escoffier c. Girel, D. 1947,J.329 and conclusions of M. le conseiller Lenoan. A provision in the Government bill (which became the 1968 Act), expressly allowing judges to moderate awards against lunatics, was expunged from the final text, presumably in the belief that judges are, in any event, free to fix the amounts of such awards and, in so doing, will inevitably take the defendant's condition into account.

49. This solution is in fact adopted in art. 1911 of the Mexican Code. Generally speaking, it would seem that the same difficulty would lie in the way of a similar argument if put before an English court. There is no very compelling authority for the proposition that a person incapable of distinguishing right from wrong cannot be liable in tort for negligence, but liability at Common law, if it existed, would have to be for the full amount of the damage, and this might seem too hard in many instances.

50. Ch. Civ. 2ème section, 18 déc. 1964, D. 1965,J.191, concl. de M. l'avocat général Schmelck.

51. Ch. Civ. 2ème section, 1 mars 1967, Bull.civ. 1967,11,no. 96;Ch. Civ. 2ème section, 30 juin 1966, Bull.civ. 1966, II, no. 720 and Durry, observations in Rev.trim.dr.civ. (1967) 828.

52. Art. 489-2 provides: 'celui qui a causé un dommage à autrui alors qu'il était sous l'empire d'un trouble mental, n'en est pas moins obligé à réparation'.

53. The leading case was Veuve Gasse c. Saby, Ch. Civ. 27 mars 1928, D.P. 1928,1.145 and Note Ripert. For an English discussion of the developments in this area see Britton in 25 I.C.L.Q. (1976). 826.

54. Henri Capitant, Les Grands Arrêts de la jurisprudence civile, 7th edn (1976), 530.

55. For example, Weill and Terré, no. 728 and notes.

56. For example, Ch. Civ. 2ème section, 5 avr. 1962, D. 1963,78; 21 déc. 1962, D. 1963,418 and Boré, 'La Chambre civile a-t-elle créé une presomption de faute à la

charge du transporteur bénévole?' D. Chron. 1963,21. See also the interesting decision of Paris, 27 juin 1967, *G.P.* 1967,2.170 (affirmed by Ch. Mixte, 20 déc. 1968, D. 1969,37) and observations by Durry in *Rev.trim.dr.civ.* (1968),152.

57. Ch. Mixte, 20 déc. 1968 (three decisions) D. 1969,37.

58. Thus, see Durry, *Rev.trim.dr.civ.* (1967), 636; (1970), 571; (1971), 160.

59. Josserand, 'Le Gardien de l'automobile, le voleur et la víctime d'un accident', D.H. Chron. 1936,37.

60. D.P. 1936,1.81.

61. 2 déc. 1941, D.C. 1942,25 and Note Ripert; S. 1941,1.217 and Note H. Mazeaud. The whole problem cannot be understood apart from the practice of third party insurance which, though spreading, was *not at that time* compulsory in France. The problem was hence whether, if thieves stole a car and after injuring someone disappeared completely or were insolvent – both the reckless driving and the disappearance being only what one would expect – the (innocent) owner (or his insurer *if there was one*) should pay compensation to the (equally innocent) victim or whether the latter should go without a remedy.

    The problem nowadays is different given the establishment (since 1958) of compulsory third party insurance, the increase of social security benefits, and the creation of various Fonds de garantie which in France took place in 1951. (Initially these covered only *dommage corporel*, but since 1966 they have also covered *dommage matériel* up to a certain limit.) The question now is who should 'foot the bill': the owner's insurer or the state? For a comparative study of traffic accident compensation see Tunc, *Encyclopedia*, XI, ch. 14.

62. See Goldman, *La Détermination du gardien responsable*; idem. *Mélanges P. Roubier*, II (1961), pp. 51 *et seq.*; D. Mayer, 'La "Garde" en commun', *Rev.trim.dr.civ.* (1975), 197; A. Tunc, 'Garde du comportement et garde de la structure dans la responsabilité du fait des choses inanimées', *J.C.P.* 1957,1.1384; *idem.*, 'La Détermination du gardien dans la responsabilité du fait des choses inanimées', *J.C.P.* 1960,1.1592. See also A. Tunc, Note to Ch. Civ. 3 nov. 1942; Ch. Req. 22 juin 1943, D. 1947,145 and, more generally, Mazeaud and Tunc, nos. 1155 *et seq.*, esp. 1160.

63. In this sense, Tunc in references given in previous note.

64. See Tunc in *J.C.P.* 1960,1.1592 and in D. 1947,145, II.B inclining in favour of the latter view.

65. Ch. Civ. 2ème section, 5 janv. 1956, D. 1957,261 and Note Rodière; *J.C.P.* 1956,2.9095 and Note Savatier; Weill and Terré, no. 777 and n. 1. See also: Ch. Civ. 11 déc. 1968, *Bull.civ.* II, no. 304 and Ch. Civ. 12 juin 1969, *Bull.civ.* III, no. 473; Durry, *Rev.trim.dr.civ.* (1970), 361; Poitiers, 20 déc. 1969, *G.P.* 1970,2.13; Durry, *Rev.trim.dr.civ.* (1971), 151 (where it is stressed that considerations of policy and equity lie behind the decisions of the courts).

66. J. Carbonnier, *Droit Civil* (8th edn), IV (1975), p. 394.

67. Ch. Civ. 21 juin 1937, S. 1937,1.350 and 1938,1.16; 9 juin 1939, D.H. 1939,449; 16 janv. 1940, S. 1940,1.97 and Note H. Mazeaud.

68. D. 1930,1.59. III.

69. Ch. Civ. 19 fév. 1941, D.C. 1941,85; Ch. Civ. 23 janv. 1945, *D.J.* 1945,317 and Note Savatier.

70. Weill and Terré, no. 711; Carbonnier, *Droit civil*, IV, § 108 and, in greater detail, Mazeaud and Tunc, no. 1211 bis.

71. Ch. Civ. 24 fév. 1941, S. 1941, I.201; A. Tunc, 'Force majeure et absence de faute en matière délictuelle', *Rev.trim.dr.civ.* (1946), 171, 194: Mazeaud and Tunc, nos. 1211–19 bis.
72. See also para. 1319 Austrian CC.
73. An English summary of their basic provisions along with further literature can be found in the first edition of A. von Mehren's *The Civil Law System* (1957), pp. 415 *et seq.* and Zweigert and Kötz, 315–22.
74. The law is now consolidated in the *Haftpflichtgesetz* of 4 January 1978 which also covers 'death, or injury to the body or health of a human being or damage to property where this is due to the effects of electricity, gas, steam or liquids that emanate from an installation for the transmission or supply of such energies or substances'. Ceilings are also established for certain kinds of liability, and in some cases liability cannot be excluded or limited by agreement.
75. See Sir Otto Kahn-Freund's remarks in the translated edition of Karl Renner's *The Institutions of Private Law* (1948, reprinted 1976) at p. 238.
76. (*RGBl.* 437) now law of 19 December 1952 (*BGBl.* I 837).
77. (*RGBl.* I 681) now law of 10 January 1959 (*BGBl.* I 9). Liability is stricter than usual since the operator of the aircraft is liable even if the accident is due to *force majeur.*
78. (*BGBl.* I 814).
79. (*BGBl.* I 1110.) Note also the *Gesetz zur Reinhaltung der Bundeswasserstrassen of* 17 August 1960 (*BGBl.* II 2125).
80. For a relatively brief but up to date description of the various Swiss statutes see H. Deschenaux and P. Tercier, *La Responsabilité civile* (1975), pp. 138–86.
81. Art. 1.
82. For example, *ATF* 63/1937, II. 204; 44/1918, II.289; 34/1908, II.444 (interpreting the terms 'construction' and 'travaux accessoires').
83. In force since 1 August 1975. For a fuller discussion see Deschenaux and Tercier, *La Responsabilité civile*, pp. 138 *et seq.*
84. *RGZ* 78, 171, at 172; *BGHZ* 51, 91; 55,229.
85. Eg. *RGZ* 147, 353. See also BGH NJW 1965,197.
86. OGH 10 September 1947, SZ XXI 46; OGH 20 February 1958, SZ XXXI 26; OGH 18 March 1953, SZ XXVI 75; OGH 30 August 1961, SZ XXXIV III.
87. Zweigert and Kötz, 294.
88. Buckland, *Text-book*, 599–603.
89. G. 4, 76. De Visscher, pp. 325–8, advances the theory that the *lex* did not establish a noxal action, which had already been established, with prospective application to all new statutes creating liability in delict, by the Twelve Tables. He thinks that if there had been an express provision in the *lex*, Celsus (in D 9,4,2,1) could not have argued so indirectly about the question whether the noxal action existed where a slave acted with his master's knowledge. However, the evidence may just as easily lead to the conclusion that while the Twelve Tables regulated the system of noxal actions, they left it to future legislation to establish specific new actions of this kind.
90. H.t. 32 pr.
91. H.t. 27, 3.
92. D 47,2,18; D 9,4,7 pr. ('Noxa caput sequitur.') The 'caput' is that of the slave.
93. H.t. 38 causes a difficulty, for the *bonae fidei possessor* is there held liable to the true owner for damage done to the latter's slave whilst in *bonae fidei* servitude to him.

Perhaps the liability was intended to be not noxal, but direct. For damage done by a slave common to both plaintiff and defendant, see h.t. 27,1.

94. B. Nicholas, *An Introduction to Roman Law* (1962), 223. Jolowicz and Nicholas, 173.

95. *D* 9,4,2 pr. Apart from the evidence of Celsus and Ulpian (*D* 9,4,2,1), which is not conclusive, the best reason for taking this view is that otherwise the damage would not be actionable under the *lex*, as being done indirectly and not *corpore* of the defendant; whereas it is nowhere in fact suggested that the proper action was an *actio utilis*.

96. H.t. 44.1; *D* 9,4,2 pr.

97. H.t. 45 pr.; *D* 50,17,50.

98. *D* 9,4,2,1; 9,4,4,2; 9,4,6.

99. *D* 47,10,17,7.

100. H.t. 37 pr.; *D* 50,17,167,1.; 169 pr.

101. *D* 43,16,1,13.

102. H.t. 37 pr.; *D* 44,7,20; 50, 17,157 pr.; 169 pr.

103. *D* 19,5,20,2; 13,6,20;13,6,10,1; An extensive discussion of these and the *locatio conductio* texts can be found in Geoffrey MacCormack's 'Culpa in eligendo', 18 *Rev.int.dr.ant.*, 3rd series (1971), 525 *et seq.*

104. H.t. 27,9; 27,11; *D* 13,6,11; 19,2,11 pr.; *Coll.* 12,7,7.

105. H.t. 27,11; *Coll.* 12,7,9. Noxal surrender in contractual actions certainly seems a monstrosity that cannot be reconciled with the classical system of actions; but once the strict action system broke down and the emphasis was thrown on to substantive grounds of liability, there would be no particular reason why the ability or inability of a master to escape personal liability by noxal surrender should depend on a technical distinction between contract and delict, especially where the action for delict was for the most part compensatory in character. Thus it was not surprising that some authorities (e.g. de Visscher, pp. 470–8) should have held that noxal surrender in contract is entirely post-classical. Since it appears in the *Collatio* (12,7,9), it must have been introduced before the time of Justinian, and in the West as well as, perhaps, in the East; and it is just possible that the *Collatio* tells the truth when it ascribes the institution to Proculus. The whole scheme of the *bonae fidei iudicia* was so flexible that the parties to contracts might have agreed to a contractual noxal surrender in certain cases, and sometimes a term to that effect might even have been implied.

106. *D* 19,2,11 pr.; 30,2.

107. We know, for instance, that the *fullo* and *sarcinator* undertook *custodia* in the time of Gaius (3,205), whereas they were probably liable only for *culpa levis in abstracto* under Justinian.

108. E.g. *D* 19,2,30,2.

109. E.g. *D* 19,2,11 pr.; 25,7.

110. *D* 44,7,5,6; *D* 49,7,4; *D* 9,3,1,4; *D* 39,4,1,6.

111. MacCormack, 18 *Rev.int.dr.ant.*, 3rd series (1971) at p. 529.

112. Though Louisiana, through Spanish rather than French influence, has retained a limited form of noxal surrender: art. 2321.

113. But note that Germany was ahead of all other countries in providing workmen's compensation. For an English flirtation with this approach see Williams, 72 *L.Q.R.* (1956), 522.

114. [1938] A.C. 57.

115. Article 55 alinéa 1 of the OR (as amended in 1971) reads as follows: *'L' employeur est responsable du dommage causé par ses travailleurs ou ses autres auxiliaires dans l'accomplissement de leur travail, s'il ne prouve qu'il a pris tous les soins commandés par les circonstances pour détourner un dommage de ce genre ou que sa diligence n'eût pas empêché le dommage de se produire.'* Originally, this was seen as establishing a simple presumption of fault which could be rebutted by the employer. But in 1908 the Tribunal Fédéral [*ATF* 34 1908, II 266 (270)] interpreted *'la preuve libératoire dans un sens purement objectif'* by refusing to release the employer unless he adduced evidence that he had taken all the precautions which were *objectively* required in the *circumstances*. The standard of care was thus raised to impose *an almost* strict liability. (See now *ATF* 96/1970, II.27(31); 97/1971, II.221(223); and Tendler, *Rev.int.dr.comp.* (1972), 677 *et seq.*) It is further interesting to note that the employer's 'duty of care' is analysed under three headings: (a) *cura in eligendo* (obligation to employ competent employees) (*ATF* 90/1964, II 86(90); (b) *cura in instruendo* (obligation to give proper instructions) (*ATF* 96/1970, II.27 and (c) *cura in custodiendo* (obligation to provide effective supervision) (*ATF* 72/1946, II.225(262). Cf. Lord Wright in *Wilsons and Clyde Coal Co. Ltd* v. *English* [1938] A.C. 57,78.

116. K. Oftinger, *Schweizerisches Haftpflichtrecht*, II.1, 2nd edn (1960), 139, 159.

117. BGH NJW 1956, 1834. For a comparative examination of Greek and German law on the subject see A. Gasis in *Festschrift for the 125 years of the Greek Supreme Court* (Athens, 1963), pp. 283 *et seq.* and in *Eranion for G. Maridakis*, II (1963), pp. 227 *et seq.*

118. Rudolf Jhering, 'Culpa in contrahendo, oder Schadenersatz bei nichtigen oder nicht zur Perfektion gelangten Verträgen', in *Jahrbücher für die Dogmatik des heutigen römischen und deutschen Privatrechts* (1861). The literature on the subject is extensive.

119. *RGZ* 78,239. See also *RGZ*, 65,19.

120. BGH NJW 1976, 712. Cf. Lyon, 5 oct. 1978, D. 1979,1. R.320 (similar facts and similar result reached, however, by relying on article 1384 CC). See also Ch. Civ. 28 nov. 1979, D. 1980,1 R.259.

121. [1906] A.C. 428.

122. BGH NJW 1965,1757.

123. *RGZ* 127,218. See also *BGHZ* 17,214.

124. Zweigert and Kötz, p. 129.

125. 32 *L.Q.R.* (1916) at pp. 226–7. See also *The Pollock – Holmes Letters,* ed. by Mark De Wolfe Howe, I (1942), pp. 233–4.

126. Art. 1384, alinéa 2.

127. The standard English monograph on the subject is by Professor P. Atiyah, *Vicarious Liability in the Law of Torts* (1967), where this matter receives extensive treatment.

128. Domat, *Lois civiles*, Civ. I, tit. XVI, sect. 3, no. 1. This passage can, probably, be read with a willing eye so as to make a master liable for wrongs committed by those whom he has employed in shipping or other enterprises, but, since it is based on the Roman *actiones exercitoria* and *institoria*, may have been intended only to make him liable in contract.

129. Pothier, *Obligations*, 456.

130. Bourjon, *Droit commun de la France*, Civ. VI, tit. II, ch. I, no. 3. This case again seems based on contract.

131. The French doctrine of *respondeat superior* has spread wherever the French Code has exercised a predominant influence (e.g. Quebec CC art. 1054; Italian CC art. 2049), though some codes prefer to base liability even in this case on fault. Cf. Mexican CC art. 1924.

132. Though see, for example, W. Sellert, 'Zur Anwendung der §§ 831, 31 BGB auf die Gesellschaft bürgerlichen Rechts' in AcP 1975, 77 *et seq.* where one can find a test very similar to that advocated by Lord Denning M.R. in *Stevenson, Jordan and Harrison Ltd* v. *Macdonald and Evans* [1952] 1 T.L.R. 101. 111 (adopted in *Beloff* v. *Pressdram Ltd* [1973] 1 All E.R. 241. In *Ready Mixed Cement Ltd* v. *Minister of Pensions and National Insurance* [1968] 2 Q.B. 497 MacKenna J. in a long and learned judgment gave a variety of criteria mostly similar to those given by the American *Restatement (Second) of Agency* § 220(2). For France see, inter alia, Ch. Civ. 14 nov. 1951, *Bull.civ.* 1951,1.238; Ch. Civ. 30 avr. 1947, *J.C.P.* 47,2.3628. For a more recent and extreme example see Ch. Crim. 20 mai 1976, *G.P.* 1976,2.545.

133. Mazeaud and Tunc, nos. 888–9; Ch. Crim. 30 juin 1943, *S.* 1943,1.124; L. Enneccerus and H. Lehmann, *Lehrbuch des bürgerlichen Rechts*, 11 (1954), § 980; *Restatement (Second) of Agency*, § 220.

134. G. Eörsi, *Encyclopedia*, XI, ch. 4. no. 52.

135. Atiyah, *Vicarious Liability*, 163; Rodière, *Rev.trim.dr.civ.* (1965), 350–1.

136. *Mersey Docks and Harbour Board* v. *Coggins and Griffith (Liverpool) Ltd* [1947] A.C. 1. Cf. Ch. civ. 4 mai 1937, D.H. 1937,363 (France); BGH *VersR.* 1956(Germany); *ATF* 42 II 617 (Switzerland); See also *RGZ* 118, 41 and *RGZ* 139, 255 (doctor prescribes X-ray treatment in a certain hospital; hospital nurse negligently exposes patient to excess radiation; whether nurse is under the control of hospital or doctor).

137. See, for example, Asquith L.J.'s judgment in *Conway* v. *George Wimpey and Co. Ltd*, [1951] 2 K.B. 266 and 276 and cf. *Limpus* v. *London General Omnibus Co.* (1862) 1 H. & C. 526.

138. *RGZ* 94, 318; *RGZ* 104, 114; *BGHZ* 1, 388, 390; 11, 151; 23, 319; 24, 188, 196; 31, 358; 49, 19. Not in the 'course of employment': *RGZ* 135, 149, 154; 161, 145, 149; BGH NJW 1958, 774.

139. BGH NJW 1965, 391 (carriage of passenger contrary to the master's instructions). The Reichsgericht appeared to be less rigid on this matter. See references given in the 1965 decision. The attitude towards 'deviations' is also strict though, once again, older decisions appeared to be prepared to treat it as within the course of employment if it were only slight. See RG LZ 1930, 589 (quoted by Zweigert and Kötz, 297 and in BGH NJW 1965, 391). Theft committed by a servant is also generally regarded as being outside the course of employment, though see *BGHZ* 11, 151.

140. Ch. Crim. 23 nov. 1928; *S.* 1931,1.153; 18 oct. 1946, *S.* 1947,1.39; 5 nov. 1953, D. 1953,698; 5 oct. 1961, *Bull.crim.* 1961, no. 386; 21 nov. 1968, *G.P.* 1969,1.40.

141. Thus, for example Ch. Civ. 1 juil. 1954, D. 1954, 628; Ch. Civ. 11 juin 1957, D. 1958, 53 and Note Savatier. The Section Sociale has taken a similar view. So, Ch. Civ. 26 mai 1961, D. 1962, *Somm.* 14.

142. See references in note 140 above and, more fully, Starck, no. 614.

143. Ch. Civ. 9 mars 1960, D. 1960,329 and Note Savatier.
144. Ch. Crim. 5 oct. 1961, *Bull.crim.* no. 386, p. 740; Ch. Crim. 10 juil. 1965 discussed by Rodière in *Rev.trim.dr.civ.* (1965), 814.
145. Ass. Plén. 10 juin 1977, D. 1977,465; Durry, *Rev.trim.dr.civ.* (1977), 774.
146. Ch. Crim. 18 juil. 1978, *Bull.crim.* no. 237 p. 627; 15 mars 1978, D. 1978,412.
147. Ch. Crim. 3 mai 1976, *Bull.crim.* no. 157, p. 447; D. 1979, I.R.530.
148. The more recent case-law suggests that the Chambre Criminelle *may be* encouraging lower courts to look for *culpa in eligendo* or *vigilando* on the part of the employer and hold him liable whenever this is found to exist. This, of course, removes the reasoning from vicarious liability proper to personal negligence of the employer; but it does allow the Chambre Criminelle to revert, via a different route, to its older practice of allowing plaintiffs to sue the master rather than the servant. Thus, Ch. Crim. 2 nov. 1978, *Bull.crim.* no. 296, p. 764; D. 1979,I.R.42 and observations by Puech; Ch. Crim. 18 juin 1979, *Bull.crim.* no. 212, p. 582; D. 1979,I.4.530 observations by Puech. On the whole matter, see Théo Hassler, 'La Responsabilité des commettants', D. Chron. 1980, 125—8.
149. Ch. Civ. 15 juin 1977, *J.C.P.* 1978,2.18780 and observations by J. Baudoin.
150. In this sense A. Tunc, 39 *Louisiana L.Rev.* (1979), 1051, 1073.

Conclusions

1. Ehrenzweig, 'Negligence Without Fault', 54 *Cal.L.Rev.* (1966), 1422, 125.
2. See A. Tunc, D. Chron. 1975, 83 *et seq.*; 39 *Louisiana L.Rev.* (1979), 1051,1071.
3. Cf. *Nova Mink Ltd* v. *T.C.A.* [1951] 2 D.L.R. 241 with *RGZ* 158, 38.
4. E.g. Ch. Civ. 17 mai 1973, *G.P.* 1974,1.71 and Note H [enri] M [azeaud]; Cour de Lyon, 26 juin 1973, *G.P.* 1974,1.4; Durry, *Rev.trim.dr.civ.* (1974), 409.
5. An excellent discussion of the French 'rescue cases' can be found in C. Roy-Loustaunau, *Du Dommage éprouvé en prêtant assistance bénévole à autrui* (1980).
6. [1953] 1 Q.B. 429.
7. [1946] A.C. 401.
8. Discussed in chapter 2, p. 75.
9. Fleming, 497—8.
10. Anson's *Law of Contract*, 23rd edn, 18,19, where this argument is said to possess 'a certain cogency'. See also the reference in the next note.
11. This was one of the arguments in favour of codification accepted by Lord Scarman when, as Chairman of the Law Commission, he delivered a lecture entitled 'Codification and Judge-Made Law' and published by the University of Birmingham in 1966 (p. 19).

INDEX

Index

Index

Fire, 21, 65, 73, 108
Fonds de garantie, 116, 170, 176, 205
Force majeure, 27, 127–8, 152
Formula, 16
Foreseeability, 29, 46, 120–1, 129
Freeman, 10–11, 36
'Fregerit', 5, 15
Furtum, 17

Garde, 116, 147, 150–7, 176
Generalisation, 39, 79
Glossators, 11, 40
Good faith, 86
Greek law, 121, 206

Habeas corpus, 49
Halter, 175
Handlungsunrecht, 100
Hebrews, 2
Heir, 35, 40
Hinwegdenken, 109
Hit-and-run, 74
Hittites, 2
Höhere Gewalt, 127
Humanists, 40
Hunting accidents, 116–17

Illicéité, 26
Immovable property, 4
Immunities, 70–1
Impact theory, 46
'Imperitia', 28
Imputability, 22
Inanimate objects
    damage caused by, 149–60
    damage caused to, 6–7
Industrial accidents, 58–61, 108, 110, 143,
    147–50, 171–4, 184
Inert objects, 151, 156
'Infirmitas', 28
Iniuria, 2, 19, 22, 70, 161, 186
    As separate delict, 2, 161
Injunction, 38
Inspection failure, 75, 81, 124
Institutes, 16
Insurance, 66, 128, 143, 176, 182, 185
'Insurance factor', 64–7

Interesse, 9, 35
'Internal balance of the code factor', 61–4
Interpolations, 23–4, 26, 28, 163
Interpretation, Extension of liability by,
    14–19, 25–6
Italian law, 201, 227, 232
Iudicatus, 12
Iudicis arbitrive postulatio, 13
Ius imperandi, 161
Ius moderandi, 120
Ius tollendi, 52

Jurists, Interpretation of lex Aquilia by,
    14–19, 35–6
Justification, 19, 22

Killing, 4–5, 10–11, 13–14, 20, 30–3,
    35–6, 161
Knowledge, 84, 95, 149

Lascivia, 29
Legis actio, 13
Legitimate interest, 68–9, 88, 93, 99
Lessor, liability of, 70
Lex Aquilia
    Chapter I, 4–5
    Chapter II, 11–12
    Chapter III, 5–11
    Date, 1
Lex Cornelia de sicariis et veneficis, 161
Lex Hortensia, 188
Lex Valeria Horatia, 1
Lis crescens, 5, 13
Locatio conductio, 162
Loss distribution, 65
Lucrum cessans, 35–6
Lunatic, 27, 152–3

Malice, 52–7, 95, 181
Manus iniectio, 12
Marriage, 50
Master, 160–3, 167–71
Measure of damages, 35–6
Meddling, 72
Medical expenses, 10, 36, 172
Medical malpractice, 71, 111, 143, 145
Membrum ruptum, 2

237

Index

Mexican law, 201, 227, 232
Mis-statement, 81-7, 186-7
Mistake, 28, 144
Mortis causam praestare, 14-16
Motive, 28, 52-7
Multiple sufficient causes, 111

Natural events, 127-8
Natural law, 28, 40-1
Nautae, caupones, stabularii, 163
Nec corpore nec corpori, 16
Necessity, as a defence, 21-2
Nervous shock, 46, 114, 135, 139, 184
New York fire rule, 65
Non cumul, 62, 87
Non-feasance, 71-80, 86
Non iure, 19, 101
Norwegian law, 208, 218
Novus actus interveniens, 114, 120, 128-9
Noxal liability, 160-3
Nuisance, 56, 122, 144

Objective standard, 26, 66, 77, 100, 118
Obligation, 40
Obligation de moyens, 62
Obligation de résultat, 62
Occupier, 58, 74, 77-8
Omissions, 18, 19, 71-80, 96, 99, 109, 181
Ordre public, 138
Os fractum, 2
Overtaking causes, 111-17

Pandectists, 89, 163
Partie civile, 138, 176
Paterfamilias, 10, 11, 26
Patricians and plebeians, 1, 11
Pecuniary damage *see* Economic loss
Pecus, 4
Penal action, 4-5
Penalty, 35-6, 182
Personal injury, 49
Physical damage *see* Damage
Plurality of causes, 126-8
Plurimi, 6
Poison, 14
Policy, 43-67, 73, 130, 135, 153, 180, 183, 185
Portuguese law, 208, 217

Positive acts, 15, 17, 71, 76, 96
Positive Vertragsverletzung, 62
Praetor, 17
Pre-contract negotiation, 165
Predispositions, 112-15
Préjudice moral, 138-40
Presumptions, 142, 149-50, 157, 167, 175
Prima facie Beweis, 142
Private right, 20
Privilege, incomplete, 21-2
Products, 75, 186
Property, defence of, 49, 51
Proximate cause, 106, 118, 135
Prussian law, 41, 148, 158, 197, 227
Psychiatric illness, 47, 139
Psychoanalysis, 80, 210
Public interest, 43, 93
Public office, 20
Public policy, 43
Putator, 29

'Quanti ea res erit', 7-8
Quasi-contract, 86
Quasi-delict, 36
Quebec law, 147, 168, 232

Railway, 158
Reasonable man, 22, 26-7, 144
Recht an eingerichteten und ausgeübten Bewerbetrieb, 90-3
Rechctsfertigungsgrund, 100
Rechtswidrigkeit, 99, 100
Rechtswidrigkeitszusammenhang, 123, 136
Rei vindicatio, 38
Relatives, 70
Remedies, 37
Remoteness of damage *see* Damage
Rescue, 72-3, 135, 184
Res ipsa loquitur, 142, 182
Respondeat superior, 167
Rights, 37
Risk, 66, 112, 136, 147, 153, 168, 182
Risk spreading, 65-6, 168
'Risk' theory, 125-6, 129-30, 150
Risque créé, 151
Road traffic, 66, 174-7
Roman law, 1-36, 52, 73, 131, 160-3, 183
Runaway slave, 161

238

Index

Ruperit, 5, 15
'Rupitias', 188–9

Saevitia, 29
Scandinavian law, 121
Schikaneverbot, 53
Schmerzensgeld, 62
Schutzgesetz, 48, 63, 92
Schutzzweck der Norm, 123
Scienter, 143
Scope of employment, 168–71
'Scope of the rule" theory, 123–6, 129, 135
Scots law, 143, 144, 206
Self-defence, 20
Servant, 167–71
    functions of, 168–71
Simultaneous causes, 110–11
Social security, 171, 173
Solidary liability, 65, 129–30
Sonstiges Recht, 89, 91
Sorgfaltspflicht, allgemeine, 100
Sorgfaltspflichtenverletzung, 101
South African law, 143
Soviet law, 21, 54, 132, 194, 201, 227
Sozialadäquanz, 101, 102
Special relationship, 80, 85–6
Standard of conduct, 22, 40, 70, 97, 100–1, 144
Statutory regulations, 24, 92, 108, 110, 123–4, 136–40, 149
Stipulation pour autrui, 85, 166, 186
Strict liability, 66, 146–60, 163, 167, 175
Subjective standard, 22, 26, 77
'Superior value factor', 49–57
Support, 81
Swedish law, 53, 204, 207
Swiss law, 39, 53, 102, 114, 121, 131, 158, 164, 175, 194, 201, 206, 216, 222, 227, 229, 231

Talio, 2–3
Taxatio, 13
Theft, 17, 119, 155, 175
Third party, 128–31, 166, 175, 186
Titre gratuit, 87

Titre onéreux, 87
Trade unions, 70, 158
Transport bénévole, 131, 153
Trespass, 15, 16, 19, 21, 69, 144, 153
Twelve Tables, 2
Typical consequence, 90
Typical harm, 182

Ubi emolumentum ibi ius, 154
Ultimate consumer, 75
Ultimate receiver, 84
Unfallsversicherung, 158
Unforeseeable plaintiff, 134–40
Unjustified enrichment, 50
Unlawfulness, 99–103, 118, 180
Unrecognised defendant, 70–1
Unrecognised manner, 71–80
Unrecognised plaintiff, 67–70, 139
Unrecognised type of damage, 80–93
'Usserit', 5, 16

Value, 4–9, 10, 12, 33, 35–6
Vendor, 70
Verhaltensnorm, 100
Verkehr, im, 78, 100
Verkehrssicherungspflicten, 74, 78–9, 166
Vermögen, 89, 99
Vermögenschaden, reine, 89
Verschulden, 100
Vertragsähnlich, 87
Vertrauensverhältnis, 86
Verwandschaft, 78
Verwerfbarkeit, 100
Vicarious liability, 82, 143, 147, 163–71
Volenti non fit injuria, 25
Vorausgegangenes gefährdendes Tun, 78

Wealth, 50
Wergild, 40
Widerrechtlichkeit, 26
Wilful acts, 17, 19, 53, 89, 181
Workmen, injuries to, 171–4
Wounding, 2, 6–8, 31–2
    mortal, 31

Zweckverband, 48

239